Encyclopedia of Job-Winning Resumes

Second Edition

Myra Fournier and Jeffrey Spin

Round Lake Publishing

Second edition

Any names and identities of individuals mentioned in this book are entirely fictitious
and no resemblance to persons living or dead is intended to be made.

Round Lake Publishing Co.
31 Bailey Avenue
Ridgefield, CT 06877

Printed in the United States of America

0987654

ISBN 0-929543-41-6

Other Helpful Books from Round Lake Publishing

The following books are available from your bookseller. If they are not in stock, you may order directly from Round Lake Publishing.

The Complete Book of Contemporary Business Letters
400 model letters for all areas of business, including customer relations, handling customer complaints, credit and collections, personnel relations, memos and reports, job search, personal letters and much more. 470 pages, soft cover, 6" x 8 3/4" $19.95

Encyclopedia of Money Making Sales Letters
Over 300 letters covering all phases of selling, from prospecting for new customers to closing sales. Includes responses to objections, keeping the customer buying, selling yourself, plus much more. *"Helps sell anything"*—The New York Times. 370 pages, soft cover, 6" x 8 3/4" $19.95

The Only Personal Letter Book You'll Ever Need
Over 400 letters cover all areas of personal correspondence, including apologies and thank you's, complaints to companies and individuals, congratulations and invitations, saying no, sympathy and condolences, and much more. 460 pages, soft cover, 6" x 8 3/4" $19.95

Step-By-Step Legal Forms and Agreements
165 legal forms for business and personal use. Includes wills, living will, power of attorney, forms for buying and selling real estate, starting a company, corporate forms, and much more. The most comprehensive book of its kind. *"Could hardly be easier to use"*—The New York Times. 440 pages, soft cover, 6" x 8 3/4" $19.95

Hiring, Firing (and everything in between) Personnel Forms Book
160 forms covering all aspects of personnel management, including job applications, interviewing guides, personnel policies, performance appraisals, orientation, attendance, salary, discipline, benefits, termination, federal regulations, and more. 370 pages, soft cover, 6" x 8 3/4" $19.95

The Complete Book of Consulting
150 forms—plus expert advice— for starting and running a successful consulting practice. Includes business plans, fee calculation worksheets, sales letters, brochures and cover letters, proposals, contracts, invoices, plus much more. Maximize your income with this extremely unusual and helpful consulting resource. 300 pages, soft cover, 6" x 8 3/4" $19.95

Order Form

Please rush me the following books: res
☐ The Complete Book of Contemporary Business Letters $19.95
☐ Encyclopedia of Money Making Sales Letters $19.95
☐ The Only Personal Letter Book You'll Ever Need $19.95
☐ Step-By-Step Legal Forms and Agreements $19.95
☐ Hiring, Firing (and everything in between) Personnel Forms Book $19.95
☐ The Complete Book of Consulting $19.95

Add $3.95 to the total order for shipping

I have enclosed ☐ Check   Bill my credit card   ☐ Am Ex   ☐ Visa   ☐ MasterCard

Credit card # _____ Exp. Date _____

Signature (required for credit card) _____

Name _____
     Please print
Company _____

Address _____

City _____ State _____ Zip _____

Round Lake Publishing
31 Bailey Avenue, Ridgefield, CT 06877   **(203) 438-6303**

Contents

Chapter 3 SPECIAL CAREER SITUATIONS

Chapter 4 ADMINISTRATION

Chapter 5 ARTS AND LEISURE

Chapter 6 COMPUTER SCIENCE AND ENGINEERING

Chapter 7 EDUCATION

Chapter 8 FINANCE AND BANKING

Chapter 9 HEALTH CARE

Chapter 10 HUMAN RESOURCES

Chapter 11 LAW AND SECURITY

Chapter 12 MANAGEMENT

Chapter 13 SALES AND MARKETING

Resumes by Job Title

Resumes by Industry

Chapter 14 STUDENTS

Chapter 15 Career Changers

What Makes This Book Unique

The Learn By Example Approach

At a glance, you can tell that *Encyclopedia of Job-Winning Resumes* is a welcome alternative to the myriad of "how-to" resume-writing books already available.

No tedious worksheets, no confusing flowcharts, no cutesy cartoons, no hype.

Instead, we present a simple, yet effective "learn-by-example" approach, one with straightforward writing tips supported by more than 400 fully-composed, fully-formatted, and fully-annotated resumes and cover letters for every career.

The wide variety of stylish formats, the professionally written text, the key "buzzwords," and the special comments that accompany each resume and cover letter are powerful learning tools. They allow you to grasp the basics quickly so that you can develop your job-winning resume and cover letter with a minimum of time and effort. And a maximum of effectiveness.

How Do We Know Our Method Works?

As professional resume writers, we have observed that the greatest obstacle hindering people from composing their own resumes is their inability to organize their information into an individualized format that presents their credentials most effectively. They are stuck, endlessly debating with themselves the benefits of a Chronological vs. Functional vs. Targeted format. And, despite an understanding of their own skills, achievements, and qualifications, they are completely overwhelmed by the formidable task of creating an entire resume format from scratch. Paralysis sets in.

And yet, in our resume writing seminars, when we present participants with fully-formatted and fully-composed samples to follow, the entire situation remedies itself. They are able to organize their information easily, integrate their key credentials quickly, and produce their own first-class resumes. Not only are they delighted with the results, but they are proud of their own writing skills and feel confident about their ability to update their resumes on their own in the future.

Inspired by their success, we developed RésumExpert®, the #1-rated resume template software for the Macintosh computer. Feedback from our software users indicates that they, too, meet with great success when they use our "learn-by-example" approach.

Eager to reach a broader audience, we have written Encyclopedia of Job-Winning Resumes because we know our method works and can save you many hours of frustration and anxiety and help you produce a job-winning resume. Whether you are a student, a CEO, a person returning to the workforce or contemplating a career change, there is a sample here for you.

The Big Secret To Writing A Resume

We know from experience that the big secret to writing an effective resume is that there is none. There is no one correct method. There is no one correct style. There is no one correct format. And there definitely is no reason why it needs to be an arduous task.

How To Use This Book

We suggest you first browse through some of the resume samples at random to gain a feel for the variety of formats, type styles, and content.

Then, review your special career situation (Chapter 3) or specific career field (Chapters 4-14) before selecting a format. Remember, it is also perfectly all right to select a format from a chapter outside of your specific field. Or, you might find several formats that are applicable to your situation. Choose the one that appeals the most to you. You can also combine elements from several resumes, e.g., a phrase from one and a heading from another. There are many combinations that will work successfully for you.

When you are ready to begin writing, it is important to read Chapter 1 for informative tips and a valuable "before" and "after" resume comparison that dramatically demonstrates the impact our approach can make on the outcome of your resume.

We wish you much success in your job search!

The Essentials of Writing Your Resume 1

GETTING DOWN TO BASICS

The Universal Lament

"I'm so boring on paper" is the common belief which causes people to procrastinate in preparing their resumes. Other inhibitors include, "I don't have enough job experience," "I need several resumes for different career goals," "I don't have a specific career objective," "I don't have a college degree," "My experience won't fit onto one page."

These are concerns we hear daily from our clients. And we know some easy remedies which we share with you throughout Encyclopedia of Job-Winning Resumes.

This chapter addresses the essentials of writing a job-winning resume. To ease your reading and eliminate your confusion, we have concentrated only on the important elements of resume writing and ignored the insignificant. It's the very same approach we utilize when writing resumes for our clients, and it's one we hope you also follow.

You will find straightforward tips, a dramatic "before" and "after" resume comparison, and a comprehensive list of action verbs to give your resume more punch. After reviewing this chapter, read or re-read the section, "How to Use This Book," in "What Makes This Book Unique."

Develop A Theme

The dual challenge in developing a resume is to present your credentials on paper in a manner that is both easy to scan and interesting to read. Prospective employers are busy, and your resume needs to make a strong impression quickly.

The first and most important step is to *develop a theme*. What message do you want to convey? Your depth of experience? Breadth of experience? Academic achievements? Technical expertise? Decide what it is you want to sell about yourself and only include information which relates to that theme.

Second, concentrate on the three components of your resume – *content, format, and finishing touches*. Each of these areas is vital to projecting your resume's theme. Comprehensive tips related to each area follow below.

Third, *do most of the writing in your head* before you even approach the typewriter or computer. During your morning commute or your weekend jog or your trip to the grocery store, think about the information you'll include or omit. Jot down pertinent phrases, discard irrelevant information, and stick to your theme. This technique will save you countless hours of frustrating revisions once you begin typing.

Content

Your resume should not read like a job description. It should not be a recreation of your past history, but a brief, focused, dynamic marketing tool which conveys your key credentials for a future position. Stress your qualifications, skills, and achievements instead of your duties and responsibilities.

Make the information interesting to the reader by describing your experience in short statements. Although your resume should be written in the first person, do not use "I" when describing your work history. And do not start any sentence with "Responsibilities include." It's a weak phrase which takes up space and prohibits the reader from getting right to your most important information. Instead, begin each sentence with an action verb. You can find a list of useful "Action Verbs" on Page 14.

Utilize narrative (paragraph style) sparingly. Instead, adopt a technical writing style – factual, clipped, to the point. Use short, simple words. Let the reader's eye glide from one important fact to another by omitting the articles, "a," "an," and "the." Try to avoid abbreviations because they detract from the overall professionalism of the resume. Some permissible abbreviations include names of states, college degrees, and Inc.

Proofread several times to ensure that your content makes sense and that there are no typographical errors. An effective method to use when proofreading for spelling errors is to start from the bottom of the page and read the sentences backwards. This method forces you to concentrate on each word separately, out of context, and lets you identify any spelling errors quickly.

How much is too much? Your resume should contain all the pertinent information needed to sell yourself effectively for the position you desire. No more, no less.

It is preferable to limit your resume to one page unless your qualifications include special areas such as certifications, publications, presentations, etc. It is also preferable to limit your information to the past ten years, unless special circumstances warrant more. However, as you will see in examples throughout this book, even 30 years of experience can be condensed effectively onto one page with the correct format.

The trick to condensing your information onto one page is to omit job descriptions of similar positions, lower level positions, and irrelevant employment.

Do you need an Objective? Probably not, because if you are like many candidates you do not know the exact title of the job you're pursuing. Therefore, the tendency is to write an Objective that is far too general. Avoid trite phrases like "challenging position" and "growth potential." They take up crucial space in which you could describe your qualifications.

Challenge yourself to write a meaningful Objective in five words or less, naming a specific job or industry. If you can't do it, consider an "Alternative to an Objective" found in Chapter 3 – Special Situations, or omit an Objective completely, stating your goals in your cover letter.

In what order should you present information? People read from the top down and from left to right, so begin with your most persuasive information. For example, do not use valuable space on the left for dates, usually the least important data on the resume, unless stressing the dates will enhance your candidacy.

Start by presenting the section which demonstrates your strongest qualifications, whether it be Education, Certification, Experience, or even Volunteer Activities. If you job title is more impressive than the company, list it first. Similarly, if your degree is more impressive than the college, list it first.

Should you include a Personal section? Rarely. Information such as age, height, weight, health, marital status, and hobbies usually has little relevance to your qualifications for the position. It might even work to your detriment by providing a reason for a prospective employer to exclude you from consideration. For example, citing membership in a controversial organization might reduce the number of prospective employers interested in hiring you because of their biases.

In some cases, however, certain personal information can promote your candidacy, so a Personal section would be appropriate. For example, if you are an older candidate, you might show vitality by citing sports and travel activities; a sales candidate might indicate unmarried status combined with a willingness to travel and/or relocate. If you are a student, a Personal section is a plus and we have elaborated on this point in Chapter 14 – Students.

How do you handle confidentiality? It is understood by most prospective employers that candidates want their search to remain confidential until they are ready to make the actual switch to a new company. However, if you want to alert prospective employers to your concern, head your resume with the phrase "Confidential Resume Of." Or, withhold the name of your present employer from your resume. Instead, state "Fortune 500 manufacturing firm."

Do you need to mention References? Candidates seriously under consideration for a position will be required to furnish references to the prospective company. Therefore, it is not necessary to end your resume with a sentence about references except as a space-filler.

Never list the actual names, addresses, and telephone numbers of your references on your resume, except for highly unusual circumstances, e.g, if individuals providing you with references are very well-known or the mention of references will compensate for gaps in employment. Instead, keep reference information on a separate sheet of paper ready to be submitted if requested. Or, even better, obtain a written letter of recommendation from each reference, and then photocopy it and submit it as needed. This method greatly reduces the annoyance of phone calls made to your references who have been kind enough to lend their name to your candidacy.

Should any information be de-emphasized or omitted? Absolutely! In general, all information that detracts from your candidacy needs special treatment. For example, weak qualifications, such as a lack of a college degree should be de-emphasized by placing the Education section at the end of the resume. A section of Special Training, Coursework, or Affiliations may be substituted. Potentially damaging information, such as poor job performance or termination, should be omitted entirely.

Some types of information, such as political party, race, or disability have no relevance to your ability to perform in the business world, so should not be addressed on your resume. If, however, you are applying for a position in the type of organization where such information would be a plus, then the data becomes a credential and you should definitely stress it.

Format
There is no single correct resume format. People in the same field require different formats because their breadth of experience, length of employment, degree of education, accomplishments, and future goals all vary. It's likely that the same person at different career stages will need completely different formats for each stage.

How can you select an appropriate format? Developing a resume takes common sense. Since there is no single correct resume format, approach the task with a sense of creativity. Your credentials can be arranged in any manner that emphasizes your strengths, and is quickly scannable by the reader.

We urge you not to think in terms of "Chronological," "Functional," or "Targeted" formats. Doing so is time-consuming, confusing, and limiting. Instead, browse through the resume samples in this book and select the formats that will consolidate your essential information and present it effectively. You might even create your own hybrid by using elements from several formats. The writing will follow easily.

How can you draw attention to the most important data? In considering formats, keep in mind that "less is more." In other words, it is more effective to present a few easy-to-read highlights than to cram a lot of information onto the page. Valuable achievements lose their impact when they compete for space with too much other data.

Surrounding your most important data with empty space on the paper ("white" space) instead of other data is the most effective method to emphasize information. Other simple graphic techniques include highlighting in bold, italics, or capital letters; using bullets; and indenting.

What is an alternative resume format? An alternative resume format is a non-traditional method to present your professional history. It is used in special circumstances to make an impact, target a particular position, or when your resume is not an effective marketing tool for a certain position. It can take the form of a letter, biographical sketch, portfolio, photograph, press release, etc.

To achieve your objective and avoid gimmicks, develop an alternative resume with the utmost care and utilize it in very few situations. Examples of Alternative Resumes can be found in Chapter 3 – Special Career Situations and Chapter 2 – Cover Letters.

Finishing Touches

What are they? While finishing touches are added to your resume near the end of the creative process, they are the elements *most likely to be noticed first* by prospective employers. That's why you should consider them carefully.

Finishing touches enhance the personalization of your resume. They include having your resume typeset or desktop published; using high quality bond paper (colored or white); choosing colored ink; selecting matching, printed letterhead and envelopes; using contemporary type styles; and inserting graphics, such as symbols, pictures, or logos.

To type or typeset? Typesetting or desktop publishing (DTP) is a must! Even students have abandoned typewriters in favor of typesetting or DTP. Typesetting and DTP are far superior to typing because of the professional look they achieve. Their many advantages include the sharp quality of the finished product; the range of type styles and sizes; bold and italics highlighting capabilities; graphic elements, such as bullets, boxes, and thin, horizontal lines; and margin justification to eliminate a ragged edge to the right margin.

If you have your own computer and laser printer, you're all set. Otherwise, consult your local Yellow Pages for area printers or DTP firms. They exist in virtually every town these days. Try to select a company that has experience processing resumes and that will store your resume on disk indefinitely so that updating is quick and cost-efficient. Or, if you are a do-it-yourselfer, you might choose to rent computer and printer time at a DTP service bureau and produce your own resume.

Remember to bring along this book or make a copy of the resume that you wish to use as your sample format.

What else is appropriate for you? Browse through this book for the resumes in your career area to see the kinds of other finishing touches that might be appropriate for you.

All the resumes in this book are shown in black and white, but in our resume writing business we use colored papers – pastel shades of gray or blue – in addition to white and ivory. We prefer black ink because of its readability, but at a client's request we also use navy blue ink on white paper or brown ink on ivory paper.

Matching, printed letterhead for cover letters and envelopes are always appropriate and can also be used as personal stationery.

Graphics should be used sparingly as a highlight, not a focal point. You can use a symbol found in your word processing software, design a logo, copy a graphic from a non-copyrighted publication, or select from among the many ready-made art ("clip art") publications or electronic "clip art" software packages available.

What if you transmit your resume via fax, modem, scanning or the Internet? Emerging technologies have greatly expanded and quickened the methods that companies and recruiting firms now use to receive, store and retrieve your resume. It is in your best interest to make it easy to do so.

When *faxing* your cover letter and resume, do so from a very clear copy on white paper. Opt for a simple format and the largest type size that fits the page comfortably. Always follow up by sending an original by mail.

Large companies *scan* resumes into their computers, retrieving your resume for a specific position by searching for key words. Certain scanning procedures capture text only, so you can facilitate the process if your resume is very simple, printed on white paper, and contains no italics, bold, underlining, boxes, shading or graphics.

The Internet is the newest tool for resume circulation, particularly effective for long distance and global job searches. Several commercial services can help you go "on-line." Make sure you fully investigate these companies and understand their fees, services, how you should compose your resume, and how the finished product will look on the "Net." If maintaining confidentiality is an issue for you, find a service that provides a database which is open only to recruiters, not to the general public or individual employers.

The Cover Letter
Cover Letters are so important that we have devoted an entire chapter to them. See Chapter 3 for writing tips and examples of cover letters for many situations.

"BEFORE" AND "AFTER" RESUME COMPARISON

To illustrate the enormous improvement that can be made in a typical resume when our principles are applied, we present a "before" and "after" comparison for you to examine. Read both resumes, then check the critique that follows which covers the topics below:

Content

- **Order of sections**
- **Job descriptions**
- **Relevant information**
- **Wordiness**
- **Theme**

Format

- **Separation of sections**
- **Dates**
- **Narrative**

Finishing Touches

- **Typesetting**
- **Graphics**

The "before" example can be found on pages 8-9 and the "after" example can be found on page 10.

BEFORE

FRANK LYNCH
36 Squire Road
Brookline, Massachusetts 02146
(617) 555-9066

EDUCATION:

BENTLEY COLLEGE • Waltham, MA
1982 **Master in Business Administration**

BENTLEY COLLEGE • Waltham, MA
1980 **Bachelor in Business Administration**

LICENSES:

Series 7 registration with the Securities Exchange Commission

Series 63 registration with the State of Massachusetts

Series 3 Commodities Licensed

Life and Disability Insurance Licensed

PROFESSIONAL EXPERIENCE:

PRUDENTIAL-BACHE • Boston, MA

1988
to
present
Vice President, Investments
I was promoted to 2nd Vice President of Investments in 1989 and then to Vice President of Investments in 1991. I was responsible for identifying high net worth individuals. Marketed to these clients a broad array of investment opportunities promoted by Prudential-Bache. Responsible for implementing a new cold calling campaign to establish contact with potential new accounts for a contingent of brokers. All accounts were established utilizing cold calling campaign. Trained Account Executives. As Account Executive, established reputation for top sales.

Frank Lynch

DEAN WITTER REYNOLDS • Boston, MA

1986   **Account Executive**
to   Responsible for the marketing of investment opportu-
1988   nities promoted by Dean Witter to the small and
medium size investor.

1982   **Sales Associate**
to   Responsible for identifying small business owners
1986   andindividuals who had needs that could be satisfied
Dean Witter products. In 1984 became a member of
the "Million Dollar Roundtable."

PROFESSIONAL ACTIVITIES:

I was invited to speak at many community and business organizations on topics ranging from "Choosing a Stockbroker" to
"The Stock Market Cycle."

PERSONAL:

I am married with two children and in excellent health. I am
interested in computers, golf, and camping, and am active in
community organizations such as PTO and Town Meeting.

REFERENCES:

My personal and professional references are available. They
will be furnished upon request once a mutual interest has been
established.

FRANK LYNCH
36 Squire Road
Brookline, MA 02146   617-555-9066

OBJECTIVE: Sales Management – Investment Services

SUMMARY:

- *10-year record of achievement in investment sales and sales management*
  Consistently ranked as top sales producer for new accounts

- *Proven ability to recruit, train, and develop account executives*
  Effective with rookies and seasoned professionals

- *Demonstrated skill planning and implementing aggressive sales campaigns*
  Direct cold calling activities – lead selection, presentation, closing

- *In-depth knowledge of a full range of financial products*
  Equities, annuities, tax advantage investments, and fixed income securities

- *Active in promoting company image throughout the business community*
  Professional speaker – "Choosing a Stock Broker," "Stock Market Cycles"

- *Hold numerous industry licenses*
  Series 7 – SEC; Series 63 – Mass; Series 3 Commodities; Life and Disability

---

EXPERIENCE:

PRUDENTIAL-BACHE • BOSTON, MA

> **Vice President, Investments** (1991 to present)
> **2nd Vice President, Investments** (1989 to 1991)
> **Account Executive** (1988 to 1989)

DEAN WITTER REYNOLDS • BOSTON, MA

> **Account Executive** (1986 to 1988)
> **Sales Associate** (1982 to 1986)

EDUCATION:

BENTLEY COLLEGE • WALTHAM, MA

> **M.B.A. – Marketing/Finance** (1982)
> **B.S.B.A. – Marketing/Finance** (1980)

"Before" and "After" Critique

Frank's "before" resume is a typical example of good intentions gone awry. On the plus side, his two-page presentation is neat and well-spaced, the information is organized into short sections, and some important data is highlighted in bold. Yet, the overall effect is lackluster and difficult to scan. Major areas were remedied in the "after" presentation:

Content

- **Order of sections**

  BEFORE: The reader should not have to read through half a page to discover Frank's career field. While Frank's Education and Licenses are excellent credentials, they are not as important or impressive as his Experience, so they should not come first.

  AFTER: Beginning with a short, very specific Objective keys the reader to Frank's career goal. Next, a Summary condenses vital career information to support his Objective. By the time the reader reaches Frank's Experience and Education sections, he or she already is aware of Frank's major qualifications.

- **Job descriptions**

  BEFORE: Frank has held similar positions in the same field and repeats very similar descriptions. He uses a hard-to-scan narrative writing style and begins sentences with the weak phrases, "I was" and "Responsible for," instead of action verbs. His achievements are not highlighted.

  AFTER: Frank's Summary of major accomplishments spans his entire career so that repetitive descriptions for each job are not necessary. He highlights his achievements in short, strongly worded, bulleted statements. For futher emphasis, he uses bold italic lettering and supports each statement with specific information. His Experience section only lists positions, with job titles demonstrating career growth, so he does not need to make a specific statement about the promotions.

- **Relevant information**

  BEFORE: Frank's "Personal" and "Reference" sections are unnecessary. They add no information to promote his candidacy and, in fact, take up valuable space.

  AFTER: Only information which supports Frank's Objective is included on the resume. Omitting irrelevant information allows his credentials to be easily condensed onto one page.

- **Wordiness**

  BEFORE: Each section is too wordy. The Education section should be condensed by abbreviating the degrees and listing both under the same college name. Licenses which are common in a field do not need elaboration. In general, the style is rambling, unfocused, and repetitive.

  AFTER: Remember, "less is more." Streamlining each section and combining information from several sections into the Summary, e.g. professional speaking engagements and licenses, dramatically improves scannability. Frank uses phrases instead of sentences in his Summary to further reduce wordiness.

- **Theme**

  BEFORE: Frank's resume is unfocused. He uses neither an Objective nor an Alternative to an Objective at the top of his resume. None of his achievements are highlighted. Consequently, without more information from a cover letter or an interview, the reader must guess which credentials are Frank's most important.

  AFTER: Frank's Objective immediately establishes a focus for his resume, although even without one, the Summary section would serve the same function. Key elements are highlighted effectively so that they document Frank's expertise in his field. The Experience and Education sections further support his competence.

Format

- **Separation of sections**

  BEFORE: The lack of horizontal lines or empty space in the left margin to separate sections presents the reader with the formidable task of sifting through all of Frank's information instead of skimming from section to section.

  AFTER: Separating the sections with horizontal lines allows the reader to focus on each section as a cluster and improves scannability. The reader's eye now travels top-to-bottom instead of left-to-right, and he or she can grasp much more information at a glance.

- **Dates**

  BEFORE: Dates are bold and placed in the left margin. Not only does this over-state their importance, it interferes with the reader's concentration on important factual material.

  AFTER: Dates appear next to the job titles and college degrees and appropriately serve as reference data in that position.

- **Narrative**

  BEFORE: Long paragraphs are cumbersome to read and do not allow for emphasis of Frank's achievements.

  AFTER: Short, bulleted statements highlight the most important information which Frank needs to communicate quickly to the reader.

Finishing Touches

- **Typesetting**

  BEFORE: Frank's typewritten resume is plain. It is uninviting to read because it lacks crispness and vitality. The hyphenation on the right edge is unattractive and impedes the flow of words.

  AFTER: Typesetting or desktop publishing equipment, with its variety of type styles and highlighting capabilities, turns Frank's resume into a dynamic marketing tool.

- **Graphics**

  BEFORE: Frank's resume is devoid of any graphic touches that would attract the reader.

  AFTER: Simple graphic touches, such as a flush-left heading, bullets, and horizontal lines distinguish Frank's resume from that of other candidates.

ACTION VERBS

Account	Decide	Invent	Reduce
Achieve	Define	Invest	Refer
Administer	Delegate	Investigate	Regulate
Advise	Deliver	Judge	Relate
Analyze	Demonstrate	Lead	Reorganize
Answer	Design	Lecture	Repair
Apply	Detect	Locate	Represent
Arbitrate	Determine	Log	Research
Arrange	Develop	Maintain	Respond
Assemble	Devise	Manage	Restore
Assess	Diagnose	Manipulate	Retrieve
Assign	Direct	Manufacture	Review
Assist	Discover	Measure	Revise
Audit	Distribute	Mediate	Revitalize
Build	Edit	Memorize	Route
Calculate	Elaborate	Modify	Search
Categorize	Eliminate	Monitor	Select
Chart	Encourage	Motivate	Sell
Classify	Establish	Negotiate	Serve
Coach	Estimate	Obtain	Simplify
Code	Evaluate	Offer	Solve
Collaborate	Examine	Operate	Spearhead
Collect	Expand	Order	Speculate
Communicate	Explain	Organize	Sponsor
Compile	File	Outline	Study
Complete	Formulate	Perform	Succeed
Compose	Gather	Persuade	Summarize
Compound	Generate	Plan	Supervise
Compute	Guide	Prepare	Supply
Conduct	Handle	Prescribe	Support
Confirm	Help	Present	Synthesize
Conserve	Identify	Print	Teach
Consolidate	Illustrate	Process	Test
Construct	Implement	Produce	Train
Consult	Improve	Promote	Translate
Contact	Increase	Protect	Troubleshoot
Contribute	Initiate	Prove	Tutor
Control	Install	Provide	Unite
Coordinate	Institute	Realize	Utilize
Copy	Instruct	Receive	Vault
Correspond	Interact	Recommend	Verify
Counsel	Interpret	Record	Volunteer
Create	Interview	Recruit	Write

Cover Letters 2

Cover Letters Are Crucial

The cover letter should be viewed as an important companion piece to the resume. Whether you are developing a cover letter to re-enter the job market, secure a promotion, or register with a recruiter, the cover letter should form a personal connection between you and the reader. Communicate information that will make your credentials stand out from all others. Try to leave a strong, positive impression in the reader's mind. Enthusiasm is essential.

Each cover letter needs to contain a *brief* summary of your qualifications and/or achievements and *specific* statements regarding your interest in that *particular* company/position and how you can *uniquely* contribute.

Never underestimate the power of a well-written, personal cover letter! It could very well influence whether a recruiter or department manager will read your resume.

Express Yourself Concisely And Logically

- **Paragraph One -** Open with an introductory statement that grabs the reader and compels him or her to continue reading. Be upbeat, but not offensive.

- **Paragraph Two -** Briefly summarize your pertinent background and refer the reader to the credentials on your resume which are relevant to your candidacy.

- **Paragraph Three** - Indicate why you are interested in the position, company, product, or service. Stress what you can contribute to the company.

- **Paragraph Four** - Emphasize your desire for a personal meeting and your intention to follow up your letter with a phone call. Then, do it!

Do Your Homework On Each Company

Find background information through library sources such as Dun & Bradstreet directories, The Thomas Register, and statewide directories of manufacturers and service industries; company annual reports and newsletters; trade journals; company public relations departments; and other company employees. This information will also better prepare you for your interview.

Do Not Include A Salary History

Never commit yourself in writing to a salary range because you might sell yourself too low or price yourself out of the job. Salary is best discussed after the first interview, in the context of a total benefits package.

Ignore the request for a salary history; instead, develop a strong cover letter and resume that will motivate the prospective employer to invite you in for an interview. Probabilities are high that if you make a strong impression on the interviewer, the issue of salary will become less important to him or her.

Tell Why You Want The New Job

This is important information to include in your cover letter. However, do not make negative statements about your present company or boss. Instead, project an ambitious attitude. If you are looking for more challenge, money, growth, or management responsibility, say so. In the event you have been *laid off* due to company reorganization or relocation, say that also. See the section below for cases of termination.

A Note About Termination

Your cover letter should not indicate that you have ever been fired from previous employment because this information could negatively affect a prospective employer's attitude about even meeting you. Write your letter exactly as if you were never fired - summarize your credentials and stress your achievements. You might need to honestly discuss your status in an interview, but never volunteer negative information.

A Word Of Caution About Letter Campaigns

Letter campaigns, or mass mailings, while tremendously efficient, usually have low impact and yield poor results. So, launching a letter campaign might make you feel as if you are busy doing something positive about securing a new job, but your time might be better spent in the library researching particular companies, conducting informational interviews with knowledgeable professionals, contacting recruiters in your profession, or attending networking meetings to try to make personal contacts.

A New Idea - The Broadcast Letter

With corporate mergers, buy-outs, relocations, and bankruptcies ever more prevalent, more and more employees are finding themselves out of a job through no fault of their own. Thus, the birth of new techniques to help laid off employees find new, suitable positions. The broadcast letter is one such method. It's highly effective for you, the job hunter, and costs your former employer practically nothing.

In effect, the broadcast letter is a letter of recommendation written for you by the highest level executive possible in your company, and then sent by him/her to top executives in *carefully researched* companies. It is far more effective than a cover letter written by you because it is an endorsement by a third party, one who is, hopefully, influential in the eyes of the reader.

The broadcast letter should include information about you describing:

- Length of service

- Scope of responsibilities

- Major accomplishments

- Value to the company

- Explanation of your current employment status

- Unconditional endorsement by the company

After The Interview - The Follow-up Letter

Common courtesy dictates that you send a personally typed or handwritten follow-up letter to each person with whom you interviewed. Such a letter should:

- Describe your appreciation for time spent together

- Review the key points discussed

- Reiterate your interest in the position and company

You can also utilize the follow-up letter as a second chance to sell yourself and as a way to keep your name and image alive in the interviewer's mind. The follow-up letter is a new opportunity to:

- Send an updated resume or other supporting data

- Suggest a relevant idea for the prospective company

- Smooth over any part of the interview in which you felt less than confident

Letters for Special Situations

Throughout your career you will be faced with the need to write various letters for special career situations, e.g., request for recommendation, thank you for an informational interview, declining an offer, resignation. For your convenience, in this chapter we have included samples of different kinds of letters which will help you project a professional image no matter what the circumstances. The letters are indexed by situation.

ACCEPTANCE OF OFFER

128 Horatio Avenue
Tampa, FL 33606

Date

Elaine Monroe
Regional Sales Manager
Belmont Industries
3342 Beach Drive
Tampa, FL 33606

Dear Elaine,

I am delighted to accept the offer of employment from Belmont Industries as District Sales Manager - Southern Territory.

As you requested, I am signing and returning the employment contract which outlines the scope of the position, compensation plan, and benefit package.

Because of my many contacts at Belmont, I really feel as if I'm "coming home" rather than starting a new position. It will be exciting to implement the many programs which you and I discussed during the interviewing process.

Happy holidays. I look forward to seeing you on January 2.

Sincerely,

Ellen Caban

Encl.: Employment contract

- ✔ Ellen has made the transition from candidate to employee.
- ✔ Her acceptance letter is brief, but enthusiastic.
- ✔ It helps set a positive tone for her first day on the job.

ALTERNATIVE TO RESUME (Achievement-oriented)

37 Preston Brook Lane
Bothell, WA 98011

Date

Pierre Marchand
Desmond Demographics Company
314 Sandy Island Way
Redmond, WA 98052

Dear Mr. Marchand,

As a marketing executive with a national computer services firm, I have had 12+ years of experience in the highly competitive information services market. This experience includes development of market strategies, key account programs, and vertical market penetration.

You may be interested in some of my accomplishments:

- Successfully directed the marketing efforts of the company's sales force to penetrate the information services marketplace with system solutions for list management.

- Sold value added systems priced between $1M and $2M.

- Five consecutive years in the company's Top Sales Club by exceeding objectives in such categories as actual P&L vs. plan, product mix, and new business goals.

I hold an M.B.A. from University of Utah's Executive Program and prior to that earned a B.A. in Marketing at Seattle University.

I would be pleased to discuss my background in greater detail and will call you next week to ask some questions about the Sales Manager opening.

Sincerely yours,

Scott Atkinson

✔ Scott's letter identifies major accomplishments which support his candidacy.
✔ He eliminates the need for Pierre to read extraneous information on a resume.
✔ To insure confidentiality, he describes his present company without naming it.

ALTERNATIVE TO RESUME (Credential-oriented)

128 Forest Street
Lowman, ID 83637

Date

Board of Selectmen
Ustick Town Hall
556 Mill Pond Parkway
Ustick, ID 83704

To Whom it May Concern:

I am interested in being considered for the position of Chief of Police as recently advertised in the Boise Tribune.

My background includes an AS in Criminal Justice, Municipal Police Officers Training at the State Police Academy, and completion of 15 training courses at the Criminal Justice Training Center.

Since 1978 I have worked as a Police Investigator for the Boise Housing Authority where I have gained valuable hands-on experience investigating and resolving public safety issues. Previously I was employed as a Federal Police Officer at the Public Health Hospital and a Special Police Officer at Boise Bible College. I am also a member of the Boise Police-Community Relations Committee.

I am well acquainted with law enforcement agencies/personnel in and around Ustick, and am knowledgeable about the numerous challenges facing suburban communities relating to crime prevention and the promotion of a positive town image.

I have established an exemplary record in the field of Law Enforcement and am proud of my ability to get things done in a professional and efficient manner. I believe I am a strong candidate for this position and would welcome the opportunity to meet in person to further discuss my qualifications.

I will call you next week to answer any questions. Thank you for your consideration.

Sincerely,

Norris Kirkland

✔ Norris' key credentials pre-qualify him as a contender for Chief of Police.
✔ He omits specific job duties because they are obvious to the Board.
✔ During the interview, Norris can provide more detailed information.

Bancroft Industries
332 Winston Place
Winston-Salem, NC 27102
919/ 555-4500

Date

Frederick Hanlon
President
GCC Components
54 Reynolds Parkway
Winston-Salem, NC 27102

Dear Fred,

I am pleased to introduce Russ Kirk, a Technical Sales Manager with an outstanding record of accomplishment at Bancroft Industries for more than a decade.

Russ came on board during a period of near chaos at Bancroft - sales were sagging due to international competition and late deliveries; communication between the engineering, production, and sales departments was nonexistent; and Bancroft was steadily losing its reputation as an industry leader.

Then, Russ stepped in and worked his magic. Combining his technical expertise, sales & marketing savvy, and boundless enthusiasm, Russ successfully analyzed major stumbling blocks, developed strategies, and implemented action plans. Most important, he fostered in-house communication and team spirit, resulting in Bancroft's re-emergence and continued standing as a key player in the industry.

We value Russ as an integral part of our management team and hate to lose him as a result of our planned relocation, but our loss could be your gain. I recommend him unconditionally.

Sincerely,

John L. Meyers
CEO

✔ John knows Fred personally, so this letter will be taken seriously.
✔ His praise of Russ is glowing, specific, and sincere.
✔ The closing sentence is vital to Russ' chances for a new position.

213 Rialto Road
Oakley, OH 45209

Date

Mr. Peter Vesterman
Vice President
Depositor's Trust Company
One Plymouth Plaza
Cincinnati, OH 45202

Dear Mr. Vesterman:

Early last month I heard you speak at our industry seminar and was impressed with the level of diligence your firm performs prior to presenting a package to a lender.

I had never considered mortgage brokering as a career option, but now feel it is one that takes full advantage of my background.

I currently work for Huntington Development Company in a financial management capacity. One recent responsibility is procurement of permanent financing for seven historic restorations. Specifically, I prepare financial projections, analyze appraisals and test assumptions used by appraisers to arrive at value. In addition, I communicate with bankers and mortgage brokers regarding occupancy, debt coverage and net operating income requirements, and loan to value ratios.

My enclosed resume will prove me a seasoned professional. I hope you'll agree that I could be an asset to your Mortgage Finance Group.

I will call you next week to discuss opportunities at Depositor's Trust.

Very truly yours,

Irene Dracut

Encl.: resume

✔ Irene captures the prospective employer's interest by opening her letter on a personal note, conveying genuine interest in Depositor's Trust Company.
✔ She stresses that her current expertise is transferable to brokering.

CAREER CHANGE (B)

3 Bolton Street
Donaldson, OK 74104

Date

Rhonda Ulrich
Human Resources Manager
Trimount Industries
788 Stadium Street
Tulsa, OK 74101

Dear Ms. Ulrich,

The heart of any organization is its Human Resources Department, an area where I can readily make a contribution.

It is my intention to pursue a new career as a Human Resources generalist, and I understand that Trimount has several openings.

As the enclosed resume indicates, I hold a BS degree and have worked for several years in teaching and educational program management at the university level.

My strengths lie in training, listening, writing, planning, and organizing. I am able to learn quickly, adapt to new situations, and perform well under pressure. And I know that there can be a tremendous amount of pressure trying to keep an organization flowing.

Above all else, I'm positive and a good motivator. I'd appreciate being considered for one of your openings, and will contact you next week to discuss available positions.

Sincerely,

Charles Seymour

Encl: resume

✔ Charles readily acknowledges that he's a novice in Human Resources, but at the same time communicates a basic understanding of the field.
✔ The good feelings which Charles communicates are his biggest asset.

CAREER CHANGE (C)

921 Joslin Road
Lincoln Park, IL 60614

Date

April Giosa
Director of Human Resources
Getaway Tours
2500 East 33rd Street
Chicago, IL

Dear Ms. Giosa:

Getaway Tours is rapidly expanding in New York, and I can contribute to that success.

The enclosed resume will indicate that my professional background
spans both business and education. Raised in France, I am widely-
travelled and multi-lingual. I have taught foreign languages,
worked as a translator, and live easily within diverse cultures.
I'm a public relations natural.

After 15 years in Chicago, I have reached a plateau in my career
and am relocating to New York. In such a culturally rich area as
New York, I believe my qualifications will be valuable.

My ability to communicate in many languages, plan and implement
creative programs, work independently or on a team, facilitate
change, energize and motivate groups, and present a mature, professional image are all vital.

I have been following Getaway's phenomenal progress very
closely, and hope to be a part of it. I will contact you next week.

Sincerely,

Jeffrey Fournier

Encl: resume

- ✔ Jeff has chosen a new career path in which he has little direct experience, but is obviously well-qualified.
- ✔ He helps the company understand how he can contribute to its goals.

2368 Morningside Drive
Agoura, CA 91301

Date

Stanley Ackerman
Sales Manager
Aviva Athletics, Inc.
29 Berkeley Street
City of Commerce, CA 90022

Dear Mr. Ackerman:

Aviva products must be easy to sell. I know because, as a golf
pro, I wear them and recommend them. That's why I was thrilled
to see your ad for a Sales Rep in today's LA Times.

As a PGA-certified golf teaching professional, I have worked for
seven years on a commissioned basis: in effect, self-employed,
generating revenues for myself and athletic clubs through the
implementation of successful instructional programs and participation in multi-pronged promotional programs. I know major manufacturers of athletic equipment and clothing, and have participated
in several wear-testing programs for them, including Aviva.

I love being a teaching pro, but am ready to move on to a more
lucrative and challenging career. For me, sales is a natural!

Aviva particularly interests me because of its high profile product
line of athletic equipment and clothing. I have many ideas for
promotional programs which I would like to share with you. I will
call you next week after you've had a chance to review the enclosed resume.

Sincerely yours,

Jean Quigley

Encl.: resume

- ✔ Jean's approach is upbeat and confident.
- ✔ She relates key aspects of her present position to the field of sales.
- ✔ Her closing paragraph is provocative enough to win telephone time.

CAREER CHANGE (E)

455 Hillman Avenue
Waverly, MI 48917

Date

Edward Beacham
Sales Manager
Alcon Computer Company
Suite 404
6722 E. Washington Street
Lansing, MI 48924

Dear Mr. Beacham,

I'm a different kind of sales candidate.

One with formal computer science and mathematics training, a strong teaching background and, like Alcon, a strong interest in the desktop publishing field. In fact, I'm a computer fanatic who can't resist the latest technology, particularly Alcon's.

Unfortunately, like many professional educators, I'm under-compensated, understimulated, and underchallenged. A sales career at Alcon can remedy all that.

Presently I work evenings so that I can use my days to prepare for this career change. I will contact your office next week after you've had a chance to review my credentials. I look forward to talking Alcon and computers.

Sincerely yours,

Hal Jarvis

Encl.: resume

- ✔ Hal is enthusiastic about his career change.
- ✔ He communicates a knowledge of Alcon products and sales.
- ✔ He is proud of his non-sales background and uses it as a selling point.

87 Balsam Shores Drive
Lake Forest, FL 32208

Date

William Sparks
Dean, Business Department
Jacksonville University
24 Kingston Avenue
Jacksonville, FL 32201

Dear Mr. Sparks:

I am definitely not the typical candidate applying for a teaching position.

After ten years as the owner of a profitable shoe manufacturing business, I decided to close the company and pursue other business/teaching endeavors including consultation to start-up companies to improve their production and material sourcing.

Teaching Economics I&II nights at Jacksonville University is the most satisfying part of my career now. I hope to use this experience and my business expertise to launch a full-time teaching career. I am confident my educational background and practical business experience would enable me to enrich the curriculum in management, marketing, economics, and accounting theory.

Reggie Adams has graciously offered to speak with you about my teaching performance. I will call you following that discussion and your review of the enclosed resume.

Sincerely,

John Merchant

Encl: resume

✔ John converts his "non-traditional" background into an asset.
✔ His part-time teaching position communicates his commitment to his career change, and affords him an influential reference.

772 Buckingham Drive
E. Atlanta, GA 30316

Date

Dr. Amanda Frangellis
Acting Director
Graduate Admissions Office
Clark Atlanta University
Atlanta, GA 30304

Dear Dr. Frangellis,

Enclosed are the necessary documents which comprise my application for entrance into Clark Atlanta University's Master of Science in Nursing Program:

> Application Form
> Essay
> Copy of R.N. License
> Residency Form
> Application fee of $20.00

If you require additional information, please do not hesitate to contact me.

I will check with your office on the status of my application in one month.

Sincerely,

Brenda Pettruzelli

Encls.

✔ Brenda sends a brief letter to accompany her college application to notify the Admissions Office that her file is complete.
✔ She supplies a checklist of each document to ease the administrator's task.

DECLINING AN OFFER

463 Arrowhead Park
Decatur, AL 35603

Date

Stephen Rich
Uncommon Scents
84 Thompson Street
Huntsville, AL 35802

Dear Stephen,

I was delighted to receive your call on Monday offering me the opportunity to manage your shop in Huntsville. As you know, I'm Uncommon Scents' #1 customer!

I had hoped from our initial conversation that the opening at your Decatur shop would become available a little sooner, but since this has not occurred, I'm in the very disappointing position of having to decline your offer.

It was a tough decision, but after much thought, I accepted another retail management position with HeartBeeps a little closer to home.

Thank you so much for the confidence you showed in me by selecting me for the Manager's position. I'd like to keep in touch from time to time in case either of our situations changes again.

Sincerely,

Laureen Brosnan

✔ Laureen frankly communicates her pleasure in having been selected for the position, and her regret in having to decline.
✔ Her gracious tone has left open the possibility for future employment.

6 Ash Street
Gladstone, MO 64118

Date

Beverly Salem
Director of Personnel
Dawson Associates
455 Lee Plaza
Kansas City, MO 64108

Dear Ms. Salem:

I am seeking the opportunity to prove myself.

As a recent graduate of Columbia College with a degree in marketing, I plan to pursue a career in advertising or public relations,
and would love to begin at Dawson as a copywriter.

In addition to my resume, I am sending a portfolio of writing
samples - from satire to sports reports. I hope they will generate
interest in speaking with me personally about career opportunities
at Dawson.

I will call your office next week. Thank you for your consideration.

Sincerely,

John Alvarez

Encl.: resume and portfolio

✔ John's letter is typical for someone seeking an entry-level position, but he goes
a step further by defining his career goals.
✔ He uses his portfolio as a marketing tool.

270 Brighton Avenue
Brighton, MA 02135

Date

Arthur Humphries
Director of Consulting
Pierce Business Consultants
56-B Causeway Street
Boston, MA 02101

Dear Mr. Humphries,

Jim Peabody of your Marketing Group suggested I contact you about an entry-level research position with Pierce. I am familiar with the scope of Pierce's consulting projects and am eager to become part of such a dynamic organization.

My personal background might be of particular interest to you, as I was born and educated in Munich and am fluent in both German and French. I am familiar with many European cultures, and could easily undertake assignments abroad.

As the enclosed resume indicates, I hold a BA in Management and throughout college have worked part-time in finance, government, and manufacturing environments. Within all of these positions I demonstrated the ability to work independently and efficiently as well as having excellent communication, organization, research, and problem-solving skills.

Jim's enthusiasm about Pierce is contagious, and he assured me that you would welcome my call next week.

Sincerely,

Maria Schulze

Encl: resume

✔ Maria has researched consulting firms and chosen to contact Pierce.
✔ She presents her strongest credentials, her personal background, first.
✔ She makes excellent use of her referral source.

FOLLOWING INTERVIEW (Brief)

34-H Maplewood Street
Egan, MN 55111

Date

Ira Nash
Belden Fulfillment Company
3289 West Park Street
St. Paul, MN 55101

Dear Ira,

Thanks for meeting with me again on Wednesday to tell me more about the administrative opening at Belden Fulfillment Company.

After seeing your set-up first hand, I am confident that I could make an immediate contribution by effectively streamlining your computer system. I would also welcome additional responsibilities in the areas of research and marketing.

I would like to say that during both meetings I felt comfortable interacting with you and your brother, and believe your operation would provide me with a positive work environment.

As we discussed, I am available to come on board at the beginning of next month. I will check with you at the end of next week about the status of my candidacy.

Sincerely,

Kevin O'Malley

✔ Kevin's letter serves as a thank-you and a reminder of his continued interest.
✔ He offers general suggestions regarding his contributions.
✔ Above all, Kevin demonstrates his willingness to expand his job description.

Gail Travers
561 Glendale Court
Newton, Massachusetts 02158

Date

Andrew S. Chesterton
Chief Operations Officer
Bushing Hospital
120 Charles Street
Boston, MA 02114

Dear Mr. Chesterton:

I thought long and hard about our discussion last week, and I wish
to offer some additional thoughts regarding key planning issues at
Bushing Hospital. I also wish to reiterate my strong interest in
the position of Director of Strategic Planning. My impression is
that a close "fit" exists between your planning needs and my
abilities, specifically my ability to develop, conduct, and implement
a strategic planning process tailored to the local environment.

1. I suggest the following immediate approach:

   • Development of a Strategic Planning Committee.

   • Interviews with board members and key personnel to
     determine orientation and issues.

   • Analysis of internal hospital operations.

   • Identification of strategic business units and determina-
     tion of future strategic directions.

   • Prioritization and development of action plans.

   • Ongoing strategy sessions for senior management.

Andrew S. Chesterton

2.   Medical Staff Issues.

You raised the question of how to determine physician needs by specialty. I suggest that solutions to this issue be examined as part of a complete medical staff profile; including an overview of the entire medical staff in terms of status and specialty composition, the age and location of practice, and utilization contribution to the hospital of the top 100 admitters.

3.   Development of business plans for the product line management of Obstetrics and Pediatrics should be accelerated through the development of strategic planning sub-committees.

Other priorities identified by hospital administration could also be implemented independent of the strategic planning process. This type of immediate planning process would allow Bushing Hospital to gain market share.

I hope these thoughts provide additional clarification regarding the potential contribution I could make as Director of Strategic Planning. I have also enclosed a statement of qualifications and experience to provide you with additional background on the firm and my project experience.

I will contact you next week to see whether you need additional information.

Sincerely yours,

Gail Travers

Encls.

✔ Gail's not yet on staff, but shows she completely understands the "big picture."
✔ She uses indentation and bullets to emphasize her main points.
✔ The letter is 2 pages, but it is easy to scan because of the white space.

Tina A. Wong

3 Sixth Street • West Allis, WI 53214   414/ 555-6892

Date

Ms. Donna Carzzo
Trimar Desktop, Inc.
17 Biltmore Avenue
Greenfield, WI 53220

Dear Donna:

I enjoyed our phone conversation and would like to meet with you
to further discuss the Customer Service job.

It is my belief that customer service is the keystone in keeping
customers and building additional business. In the past, I knew
that many companies where I worked could have increased sales if
they had also provided services which maximized the use of their
products. It would be very exciting to me to become involved with
researching and implementing various customer support services.

The skills I have acquired while selling would be very beneficial in
this type of marketing position. Having worked in the field, I
know what customers need and how to uncover those needs. As I
sold sophisticated systems in the high tech marketplace, I am
confident that the transition to the desktop publishing market
would be a smooth one.

I hope the enclosed resume answers some of your questions. I will
be in touch with you by the end of next week to arrange for a
convenient meeting time. Thank you for your consideration.

Sincerely,

Tina A. Wong

Encl.: resume

✔ Tina has established that her sales philosophy is the same as the company's.
✔ Her letter continues to establish rapport with her prospective employer and
   sets a positive tone for her upcoming interview.

45-D Yarnell Drive
Rincon, AZ 85710

Date

Dr. Carol Stokely, Chair
Department of Physical Education and Athletics
Southwestern College Sports Center
Phoenix, AZ 85032

Dear Dr. Stokely,

I am enthusiastic about working with young people, and hope that I will be able to continue in this pursuit as an intern in the Recreational Management Program at Southwestern College.

Currently I am a candidate for a Master's Degree in Sports, Recreation and Fitness Management at University of Arizona, where I have been exposed to a varied curriculum encompassing all phases of facilities management, case studies, and on-site visits to recreational centers.

At the University I teach tennis to college students. Prior to this, I coached a coed YMCA tennis team for youngsters ages five to eighteen. I am also qualified to teach swimming: recently I coached two "A" level competetitive junior teams in Tucson.

Both Dr. Kenneth Fillmore and Dr. Arleen Drayton, faculty members at University of Arizona, have offered to answer any questions about my academic program. After you have discussed my candidacy with them and have had a chance to review the enclosed resume, I will contact you for your reactions.

Sincerely,

Timothy Fulton

Encl.: resume

✔ Tim stresses academics, extracurricular activities, and references.
✔ References from professors are especially impressive to other professors.
✔ His closing sentence invites a dialogue between himself and Dr. Stokely.

JOB-SHARING

24 Lynnway Arms
Beatrice, NE 68310

Date

Yvette Stone
Personnel Director
Beatrice Advertising
744 Main Street
Beatrice, NE 68310

Dear Ms. Stone,

Many proponents of job-sharing swear that two part-time people are significantly more productive than one full-time person.

Jane Jones and I share this philosophy, and so are applying as a seasoned team for your Account Executive position.

As outlined in the enclosed resumes, Jane and I have impressive credentials to contribute to a working partnership:

- 20 years combined experience in top advertising agencies, the last 2 in a job-sharing capacity.

- Solid record of achievement in copywriting, graphic design and production, and media planning.

- Success in conducting market research, as well as designing and implementing creative marketing campaigns.

- Ability to service established accounts and develop new business within the consumer market.

We sincerely hope you will consider our proposal and allow us to meet with you to further share our ideas on the possibilities a team approach might offer. We will call you in two weeks after you've had a chance to review our credentials.

Sincerely yours,

Phyllis Geld

Encl.: resume

✔ Phyllis and Jane are pioneers, and their sell job is extremely difficult.
✔ Their letter reflects sincerity, tact, and determination.
✔ The professional tone of the letter gives credibility to their ideas.

LAY-OFF

29 Hunt Club Lane
Oyster Bay, NY 11771

Date

Kathleen Everett
Regional Sales Manager
Marden Lawn Care Company
5 Noanett Road
Hicksville, NY 11802

Dear Ms. Everett:

As you may know, Kraft has recently been purchased by Carson Industries and the company reorganization will necessitate a career move for me in the very near future.

Marden Company particularly interests me because of its close association with Kraft. I believe that when you review the enclosed resume, you will agree that I am a strong candidate for a District Manager position because of my in-depth knowledge of your product lines and distribution channels.

Since 1985 I have worked as Area Sales Manager at Kraft Hardware Co., where I am currently responsible for developing and implementing sales strategies for their fastest growing territory. Prior to that I was with Folsom Company as Union District Sales Manager.

Throughout my fifteen years in the industry I have a established a solid record for successful sales and marketing techniques, fostered a large customer base, and gained in-depth knowledge of the major industry competitors.

I welcome the opportunity to further discuss my qualifications and how I might contribute to the sales and marketing programs at Marden Company. I'll contact you next week to set up a meeting.

Sincerely yours,

Michael Gregorio

Encl.: resume

✔ Michael addresses his impending lay-off immediately.
✔ He establishes his familiarity with Marden product lines, and states that his move to Marden would also be extremely beneficial for the company.

1606 Connecticut Avenue
Brookside, DE 19711

Date

Harvey Feinstein, Esquire
Legal Department
Arlwood Companies
18 Cheshire Street
Washington, DC 20027

Dear Attorney Feinstein:

The enclosed resume is an expression of my interest in an associate position in the Legal Department at Arlwood.

I have a strong academic background and several years of legal work experience. Prior to my current legislative work, I was employed as a law clerk in the District Court of Newark.

Presently at the Delaware Senate, I plan and coordinate efforts of lawyers, technical consultants, public relations agents and fund raisers in order to realize various legislative committee projects. At the District Court of Newark, I researched and wrote judicial opinions addressing complex legal issues, and participated in settlement negotiations and all aspects of trial advocacy.

My current Senate Committee directorship with the Delaware Senate will conclude in two months. I am planning to visit family in Washington then and would appreciate the opportunity to arrange an interview at that time. I will call your office next week to determine the possibility of scheduling a personal meeting with you.

Thank you for your time and consideration.

Sincerely yours,

Wendy Sharton

Encl.: resume

✔ Wendy is quickly canvassing numerous local firms for a legal position, so she does not cite specific reasons for her interest in Arlwood.
✔ Her letter is appropriately conservative for a legal position.

7 Rawlings Road
Forest Hill, VA 23225

Date

Glynnis Hines, C.P.A.
Carson & Griffin, C.P.A.'s
981 River Street
Richmond, VA 23219

Dear Ms. Hines:

I am contacting area CPA's whose list of client companies might include start-up or small firms seeking an experienced Controller.

The enclosed resume outlines nearly twelve years of broad-based experience encompassing finance, sales management, and operations. I am particularly expert at analyzing businesses and implementing controls, developing business plans, and computerizing systems.

Presently I am employed as a Controller at LeeTech, a small manufacturer of air quality monitoring devices. While I have thoroughly enjoyed my affiliation with Lee, I am exploring alternative positions within a larger environment.

If you feel my qualifications suit the needs of any of your clients, I would appreciate it if you could refer my name to them. I will be in touch with you in two weeks to introduce myself and answer any questions.

Thank you for your consideration.

Sincerely yours,

Iris Mendelson

Encl.: resume

- ✔ Iris cleverly is seeking to secure a new position through professional networking.
- ✔ In effect, she's letting the CPA firms function as personnel agencies for her.
- ✔ She states her specific goals and her intent to follow up with a call.

NEW BUSINESS ANNOUNCEMENT

VICTOR NEWSOM
P.O. Box 51
Waltham, MA 02154
(617) 555-6060

Date

Dear Friends, Associates, and Potential Clients:

As you may know, after six years as a senior manager at Malden
Community Health Plan, I recently resigned to form Lexington
Associates, a consulting firm specializing in the research, analysis,
planning, and implementation of health care programs for the
private and public sectors. The attached summary briefly describes the wide range of services and areas of expertise which I
offer. My resume is also available at your request.

As I utilize a network of outstanding professional colleagues, I can
effectively collaborate with each client to develop a flexible and
integrated set of services to meet the specific needs of any organization. Currently my client list includes a managed health care
association, a nursing home franchise, and a medical consulting
firm. I am now eager to expand my client base and welcome the
opportunity to discuss the needs that you or your associates might
have now or in the future.

I will call you next week to answer your questions.

Sincerely yours,

Victor Newsom, DPA

Encl.: Summary of Consulting Services

✔ Victor first canvasses his friends and colleagues for potential clients.
✔ He reviews his professional bacground and explains his firm's services.
✔ The personal follow-up call is key to his success in securing referrals.

PROMOTION (A)

738 Fenton Way
Dutton, MI 49511

Date

Oscar Nyman, Ph.D
Superintendent of Schools
Walker Public Schools
122 Bishop Lane
Walker, MI 49504

Dear Dr. Nyman:

As you may know, I have been an Elementary Teacher with the Walker Public Schools since 1973. Currently I am at the Elmwood Education Center with the Be Happy Program. Prior positions included Grade 2 and Grade 4 assignments in both self-contained and team teaching environments.

I hope you agree that my 18 years with the Walker Public Schools uniquely qualify me for the recently vacated Administrative Intern position.

My strengths include: dedication, maturity, and flexibility; positive relationships with students, interns, parents, teachers, and administrators; classroom and supervisory experience; leadership experience in the Walker Teachers Association; insight into the many ways teachers and administrators in Walker can collaborate for the betterment of the children.

I am very eager to be considered for this new challenge and look forward to the opportunity to contribute to the Walker Public Schools in a new capacity. I am enclosing a current resume for your convenience.

Sincerely yours,

Deborah Titus

Encl.: resume

✔ Deborah's approach is straightforward and simple.
✔ Although her credentials are already known, she reiterates them to refresh the reader's memory.

Date

Winona Brown
Personnel Manager
Exeter Hospital
74443 Hanscom Blvd.
Mobile, AL 36601

Dear Winona,

I am writing to express my interest in being considered for the
position of Medical Services Coordinator at Exeter Hospital.

It is my understanding that the role of Medical Services Coordinator requires a mature, high energy professional who can interact
with physicians and managers, analyze problem areas, and negotiate outcomes - very similar to what I currently do at Exeter.

As you know, I hold a BS in Nursing and an MS in Educational
Administration. In 1987 I was hired by Exeter as an Instructor
and rapidly assumed greater responsibilities. Since 1989 I have
facilitated the development of educational programs from concept
through design and presentation to both educate professionals and
promote Exeter Hospital.

While at Exeter, I have developed effective relationships with all
professional staff, and have been able to facilitate the change
process in concert with institutional goals and objectives. I have
created an atmosphere in which physicians are receptive to new
services, products, and protocols that may potentially affect the
quality of patient care.

I hope you agree that these steps are a solid foundation for assuming the position as Medical Services Coordinator.

As you requested, I will provide you with a current resume and
other information which you require during the selection process.

Sincerely,

Rhonda Estep

✔ Rhonda knows her target audience, and tempers her letter accordingly.
✔ She must market herself for the new position in a tactful manner that will not
jeopardize her career at Exeter if she does not land the promotion.

346 Foster Village
Whippany, NJ 07981

Date

Myrna Olsen
Personnel Director
LoveNotes Greetings, Inc.
Parsippany, NJ 07054

Dear Myrna:

You may know me as LoveNotes' HiThere Manager in Parsippany,
but I'm really a sales trainer at heart!

Please consider my proposal: A training team is needed for new
and existing LoveNotes-owned stores to school others in store
policies and procedures. The most important challenge we have is
to TRAIN - success for individual stores as well as large corporations depends upon this. I would like to lead such a team.

I know first-hand about training needs. We both know it was a
challenge to install HiThere, a new concept store: to conquer the
computer system, to work with unique, non-traditional fixtures, to
train staff and manage this high volume store. How I delighted in
its success.

Previously I was Assistant Manager of Ellen's in Whippany. I
participated in a store remodel there and also recruited and
trained a store manager for the Ellen's in Edison.

Consider this probability: A district manager acquires several
stores at once - the training he/she could provide would be insuffi-
cient. As a trainer, I would ensure success for the manager and
staff.

Please review the brief proposal and resume you find attached,
and I will call you soon for your comments.

Sincerely yours,

Ursula Graves

- ✔ Ursula's tone is upbeat, but professional.
- ✔ She establishes herself as a dedicated employee and team player.
- ✔ Her closing indicates that she is willing to listen to alternative ideas.

RECRUITING AGENCY

2689-A Royal Crest Arms
Houston, TX 77002

Date

Louis Giles
Saxon Placement Company
5 Winston Place
West Palm Beach, FL 33401

Dear Mr. Giles:

As we previously discussed by telephone, I am forwarding you a current resume in the hope that your firm might be helpful in securing me a management position in the hotel industry.

I hold an AS Degree in Hotel and Restaurant Management and most recently worked for Brighton International Hotels as a Front Desk Manager in both Atlanta and Houston. I have established a solid record for both knowledge of hotel operations and the ability to run an efficient, cohesive organization. I am particularly aware of the necessity for a well-trained, highly-motivated staff in order to achieve company goals.

The following information might be useful to you in placing me:

1.   I am primarily interested in a position in Miami.

2.   My salary expectation is $30K+, with important factors being benefits, area, and growth potential.

3.   Two references to contact at the Atlanta Brighton (404/ 555-2000) are Evelyn Meany, General Manager and Brian Snipes, Restaurant Manager.

If you need further information, please feel free to contact me days or evenings at 713/ 555-5050. I look forward to a productive working relationship with your organization.

Sincerely yours,

Marsha Whittier

Encl.: resume

✔ Marsha summarizes her background and supplies references.
✔ She stresses her desire to help attain company goals, be a team player.
✔ She outlines specific job requirements to avoid inappropriate interviews.

909 Delta Court
Plain, MS 39218

Date

Eileen Castro
Office Manager
Law Offices of Harrington Harvey
One Roswell Plaza
Jackson, MS 39205

Dear Ms. Castro,

I'm celebrating my last child's college graduation, and my own
return to work as a Paralegal.

I completed Paralegal Studies at Rider College and worked for 5
years in a general law office, but interrupted my career to raise
three terrific kids.

During that time, I owned a clothing consignment shop, served as
an interior designer on a private residence, and spearheaded successful charity fundraisers. Now that my children are adults, I
am seeking to channel all my energies back into my paralegal
career.

I recently returned to Jackson from the New Jersey area, and am
temporarily employed in the Corporate Law Offices of the Jackson
People's Bank, but would prefer the stimulation a litigation firm
such as Harrington Harvey offers.

I would welcome the opportunity to meet in person, and I will
contact you next week after you've had the chance to review the
enclosed resume.

Sincerely,

Sally MacIntyre

Encl.: resume

✔ Sally is open about her previous status as a full-time homemaker and mother.
✔ She portrays herself as personable and competent, a person whose life
   experience more than compensates for her gap in employment.

RE-ENTERING JOB MARKET (Self-employed)

JUDITH HOLT • 2 Oak Road • Ensley, AL 35218 • 205/ 555-4336

Date

Ruth Stevens
Office of Career Services
Birmingham-Southern College
124 East Main Street
Birmingham, AL 35203

Dear Ms. Stevens:

I am excited about the impending sale of my career consulting business and the prospect of applying my expertise as a Career Counselor at Birmingham-Southern.

As the enclosed resume indicates, I hold Masters degrees in both counseling and education and have worked in diverse environments including business, education, and health care.

In 1982 I founded and have since operated Resumes, etc., whose services include testing, counseling, resume preparation, videotaped interview practice, and workshops. My area of specialization has always been college students entering the job market; in fact, I participate each year in Birmingham-Southern's Job Fair.

I would welcome the opportunity to further discuss my qualifications and learn more about Birmingham-Southern's career development programs for students. I will contact you shortly to answer any questions.

Sincerely yours,

Judith Holt

Encl.: resume

- ✔ Judith hopes to impress college personnel without intimidating them.
- ✔ She establishes only her basic credentials to gain an interview.
- ✔ Her annual connection with the school's Job Fair is a plus.

REFERRAL

Rachel P. Flood

46 Belleville Place
Lester, PA 19113

(215) 555-1512

Date

Edward Collins
Director of Production
WELM-TV
5422 Armstrong Blvd.
Philadelphia, PA 19104

Dear Edward:

Our mutual friend Joyce Kay insists you're the best person to work for at WELM-TV! Consequently, this letter. My background and interest lie in educational programming, and I'm currently earning an M.Ed with a specialization in educational television.

Presently I work as an Associate Producer at a major advertising agency where I've planned and produced award-winning television commercials for local and national clients. Enclosed is a resume and video portfolio which feature many of my projects.

I am interested in broadening my experience in film and video by seeking out a new challenge in television. WELM-TV interests me because of its quality programming and funding, and how can I pass up Joyce's recommendation?

If you have time, I'd really appreciate hearing your views about my work and my chances at WELM. I will call you next week.

Thanks for your consideration.

Rachel P. Flood

Encls.: resume, video portfolio

✔ A mutual friend serves as an icebreaker, and allows Rachel some latitude to write candidly and humorously without appearing pushy.
✔ Her professionalism is still very apparent, however.

RELOCATION

Paradise Bay Resort
King George's, JAMAICA

Date

Virginia Day
Personnel Manager
Northside Princess Hotel
18 Treble Cove Road
Fort Lauderdale, FL 33310

Dear Ms. Day:

I am permanently relocating to Fort Lauderdale so that my wife
may pursue her education as a surgical nurse.

Since 1980 I have been employed as the On-site Manager at the
Paradise Bay Resort, the #1 small resort in Jamaica. My efforts
in sales & marketing, public relations, and operations contributed
significantly to its present respect within the industry.

The Northside Princess Hotel is definitely Fort Lauderdale's pre-
mier resort, and I'm confident I can contribute to its continuing
excellence even in light of today's competition.

The enclosed resume outlines the specifics of my career, including
a BS degree in Hotel and Restaurant Management and prior experience in management and culinary arts. I think you'll find my
credentials interesting.

I will call you in two weeks when I'm settled. I'd love it if you
could brief me on the current state of Florida's travel industry.

Sincerely yours,

Jackson Emery

Encl.: resume

✔ Jackson's opening statement clarifies the permanence of his relocation.
✔ He establishes himself as a colleague rather than a job-hunter.
✔ Jackson's questions about the general industry will be ice-breakers.

REQUEST FOR INFORMATIONAL INTERVIEW

667 Winnisimet Street
Hartford, CT 06101

Date

Events, Intl.
8765 A Street
Coronado, CA 92118

Gentlemen:

I am writing to introduce myself and ask about your willingness to meet with me to discuss career opportunities in southern California. After residing and working in New England for nine years, I am relocating in two months to rejoin friends and family.

As the enclosed resume indicates, my background spans a wide range of business environments. I have proven myself an apt administrator and am particularly interested in pursuing opportunities in management or meeting planning.

I am bi-lingual, willing to travel, and full of energy and enthusiasm! While I have been receiving newspapers from southern California to try to assess the job market, this route has proved disappointing. I am hoping that you might provide me with fifteen minutes of your time to discuss the current job climate there.

It is my plan to contact your office when I arrive in California next month to determine the possibility of setting up a short meeting at your earliest convenience.

Thank you for your consideration.

Sincerely,

Joseph Esteban

Encl: resume

✔ Joseph is up front about his need for specific information.
✔ He describes his other concrete attempt to assess the job market.
✔ He respectfully asks for only 15 minutes of valuable time.

REQUEST FOR RECOMMENDATION

6-H Oakland Park Street
Linnton, OR 97231

Date

Dr. Paul Connors
Director of Clinical Periodontics
Portland Dental School
890 Maplewood Avenue
Portland, OR 97208

Dear Dr. Connors,

Thank you for agreeing to recommend me for admission to a post-graduate program in periodontics.

Enclosed are the documents which you requested - Curriculum Vitae, Student Appraisal Form, Transcript, and Accomplishment Report.

These documents will attest to both my strong interest in periodontal research and my solid record of academic and professional achievements while at Portland Dental School. Of note:

- Grades of 95% or above in practical coursework.
- #2 student in clinical points.
- President of Dental Honor Society.
- Member of Surgical Procedures Committee.
- Periodontal Lab Instructor.
- Research Fellow at Knight School of Medicine.
- Numerous Research Assistantships.
- Clinical Assistant at Surgical Clinic.

I am well aware of the high caliber of competition facing me in applying for a post-graduate program in periodontics. Your strong recommendation would boost my candidacy enormously. I greatly appreciate your time and effort on my behalf.

Sincerely yours,

Bernard Driscoll

Encls.

✔ Bernard's letter is obviously a follow-up to a previous conversation.
✔ Bernard provides the needed documentation, and then goes a step further by summarizing his achievements as a reminder to his mentor.

REQUEST FOR SPONSORSHIP

168 Renner Way
Lake Andes, SD 57356

Date

Mr. Herbert Oldham, C.F.A.
Treasurer
Bullhead Company
1 Industrial Lane
Ravinia, SD 57357

Dear Mr. Oldham,

As you graciously suggested during our recent telephone conversation, I am forwarding you the enrollment form for the C.F.A. federation.

I want you to know how much I appreciate your willingness to act as my sponsor, and wish to thank you for the encouragement you provided me during my efforts to find a job in the industry.

I am extremely happy to be able to report that I accepted a position at the Gross Point Company in Rockerville and begin next month.

Again, please accept my thanks for your time and interest in me. If you need further information regarding the application, please do not hesitate to contact me.

Sincerely yours,

Hugo Branson

Encl.: C.F.A. federation enrollment form

✔ Hugo's letter appropriately reflects his deep appreciation for his mentor's time and effort in guiding his career.
✔ He should continue to keep his sponsor informed of his career progress.

RESIGNATION

182 E. 30th Street - #5-A
New York, NY 10016

Date

Ms. Ruth Kelleher
Account Manager
Arrowhead Advertising Co.
3 Park Avenue - Suite 504
New York, NY 10018

Dear Ruth,

As you know, I have enjoyed immensely working for you these past three years as a Junior Account Executive. Your continual support and enthusiasm greatly contributed to my productivity and satisfaction at Arrowhead.

You concur that I am ready to move into an Account Executive's role. Unfortunately, no positions at this level are presently available at Arrowhead, nor do the prospects look promising.

I have, therefore, accepted a new position as Key Account Manager at Bancroft Advertising, where I will begin on the first of next month. Of course, I will remain at Arrowhead until that time to ensure a smooth transition of my accounts to a new manager.

Please know that I leave with mixed emotions. I am excited about the new challenges in store for me, but also saddened to leave terrific colleagues and a wonderfully creative atmosphere.

Again, my thanks for being a wonderful manager and friend.

I hope we'll keep in touch.

Sincerely,

Elisa Bootman

✔ Elisa infuses the right amount of personal warmth into a difficult letter.
✔ She cites career growth as the only reason for her resignation.
✔ She demonstrates professionalism through her concern about her accounts.

RESPONSE TO AN ADVERTISEMENT

99 Common Street
Potomac, MD 20854

Date

Deborah Lyons
Director of Human Resources
Bank of Maryland
4200 East Carlysle
Potomac, MD 20854

Dear Ms. Lyons,

I am responding to your recent ad in the Potomac Gazette for an Assistant Director of Business Development. It greatly interests me because I share your excitement about the challenges facing Maryland's banking industry. To meet those challenges, it is critical to recruit a highly experienced, creative Assistant Director of Business Development who can support in the development and implementation of programs to promote both community relations and business development.

I consider myself such a professional.

As my resume indicates, I am knowledgeable about all areas of banking operations, but shine in community relations and business development. I am recognized as a positive catalyst, a motivator, a change agent. I have proven particularly effective in:

- delivering seminars to targeted segments of the community
- conducting staff training in new product sales
- maintaining networks with key community leaders
- conducting market research to determine customer needs

I would welcome the opportunity to further discuss my qualifications, and will contact you next week to answer any questions.

Sincerely yours,

Janice Phillips

Encl.: resume

✔ Janice opens her letter by naming the advertisement and position.
✔ To connect with the reader, she echoes a specific statement from the ad.
✔ Short, bulleted phrases present her key credentials for the position.

578 Cushing Avenue
Oak Park, IL 60301

Date

Jonathan Dillworth
General Manager
Armstrong Hotel
3889 Pennsylvania Avenue
Chicago, IL 60607

Dear Mr. Dillworth,

I appreciate your taking time from your busy schedule to meet with me to share information about the hospitality industry. From our discussion I gained a very accurate and comprehensive picture of the future of the hotel industry, and have decided to aim my future career plans in that direction.

The Armstrong Hotel is quite an impressive place. The decor and atmosphere reflect the overall excellence of the operation, and its location near the top tourist attractions in the city gives it direct exposure to thousands of potential customers. What an exciting place to work!

As you suggested, I am enclosing a copy of my new resume. I am eager to meet with Personnel at a convenient time to discuss available positions.

Last week the Chicago Times mentioned that you and your executive chef were enroute to Hawaii. I hope you had a successful trip.

Thank you again for your time and your interest. I will stop by your office to say hello on the day of my interview.

Sincerely,

Alex Roper

Encl.: resume

- ✔ Alex expresses his appreciation for the meeting, and shows initiative by sending his resume as a follow-up.
- ✔ He lays a foundation for communication in the future.

671-C Drury Lane Apartments
Waynedale, IN 46809

Date

Richard Heller
President
Computer Directions
66 Kings Mall Road
Fort Wayne, IN 46802

Dear Richard,

I enjoyed meeting with you Monday and very much appreciated the
generosity you showed by rescheduling our appointment to such an
early hour to accommodate my unexpected family commitment.

It was extremely informative to learn about the major milestones
that have occurred during the phenomenal growth of Computer
Directions. Obviously, targeting specific vertical markets was
really the breakthrough.

I have given both available positions considerable thought, and am
very interested in joining your Corporate Marketing Department.
We've already discussed two of my ideas for generating revenues:
tax write-offs for donating used equipment to educational institutions, and the giveaway of inexpensive, but popular "template"
software with each system. In such a creative atmosphere, I know
more ideas will come easily.

I will contact you next week to see how I stand in your selection
process. Thanks again for your time and consideration.

Sincerely yours,

Francine Bellows

✔ Francine uses her letter to thank Richard for his courtesy, refresh his memory
 about her, and express her interest in being considered for a specific position.
✔ She conveys enthusiasm, intelligence, and professionalism.

TRAINING PROGRAM

12 Wincrest Drive
Burlington, MA 01803

Date

Julie Reese
Director of Executive Training
Harwood's
Burlingon Mall
Burlingon, MA 01803

Dear Ms. Reese,

As you know from Jesse Rourke, I am interested in applying for acceptance into Harwood's Executive Training Program.

I recently received my BSBA with a concentration in Marketing and Advertising. My retail experience includes 4 years of employment as a Sales Assistant at His & Hers in the Woburn Mall.

Earlier this week I contacted Nell Gibson, an Assistant Buyer at Harwood's, whose enthusiasm for the program was contagious. She indicated that Harwood's Executive Training Program is excellent preparation for a career in retailing, offering growth potential within a challenging, fast-paced environment. I am confident that I could excel in the program and contribute to Harwood's success.

I very much appreciate your willingness to review my resume and look forward to meeting you to further discuss the Executive Training Program and my own qualifications. I will contact you next week to answer any questions.

Enclosed with my resume is a personal note from Jesse.

Sincerely yours,

Gloria Barnes

Encls.

✔ Gloria has demonstrated her initiative by identifying two good contacts at Harwood's and by following up on the leads.
✔ Her job experience conveys her seriousness about pursuing a retail career.

Special Career Situations 3

You Are Not Alone

Like many job-seekers, you may be unable to tackle your resume because you perceive that there are unfavorable or unusual circumstances in your employment and/or educational background. Or, perhaps you can't decide how to capitalize on certain strengths.

You probably feel that the obstacle you face in writing your resume is unique and, at the same time, overwhelming. It might help you to know that *most* people face some kind of challenge in developing an effective resume.

In this chapter we have identified 23 commonly-encountered career situations which are often stumbling blocks. We have provided one or more resume samples for each situation and have included explanations about how and why to remedy each obstacle.

Are Your Negatives Really So Negative?

Just as no two job candidates are alike, so are no two prospective employers alike. Priorities vary from company to company and from manager to manager. Some candidates are valued for trainability, some for technical expertise, some for leadership qualities, and others for academic prowess.

If you research your targeted field and company you might find that what you perceive as a negative about your background is actually insignificant. It might even be a positive in the eyes of a prospective employer.

Turn Negatives Into Positives

If you have determined that there is an unfavorable circumstance in your background, there is nothing you can do to change the actual condition. However, you can, and should *change your attitude* about the obstacle.

You needn't lie. Just ignore the negative aspects and emphasize the positive. For instance:

- If you are an *older candidate*,
  DO: emphasize your depth of experience and maturity in decision-making
  DON'T: portray yourself as lacking in vitality or rigid in your attitudes

- If you have held *unrelated jobs*,
  DO: stress your breadth of experience and risk-taking ability
  DON'T: portray yourself as indecisive or irresponsible

- If you have a *weak education*,
  DO: demonstrate how much you have accomplished despite this drawback
  DON'T: portray yourself as unable or unwilling to learn new skills

- If you are *changing careers*,
  DO: present your transferable skills and knowledge of the required duties
  DON'T: stress unrelated accomplishments

- If you are undecided about your *Objective*,
  DO: identify a range of your areas of interest and expertise
  DON'T: write a general, rambling Objective that appears unfocused

- If you have held all *similar jobs*,
  DO: condense your overall experience
  DON'T: repeat the same description under each position

Confidence Is The Key

A natural tendency for all of us is to overlook our many strengths and fixate on our few weaknesses. In resume-writing, this predisposition can be deadly. Remember, no career situation is so adverse that it cannot be remedied. Concentrate on your strengths and project confidence. If you can do this, it is likely that you will create a positive impression as a candidate and be pleased at the outcome.

ACCENTUATE PROMOTIONS

DENNIS FOY
226 Higgins Road
Hoffman Estates, IL 60172
(312) 555-6023

PROFESSIONAL EXPERIENCE:

SEARS-ROEBUCK COMPANY   CHICAGO, IL
PLANNING MANAGER   **1990 to present**

- Manage staff of six in the tracking, expediting and billing of shipments of goods valued at $68M monthly from US manufacturers.
- Keep current on import and liability regulations.
- Coordinate with Inventory Control Manager and Traffic Manager.
- Assisted MIS staff in conversion from Prime to DEC computer system.
- **Promoted from Assistant Planning Manager (1989 to 1990).**

ASST. PLANNING MANAGER   **1987 to 1989**

- Analyzed sales and inventory trends; modified unit/dollar forecasts.
- Evaluated store performance and recommended action plans.
- Researched and developed new store layouts and budgets.
- **Promoted from Assistant Distribution Manager (1986 to 1987)**.

QUAL-RITE SHOE CORPORATION   SCHAUMBURG, IL
SALES MANAGER   **1984 to 1986**

- Developed sales projections, assisted in costing, and coordinated transportation of raw materials and finished products.
- Established new division within 8 months and implemented training.
- Received numerous company awards for outstanding contributions.
- **Promoted from Sales Representative (1983 to 1984).**

EDUCATION:

DEPAUL UNIVERSITY   CHICAGO, IL
BACHELOR OF ARTS DEGREE IN SOCIOLOGY   **1983**

IN-HOUSE TRAINING
Logistics, Planning, Operations, Management

✔ Dennis' promotions, incorporated into his job descriptions, demonstrate his consistent job advancement and eliminates the need for repetition.
✔ He accentuates his promotions and dates in bold for further emphasis.

CHET MINTER
289 Riggs Road
Adelphi, MD 20783
301/ 555-4239

EXPERIENCE

HAMILTON & GILBERT TAX CENTERS

Regional Manager • Bethesda, MD	1988 to present
District Manager • Rockville, MD	1986 to 1988
Asst. District Manager / Tax Preparer • Washington, DC	1984 to 1986

Manage 9-office region in the preparation of 18,000+ tax returns, grossing $1M in annual sales. Prepare budgets, manage staff, and direct operations of all tax programs. Consistently exceed sales goals, increasing annual net profit by 23%.

Scope of responsibilities:

- **Accounting** – Hire and direct bookkeepers in payroll, employee bonuses, end of month, quarterly and year-end reporting functions.

- **Personnel Management** – Hire, schedule, and train tax preparers, receptionists, bookkeepers, and processors.

- **Office Establishment** – Located, leased, renovated, and equipped 4 district offices.

- **Training** – Institute and administer annual tax schools in 4 locations. Arrange physical space, hire instructors, recruit and register students, and teach tax preparation course.

- **Marketing** – Deliver presentations and design ads for business development and public relations purposes.

- **Customer Service** – Provide extensive customer service in order to alleviate problems and ensure customer satisfaction.

EDUCATION

BOWIE STATE UNIVERSITY • Bowie, MD
Bachelor of Science in Accounting   1984

✔ Chet combines two key methods of handling all experience in one company – to avoid repetition he lists, but does not describe, each job position, and he organizes his major job functions under Scope of Responsibilities.

ALL EMPLOYMENT IN ONE COMPANY (B)

184 Beacon Pond Road
Portland, ME 04101

Date

Ms. Anne Holmes
Director
Kramer Travel Agency
New York City, NY 10018

Dear Ms. Holmes:

As the Program Director of the highly successful Country Inn
Travel Pak Program at Jameson Travel for nearly ten years, I am
well aware of the complexities of the tour industry today. Since
our program's inception under my direction, it has grown to service 10,000 tourists annually. The revenues represent a sizeable
percentage of the total income for Jameson.

I can do the same for you.

I direct all phases of program development, policy negotiations,
procedural and budgetary decision making, and staff training and
supervision. Ever on the look-out for new and exciting programs
to add to our basic Travel Pak, I have created tour packages that
have received rave reviews in numerous industry magazines.

In addition to my ten years of experience at Jameson, I hold a
Bachelor of Arts Degree in Business Administration from the University of Maine and have received numerous certifications for
advanced training within the travel industry.

Travel is in my blood and I love it. The challenge of beginning a
new Bed and Breakfast program from the ground-up is exciting.
My schedule includes frequent visits to New York, and I would
welcome the chance to meet with you to discuss some of my ideas.

Please feel free to contact Mr. Harvey Moore, president of the
National Association of Innkeepers, a personal acquaintance and
business associate of mine. He can provide you with a reference.

Sincerely yours,

Melissa Montez

✔ Melissa's Alternative Resume combines a cover letter and job history.
✔ It allows her to adopt a personal approach and also eliminates the possibility
that a conventional resume, listing only one job, would look weak.

CHARLES LAVOIE

173 Dunbar Avenue
Dunbar, WV 25064

Residence: 304/ 555-2876
Business: 304/ 555-4040

EXPERIENCE: ACE AUTO PARTS COMPANY   CHARLESTON, WV

Director of Operations	**1988 to present**
Retail Manager	**1985 to 1988**
Management Trainee	**1983 to 1985**

Supervise total operations of seven retail stores for this regional manufacturer of aftermarket automotive parts. Act as Manager for 5,000 square foot retail store with 8 full- and part-time staff.

Regional Manager ~

- Monitor schedules, training, salaries, hours, and expenditures.
- Conduct regular store visits to resolve operational problems.
- Review performance of store managers.

Store Manager ~

- #2 in sales during off-season promotions.
- Significantly reduced merchandise return rate.
- Devised merchandising strategies adopted by regional stores.

Coordinator of New Store Openings ~

- Design physical store layout.
- Supervise construction schedules and costs.
- Purchase signage, equipment, supplies, and maintenance services.
- Recruit, hire, and train sales staffs.
- Establish all operational systems and procedures.

EDUCATION: UNIVERSITY OF PITTSBURGH   PITTSBURGH, PA

A.S. in Retail Management   **1983**

REFERENCES: AVAILABLE UPON REQUEST

- ✔ Charles demonstrates growth in one company from management trainee.
- ✔ He describes only his most current position to avoid repetition.
- ✔ Charles includes information about each of the separate roles he holds.

ALTERNATIVE TO AN OBJECTIVE (A)

CHERYL NILES

124 Floral Canyon Drive
Cottonwood, UT 84121
801/ 555-8033

Areas of Interest

MARKETING • PROMOTIONS • CUSTOMER SUPPORT

Professional Experience

CORPORATE CREATIONS ENTERPRISES
Murray, UT   1989 to present

Marketing Assistant
Perform all aspects of marketing and customer support for this growing distributor of unique corporate gifts. Prospect corporate and retail accounts through cold-calling, telemarketing, trade shows, and professional networking. Monitor sales programs, plan marketing strategies, and devise creative product applications. Assist customers with application, product, pricing, and delivery information.

BOYLE ADVERTISING AGENCY
Salt Lake City, UT   1987 to 1989

Sales Representative
Travelled throughout Utah promoting Graphic Arts and PR services to small businesses. Familiar with advertising design, creation, and placement.

Education

WEBER STATE COLLEGE
Ogden, UT   1987

B.S. in Graphic Arts

- ✔ Cheryl identifies several career interests rather than a specific Objective.
- ✔ The areas are all related to each other and allow flexibility in her job search.
- ✔ Cheryl's job experiences strongly support her Areas of Interest.

Sales
Marketing
Public Relations

GLORIA ARVIDES

34 Clay Road • Barberton, OH 44203 • 216/ 555-7813

Experience:

SALES REPRESENTATIVE
WALTON SALES • Akron, OH   1989 to present

Develop and expand accounts for a $2M sales incentives company. Consistently meet or exceed quarterly quotas. Achieved #1 standing in sales performance in 1990.

MARKETING ASSISTANT
GRADIENT CORPORATION • Canton, OH 1986 to 1989

Contributed to the planning, design and production of collateral materials to support a new suite of software products. Conducted market research, developed copy, and collaborated with graphic design, photography, and printing professionals to produce the final products.

Coordinated promotional events to local computer user groups and assisted in product demonstrations.

PUBLIC RELATIONS ASSISTANT
TOWN OF TALMADGE • Talmadge, OH   1984 to 1986

Supported in the design and implementation of regional public relations campaigns designed to increase the visibility of the town as a viable alternative to Akron shopping and entertainment.

Education:

BACHELOR OF ARTS IN MARKETING
CAPITOL UNIVERSITY • Columbus, OH   1984

DALE CARNEGIE SALES COURSES

TOASTMASTERS

✔ Gloria's career interests are presented in the upper left corner to spark interest.
✔ The three areas both summarize her career and express her future goals.
✔ A prospective job may encompass one or more of the three fields.

GRACE HORNSBY

179 Alma School Road • Mesa, AZ 85201 602/ 555-0253

SUMMARY OF QUALIFICATIONS:

Results-oriented marketing manager with extensive business and technical training • Experience in product development • Demonstrated success planning, developing and implementing marketing programs under deadline and within budget • Proven ability to work independently or on a team • Effective training and presentation skills • Budgetary and supervisory responsibilities.

PROFESSIONAL EXPERIENCE:

Marketing Manager
BIO-TRIM MANUFACTURING • Scottsdale, AZ 1988 to present
(Producer of high-end exercise equipment)

- Establish comprehensive sales and marketing strategies to target new markets, track leads, and improve the customer feedback process.
- Conceptualize, design, and produce written and audiovisual materials for both domestic and foreign sales and marketing support.

Project Manager
NEUROMOTION CORPORATION • Tempe, AZ 1986 to 1988
(Manufacturer of sports training equipment)

- Directed successful product testing program; developed testing parameters and data sheets; gathered and compiled data; wrote and submitted final performance report.
- Established administrative systems that increased the quality and improved the delivery of products to customers.

Radiology Lab Technologist
ST. JOSEPH'S HOSPITAL • Phoenix, AZ 1982 to 1986

EDUCATION:

B.S. in Health Care Management
SOUTHWESTERN COLLEGE • Phoenix, AZ 1986

Certified Radiology Lab Technologist
ARIZONA STATE HOSPITAL • Phoenix, AZ 1982

✔ Grace condenses her career history in a Summary of Qualifications section.
✔ Her Qualifications will allow her to apply for various positions.
✔ Her resume includes specific facts which support her Summary.

WILLIAM HUGGINS
1209 Decatur Road
Scottdale, GA 30079
404/ 555-2669

TRANSPORTATION TECHNOLOGY

EDUCATION

DEVRY INSTITUTE OF TECHNOLOGY • Decatur, GA
Bachelor of Science in Transportation Technology   **1989**
Associate of Science in Business   **1987**

EXPERIENCE

GEM CHARTER FLIGHTS • Atlanta, GA
Dispatcher   **1991 to present**

Calculate pre-flight information including times, routes, and fuel consumption. Prepare releases, obtain FAA clearances, and brief Captain. Thoroughly trained in system operations of charter aircraft.

SOUTHERN COMMUTER AIRLINES • Atlanta, GA
Passenger Service Supervisor   **1989 to 1991**
Passenger Service Agent   **1987 to 1989**

Supervised Agents in the preparation of planes and the assistance of passengers prior to departures and arrivals. Ensured the smooth flow of passengers and baggage through x-ray and metal detectors. Maintained a professional image at all times to promote the company's services.

ACTIVITIES

Member, National Association of Transportation Technology
Member, Airline Operators & Pilots Association

REFERENCES

Available upon request

✔ William's heading names his career field, but not a specific job title, so he can use his resume for different positions within his field.
✔ His Education, Experience, and Activities directly relate to his career field.

JAMES MONAHAN

High Pine Development Company
184 Winnisquam Road
Laconia, NH 03246
603/ 555-7080

Professional Experience

PARTNER	1985 to present
High Pine Development Company	**Laconia, NH**

Plan and direct day-to-day operations, legal activities, and the coordination of projects for a real estate development firm specializing in custom-built log cabin dwellings. Within six years increased annual gross revenues from $1M to $14M.

Areas of expertise:

- Site selection
- Property negotiation
- Municipal approval process
- Mortgage package development
- Materials transportation

- Land development
- Building erection
- Road construction
- Marketing
- Sales

SUBCONTRACTOR	1978 to 1985
Rockingham Construction	**Fremont, NH**

Current Projects – High Pine Development Company

- Development of a large 4-unit commercial retail center.
- Construction of roads and single-family dwellings on a 22-lot subdivision.
- Site plan review process for an 8-home subdivision.
- Site plan review process for a 32-unit cluster project.

Professional and Personal References available upon request

✔ James' resume is designed to secure customers, financing, or a new job.
✔ It highlights both his business expertise and technical know-how.
✔ Specific facts and figures indicate his range of experience and success level.

ANITA WOLPER
227 Westmore Avenue
Lombard, IL 60148
312/ 555-3367

OBJECTIVE: Human Resources position in Training or Employee Assistance

QUALIFICATIONS:

- M.S.W. with Certification in Human Resources Management.
- Management experience in program development, staff training, and PR.
- Expertise in assessing organizational need and planning new strategies.
- Strong background in curriculum development, teaching, and training.
- Facility in crisis management and creative problem-solving.
- Comfortable interacting with people of diverse ages and backgrounds.

EXPERIENCE:

- Initiated and administered regional sheltered workshop program for a developmentally disabled adult population residing in group homes.
- Planned and implemented multi-pronged marketing program to promote the benefits of disabled workers in the workforce to prospective employers.
- Recruited and provided orientation sessions for employers in business, medical, and educational organizations.
- Monitored individual progress of participants and provided trouble-shooting to employer and employee as needed.
- Taught college-level courses in Family Dynamics, Work/Family Issues, Substance Abuse, and Developmental Psychology.
- Hired, trained, and evaluated case workers providing family planning, infertility support, and AIDS prevention.
- Coordinated educational, legal, medical, and mental health services for a caseload of geriatric clients.
- Provided direct short-term intervention for clients in crisis.

Anita Wolper

EDUCATION:

KENDALL COLLEGE   EVANSTON, IL
M.S. in Social Work   **1985**
B.S. in Sociology   **1983**

ELMHURST COLLEGE   ELMHURST, IL
HR Management Certificate Program   **1991**

EMPLOYMENT:

DEPARTMENT OF MENTAL RETARDATION   CHICAGO, IL
Program Manager   **1989 to present**

DEPARTMENT OF MENTAL HEALTH   CHICAGO, IL
Social Worker Consultant   **1985 to 1989**

AFFILIATIONS:

National Association of Social Workers

American Society for Training and Development

Regional Roundtable for Human Resources Professionals

REFERENCES:

Available upon request

✔ Anita's resume will enhance her career switch because she has stated a clear Objective and has developed her Qualifications and Experience sections to support her Objective.

MARGARET MAHONEY

304 Watchung Avenue • Montclair, NJ 07042   201/ 555-3081

AREAS OF EXPERTISE:

- Teaching / training
- Recruitment
- Negotiation
- Group decision-making
- Program development
- Stress management
- Crisis management

- Staff supervision
- Employee relations
- Meeting facilitation
- Organizational consultation
- Team building
- Report writing
- Goal setting

PROFESSIONAL HIGHLIGHTS:

Clinical Director   **1988 to present**
SAFE HARBOR SHELTERS   NEWARK, NJ
(Direct clinical programs and professional staff in milieu therapeutic setting)

Training Supervisor   **1985 to 1988**
JASON ASSOCIATES   BELLEVILLE, NJ
(Supervised clinical and teaching staff in university-affiliated medical setting)

Therapist   **1980 to 1985**
V.A. MEDICAL CENTER   EAST ORANGE, NJ
(Provided consultation and coordination of adult therapeutic services)

EDUCATION:

Master of Social Work   **1980**
KEAN COLLEGE   UNION, NJ

Bachelor of Science in Psychology   **1978**
RAMAPO COLLEGE   MAHWAH, NJ

Continuing Education – Organizational Development, Human Resources, Systems, Marketing, Management

---

- ✔ Margaret's Areas of Expertise are transferable to a new career in business.
- ✔ She de-emphasizes her Human Services placements with brief descriptions.
- ✔ Margaret includes Continuing Education courses relevant to business.

HANNA SPIEGEL
2044 Wells Road
Wethersfield, CT 06109
203/ 555-1184

PERSONAL STATEMENT

I am seeking to pursue a career in business which will utilize my *teaching, sales, and multi-lingual background.* Employment in diverse environments has fostered my ability to learn quickly and be flexible. I am confident I can succeed in a responsible position requiring maturity, flexibility, and enthusiasm.

EDUCATION

Bachelor of Arts in Secondary Education   **1989**
BOSTON COLLEGE   BOSTON, MA

- Concentration in Foreign Languages – German, Russian
- Junior Year Abroad – Germany and Russia

EXPERIENCE

Sales Associate   **p.t., 1991 to present**
MARY KAY COSMETICS   HARTFORD, CT

Conduct at-home sales presentations for small groups of qualified buyers. Develop and implement promotional activities, provide excellent customer service in the form of product knowledge and follow-up on satisfaction. Named "Rookie of the Month" for sales performance in June, 1991.

Foreign Language Teacher   **1989 to present**
SILAS DEANE HIGH SCHOOL   NEW BRITAIN, CT

Planned and taught introductory German to freshmen, sophomore, and junior students. Integrated conversation, history, and culture into the curriculum. Conducted field trips to museums, theaters, cinemas, and other cultural activities when appropriate. Encouraged prominent German guest speakers to address classes on timely topics.

✔ Hanna's Personal Statement emphasizes her special skills and qualities.
✔ Her part-time sales position shows her interest in the business world.
✔ Hanna's sales award demonstrates her business skills.

CURRICULUM VITAE

DARREN HOROWITZ, DVM

1602 Gardner Street
Independence, MO 64051

Residence: 816/ 555-3048   *Office: 816/ 555-4045*

EXPERIENCE:

1991 to present	**Doctor of Veterinary Medicine** THE CAT DOCTOR Kansas City, MO

EDUCATION:

1989	**Doctor of Veterinary Medicine** AVILA COLLEGE SCHOOL OF VETERINARY MEDICINE Kansas City, MO
1983	**BS in Biology** ROCKHURST COLLEGE – SCHOOL OF MEDICINE Kansas City, MO

TRAINING:

1985 to 1989	**Veterinary Assistant** BISHOP ANIMAL HOSPITAL Kansas City, KS
1989	**Pathology Lab Instructor** AVILA COLLEGE SCHOOL OF VETERINARY MEDICINE Kansas City, MO
1988 to 1990	**Clinical Assistant - Feline Surgery** AVILA COLLEGE SCHOOL OF VETERINARY MEDICINE Kansas City, MO

LICENSES:

Missouri and Kansas

- ✔ Darren's C.V. is standard for medical, legal, and academic professionals.
- ✔ He lists, but does not describe, Education, Training, Experience, and Licenses.
- ✔ Other credentials might include Publications, Presentations, and Affiliations.

Joseph Weymouth
1117 Petrovitsky Road
Renton, WA 98055
206/ 555-0777

PURCHASING

Professional Experience:

Purchasing Manager
FOOT JOY MANUFACTURING • Seattle, WA   1990 to present
($500M athletic shoe manufacturer)

- Purchase raw materials for 12 men's athletic shoe lines.
- Research vendors and maintain price/quality comparisons.
- Negotiate favorable price and delivery.
- Assist Marketing to develop cost-effective design options.
- Coordinate shipments of raw materials from vendors and shipments of finished product to distribution centers.
- Maintain physical inventory of distribution center.
- Received promotion from **Senior Purchasing Agent** (1988 to 1990).

Purchasing Agent
GEE WILLIKERS TOY STORE • Bellevue, WA   1986 to 1988
($2M toy store)

- Purchased toys and games for pre-school market.
- Selected vendors and maintained vendor performance files.
- Developed a child test market focus group.

Purchasing Assistant
DEAN MEDICAL SYSTEMS • Issaquah, WA   1982 to 1986

Sales Assistant
ROYCO INSTRUMENTS COMPANY • Redmond, WA   1979 to 1982

Education:

BS in Business Management
UNIVERSITY OF PUGET SOUND • Tacoma, WA   1979

References available upon request

✔ Joseph lists all jobs, but omits earlier company and job descriptions.
✔ This technique avoids repetition, condenses a lengthy career onto one page, and allows the mention of earlier company names, if prominent.

MALCOLM HINES
715 Bald Hill Road
West Warwick, RI 02893
401/ 555-2589

PROFESSIONAL EXPERIENCE

President   **1990 to present**
GRAYSON MORTGAGE COMPANY   PAWTUCKET, RI

Participated in the formation of a mortgage company. Established guidelines and procedures for the processing, underwriting and placement of residential mortgages.

- Gained approval as a subcontractor for the Resolution Trust Corporation.

Vice President   **1988 to 1990**
PROVIDENT HOME LENDING COMPANY   PROVIDENCE, RI

Planned and managed all operations of the Secondary Marketing, Program Administration, Closing, and Quality Control departments for a wholly-owned subsidiary of The Provident Savings Bank.

- Manager on due diligence and sale of parent bank's residential loan portfolio.
- Ensured program compliance with govt. and secondary market regulations.
- Established successful risk management policies and procedures.
- Implemented budgets that satisfied prescribed limits and variances.

Director of Secondary Marketing   **1986 to 1988**
Secondary Market Sales   **1984 to 1986**
PROVIDENCE SAVINGS & LOAN   CRANSTON, RI

Directed the strategic planning, new product development, inventory control, and secondary sales for an affiliate of a bank holding company.

EDUCATION

M.B.A. Candidate in Finance
RHODE ISLAND COLLEGE   PROVIDENCE, RI

B.S. in Finance   **1984**
BOSTON UNIVERSITY   BOSTON, MA

✔ Malcolm's job titles, job descriptions, and college degrees indicate steady growth in the same field.
✔ Earlier positions are combined to avoid repetition.

EDUCATION BACKGROUND WEAK

GEORGE DIGBY
619 Katella Avenue
Santa Ana, CA 92702

Residence: 714/ 555-3915   *Business:* 714/ 555-4000

PROFESSIONAL EXPERIENCE:

VICE PRESIDENT OF OPERATIONS • National Electronics of America	1986 to present
OPERATIONS MANAGER • Regency Telecommunications	1983 to 1986
ASSISTANT OPERATIONS MANAGER • Regency Telecommunications	1980 to 1983
PRODUCT MANAGER • Future Manufacturing Company	1978 to 1980

PROFESSIONAL HIGHLIGHTS:

- Participated in the development of corporate policies, procedures, and benefits.
- Directed warehousing and shipping of $20M in inventory to support $70M in annual sales.
- Authorized corporate purchases including capital equipment up to $150K.
- Directed all accounting functions including accounts payable, receivables, and payroll.
- Oversaw collections of $10M in receivables and authorized credit limits exceeding $40K.
- Supervised the design and fabrication of a 150,000 square-foot distribution center.
- Researched, selected, customized, and oversaw installation of minicomputer software for order entry, order tracking, purchasing, shipping and receiving, inventory control, and credit.
- Developed a company-wide computerized distribution system for local and off-site locations.
- Assured working conditions and procedures in accordance with OSHA regulations.
- Headed Acquisition Committee researching the possible purchase of a small R&D firm.

CONTINUING EDUCATION:

Certificate Programs in MIS, Purchasing, Production, Management, Operations

AFFILIATIONS:

Member, National Association of Executive Managers
President, Electronics Business Roundtable

✔ George begins with Experience and Highlights sections because they are strong indicators of his high level of functioning in the business world.
✔ He lacks a college degree, but includes relevant business certificate programs.

ENTERING WORK FORCE AFTER RAISING FAMILY

JOYCE LEVINE

1307 Wakefield Chapel Road
Annandale, VA 22003
703/ 555-3878

I am seeking a full-time administrative position within a small professional office which requires a mature, personable, responsible professional with strong secretarial and bookkeeping skills.

I hold an A.S. degree in Business Administration from Lynchburg College and have recently completed PC courses in word processing, database management, and spreadsheets.

While successfully meeting the many challenges of raising a family, I also continued to pursue both personal and career growth activities in order to prepare myself for a long-anticipated business career. Some of my activities include:

- *Part-time Bookkeeper*, The Loft – family-owned retail store (6 years)

- *Treasurer*, Hayden School P.T.O. (2 years)

- *District Fund Raising Chairman*, United Way (3 years)

- *Volunteer*, Allandale General Hospital – Unit Secretary (2 years)

- *Certificate of Completion*, Virginia Computer Center (6 month program)

- *Writing Courses*, Allandale Adult Education Program (1 year)

In performing the above activities, I found myself particularly adept at organizing, following through, solving problems, and attending to detail. I was able to work well with a variety of people and to depend on my positive outlook and sense of humor on hectic days.

For your convenience, I am enclosing two letters of reference – one from Regina Malden, Regional Fund Raising Chairman of the United Way, and one from Richard Swartz, Director of Volunteers at Allandale General Hospital.

✔ Joyce's resume focuses on her strengths and projects self-confidence.
✔ She presents specific business activities which prepare her for a career.
✔ Including references is a powerful statement about her professionalism.

BARBARA PAULUS
29 Haviland Street
Vestavia Hills, AL 35216
205/ 555-3927

PROFESSIONAL EXPERIENCE

Sales & Marketing Assistant • METRACORP • Bessemer, AL   1990 to present

- Support National Director of Sales & Marketing in the creation of promotional literature and the placement of advertisements. Conduct market research and testing to determine future product viability.
- Assist the International Sales Division during the Manager's extensive travel. Provide foreign representatives with business agreements, applications and sales assistance, promotional materials, and order shipment information and status.

Position will be eliminated due to departmental reorganization.

Telemarketing Representative • PHONE ONE • Birmingham, AL   1989 to 1990

- Solicited residential customers for a long distance telephone service company.
- Assisted in implementing a PC-based contacts system to streamline operations.
- Participated in the development of a direct mail marketing program.

Position was eliminated due to economic considerations.

Customer Service Agent • PROCTER APPLIANCES • Homewood, AL   1988 to 1989

- Assisted network of representatives in the servicing of nationwide accounts.
- Resolved customer problems and technical inquiries.
- Developed client questionnaires to assess customer satisfaction.

During company strike, recruited by PHONE ONE President.

EDUCATION

Bachelor of Arts in Liberal Arts • OAKWOOD COLLEGE • Huntsville, AL   1988

References available upon request

✔ Barbara closes each job description with a short explanation of the circumstances surrounding her job change, including lay-off. If she were fired,
however, she *would not* mention it in her resume or cover letter.

VICTOR GRESHAM

19 Nonquit Lane
Billings, MT 59101
406/ 555-1758

I am seeking a senior administrative or finance position within a not-for-profit organization.

I hold an MBA in Finance and since 1975 have been affiliated with national fund raising and human services organizations in financial management positions. Within these organizations, I proved myself able to generate new ideas, develop procedures to implement them, train and motivate staff, and maintain budgetary controls. I was successful at getting the job done independently or as part of a team, and consistently meeting organizational goals.

A lifelong resident of Billings, I am an active member of the community. I hold directorships on numerous civic and educational Boards and coach both adult and youth sports teams. I am well-travelled and enjoy studying foreign languages and cultures.

Professional Highlights:

- Analyzed, interpreted, and reviewed budgets up to $7M for the financial requirements of local and national charitable organizations.

- Managed all A/R and collections functions involving communication with private donors, financial institutions, and top management.

- Designed work simplification procedures for efficient processing of $15M in charitable donations, record keeping, cash flow and records maintenance.

- Recruited, scheduled, motivated, and supervised paid and volunteer staffs, achieving significant reduction in force without compromising productivity.

- Planned layout of a new corporate facility and directed the relocation at more than $30,000 under budget.

References:

Robert Fogel, President – Bank of Montana – 406/ 555-2354
Claire Hyland, Natl. Fund Raising Chairman – American Cancer Society – 213/ 555-3349

- ✔ Victor's Alternative Resume describes his career and related activities.
- ✔ He omits references to specific companies and dates.
- ✔ Professional Highlights and References validate his professionalism.

BRENDA COCHRAN
2067 Starlight Drive
Novato, CA 94947
707/ 555-0391

EXPERIENCE:

CHANDLER OFFICE PRODUCTS   SANTA ROSA, CA

Territory Manager   **1990 to present**

Recruited to revitalize the dormant northern California territory. Rapidly expanded business in stationery stores and office supply franchises. Collaborated with clients to establish sales forecasts, stock plans and advertising programs. Provided excellent account troubleshooting and follow-up to maintain productive working relationships.

- Increased sales 32% in largest department store in first 8 months.
- Received national sales award in 1991.
- Exceeded every assigned sales quota.

CROSS PEN COMPANY   SAN FRANCISCO, CA

Territory Manager   **1988 to 1990**

Performed similar functions in the territory described above.

- Increased annual sales by 25% in existing accounts.
- Designed successful sales contest for national stationery account.
- Trained retail sales representatives in product lines.
- Exceeded every major sales quota assigned for territory.

District Manager	**1986 to 1988**
Account Manager	**1984 to 1986**
Sales Representative	**1982 to 1984**

EDUCATION:

GRAND CANYON UNIVERSITY   PHOENIX, AZ

A.S. in Retail Management   **1982**

✔ Brenda describes only one of her Territory Manager positions – she references the other and lists achievements for both.
✔ She lists, but does not describe previous positions to avoid further repetition.

PAUL HERRELL
173 Tufts Street
Medford, MA 02155
617/ 555-2247

QUALIFICATIONS:

- 25+ years production experience in the electronics industry.

- 10+ years experience as a Production Manager.

- Proven ability to plan and complete projects under deadline and budget.

- Comfortable motivating and supervising culturally diverse work forces.

- Expertise in all production planning, scheduling, and assembling stages.

- Capable of communicating with staff in all departments and at all levels

---

EXPERIENCE:

HEWLETT-PACKARD COMPANY	WALTHAM, MA
PRODUCTION MANAGER	**1987 to present**
RCA CORPORATION	BOSTON, MA
PRODUCTION MANAGER	**1983 to 1987**
ASSISTANT PRODUCTION MANAGER	**1979 to 1983**
PRODUCTION SUPERVISOR	**1975 to 1979**

Held various Production positions (1965 to 1975)

EDUCATION:

WENTWORTH INSTITUTE	BOSTON, MA
B.S. IN BUSINESS ADMINISTRATION	**1975**
A.S. IN MECHANICAL ENGINEERING	**1965**

IN-HOUSE TRAINING
Production Management, MRP, Just-in-Time Manufacturing

✔ Paul condenses 25+ years of experience onto one page by tightly summarizing his career in both his Qualifications and Experience sections.
✔ Job details at each company can be discussed at an interview.

THOMAS GROSS 796 Huron Road, Offutt AFB, Omaha, NE 68113

Office: 402/ 555-6060   Home: 402/ 555-6239

PLANNING AND OPERATIONS MANAGEMENT

SUMMARY
More than fifteen years of top management positions in complex, diversified organizations. Extensive hands-on experience in organizational structuring, strategic planning, policy development, professional training, and MIS. Persuasive writing and presentation skills that articulate organizational goals, objectives and direction.

MANAGEMENT
Currently Associate Director of Training at a large Federal Agency with operations at nine US and six overseas locations. Previous experience as Director of Operations for a specialized agency responsible for the implementation of MIS systems.

PLANNING
Implemented national-level MIS studies and analyses. Devised contingency plans for recording and monitoring intelligence information about US civilians from hostile foreign countries. Designed and coordinated the MIS portion of joint programs to test and validate relevant plans and initiatives.

POLICY
Directly contributed to the development of US national MIS policy affecting both conventional and intelligence operations. Proposed US Armed Forces national training goals and objectives and contributed to related national policy and program initiatives. Authored US Armed Forces worldwide MIS training policy.

OPERATIONS
Managed and directed MIS line organizations responsible for operations and maintenance of US intelligence gathering in the eastern bloc. Implemented modernization program for facilities in East Germany and initiated plans for subsequent expansion.

EDUCATION
BA in history, Hood College
MS in Political Science, Temple University

MILITARY
HONORABLE DISCHARGE, Lt. Colonel

Top Secret Clearance

✔ Thomas eliminates all military jargon from his resume.
✔ He organizes his career information into accepted business functions.
✔ Military information is included only to lend credence to his experience.

NO CLEAR CAREER PATH (A)

ROSE MULLIGAN
108-B Wheaton Place
Garner, NC 27529
919/ 555-8216

OBJECTIVE: Retail Management Trainee program

QUALIFICATIONS: Experience in retail sales and operations.

Quick learner with excellent work record in varied environments.

Professional image and excellent communication skills.

Ability to interact effectively with all types of people.

EXPERIENCE:

Flight Attendant	1990 to present
Omni Airlines	Raleigh, NC

Assure passenger safety and comfort for charter airline servicing corporations, professional athletic teams, and individual groups.

Sales Associate	1988 to 1990
Lingerie Elegance	Chapel Hill, NC

Assisted upscale customers in the selection and purchase of fine lingerie. Supported Owner in planning and implementing merchandising and promotional programs. Accompanied Owner on European buying trips. Established a solid repeat clientele. Assumed responsibility for entire store in Owner's absence.

Cashier	1986 to 1988
OSCO Drugs	Durham, NC

EDUCATION:

DIPLOMA	1986
Carrboro High School	Carrboro, NC

REFERENCES: Available upon request

✔ Rose's Objective displays a new attempt at a career path.
✔ Her Qualifications section identifies commonalities of her unrelated jobs.
✔ Retail experience is emphasized to support her Objective.

HENRY THEIL
3022 Barbur Blvd.
Garden Home, OR 97223
503/ 555-0392

SUMMARY

Hands-on manager with background in entrepreneurial and established firms • Able to integrate all business functions • Strong sales, marketing, and customer-service orientation • Ability to train, motivate, and supervise staff.

PROFESSIONAL EXPERIENCE

OPERATIONS MANAGER   **1990 to present**
SPARKLE CLEANERS   **BEAVERTON, OR**

- Manage family dry cleaning business.
- Oversee on-site managers at 3 shops and 1 cleaning plant.
- Relocated one shop and implemented aggressive marketing program.
- Establish pricing and promotional specials.
- Train, orient, schedule, and supervise route drivers.

PRODUCTION MANAGER   **1988 to 1990**
ELECTRASOUND ACOUSTICS CORPORATION   **GRESHAM, OR**

- Recruited to streamline production department for a speaker maker.
- Initiated order tracking, expediting, and pricing systems.
- Hired, trained, and supervised new staff.

SALESMAN   **1985 to 1988**
PHONE U.S., INC.   **PORTLAND, OR**

- Sold long distance telephone service exclusively to very large accounts.
- Secured leads through telephone sales presentations.
- Consistently ranked as company's top sales performer.

EDUCATION

B.S. IN MATHEMATICS   **1985**
PORTLAND STATE UNIVERSITY   **PORTLAND, OR**

✔ Henry's Summary emphasizes the positive aspects of his diverse positions.
✔ He mentions his "family-owned" business to imply that his joining the firm was a temporary obligation rather than a solid career choice.

JACK HARDIN
306 Wallisville Road
Houston, TX 77027
713/ 555-7800

QUALIFICATIONS:

- Extensive management/engineering experience on diverse commercial real estate development, construction, and rehabilitation projects. *Received Prism Awards for design and creativity.*

- Expert in all phases of project management including acquisition, cost estimating, permitting, bidding, negotiating with subcontractors, monitoring construction schedules, and supervising occupancy schedules. *Introduced an innovative, in-house method of forming and placing concrete, resulting in significant time and budget savings on projects.*

- Effective in coordinating and negotiating with owners, realtors, property managers, attorneys, government agencies, and FDIC. *Initiated a positive development trend and instilled neighborhood pride as a result of construction and full occupancy of an inner city commercial office park.*

- Strong appraisal background based on sound assessment of value of land, integrity of finished product, and prevailing market conditions. *Licensed by the National Association of Property Appraisers.*

EXPERIENCE:

INDEPENDENT DEVELOPER
HARDIN DEVELOPMENT

SUB-CONTRACTOR
EMPIRE MECHANICAL CONTRACTORS

PROJECT ENGINEER
HOUSTON CONSTRUCTION

EDUCATION:

RICE UNIVERSITY
M.S. IN STRUCTURAL DESIGN
B.S. IN CIVIL ENGINEERING

- ✔ Jack omits dates from his resume to guard against age discrimination.
- ✔ He emphasize his extensive experience to boost his candidacy.
- ✔ His strong credentials will be seriously considered despite the lack of dates.

PATRICIA BABCOCK
3566 Montchannin Road
Talleyville, DE 19803
302/ 555-1873

OBJECTIVE: Administrative Assistant in a small professional office

EDUCATION:

WILMINGTON COLLEGE   NEW CASTLE, DE
Associates Degree in Secretarial Arts   **June 1991**

NEWPORT HIGH SCHOOL   NEWPORT, DE
Diploma - College Preparatory   **June 1987**

SKILLS:

Office Equipment: FAX, Dictaphone, telephone switchboard

Secretarial: Typing – 80 wpm; Speedwriting – 102 wpm

Computer: IBM-PC, DOS, WordStar, Lotus 1-2-3

EMPLOYMENT:

EARTH RESOURCES COMPANY   ELSMERE, DE
Administrative Assistant   **1988 to present**

Provide customer support for an environmental services company. Respond to customer inquiries, schedule sales presentations, maintain in-house direct mailing list, and performed secretarial functions.

REED TEMPORARY AGENCY   WILMINGTON, DE
Receptionist   **p. t., 1987 to 1988**

Performed a variety of reception and secretarial duties at DuPont Corporation.

REFERENCES:

Furnished upon request

✔ Patricia acknowledges her part-time status with "p.t." next to the date.
✔ With only one full-time position, previous part-time jobs add to her credentials.
✔ Her Education and Skills sections strongly support her Objective.

NANCY VACHON 12 Van Born Road, Wayne, IL 48184 ■ 313/ 555-2033

Summary of Qualifications:

- Administrative background in both business and academic environments.
- Expertise in program development; staff recruitment, training, and evaluation; office management; budget preparation; grant writing; and public relations.
- Strong communication, negotiation, organization, and problem-solving skills.
- Able to manage simultaneous projects and successfully meet deadlines.

Employment Highlights:

ADMINISTRATOR • Montessori School (6 years)

- Established initial guidelines, budgets, and staffing for a new concept school.
- Wrote and submitted proposals to obtain private funding from corporate sources.
- Recruited, trained, supervised, and evaluated staffs.
- Planned and implemented public relations programs within the community.

OFFICE MANAGER • Westland Medical Practice (4 years)

- Managed administrative operations of a 3-physician group practice including patient scheduling, staff management, A/R, A/P, billing, correspondence, and purchasing.
- Utilized word processing and accounting software packages on PC.

PERSONNEL GENERALIST • Dearborn Manufacturing (3 years)

- Recruited, hired, trained, and internally placed administrative staff.
- Provided orientation for exempt and non-exempt employees.
- Established and implemented a data processing training program.

Education:

M.A. IN EDUCATIONAL ADMINISTRATION • Marygrove College

B.S. IN SOCIOLOGY • Concordia College

✔ In order to de-emphasize an extended absence from the workforce, Nancy cites number of years rather than dates next to each position. This technique allows her resume to reflect competence, stability, and currency.

GUY KERTZMAN
908 West Liberty Road
Dormont, PA 15216
412/ 555-3489

OBJECTIVE:	Field Sales position with a large manufacturer

EDUCATION:	LA ROCHE COLLEGE	
	Pittsburgh, PA	
	B.S.B.A. in Marketing	1990

EXPERIENCE: MYERS STEEL DISTRIBUTORS
Pittsburgh, PA

Sales Administrator 1991 to present

Track and process orders for ten $1M+ key accounts. Resolve vendor problems via telephone. Use an IBM PC for word processing, correspondence, and maintaining sales logs and shipping schedules. Familiar with PC databases, spreadsheets and other business software.

Customer Service Representative 1990 to 1991

Aided fabricators in the selection of the proper type and size of steel for a particular construction project. Scheduled and tracked deliveries using an IBM PC.

ORGANIZATIONS: National Sales & Marketing Society

INTERESTS: Sports, sketching, piano

References available upon request

✔ Graphic elements compensate for Guy's lack of experience, e.g., horizontal dividing lines, large left margins, double spacing between job descriptions.
✔ He includes Organizations, Interests, and References to use space.

ANNETTE TREACHER
458 Ludlam Road
Kendall, FL 33156
305/ 555-3499

TRAVEL CONSULTANT / MANAGER

Qualifications:

- Manager of a full-service agency after only two years in the industry.
- Experience as a travel consultant for corporate, individual, and group accounts.
- Certified to book all accommodations for domestic and international travel.
- Highly accomplished at managing multiple tasks in an efficient manner.
- Expert at directing administrative, sales, training, and customer service operations.
- Superb communication, organizational, and problem-solving skills.
- Considerable travel experience in the US and abroad.

Experience:

TRAVEL CONSULTANT / MANAGER • Miami Beach Travel   1987 to present
SALES REPRESENTATIVE • Miami Sporting Goods Mfg. Co.   1982 to 1987

Education:

SABRE COMPUTER TRAINING PROGRAM • Eastern Airlines • Miami, TX   1988
SALES & MARKETING SEMINARS • Cruises International • New York, NY   1988
TRAVEL & TOURISM PROGRAM • Nova University • Fort Lauderdale, FL   1987
BACHELOR OF SCIENCE • Florida State University • Tallahassee, FL   1982

Affiliations:

INTERNATIONAL TRAVEL ASSOCIATION
SALESWOMEN OF MIAMI
MIAMI CHAMBER OF COMMERCE

- ✔ Annette begins her resume with a prominent heading targeting one job.
- ✔ Her resume only includes very specific credentials supporting her goal.
- ✔ Annette would have to create a new resume to seek other kinds of positions.

DEBORAH MULDOWNEY
1704-E West Ninth Street
New York, NY 10013
212/ 555-4661

SUMMARY OF QUALIFICATIONS:

- Strong administrative background within high tech environments.
- Proven ability to interact effectively with clients and staff at all levels.
- Proficient in handling simultaneous projects and meeting deadlines effectively.
- Skills include technical typing, editing, dictaphone, and meeting planning.

EMPLOYMENT:

Temporary   *1990 to present*

WEBB ENGINEERING • Hoboken, NJ • Computer Applications Department
VIZCOMM CORPORATION • Jersey City, NJ • Systems Software Department
HANSON PRINTER CORPORATION • Yonkers, NY • Documentation Department

Permanent   *1984 to 1990*

RYCO AUDIOSONICS • New York, NY
Administrative Assistant – Assembly Department (1987 - 1990)

NEWTECH COMPUTER SYSTEMS • New York, NY
Secretary – Engineering Design Department (1984 - 1987)

EDUCATION:

KEAN COLLEGE • Union, NJ
A.S. in Secretarial Sciences (1984)

CURRENT ASSOCIATIONS:

New York City Women's Business Association • National Secretaries Association

---

REFERENCES:

Available upon request

✔ Deborah's Summary of Qualifications emphasizes her administrative skills.
✔ She lists Temporary positions to show currency and diversity of experience.
✔ Current Associations demonstrate her seriousness about her field.

PROFESSIONAL HISTORY

Maria Morales
455 Zuni Road
Albuquerque, NM 87101
505/ 555-2773

I would like to introduce myself by way of the following professional history. I offer a unique bilingual background, success in many professional endeavors, and a blend of maturity, flexibility, high energy, and the ability to learn quickly and make effective decisions. Throughout my career I have proven myself a personable, dedicated, committed professional who has contributed significantly to getting the job done.

Diverse opportunities have come my way and I have seized them. While my experience has been diverse, several common threads hold it all together. One, a love of and ability to relate to all types of people. Two, excellent organization skills. Three, a polished professional image. Four, company loyalty. Five, a strong achievement orientation.

These valuable qualities can simultaneously promote my own professional growth as well as contribute to the success of any organization with which I am affiliated. It is my hope to find a mutually beneficial fit.

- Raised and college-educated in Puerto Rico
- Fluent in English and Spanish; familiar with Italian
- Travelled throughout Europe, United States, Caribbean, Bahamas
- Resident of various U.S. regions – New England, South, and West Coast
- Interpreter for hotel chain
- Management experience in retail and restaurant businesses
- Professional nanny for newborn and three year-old
- Executive secretary in high tech companies
- Public speaking background
- Meeting planning experience
- Business Manager for self-employed artist

✔ Maria's personal attributes and career experiences fit no mold, so she selects an Alternative Resume format which celebrates her unique background.
✔ An atypical presentation can attract a unique prospective employer!

Administration 4

The Buck Stops With You

Administration is the heart of any organization, the momentum that keeps it running. As administrators, you implement policy, motivate personnel, and track paperwork. Your job description is frequently open to interpretation, so all the loose ends are dropped onto your desk. You juggle a multitude of details, ensure that important deadlines are met, and pinch hit for your boss when a quick decision is needed.

Administration is a formidable task, and without you any organization would come to a screeching halt. Therefore, your resume needs to communicate that you are up to the challenge. In addition to competency in your area of specialization, you need to demonstrate coping skills. Maturity, flexibility, tact, and problem-solving ability are key qualifications.

The Many Facets of Administration

The range of duties in administration is so vast that it can be difficult to integrate all of your responsibilities, skills, and credentials so that your resume is still well-organized and concise. Three easy methods discussed below are demonstrated in the resume samples in this chapter.

The first technique is to begin your resume with a Summary of Qualifications section. It identifies and condenses the *major* points about your career and capabilities which you want to communicate to a prospective employer. For example, you might include the number of years in an industry, secretarial skills, accounting knowledge, and supervisory ability. This section allows the reader to quickly scan a synopsis of your entire career.

The second technique is to include a Special Skills section. It lists technical proficiencies related to computer usage, office equipment, foreign languages, and other special areas. This technique eliminates the need for you to repeat the same skills in each job description.

The third technique is to group your job duties under specific functions such as Office Management, Personnel Management, and Sales Support. This technique not only organizes your experience, but highlights your strengths at the same time.

In addition to aiding you in producing a more organized resume, these techniques will facilitate your thinking about your career and help you realize how proficient you really are. They're a tremendous morale booster!

Consider A Specific Objective

If you can pinpoint the exact new position you're seeking, e.g. "Executive Secretary in a Fortune 500 company," or "Office Manager in a general law firm," it is beneficial to state your goal at the top of your resume. Your Objective will connote that your career is purposely headed in a certain direction, and it also allows a recruiter or prospective employer to easily prequalify you for a position they are seeking to fill.

If, however, you are qualified for, or interested in, several different kinds of positions, then using an Alternative to an Objective, such as one found in Chapter 3, is recommended. Some of these Alternatives can also be found in the resume samples in this chapter.

Is Your Career Upwardly Mobile?

Administration is a catch-all phrase used to describe a variety of personnel ranging from filing clerks to executive directors. As can be seen by scanning the resumes in this chapter, administration is still heavily female-oriented. For many reasons, some professionals consider the term *administration* a stigma. Consequently, many administrators are seeking to move from administration into management, an area which they perceive commands more respect.

Administration is indeed a stepping-stone to supervisory and management roles. If your career is upwardly mobile, your resume should stress any current management responsibilities, including instances when you temporarily assumed your manager's role. Remember to list any training, coursework, or degrees related to management which you have completed or are currently pursuing. These added credentials demonstrate that you are preparing for more decision-making authority, more challenge, and more financial reward.

ADMINISTRATIVE ASSISTANT (Brokerage)

BRENDA DOBBS
108 Rusk Road
Elk Mound, WI 54739
715/ 555-8036

EXPERIENCE:

HERRELL-KLEINMETZ   EAU CLAIRE, WI
Administrative Assistant   **1990 to present**

Support the Director of Institutional Sales for this 150-person brokerage firm.

- Hire and supervise support personnel.

- Oversee the administration of personnel benefits.

- Coordinate off-site corporate luncheons for institutional clients and newly-public company executives.

- Notary Public – perform signature guarantees.

BEAL PROPERTY MANAGEMENT COMPANY   EAU CLAIRE, WI
Administrative Assistant   **1988 to 1990**

Performed collections and bookkeeping functions for 200 commercial and residential rental units.

- Assisted Principal with correspondence, meeting planning, and community relations activities related to his affiliation with the Chamber of Commerce.

EDUCATION:

UNIVERSITY OF WISCONSIN   MENOMONIE, WI
A.S. in Business Administration   **1988**

References available upon request

✔ Brenda begins each job description with a general statement of duties.
✔ She highlights specific functions with bullets for easy scanning.
✔ Brenda uses a wide left margin and maximum white space to fill the page.

DIANE FREUHAUF

178 Trammel Road • Jacksonville, AR 72076   501/ 555-8178

SUMMARY:

- Successful administrative support experience within corporate and not-for-profit areas.
- Strong secretarial skills including word processing, shorthand, and bookkeeping.
- Proven ability to work independently, handle simultaneous projects, and meet deadlines.
- Solid communication, organization, and problem-solving skills.
- Notary Public.

EXPERIENCE:

ADMINISTRATIVE ASSISTANT   1989 TO PRESENT
G.T. Joyce Management Consultants   Little Rock, AR

Provide administrative support for this management consulting firm with six national offices. Assist Office Manager and Accounting Manager in the areas of A/P, billing, purchasing, correspondence, notarizing, and travel / meeting arrangements.

- Attend weekly staff meetings to monitor current case work and discuss office procedures. Provide liaison to out-of-state offices.
- Assign new case numbers, update monthly case list, and charge incoming invoices to appropriate case numbers for billing purposes.
- Prepare and disburse checks for A/P and reimbursement of employee expenses.
- Monitor inventory, order supplies and equipment, and rectify account problems.
- Perform word processing and data entry functions on an IBM PC.

ADMINISTRATIVE ASSISTANT   1987 TO 1989
Junior League   North Little Rock, AR

- Administered banking procedures and prepared monthly financial report.
- Coordinated all details of major fund raisers to expand philanthropic programs.
- Provided orientation to a volunteer staff.

EDUCATION:

ASSOCIATE DEGREE / SECRETARIAL STUDIES   1987
University of Central Arkansas   Conway, AR

✔ Diane's opening Summary highlights important skills and credentials.
✔ Her company description lends importance to her own position.
✔ Less space is devoted to her earlier position because it is less relevant.

ADMINISTRATIVE ASSISTANT (Customer Support)

BETTE JOHANSEN
202 Waverly Place
Greenwood, NE 68366

Residence: 402/ 555-9032   *Messages:* 402/ 555-9033

OBJECTIVE: Administrative Assistant in a small professional office

EDUCATION:

UNION COLLEGE   LINCOLN, NE
Associates Degree in Secretarial Arts   **June 1991**

BENNINGTON HIGH SCHOOL   BENNINGTON, NE
Diploma - College Preparatory   **June 1989**

SKILLS:

Secretarial: Typing - 70 wpm; Speedwriting - 98 wpm

Computers: IBM-PC, WordPerfect, Lotus, dBase

Office Equipment: Dictaphone, FAX, AT&T Merlin phone system

EMPLOYMENT:

CHAR-FLO CORPORATION   OMAHA, NE
Administrative Assistant - Customer Support   **p.t., 1990 to 1991**

    Customer liaison for a new water filtration product. Responded to customer inquiries, scheduled product demos both in-house and on-site, maintained customer database, and performed secretarial functions.

PENACOOK TEMPORARY PERSONNEL   FREMONT, NE
Receptionist   **p.t., 1989 to 1990**

    Performed a variety of reception and secretarial duties at Craddock Life Insurance Company, Omaha and Northstar Brokerage, Fremont.

REFERENCES: Furnished upon request

✔ Bette's special telephone number for messages is an aid to an employer.
✔ Her special skills command a separate section with italicized headings.
✔ Using "p.t." before dates acknowledges, but de-emphasizes part-time status.

ANNE MANVILLE
189 Old Georgia Road
Glendale, SC 29346
803/ 555-3518

SUMMARY

Administrative experience in environments requiring heavy contact with senior citizens, volunteer workers, and professional staffs • Solid organization and problem-solving skills • Demonstrated ability to work independently, handle simultaneous tasks, and meet deadlines • Well-developed communication and supervisory skills.

EXPERIENCE

Administrative Assistant   **1990 to present**
SENIOR ACTION VOLUNTEER ENTERPRISES (SAVE)   SPARTANBURG, SC

- Manage office procedures for 600 retired senior volunteers.
- Supervise 6 volunteer administrative staff members.
- Liaison to 60 SAVE offices in order to ensure proper program administration.
- Assist SAVE Director to organize recognition events and other special projects.
- Maintain accurate records of volunteer hours, reimbursements, and enrollments.
- Word process newsletters, minutes, letters, and volunteer lists.

Patient Coordinator   **1987 to 1990**
MARY BLACK MEMORIAL HOSPITAL   SPARTANBURG, SC

- Organized and set up physical operations of new out-patient Elder Well Clinic.
- Coordinated patient scheduling with all departments.
- Received new patients and thoroughly explained clinic procedures.
- Resolved patient inquiries via telephone and during office visits.
- Maintained computerized database of patients.

EDUCATION

Associate of Arts in Liberal Arts   **1987**
BENEDICT COLLEGE   COLUMBIA, SC

References available upon request

✔ Horizontal lines segment Anne's resume into easy-to-read sections.
✔ Her first Summary statement differentiates her from other candidates.
✔ Bullets assist the reader to scan her lengthy job descriptions.

ADMINISTRATIVE ASSISTANT (Marketing)

_____ **MAE CRANE** _____

603/ 555-4196   124 High Rock Lane • Durham, NH 03824

EXPERIENCE: **Administrative Assistant – Marketing**
Hamilton Wood Designs
Portsmouth, NH   1991 to present

Provide administrative support to national marketing manager for this manufacturer of custom executive furniture. Key accounts include Sanders Associates, Green Mountain Banks, MacConnection, and NE Life Insurance.

Utilize IBM-PC to maintain customer data base, track office inventory, and generate general correspondence, new customer letters, product notes, and reports for executive management.

Arrange travel plans corporate-wide. Perform telephone and filing duties.

Consistently receive excellent evaluations in the areas of organization, personal interactions, independent work habits, and quality and quantity of work.

Customer Service / Administrative Assistant
New Hampshire People's Bank
Durham, NH   1990 to 1991

Provided teller and general office assistance.

EDUCATION: **Diploma (Business Curriculum)**
Samuel Adams High School
Dover, NH   1990

National Honor Society, Student Council President

Planning to pursue college degree on a part-time basis.

References available upon request

✔ Mae's heading and modern type style differentiate her resume.
✔ The mention of her positive performance evaluations is a key asset.
✔ Mae presently lacks college, so she highlights her plans to pursue a degree.

ADMINISTRATIVE ASSISTANT (Operations)

GAIL CLIFFORD
407 Overland Road
Meridian, ID 83642
208/ 555-8249

EXPERIENCE:

OLIVETTI COMMUNICATIONS • Boise, ID
Administrative Assistant – Operations (1989 to present)

Maintain operations on computer system including inventory; orders; month-end sales figures; vendor debits; A/P vouchering; customer, vendor, and manufacturer files. Generate sales and financial reports. Collaborate with programmers to resolve system problems.

Assume responsibilities of Department Manager in her absence. Train administrative personnel. Purchase computer supplies and office supplies. Greet visitors; resolve telephone inquiries; schedule travel arrangements; perform word processing.

PEABODY TEMPORARY AGENCY • Caldwell, ID
Administrative Assistant (1987 to 1989)

Performed a wide range of administrative functions for diverse client companies in banking, high tech, and health care.

B/W MANUFACTURING • Nampa, ID
Bookkeeping Assistant (1986 to 1987)

Performed A/P, A/R and Collections functions. Recorded daily sales, reconciled accounts, processed time cards, paid invoices, and prepared checks for deposits.

Receptionist (1985 to 1986)

EDUCATION:

NAMPA VALLEY JUNIOR COLLEGE • Nampa, ID
Executive Secretarial Studies (1987)

REFERENCES:

Available upon request

✔ Gail's description of her current job includes occasional management duties.
✔ The types of companies for which she previously worked are important to mention because they demonstrate her familiarity with various environments.

RANDALL SHAW
45 Madison Pike
Madison, AL 35758
205/ 555-0377

OBJECTIVE: Office Manager with a start-up company

QUALIFICATIONS:

- 7+ years as an administrative assistant reporting directly to company presidents.
- Solid experience in establishing, organizing, and managing office procedures.
- Proficiency in bookkeeping, word processing, billing, and correspondence.
- Strong background in both client and vendor relations.
- Current appointment as a Notary Public.

EMPLOYMENT:

ADMINISTRATIVE ASSISTANT 1989 TO PRESENT
Redstone Property Management Company Huntsville, AL

ADMINISTRATIVE ASSISTANT 1985 TO 1989
Johnson Real Estate Company Decatur, AL

HIGHLIGHTS:

- Planned physical layout of offices and established all office management systems.
- Administered A/P, A/R, payroll, and tax deposits.
- Handled office correspondence, files, and purchasing.
- Administered personal financial affairs of corporate presidents.
- Scheduled and conducted client viewing of rental and sales properties.
- Maintained leases on rental properties and supervised collection of condo fees.
- Coordinated with maintenance staff to ensure high quality property upkeep.

EDUCATION:

BUSINESS COURSEWORK 1985
Oakwood College Huntsville, AL

✔ Randall's Objective targets a very specific position.
✔ Both the Qualifications and Highlights sections support his Objective.
✔ Randall lacks a degree, but includes related college coursework.

ADMINISTRATIVE ASSISTANT (Sales)

PATRICIA CUMMINGS • 2309 Rahway Avenue • Midland, TX 79701 • 915/ 555-3729

EDUCATION:

AMANDA HALL SECRETARIAL SCHOOL • Odessa, TX
Certificate in Secretarial Studies (1989)

CHARLES E. CARY HIGH SCHOOL • Midland, TX
Diploma – college curriculum (1988)

SECRETARIAL SKILLS:

Typing • Dictaphone • Telephone Switchboard • Duplicating and Fax machines • IBM PC • MS-DOS • WordPerfect • Lotus 1-2-3 software.

PROFESSIONAL EXPERIENCE:

Transonics Corporation • Odessa, TX
(Electronics firm specializing in Data Acquisition Systems)

Administrative Assistant – Sales Department (1991 to present). Provide administrative support for this busy department consisting of a national sales manager, seven outside sales representatives, and four customer service support staff. Administer billing, sales tracking, and sales correspondence procedures. Provide customer support as needed.

Perform secretarial duties for the sales, customer service, production, and purchasing departments. Organize correspondence, travel arrangements, and office meetings. Successfully work independently during Manager's frequent travel.

DataQuery • Odessa, TX
(Electronics firm specializing in hand-held Data Acquisition Instruments)

Secretary – Sales and Marketing Department (1989 to 1991). Responsibilities were similar to those stated above. Accepted position offered by upper level management when they joined Transonics Corporation.

References available upon request

✔ Education credentials and Secretarial Skills "prequalify" Patricia for her field.
✔ Her DataQuery job description avoids repetition of her most current duties, and also demonstrates her value to her superiors.

ADMINISTRATIVE DIRECTOR

ALLAN RAUSEO   40 Wainwright Road • Troy, NY 12182 • 518/ 555-9233

Qualifications:

- Efficient administrator with a record of success in non-profit organizations.
- Experienced in budget administration, staff management, and marketing.
- Strong oral and written communication, organization, and problem-solving skills.
- Capability managing simultaneous projects and successfully meeting deadlines.
- Ability to master and integrate all aspects of business operations.

Experience:

THE JIMMY FUND   ALBANY, NY
Administrative Director – New Program Development   **1988 to present**

- Wrote initial Procedural Manual outlining steps for new program development.
- Recruited, trained, and supervised a new administrative staff.
- Coordinated the renovation of enlarged office space in a new facility.
- Administered the annual budget of $1M.
- Participated in computerization, advertising, and public relations functions.
- Liaison to American Coalition of Non-profit Organizations.

GOODWILL INDUSTRIES   ALBANY, NY
Administrative Coordinator   **1985 to 1988**

- Initiated and directed day-to-day operations of off-site pick-up locations.
- Oversaw marketing, staff recruitment, inventory processing, and bookkeeping.
- Closely coordinated with all departments to ensure smooth operation.
- Instituted new marketing program emphasizing tax benefits to donors.

Formerly held positions in **Retail Management (1980 to 1985)**.

Education:

NORTHEASTERN UNIVERSITY   BOSTON, MA
Bachelor of Arts in Retail Management   **1980**

✔ Allan's Qualifications section combines both specific and general capabilities.
✔ His bulleted format is easy to scan and demonstrates breadth of experience.
✔ Allan's former career supports his current management status.

EXECUTIVE ASSISTANT

LUCILLE GIORDANO

872 Great Southern Avenue • North Miami, FL 33161   305/ 555-1107

SUMMARY:

- 12+ years professional experience in sales companies and high tech industries.
- Business background in administration, meeting planning, and personnel.
- Ability to assess organizational need and implement administrative procedures.
- Bilingual; informal experience as an interpreter.
- Able to work independently and meet deadlines.
- Strong management, problem-solving, and supervisory skills.

ACCOMPLISHMENTS:

- *Managed regional office of #1 national radar detector company.*
  Recruited, trained, supervised, and evaluated eight administrative personnel. Supported senior executive staff in facilities planning and redesign. Established and implemented human resources and purchasing functions. Planned and maintained administrative budgets. Facilitated problem-resolution between departments, company, representatives, distributors, and customers.

- *Established and administered sales branch of national hardware company.*
  Researched and selected phone, courier, and postal services; office equipment; and office supplies. Negotiated with vendors for substantial discounts and free delivery to regional offices.

- *Organized and attended national trade shows, conferences, and conventions.*
  Coordinated registration, booth set-up, security, transportation, hotel accommodations, customer relations, and sales support. Provided on-site trouble-shooting and monitored customer concerns for use in future planning.

- *Provided administrative support and input to CEO.*
  Recommended organizational changes which facilitated effective staff utilization, efficient reporting of sales information, and significant improvement in company morale. Trained and supervised support staff.

- *Performed executive secretarial functions for Director of Sales & Marketing.*
  Scheduled and prepared paperwork for the Board of Directors meetings. Maintained appointment calendars, prepared correspondence, and coordinated travel arrangements. Prepared contracts and pre-qualified sales leads.

LUCILLE GIORDANO

EMPLOYMENT:

Executive Assistant
Uni-Sound Medical Electronics Company

1990 to present
Miami, FL

Administrative Director
Edutech Video Corporation

1987 to 1990
Hollywood, FL

Office Manager
Protron Instruments, Inc.

1983 to 1987
Kendall, FL

Executive Secretary
Zyquest Printer Company

1979 to 1983
Miami, FL

EDUCATION:

Bachelor of Arts
Orlando College

1979
Orlando, FL

Management Coursework
Florida Atlantic University

1988
Boca Raton, FL

AFFILIATIONS:

National Association for Female Executives, Toastmasters

INTERESTS:

Single; willing to travel and/or relocate.
Bi-lingual in Italian.
Well-travelled throughout Europe and Canada.

REFERENCES:

Available upon request

✔ Lucille's resume utilizes bullets, italics, and white space to ease scanning.
✔ Page 1 summarizes her career and identifies high-level accomplishments.
✔ Page 2 lists supporting employment, educational, and related data.

EXECUTIVE SECRETARY (Communications)

DOROTHY GARRETT

716 Rockwell Road • Catonsville, MD 21228   301/555-2771

EXPERIENCE:

GEOTEX CORPORATION   BALTIMORE, MD
Executive Secretary - Corporate Communications   1989 to present
Executive secretary, special events coordinator, project traffic controller, and information conduit for the Corporate Communications Department whose primary audience includes the highest levels of the Company plus the Executive Board.

Areas of responsibility:

- **Executive Secretarial:** organize and maintain PC data bases; develop graphic presentations; run pre-programmed MIS reports; prepare correspondence; administer budget, financial, and personnel forms and reports; maintain office supplies and equipment; resolve phone and mail inquiries.

- **Marketing:** collate and distribute corporate press clips; maintain inventory of corporate literature and videotapes; plan monthly activities with department directors; update calendars; liaison with various divisional managers and staff and outside vendors.

- **Special Activities:** meeting facilitation; research projects; library searches.

Executive Secretary – Product Marketing   1987 to 1989
Administered daily departmental operations. Provided liaison to all other departments and international offices. Coordinated large executive conferences.

HEURACHRON, INC.   TOWSON, MD
Executive Secretary to V.P. of Administration   1984 to 1987

EDUCATION:

TOWSON STATE UNIVERSITY   TOWSON, MD
Associates Degree in Business Candidate
Completed Business Law, Introduction to Marketing, and Business Writing.

REFERENCES:

Available upon request

✔ Dorothy projects a breadth of experience through her current job description.
✔ She organizes all functions under 3 key areas of responsibility.
✔ Education includes her current standing as a degree candidate.

EXECUTIVE SECRETARY (High Tech)

EILEEN BUCHANAN
204 Mountainside Road
Cranford, NJ 07016
201/ 555-4088

OBJECTIVE: Executive Secretary with an established high tech corporation

QUALIFICATIONS:

- 7+ years experience as an *Executive Secretary* within high tech industry.
- Background in *staff training, meeting planning, and customer support.*
- *Outstanding office skills* and knowledge of office management procedures.
- *Ability to communicate* with customers, management, and all staff.
- Skilled at independent *problem-solving and follow-through.*

EXPERIENCE:

EXECUTIVE SECRETARY   1989 TO PRESENT
ELKAY Home Electronics Corporation   Elizabeth, NJ

- Manage office procedures for area headquarters of a national electronics manufacturer.
- Provide liaison between Area Manager and field management.
- Train and supervise branch office personnel.
- Investigate customer complaints and support in the resolution of problems.
- Maintain personnel records for 300 employees and assure execution of contracts.
- Coordinate meetings, seminars, and social functions.

EXECUTIVE SECRETARY   1986 TO 1989
Nuclear Products of America, Inc.   Rahway, NJ

ADMINISTRATIVE ASSISTANT   1984 TO 1986
Princeton Medical Company   Edison, NJ

EDUCATION:

A.S. IN BUSINESS ADMINISTRATION   1984
Upsala College   East Orange, NJ

✔ Eileen's Objective is concise and specific.
✔ She includes management functions in her current job description.
✔ To avoid repetition, Eileen lists, but does not describe, previous employment.

OFFICE MANAGER / ACCOUNTANT

RUSSELL ZEKIS
4 Monmouth Street
Gastonia, NC 28052
704/ 555-4545

EMPLOYMENT:

Office Manager   **1980 to present**
JUDSON CONSULTING   Charlotte, NC

Accountant   **part-time**
FITZWRIGHT SHOE STORES   Charlotte, NC

Bookkeeper   **part-time**
POP'S PRINTSHOPS   Belmont, NC

HIGHLIGHTS:

Office Management

- Manage daily operation of large consulting firm including office administration, staffing, client contact, payroll and benefits administration, purchasing, billing, cost accounting, and general accounting.

- Administer a complete range of accounting and investment functions related to business income and consultants' personal portfolio.

- Designed, implemented, and updated all office procedures including total computerization of billing and accounting functions.

Accounting

- Perform accounting activities from worksheet through general ledger, preparation of financial statements, and the preparation for annual audits.

- In-depth knowledge of A/R, A/P, collections, cost accounting, billing, payroll and benefits administration, tax returns, pension and profit sharing plans.

- Knowledge of AccPac accounting software and Lotus 1-2-3 spreadsheet software.

EDUCATION:

Accounting Coursework (18 credits)   **1978 to 1980**
UNIVERSITY OF NORTH CAROLINA AT CHARLOTTE

> ✔ Russell includes part-time positions because they are relevant to his field and demonstrate experience in a diversity of environments.
> ✔ He organizes his experience into 2 main functions of equal importance.

OFFICE MANAGER (Corporate)

CONSTANCE FLAGG
3-A Bishop's Place
Port Allen, LA 70767
504/ 555-4071

JOB OBJECTIVE

Office Manager

EXPERIENCE

Office Manager   **1990 to present**
SASSY CISSEY'S   Baton Rouge, LA

- Manage corporate office function for $8M clothing manufacturer.
- Coordinate activities of data processing, accounting, sales support, and reception.
- Maintain updated computerized database of customers.
- Utilize customized software for inventory and A/P applications.
- Write basic computer programs to compute pricing formulas.
- Process bank reconciliations and tax reports for eight-state trucking fleet.
- Prepare weekly P&L statement for Corporate President.
- Compile and verify all financial data necessary for utilization by CPA firm.

Office Manager   **1988 to 1990**
LAWSON CONSULTING COMPANY   Baton Rouge, LA

Bookkeeper   **1985 to 1988**
Assistant Bookkeeper   **1983 to 1985**
ATI SYSTEMS CORPORATION   Plaquemine, LA

EDUCATION

Business and Accounting Studies   **1980 to 1983**
UNIVERSITY OF SOUTHWESTERN LOUISIANA   Lafayette, LA

Diploma – Business Curriculum   **1979**
EUSTIS HIGH SCHOOL   Henderson, LA

✔ Constance's centered section headings draw the eye to each section.
✔ Her Bookkeeping positions support current duties as an Office Manager.
✔ Lacking a college degree, she cites her diploma and college studies.

GAVIN O'ROURKE
316 Ewing Avenue
South Bend, IN 46624
219/ 555-1339

PROFESSIONAL EXPERIENCE:

OFFICE MANAGER   1989 TO PRESENT
Crowe Wine Imports   South Bend, IN
(Wine distributors • $3.2M annual sales)

- Report to CEO in the administration of accounting, personnel, and customer service.
- Hire, train, and supervise administrative and customer service personnel.
- Maintain complete bookkeeping system through monthly financial reports.
- Assisted software developers in the conversion to a computerized accounting system.
- Control inventory, invoicing, cash receipts, and collections activities.
- Compute payroll and quarterly tax returns.
- Hold signature and decision-making authority for bank accounts and a revolving loan.

OFFICE MANAGER   1986 TO 1989
Pencraft Office Supplies Distributors, Inc.   Mishawaka, IN

BOOKKEEPER   1984 TO 1986
Action Automotive Parts Wholesalers   Elkhart, IN

EDUCATION:

BUSINESS COURSEWORK   1982 TO 1984
Bethel College   Mishawaka, IN

INTERESTS:

Amateur photographer and poet. Travelled extensively through England, Ireland, and Scotland.

REFERENCES:

Available upon request

✔ Gavin briefly describes his company to cue the reader.
✔ He identifies the breadth of his experience in short, concise statements.
✔ His Interests celebrate his heritage and spark the reader's interest.

OFFICE MANAGER (Medical)

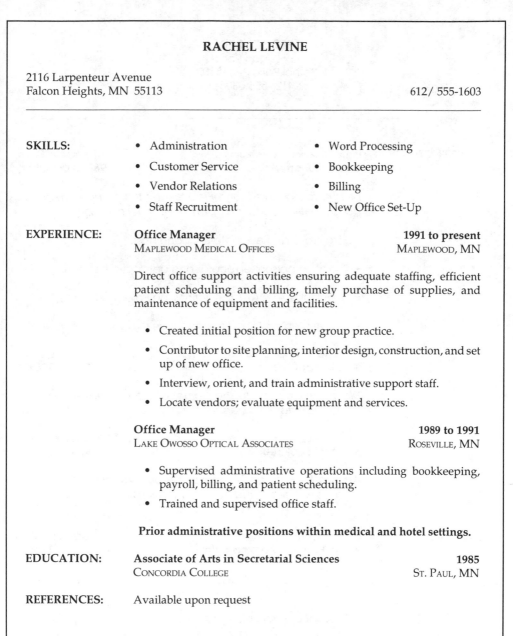

RACHEL LEVINE

2116 Larpenteur Avenue
Falcon Heights, MN 55113

612/ 555-1603

SKILLS:
- Administration
- Customer Service
- Vendor Relations
- Staff Recruitment
- Word Processing
- Bookkeeping
- Billing
- New Office Set-Up

EXPERIENCE:

Office Manager   **1991 to present**
MAPLEWOOD MEDICAL OFFICES   MAPLEWOOD, MN

Direct office support activities ensuring adequate staffing, efficient patient scheduling and billing, timely purchase of supplies, and maintenance of equipment and facilities.

- Created initial position for new group practice.
- Contributor to site planning, interior design, construction, and set up of new office.
- Interview, orient, and train administrative support staff.
- Locate vendors; evaluate equipment and services.

Office Manager   **1989 to 1991**
LAKE OWOSSO OPTICAL ASSOCIATES   ROSEVILLE, MN

- Supervised administrative operations including bookkeeping, payroll, billing, and patient scheduling.
- Trained and supervised office staff.

Prior administrative positions within medical and hotel settings.

EDUCATION: **Associate of Arts in Secretarial Sciences**   **1985**
CONCORDIA COLLEGE   ST. PAUL, MN

REFERENCES: Available upon request

✔ Rachel's Skills section is an easy-to-scan summary of her specific capabilities.
✔ Her job descriptions support all the functions in her Skills section.
✔ Rachel omits descriptions of less responsible positions between 1985 and 1989.

OFFICE MANAGER (R & D)

FRED SCHMIDT
117 Logan Road
Bethel Park, PA 15102
412/ 555-0306

EXPERIENCE:

POLAR RESEARCH CORPORATION   PITTSBURGH, PA
Office Manager   **1988 to present**

Directly responsible to the President for the management of administrative, accounting, and personnel operations:

- Hire, train, and evaluate 3 support staff.

- Maintain personnel records and administer benefits.

- Administer A/P, A/R, collections, payroll, and taxes.

- Monitor job costs and performance using MRP software.

LEE INDUSTRIAL PUMP COMPANY   MILLVALE, PA
Bookkeeper   **1986 to 1988**

Directly responsible to the Comptroller for bookkeeping, inventory control, and personnel functions.

GENELCO ELECTRONICS   MCKEES ROCKS, PA
Assistant Bookkeeper   **1984 to 1986**

Assisted Full Charge Bookkeeper in bookkeeping, invoicing, credit, collections, and payroll operations.

EDUCATION:

CARLOW COLLEGE   PITTSBURGH, PA
A.S. in Business Administration   **1984**

References available upon request

✔ Fred's job titles indicate a straight progression in career growth.
✔ To avoid repetition, he only elaborates on his most current position.
✔ The use of italics highlights his general areas of responsibility.

Sales Administration
Office Management
Marketing Support

SHARON BRECKER

21 Tom Road • Hartford, CT 06101 • 203/ 555-3734

Experience:

OFFICE MANAGER	**1989 to present**
CRONIN ENGINEERING	Hartford, CT

Administer office procedures for an environmental engineering company including lead processing and follow-up; file centralization and maintenance; cash reconciliation; processing of A/R and A/P; purchasing of office supplies, equipment and furniture.

ADMINISTRATIVE ASSISTANT/Sales	**1987 to 1989**
TITAN TELEMARKETING	New Britain, CT

Coordinated activities for an active ten-person sales office. Researched and prepared monthly sales summaries, communications cost summaries, customer complaints and credits, and affirmative action reports.

Processed A/P; prepared and forecasted budgets; administered petty cash fund; and purchased supplies, furniture, and equipment. Provided customer support.

Trained and supervised a junior secretary.

SALES COORDINATOR	**1985 to 1987**
UNITED TECHNOLOGIES	Middletown, CT

Coordinated the sales efforts of five area managers through follow-up customer support. Maintained sales records; prepared correspondence; forwarded appropriate literature; and resolved customer problems. Assisted in preparing quarterly taxes, quarterly budget revisions, sales forecasts, and annual projections.

Education:

B.S./Business Administration	**1985**
UNIVERSITY OF CONNECTICUT	Stamford, CT

✔ Listing several career interests allows Sharon flexibility in her job search.
✔ Her job descriptions are a series of tasks showing breadth of experience.
✔ Bold lettering separates paragraphs for easier reading.

OFFICE MANAGER (Test Lab)

BURTON HANKS
109 Trask Pond Road
Sun City, AZ 83551

Residence: 602/ 555-2004   *Business:* 602/ 555-6700

Areas of Interest

OFFICE MANAGEMENT • CUSTOMER SERVICE • SALES & MARKETING

Professional Experience

Office Manager   1991 to present
EATON TEST LABORATORIES   Phoenix, AZ

Schedule, manage and evaluate staff in the effective operation of a demanding laboratory office. Establish efficient office procedures, recordkeeping, and invoicing systems. Collaborate with systems analyst to develop computer programs for data management and water sample tracking.

Support in sales, marketing, and customer support activities. Follow up leads, send literature, and refer clients for technical information.

Manager – Customer Service Department   1987 to 1991
HYGIENIA LABS   Tempe, AZ

Performed a wide range of customer service functions including scheduling of asbestos sample tests, order expedition, and volume pricing. Developed computerized system for sample tracking. Hired, trained, and evaluated customer service representatives. Closely coordinated programs with Sales, Purchasing, Credit, and Data Processing Departments.

Customer Service Representative   1984 to 1987
ECHO DATA SERVICES   Scottsdale, AZ

Education

B.S. in Business Administration   1984
ARIZONA STATE UNIVERSITY   Tempe, AZ

Continuing Education in Sales, Customer Support, and Computer Applications.

✔ Burton's Areas of Interest are an effective alternative to an Objective.
✔ His job descriptions directly relate to his Areas of Interest.
✔ Computer experience is specifically noted under Experience and Education.

SECRETARY (Contracts)

MARISA BONNELL
216 Elmhurst Drive
Houston, TX 77045
713/ 555-2357

WORK EXPERIENCE:

TEXAS MICROWAVE SYSTEMS   HOUSTON, TX
SECRETARY   **1990 to present**

Report to the Manager of Contract Administration and five Administrators. Perform contract-specific tasks including issuing contract numbers, typing and distributing contract abstracts, maintaining a 3,200 record database, and general office duties.

Administer a comprehensive contract cost tracking system. Issue tracking numbers, obtain management approval, maintain a written log and permanent files, and issue weekly reports using Lotus 1-2-3 and dBase.

UNITED STATES TENNIS ASSOCIATION   HOUSTON, TX
SECRETARY   **1988 to 1990**

Oversaw 3 full-time and 6 volunteer personnel in the administration of a large professional organization. Updated memberships and mailing lists. Designed and distributed newsletters. Planned and coordinated conferences and meetings.

EDUCATION:

HOWARD PAYNE UNIVERSITY   BROWNWOOD, TX
EXECUTIVE SECRETARIAL STUDIES   **1987 to 1988**

COLEMAN HIGH SCHOOL   COLEMAN, TX
BUSINESS CURRICULUM   **1987**

References available upon request

✔ Marisa lists prominent company names before job titles.
✔ She mentions experience with specific computer software programs.
✔ She lacks a college degree, so she includes her high school diploma.

JILL VASQUEZ
71 Branham Lane
San Jose, CA 95124
408/ 555-9023

SUMMARY OF QUALIFICATIONS:

- Strong administrative background within high tech and engineering environments.
- Skills include technical typing, editing, dictaphone, meeting planning, and switchboard.
- Proven ability to interact effectively with clients and staff at all levels.
- Proficient in handling simultaneous projects and meeting deadlines effectively.

EMPLOYMENT:

Temporary   *1988 to present*

APPLE COMPUTER • Cupertino, CA • Engineering Drafting Department

PARACOMP, INC. • San Francisco, CA • Hardware Design Department

ASANTE TECHNOLOGIES • Sunnyvale, CA • Software Testing Department

Permanent   *1980 to 1988*

GENERATION SYSTEMS, INC. • Sunnyvale, CA
Secretary - Quality Assurance Department (1984 - 1988)

SIGMA DESIGNS • Fremont, CA
Administrative Assistant - Technical Library (1980 - 1984)

EDUCATION:

GOLDEN GATE UNIVERSITY • San Francisco, CA
A.S. in Secretarial Sciences (1980)

ASSOCIATIONS:

Professional Secretaries International • Toastmasters • Secretary of Junior League

---

✔ Horizontal lines segment Jill's resume into short, scannable sections.
✔ Temporary and Permanent headings organize her many job listings.
✔ Jill notes specific departments to show a wide range of experience.

LOIS KINSELLA
191 Nieman Road
Merriam, KS 66203
913/ 555-0346

HIGHLIGHTS:

- 10+ years of secretarial experience in a human resources environment.
- Excellent word processing, shorthand, telephone, and reception skills.
- Proven ability to train and coordinate administrative staff.
- Demonstrated skill teaching speed writing at an accredited evening school.
- Strong oral and written communication skills.
- Proficient in developing office procedures and forms to improve efficiency.
- Successful independent or team worker; conscientious; well-organized; problem-solver.

EXPERIENCE:

SECRETARY FOR THE HUMAN RESOURCES MANAGER   1991 to present
Hyperion Truck Body Company • Lenexa, KS

SECRETARY – HUMAN RESOURCES DEPARTMENT   1988 to 1991
Thorus Construction Company • Shawnee Mission, KS

SECRETARY – HUMAN RESOURCES DEPARTMENT   1985 to 1988
Diebold Financial Services Corporation • Kansas City, KS

TRAINING:

HUMAN RESOURCES MANAGEMENT   1986 to 1987
National College • Kansas City, MO

WORD PROCESSING, SHORTHAND   1985
Harper Secretarial School • Lenexa, KS

DIPLOMA – BUSINESS CURRICULUM   1984
Vanderbilt High School • Overland Park, KS

- ✔ The Highlights section summarizes skills to avoid repetition in job descriptions.
- ✔ HR experience and HR coursework demonstrate Lois' specialty.
- ✔ Lois lacks a college education, so she heads the last section as Training.

SECRETARY (Legal)

VALERIE BROOMLEY
1202 Coldwater Road
Morrice, MI 48857
313/ 555-2773

EXPERIENCE:

GENESEE COUNTY LEGAL ASSOCIATES   FLINT, MI
Legal Secretary   **1990 to present**

Provide secretarial support to four litigation associates. Draft correspondence and legal documents in Microsoft Word; file court documents; docket court deadlines, hearings, and motions; schedule appointments and interact with clients.

MANN, REID, CLARK, JONES & CUSHING, P.C.   LANSING, MI
Correspondence Manager   **1988 to 1990**
Legal Secretary   **1987 to 1988**

Managed complete operations of Correspondence Department consisting of 2 Supervisors and 40 Specialists. Hired, trained, scheduled, supervised, and evaluated staff. Implemented efficient workflow procedures. Drafted and revised staff manuals.

Received excellent evaluations for job knowledge, commitment, and management performance.

LAW OFFICE OF ROGER TILTON   FLINT, MI
Legal Secretary   **1984 to 1987**

EDUCATION:

BAKER COLLEGE   OWOSSO, MI
A.S. Degree in Legal Secretarial Science   **1984**

References available upon request

✔ Valerie's resume demonstrates both secretarial and management ability.
✔ To avoid repetition, she only describes her current Legal Secretary position.
✔ Her excellent performance evaluation boosts her credentials.

SECRETARY (Real Estate Development)

RHONDA WEST
2401 Panola Mountain Drive
Forest Park, GA 30050

Residence: 404/ 555-4868   *Business:* 404/ 555-9600

EXPERIENCE

Executive Secretary
JACKSON DEVELOPMENT COMPANY • Atlanta, GA   1990 to present

- Support five Managers in a fast-paced real estate development office.
- Collaborate with Construction Manager to assure punctuality with contractors.
- Create and administer a PC-based project tracking system.
- Maintain time-billing record for four development projects.
- Prepare and update financial statements for each project budget.

Department Secretary
LASERTRON CORPORATION • College Park, GA   1988 to 1990

- Supported Marketing Manager and five Regional Sales Managers.
- Supervised two secretaries and coordinated workflow.
- Provided liaison to all divisions regarding price and product changes.
- Calculated price changes and notified customers and agents.
- Prepared correspondence, reports, market studies, memos, and newsletters.
- Coordinated special events and departmental meetings.
- Familiar with MS-DOS, Lotus 1-2-3, WordPerfect, and dBase.

Administrative Assistant
PAYTON PROPERTIES • East Point, GA   1985 to 1988

EDUCATION

B.S. in Business Management
CLARK ATLANTA UNIVERSITY • Atlanta, GA   Candidate

A.S. in Business Management
CLARK ATLANTA UNIVERSITY • Atlanta, GA   1985

✔ For convenience, Rhonda provides a Business phone number.
✔ Her concise, bulleted statements demonstrate a breadth of experience.
✔ Her Candidacy for a B.S. indicates a potential for career growth.

ELLEN MILES

438 San Marcos Drive
Starkville, MS 39759
601/ 555-7888

EXPERIENCE: | **Staff Assistant - R&D Library** | **1987 to present**
Demco | **Starkville, MS**

- *Primary information source* for engineers and technical staff of the R&D branch of a medical products company.

- *Coordinate* the distribution of pertinent newsletters and technical data to department managers.

- *Word process* requests for information and inter-office memos.

- *Catalogue* books, periodicals, and technical notes.

- *Expedite and track* special information requests.

- Perform *administrative tasks*, e.g., phones, filing, and xeroxing/ collating of manuscripts for presentations.

- *Coordinate* special in-house technical meetings.

- Highly experienced on *Macintosh* and *IBM* computers.

- *Competent* using library information systems.

EDUCATION: | **Associate of Science** | **1987**
Starkville Community College | **Starkville, MS**

- Major: *Secretarial/Library Sciences*

- *Honors Graduate*

✔ Ellen has only one position to describe, so she chooses formatting elements that fill up the page, such as wide margins and large spacing between lines.
✔ Italics highlight her concise, bulleted statements.

Arts and Leisure 5

Anything Goes

Resume-writing can be fun for professionals in the Arts and Leisure fields. As a group, you are talented, creative, offbeat. You march to the beat of a very special drummer. Many of your job titles hold a distinct allure for 9-to-5'ers — they conjure up travel, romance, excitement, celebrity. It is *your* careers about which most people fantasize when they feel stifled in their own.

It makes sense, then, that the creative nature of your profession allows you the most opportunity for creativity in writing your resume. Whereas businesspeople have only a small degree of latitude in deviating from the norm, for you there is hardly a norm at all. Almost anything goes.

Make A Strong Visual Impact

Your resume is not only a written statement of your professional credentials, but an artistic statement as well. If you use this medium effectively, you can graphically communicate your creativity. Visual excitement can be infused throughout your resume if you incorporate some of the following simple suggestions:

- Use stylish typefaces such as Bookman, Avant Garde, *Zapf Chancery*.

- Insert accent symbols such as ~ (Tildes), • (Bullets), ■ (Boxes), ✔ (Checkmarks),

◆ (Diamonds), * (Stars), > (Arrows), etc.

- Create original drawings related to your field, e.g., musical notes for a Musician, balloons for an Events Planner, a camera for a Photographer.

- Incorporate your initials into a special logo.

- Include a photograph.

- Place a border around the entire resume.

- Use full lines or half-lines to divide sections.

- Create distinctive name and address headings and/or section headings using larger-than-normal type sizes or all lower case letters.

- Design an alternative resume, e.g., folded-style, narrative, or press release.

- Select a unique presentation, e.g., 8-1/2" x 11" horizontal, or side-by-side columns.

- Print on colored or glossy paper.

Throughout this chapter you will find examples of the graphic touches cited above.

Your Job Title May Be Self-Explanatory

Arts and Leisure careers have such a wide appeal to the general public that most people understand the duties inherent in many positions. Job titles such as actress, flight attendant, and travel agent need no explanation. Instead, utilize the valuable space on your resume to describe special achievements or skills.

A Word About Education

Often it is talent, specialized training, and hard work rather than a college degree that are the keys to a successful Arts and Leisure career. So, it is very likely that education might play a more minor role on your resume, if one at all. Several resume examples in this chapter include specialized training under Education or omit an Education section altogether.

Selling Yourself As a Freelancer

Freelancing is very common to Arts and Leisure professionals, either as a deliberate career choice, an occasional necessity between permanent jobs, or a temporary hiatus while preparing for a career change. Typically, a resume for a freelancer does not differ from that of a permanent job-seeker. Yet, freelancing itself is a definite skill.

In effect, you are in business for yourself, marketing a precious commodity, your talent. Therefore, if circumstances warrant, on your resume you can highlight your business savvy as well as your creativity. We have included several examples of resumes for freelancers in this chapter.

Testing Entrepreneurship

Frequently Arts and Leisure professionals go even a step further than freelancing. They become entrepreneurs. Caterers, graphic designers, and photographers often establish their own companies, combining their artistic bent with business know-how. So, in addition to executing projects, they also plan budgets, manage staff, and control inventories.

Many are happy in their new endeavor; many are not. Many succeed; many do not. Many continue to feel ambivalent about their dual roles even after several years, so they design a resume which can either win them clients or a new job. We have included several examples in this chapter.

Vital Statistics For Entertainers

It has been eons since job candidates listed personal statistics such as height, weight, and state of health on their resumes. In fact, we know that federal law prohibits a prospective employer from inquiring about most areas of an applicant's personal life. Yet, much of what an entertainer is selling is his or her personal appearance, so providing data about height, weight, hair color, and eye color is a given. Even a photo is appropriate.

References and Portfolio

Chapter 1 mentions that References on a resume are optional. That statement does not pertain to most Arts and Leisure professionals. If at all possible, close your resume with a statement about the availability of References *and* Portfolio. These are probably your most important marketing tools, even more critical than your resume because your field is so competitive and talent is so hard to measure objectively.

❦ LOLA BERGERON ❦

2466 Newbridge Street
Livingston, NJ 07039
201/ 555-0348

ACTRESS (Resume)

❦ LOLA BERGERON ❦

Actress

2466 Newbridge Street
Livingston, NJ 07039
201/ 555-0348

Height: 5'6" *Weight:* 125 lbs.
Eyes: Brown   *Hair:* Brown
Voice: Soprano

THEATER HIGHLIGHTS

Character	Show	Theater
Julie	Carousel	Back Alley
Girl	The Fantasticks	Back Alley
Joanne	A Chorus Line	Repertory I
Ensemble	Contemporary Insanity	Repertory I
Ensemble	Jacques Brel *	Stage Right
April	Hot L. Baltimore	Drew University
Grace	Joe Egg **	Drew University
Juliet	Romeo & Juliet	Drew University
Maria	West Side Story	Drew University

* Regional Winner of American Amateur Theater competition for "Jacques Brel."
** Regional Finalist of American Amateur Theater competition for "Joe Egg."

EDUCATION

B.F.A. in Drama • DREW UNIVERSITY • 1991

Curriculum included TV acting, commercials, and soap opera workshops.

SPECIAL SKILLS

Dialects - Italian, French, Irish, Slavic, American Southern.
Directing • Coaching • Character Roles

✔ Physical stats, key roles, awards, and special skills are all vital information.
✔ Graphics surrounding Lola's name coordinate her resume and letterhead.
✔ The barmaid graphic is a touch of whimsy to emphasize character roles.

ANTIQUES CONSULTANT

Art
Architecture
Antiques

ANGELA LAQUADERA

4652 Broadway, New York, NY 10011 • 212/ 555-2589

Highlights:

MASTERPIECES, INC.   **NEW YORK, NY**
Founder/President (1988 to present). Manage artwork search and buying service for select corporate and residential clients. Administer appraisal, restoration, repair, and sale of private original pieces. Maintain relations with top domestic and international galleries.

GALLERY MOZAMBIQUE   **NEW YORK, NY**
Assistant Manager (1986 to 1988). Planned and executed sales, marketing, advertising and PR activities for a new gallery specializing in Afro-American art. Coordinated exhibition and sale events at the Institute for Afro-American Studies, Swanton Mall, and Civic Center.

INDEPENDENT CONSULTANT (1983 to 1986)
NY Historical Society. Researched, organized, and valued a fragile collection of turn-of-the-century postcards. Researched the artists and recommended conservation methods. Submitted a proposal to the Arts Commission to preserve the most valuable as historical documents.

76 Third Avenue, New York City, NY. Conducted extensive research of a 20-room, fully-appointed Victorian estate currently utilized as university V.I.P. lodging. Ascertained the history of ownership and construction date information conforming to the professional standards of historical documentation.

Education:

MILLIKIN UNIVERSITY   **DECATUR, IL**
B.S. in Fine Arts (1980). History of Art.

UNIVERSITY OF FLORENCE   **FLORENCE, ITALY**
Art Studies (1981 to 1983). Classical Architecture.

✔ Since Angela is in a creative field, she selects a type style with an especially attractive "Q" to further highlight both "Laquadera" and "Mozambique."
✔ Her areas of expertise in the upper left hand corner add artistic flair.

ANTIQUES DEALER

MARY JAMISON

---

702 Amity Avenue
Nampa, ID 83651
(208) 555-2047

EMPLOYMENT:

ANTIQUITIES, INC. • Boise, ID   1990 to present
Associate Buyer – Purchase inventory for this retail / wholesale antique dealer specializing in fine antique jewelry, lamps, glass and china, and period furniture. Attend major regional auctions to purchase for store, clients, and proprietor's private collection. Authorized to make purchases up to $15,000.

Support merchandising and customer service activities in three shops. Write copy for a variety of mail order publications. Attend seminars and keep current through trade journals.

TEE HEE'S • Boise, ID   p.t., 1986 to1990
Partner – Co-founded and co-operated high quality hand-painted tee shirt business catering to the student population. Participated in all operational, artistic, and technical activities.

Generated profits which accounted for 50% of college tuition.

EDUCATION:

BOISE STATE UNIVERSITY • Boise, ID   1990
Bachelor of Arts (Major: Art History)

AFFILIATIONS:

National Society for the Preservation of Antiquities
American Association of Antique Dealers

REFERENCES:

Available upon request

✔ Mary stresses industry knowledge, marketing activities, and customer service experience in her current position.
✔ Her part-time position demonstrates both artistic and business savvy.

ARTIST

MICHELLE COLES
327 East Dutton Street
Oak Park, MI 48237
313/ 555-6605

Education:

MCGILL ART INSTITUTE   1986
Bachelor of Science in Fine Arts

Artistic Consulting:

TRAVELART COMPANY • Detroit, MI   1991 to present

Assist corporate clients in the selection and presentation of fine art reproductions. Coordinate all aspects with sensitivity toward client space, time, budget, and style parameters.

Free-lance Design:

LOFTUS DESIGN • Highland Park, MI   1988 to 1991
Created 50 award-winning original stencil designs for residential space for this interior design firm.

EDUCATIONAL ART COMPANY • Detroit, MI   1987 to 1988
Created child-focused murals for chain of daycare centers.

FURNISHINGS BY PAUL • Dearborn, MI   1986 to 1987
Created paintings for department store food emporiums.

Teaching:

MANNING ART SCHOOL • Detroit, MI   1988 to present
Adult Education Instructor

IDYLWYLD PUBLIC SCHOOLS • Livonia, MI
Substitute Art Teacher   1988 to present

Exhibits:

GROUP EXHIBIT - Detroit Art Museum, Detroit, MI   1988

ONE-MAN EXHIBIT - Côte St. Luc Gallery, Montreal   1986

✔ Michelle includes important facets of her career as an artisit, e.g., education, consulting, design, teaching, and exhibits.
✔ Horizontal lines segment information into scannable sections.

ARTS ADMINISTRATOR

HAL MALCOLM
244 Winfield Road
Wheaton, IL 60187
312/ 555-9167

EXPERIENCE:

Director   **1988 to present**
ARTISTS-IN-RESIDENCE PROGRAM   CHICAGO AREA

Originated and currently direct this highly successful program to promote the arts to residents of all ages within an 8-city region. Assist neighboring towns in establishing similar programs.

- Wrote grant which obtained government funding.
- Recruited and hired 60 artists to present creative programs.
- Created promotional materials, e.g., brochures, press releases.

Provide consultation in the design of individual projects including theater and musical productions, art exhibits, workshops, art contests for gifted and talented youngsters, portraits of elderly citizens, and production of advertising materials.

Design Consultant   **1986 to 1988**
MUSEUM OF FINE ARTS   CHICAGO, IL

Created original designs for color, theme, and special effects at preview parties promoting opening exhibits including Egyptian Treasures, Early Period of Picasso, Photography of Ansel Adams.

Board Member   **1984 to 1986**
SCHAUMBURG ARTS COUNCIL   SCHAUMBURG, IL

Practicing Artist   **1980 to present**
SPECIALIZE IN OIL PAINTING   *Award Winner*

EDUCATION:

Artistic Training   **1975 to present**
CHICAGO MUSEUM ART SCHOOL   CHICAGO, IL

REFERENCES: **References and portfolio available upon request**

✔ Hal's resume equally reflects his excellence as an artist and administrator.
✔ His current job description is comprehensive, but still easy to read because he uses bullets to highlight major achievements.

JOHN CENNERAZZO
55 Calcutta Way
Reading, OH 45215
513/ 555-5029

EDUCATION:	**University of Cincinnati**	**Cincinnati, OH**
	B.S. IN PHYSICAL EDUCATION	Spring 1991
	Specialization in athletic training	

g.p.a.: 4.0

coursework: Orthopedic Assessment, Therapeutic Modalities, Anatomy, Physiology, Kinesiology, Emergency Care, Issues in Athletic Training, Independent Study

varsity sports: Swim Team - 1988-1991

certification: NATA Certification Test - January 1991

	Brookhaven High School	**Glenmary, OH**
	DIPLOMA	Spring 1987

g.p.a.: 3.85

varsity sports: Golf - Captain
Hockey - Captain
Swimming

awards: MVP, Golf - 1987
MVP, Hockey - 1986
Brookhaven High School Sportsmanship Award - 1986

EXPERIENCE:	**University of Cincinnati**	**Cincinnati, OH**
	STUDENT TRAINER	1989 to 1991

Co-head Trainer for track team. Student Trainer for basketball team. Received Student Trainer of the Month Award.

RESIDENT TRAINER OF HOCKEY FLOOR	1989 to 1991

Reading Hospital	**Reading, OH**
INTERN - Sports Medicine Clinic	Spring 1988

ATHLETIC TRAINER (continued)

EXPERIENCE
CONTINUED:

Camp Evergreen	**Norwood, OH**
SWIMMING DIRECTOR	1989
SPECIAL EVENTS DIRECTOR	1989
LIFE GUARD	1988 to 1989
Winton Tennis & Swim Club	**Green Hills, OH**
SWIMMING INSTRUCTOR	1987
USPGA Schools Program Volunteer	**Southern OHIO**
(Golf Instructor for local public school students)	1990

CERTIFICATION: Life Guard - Red Cross

CPR - Red Cross

First Aid - Red Cross

AFFILIATIONS: Active member of NATA, USPGA, and RED CROSS

ACTIVITIES: Marathon Runner

Triathlete

USPGA sectional Golf Tournament Competitor

Mountain Climbing

REFERENCES: Personal and Professional References available upon request

---

✔ Although all of John's experience occurred during college, his impressive list of sports activities, certifications, and affiliations requires 2 pages.
✔ His high school sports record is noteworthy and directly related to his career.

BURTON SOHM
18 Pierce Drive
Lawrence, IN 46226
317/ 555-9731

EXPERIENCE

Author   **1980 to present**
BAILEY PUBLISHING   **INDIANAPOLIS, IN**
Contracted to write and revise high school textbooks, student workbooks, teacher guides, audio-visual materials, and testing programs in Italian, German, and English for this leading educational publisher, a division of Houghton Mifflin.

- Undertook six revisions to meet the needs of a growing market.
- Produced sales training materials for national sales meetings.
- Presented multi-media training sessions to publisher's sales reps.
- Accompanied sales staff on calls to promote product lines.

Publisher   **1987 to present**
ACCELERATED LANGUAGE VIDEOS   **INDIANAPOLIS, IN**
Produce videotapes and manuals for language immersion programs.

- Successful marketing efforts resulted in several reprints and a steady rise in domestic and international sales since the product's inception.

Foreign Language Instructor   **1970 to 1980**
JEREMIAH PARKS HIGH SCHOOL   **SPEEDWAY, IN**
Implemented foreign language curriculum, using the latest technology.

- Initiated German program, now the leading foreign language elective.
- Motivated numerous students to earn local and national awards.
- Recognized as a Merit Teacher for outstanding performance.

EDUCATION

MA in English
INDIANA UNIVERSITY   **INDIANAPOLIS, IN**

BA in German
INDIANA UNIVERSITY   **SOUTH BEND, IN**

✔ Burton's knowledge of foreign languages is so central to his success as an author that he stresses work experience dating back to 1970.
✔ To avoid age discrimination, he omits the dates of his college degrees.

KAREN DONAHUE

904 Hubbard Street
South St. Paul, MN 55075

612/ 555-3582

PROFESSIONAL EXPERIENCE:

PICKWICK PROMOTIONS • St. Paul, MN
Associate Broadcast Producer (1990 to present)

- Manage all aspects of radio commercial production for major local and national accounts including IBM Corporation, FMC Corporation, and Scotch Company.

- Provide leadership during both pre-production planning and production. Select and coordinate directors, production houses, editors, and talent.

- *Murrow Award for Outstanding Program* (Pathways; 1990)

Audio/Video Manager (1988 to 1990)

- Created new A/V Department and Library and managed all planning and day-to-day operations of in-house and sub-contracted broadcast projects.

- Supervised staff, devised and administered large budgets, and selected and purchased capital equipment in excess of $500K.

KSTP • Minneapolis, MN
Traffic Coordinator (1985 to 1988)

- Scheduled and trafficked all commercials for a national AOR leader.

- Dealt directly with reps and clients on availability, rates, orders, and copy.

- Coordinated with program directors to ensure smooth daily programming.

MINNESOTA POLITICAL PARTY • St. Paul, MN
Advertising Consultant (Summer 1985)

EDUCATION:

NORTHWESTERN COLLEGE • St. Paul, MN
B.S. in Broadcast Management (1985)

✔ Karen's use of half-lines adds a subtle graphic touch to attract interest.
✔ She italicizes her broadcast award for emphasis.
✔ To avoid conflict, she omits the specific political party for which she consulted.

CATERER

CYBIL MUNROE
443 Poplar Street
Bloomfield, NJ 07003
201/ 555-3422

EXPERIENCE:	**President** CULINARY CREATIONS, INC.	**1985 to present** MONTCLAIR, NJ

Plan, organize, and coordinate all phases of off-premises catering for a variety of prestigious clients including Merck, Sharp & Dohme, Rutgers University School of Education, Fiat Motor Corporation, Newark Chamber of Commerce, U.S. Shipbuilding, and Schering-Plough Corporation.

Design and execute all aspects of theme functions encompassing flower arrangements, table settings, menu planning, food displays, and entertainment bookings.

Received Culinary Arts Awards - 1989 and 1990

Instructor - Food Presentation   **1989 to present**
BLOOMFIELD COLLEGE   BLOOMFIELD, NJ

Head Chef   **1982 to 1985**
CAFE BUDAPEST   NEW YORK, NY
(Hungarian Cuisine • 160 seats)

Sautée Chef, Pastry Chef   **1980 to 1982**
PAPILLION   FAIR LAWN, NJ
(French Bistro • 75 seats)

EDUCATION: **Bachelor of Culinary Arts**   **1980**
                       GRATZ COLLEGE   MELROSE PARK, PA

ACTIVITIES: **Charter Member**
                       AMERICAN CULINARY GUILD

                       Food Chairman - Special Events Committee
                       AMERICAN CANCER SOCIETY

References & Portfolio available upon request

✔ Cybil's description of her business is strengthened by key clients and awards.
✔ Brief descriptions of restaurant jobs demonstrate her breadth of experience.
✔ The mention of a portfolio enhances Cybil's professionalism.

CHEF (Head)

EDWARD SANCHEZ
Rio Barona Drive
Del Mar, CA 92014

Residence: 619/ 555-4288   Business: 619/ 555-3434

OBJECTIVE: Head Chef in a small Hawaiian resort

EDUCATION: **B.S. in Hotel and Restaurant Management**   **1984**
ANTIOCH UNIVERSITY   Marina Del Rey, CA

Diploma (Culinary Arts Major)   **1980**
PACIFIC VOCATIONAL HIGH SCHOOL   Carlsbad, CA

EXPERIENCE: PROSPECT PALMS   La Jolla, CA
(Exclusive resort • 96 rooms • 128-seat oceanside dining)

Head Chef   **1988 to present**
On-site Manager   **1986 to 1988**

Plan and prepare new menus daily in the Continental tradition for breakfast, lunch, dinner, brunch, and special functions. Manage kitchen operations including pricing, costing, ordering, inventory control, and staff supervision.

- Significantly increased patronage by expanding menus and introducing Sunday brunches.

- Significantly decreased costs by establishing efficient inventory and portion control procedures.

- Receive numerous recipe requests from Bon Appetit.

- Regularly cited in national publications, e.g. Travel's Dining Guide and Lifestyles Magazine.

PREVIOUS POSITIONS (1984 to 1986) include Chez Charles (wine steward) and the Rialto Restaurant (bartender).

REFERENCES: **Available upon request**

✔ A traditional format with a modern type style is an attractive combination.
✔ Edward presents Education first as a "prequalifier" for an industry position.
✔ He describes only his present position as it directly supports his Objective.

CHEF (Pastry)

ARTHUR FERRANTI
2367 Blake Canyon Road
Flagstaff, AZ 86001
602/ 555-0958

EDUCATION:

Paradise Valley College
A.S. IN CULINARY ARTS (1984)

Scottsdale Vocational Technical High School
DIPLOMA IN CULINARY ARTS (1982)

EXPERIENCE:

Arnold Palmer Golf & Tennis Resort • Flagstaff, AZ
HEAD PASTRY CHEF (1990 TO PRESENT)
(Supervised pastry cooks in the preparation and serving of pastries, tortes, and sorbets. Planned seasonal menus and desserts of the day.)

Cottonwood Cafe • Mountainaire, AZ
PASTRY CHEF (1988 TO 1990)
(Developed entire dessert menu for new southwestern fare upscale restaurant)

Epicurean Bakeries, Inc. • Flagstaff, AZ
PASTRY COOK (1986 TO 1988)
(Produced high volume bakery items including European pastries and breads)

Sunset Country Club • Winona, AZ
HEAD CHEF (1984 TO 1986)
(Supervised cooks in the planning and preparation of daily meals and special events)

AWARDS:

1st place, Ritz Pastry Bake-Off (1991)

1st place, Gourmet Food Show (1990)

2nd place, Maison Henri Continental Pastry Contest (1990)

✔ Arthur's resume is softened by italics and by dates tucked next to his job titles.
✔ Job descriptions are brief, but demonstrate a breadth of experience.
✔ Arthur's Award section demonstrates excellence in his field.

resume
of
belinda davis hamilton

108 highland view terrace
powderly, alabama 35221
205/ 555-8127

COLOR CONSULTANT (Folded Resume – Inside Left)

background

Belinda Davis Hamilton entered the exciting field of color consulting in its infancy. As a student of health education and communication, she first became aware of the dramatic physiological and emotional impact that color has on human beings.

She studied, trained, and conducted research in New York before beginning a successful career in the Birmingham area as a personal color consultant. The exclusive color consultant to the Southern Salons of Maybelline, she also addressed modeling agencies, retailers, businesses, colleges, and professional organizations.

Currently an environmental color specialist, she lectures widely and undertakes ever more challenging projects requiring not only expertise in design, color, and materials, but an understanding of and respect for human nature.

education

BACHELOR OF ARTS in health education / communication
University of Alabama (1982)

CONTINUING EDUCATION SEMINARS in Leadership, Business Building, and Management.

professional organizations

American Business Designers • National Society of Interior Designers • American Institute of Architects

References available upon request

professional accomplishments ————————

ENVIRONMENTAL COLOR SPECIALIST

- Taught "Color Theory: A New Challenge" at the Birmingham Architectural and Birmingham Design Centers.

- Pioneered a new marketing approach for the showroom of a custom-design paint store in the Birmingham Art Center.

- Supervised architectural students in developing the floorplan for Birmingham business offices. Personally selected color scheme, furnishings, fabric, paint, art, and accessories, and directed contractors.

- Proposed and implemented color scheme for logo, menu, and complete interior of Birmingham department store.

- Designed color scheme for 9 rooms of an elder care center.

- Designed the paint restoration of a pre-civil war plantation utilizing a stained-glass window as a focal point.

- Selected materials and developed color scheme utilizing unique paint products for a new wallpaper business.

related ————————————————

Single • Willing to Travel • Interested in dance, art, theatre, jazz, tennis, thouroughbred horses, and golf.

> *Portfolio available upon request*

presentations _____

Birmingham Design Center

Birmingham Architectural Center

University of Alabama

University of Alabama Fashion Design Program

Bloomingdale's - Birmingham

Belk's - Birmingham and Atlanta area stores

Nieman Marcus - New York City, NY and Chicago, IL

Sebastion Models Agency

W.C. Anderson Modeling Agency

Convention Program - Reunion Center, Dallas, TX

Radio & TV - Atlanta, Birmingham, Mobile

Evening Magazine - Birmingham

Southern Women Business Owners Association - Atlanta chapter

IBM Corporation

Princess Cruises Lines

✔ Belinda's unique resume is 8-1/2" x 11" held horizontally and folded in half.
✔ Headings are in large, bold, lower case letters for an original effect.
✔ Pastel colored paper is a must for Belinda's field.

COMEDIAN / MAGICIAN

SCOTT ROWLEY

Comedian / Magician

329 Beaver Run • Sioux Falls, SD 57101 • 605/ 555-7205

SUMMARY

10 years as a stand-up comedian and magician performing nationally • Specialize in political satire, but expert at creating and presenting routines appropriate to diverse audiences such as college students, children, senior citizens, businesspersons, and young marrieds • Recipient of the 1989 Catch A Rising Star Comedy Award recognizing promising young comedians • Frequent appearances on The Tonight Show and HBO Comedy Specials.

APPEARANCE HIGHLIGHTS

COMEDY CLUBS ~

Catch A Rising Star • Hollywood, CA (1986, 1987, 1990)
The Improv • New York, NY (1987, 1988, 1989)
The Comic Strip • San Francisco, CA (1989, 1991)

COLLEGE SHOWS ~

UCLA • Los Angeles, CA (1985)
University of Michigan • Ann Arbor, MI (1986)
USC • Los Angeles, CA (1986)

PRIVATE FUNCTIONS ~

AT & T • New York City, NY (1983)
March of Dimes Benefit Show • Chicago, IL (1988)
AIDS Action Organization • San Francisco, CA (1990)

CRUISE SHIPS ~

Princess Cruise Line • Miami, FL (1981)
Cunard Cruise Lines • New York, NY (1982)
Carnival Cruise Lines • New York, NY (1983)

References and Video Portfolio available

✔ Scott's opening section summarizes his 10 years as a performer.
✔ His varied performance venues demonstrate his diversity of audiences.
✔ Identifying specific "gigs" validates Scott's credibility.

RITA CHAVEZ

Dancer / Singer

1224 Joy Street • Washington, DC 20004 • 202/ 555-9994

PERSONAL DESCRIPTION

Height: 5'8"   *Weight:* 108 lbs.

Eyes: Blue   *Hair:* Blonde   *Voice:* Alto

PROFESSIONAL EXPERIENCE

IMPULSE DANCE TROUPE • Washington, DC
Dancer / Choreographer (Feb 89 to present)
Travel extensively throughout the region performing for children, senior citizens, and disabled audiences.   Headliner at the Special Olympics annual conference.

DISNEYWORLD • Orlando, FL
Feel the Beat (Aug 88 to Jan 89)

AVERY FISHER HALL • New York City, NY
Rhythms for Peace (Jul 88)

AMERICAN DANCE INTERNATIONAL • Miami, FL
Dancer (Dec 86 to Jun 88)
Performed American period, popular, and musical theater dance on cruise ships. Also performed in holiday jazz concert with the Greater Miami Symphony Orchestra.

TELEVISION EXPERIENCE

UNIVERSAL STUDIOS • Los Angeles, CA
Commercial shoot for 1991 promotion (Fall 90)

DANCIN' U.S.A. • Hollywood, CA
Represented City and State (Nov 90)

References / Video available upon request

- ✔ Rita highlights her specific fields of entertainment under her name.
- ✔ Her opening section provides a necessary personal description.
- ✔ Prestigious dance troupes and sites are highlighted in capitals.

JOEL FARB
48 Stoney Brook Road
Westville, CT 06515
203/ 555-8327

EVENTS PLANNER

ArtsEvents, Inc. • New Haven, CT   1987 to present

Principal • Plan and coordinate social, educational, and fund raising events for prominent organizations within the artistic community • Supervise in-house and sub-contracted staffs in the implementation of schedules, facilities, menus, decorations, entertainment, speakers, invitations, and promotions.

Key Events:

- **"Lunch With Degas"**
  Coordinated joint Folk Art Museum & Women's Guild luncheon requiring collaboration with the Museum's Function Manager and Director of Group Sales. Created publicity and handled registration details.

- **"Kids Back Then"**
  Organized Colonial Day celebration at the Children's Museum. Recruited artisans, storytellers, and musicians. Planned crafts, activities, food, displays, and costumes. Organized floor space and rotation of activities.

- **"Holiday Art"**
  Located and negotiated contracts with 50 local artisans to display crafts on consignment at Women's Guild Christmas Bazaar. Prepared and decorated booths. Recruited, scheduled, and oversaw volunteer staff.

- **"Swan Lake Gala"**
  Managed annual P.R. event for Hartford Ballet Company. Planned list of prominent guests from business, entertainment, and government. Designed publicity and invitations. Negotiated contracts with caterer, musicians, and function hall. Provided on-site management of function.

- **"Art Smart"**
  Recruited educators to plan, develop, and present educational programs to inner city students to acquaint them with the Afro-American Museum. Supported in the administration of grant funds.

✔ Joel's specialty is displayed as a bold banner at the top of his resume.
✔ He also highlights company name and key events in bold.
✔ Bullets help the reader scan down the list of events.

URSULA MEINZ

20 Parson Lane ~ Parkville, MD 21234 ~ 301/555-1087

EXPERIENCE:

President & Founder • WHAT'S NEXT, INC.   1987 to present
Public Relations firm specializing in large-scale public special events

~ Originated and organized all facets of the annual New Year's Eve celebration "First Night" growing this city tradition from 2,000 participants to 80,000 in five years. It now boasts 53 social events sponsored by 275 organizations and corporations, a paid staff of 15, and a volunteer staff of 250.

~ Supported in the planning and implementation of media coverage and logistics for large city-wide celebrations including outdoor concerts; previews of major motion pictures; unveiling of the Civic Center; the city's 300th Birthday Celebration; the arrival of the U.S.S. Kennedy; and a visit by Mother Theresa.

~ Organized and promoted high-visibility spoofed sporting events including "Battle of the Bulge," "The Couch Potato's Triathalon," "Women on the Move," and "Let's Wear out the Kids."

~ Designed and implemented fund raising events, e.g. dinner dance, silent auction, jazz cruise for politically-motivated organizations including the Women's Voting League and the American Council on Health Insurance.

Director • WBMD-TV's "YOU AND THE ARTS"   1985 to 1987
Spearheaded a public service campaign that solicited $1.5M from corporations and individuals and appeared to significantly increase ratings.

Asst. Director of Special Events • PRO BASEBALL CORP.   1983 to 1985
Assisted in the development and coordination of ticket promotions, give-away campaigns, college nights, retirement ceremonies, old timers games, and clinics.

EDUCATION:

B.S.B.A. in Marketing • TEMPLE UNIVERSITY   1983

REFERENCES:

References and portfolio available upon request

✔ Tildes (~), bullets, attractive spacing, and a delicate type style all contribute to the readability of Ursula's information-packed resume.
✔ Ursula only includes well-recognized events within her company description.

FILM / VIDEO PRODUCER

FIONA SCARBORO

Film and Video Production

3882 Ranier Avenue South
Seattle, WA 98160

Residence: 206/ 555-7552
Business: 206/ 555-4039

EXPERIENCE:

Free-lance Film and Video Producer   **1987 to present**

Directed a full-length nature film previewed at the Audubon Society. Responsible for camera work and editing.

Produced a "70's horror film" previewed on KDDY's Graveyard Shift. Responsible for writing, camera work, directing, and editing.

Produced an 8mm video of above film previewed at Viceroy Museum Art School. Responsible for writing, camera work, directing, and editing.

Free-lance Musician   **1980 to present**

Flutist with area jazz bands. Record commercials and sound tracks.

Radio Personality   **1985 to 1987**
KSWA   SEATTLE, WA

D.J. and talk show host for a news radio station.

TRAINING:

16mm Film Production • 16mm Film Editing
Video Production • Super 8 Film Production   AMERICAN VIDEO INSTITUTE

Video Production • Special Effects   VICEROY MUSEUM ART SCHOOL

Super 8 Production, Editing and Sound   SUPER SCREENINGS, INC.

EDUCATION:

A.S. in Communications   1985
UNIVERSITY OF SOUTHERN CALIFORNIA   LOS ANGELES, CA

References and film portfolio available

✔ Fiona includes various film projects to show her breadth of experience.
✔ Musician and D.J. positions support her creative background.
✔ Fiona presents Training before Education because of its relevancy.

FLIGHT ATTENDANT (Entry-level)

EILEEN BOUQUIN
3471 Bouldercrest Road
Gresham Park, GA 30316
404/ 555-1156

OBJECTIVE: Flight attendant with a national airline. Willing to relocate.

QUALIFICATIONS:

Outstanding employment record. Long-standing Field Salesperson for one of the nation's largest distributors of school supplies. *Salesperson of the Year.*

Proven ability to satisfy large numbers of people. Activities coordinator for one of the leading elderly care facilities in the United States. *Organized many highly successful social events for more than 600 residents at one time.*

Demonstrated skill in providing excellent customer service. As Customer Service Representative, successfully alleviated customer complaints and allayed customer concerns via telephone. *Promoted to Manager.*

Proficiency in staff training. Trained and managed a staff of 3 Customer Service Representatives. *Staff consistently resolved customer complaints efficiently.*

Capacity to interact effectively with a wide variety of people. Volunteer as evening events planner at local community center. *Interact with people of all ages and all walks of life.*

EMPLOYMENT:

T.J. Holcomb School Supply Corporation • Decatur, GA	1988 to present
Belmont Business Products Company • Atlanta, GA	1985 to 1988
Lakewood Elder Community • Atlanta, GA	1983 to 1985

EDUCATION:

B.S. in History   **1983**
KENNESAW STATE COLLEGE   Marietta, GA

Certified in CPR.

✔ Eileen's resume identifies her professional achievements which are transferrable to a career as a flight attendant.
✔ Important phrases are highlighted in bold and italics for emphasis.

FLIGHT ATTENDANT (Experienced)

ROBIN MOLINEAUX
202 Morningside Drive
Las Vegas, NV 89114
702/ 555-1107

Objective:

FLIGHT ATTENDANT - INTERNATIONAL CARRIER

Qualifications:

- 10+ years as a flight attendant on a major domestic carrier.
- 7+ years experience as a flight attendant supervisor.
- Recipient of numerous Customer Service Awards.
- Certified in airline safety and passenger service.
- Fluent in Italian and Portuguese.
- Well-travelled throughout Europe and South America.
- Associate of Arts Degree in Business.
- Previous employment as a medical secretary.

Employment:

Flight Attendant (1980 to present)
UNITED AIRLINES

Medical Secretary (1978 to 1980)
ALBERT HARMON, M.D. • EVANSVILLE, IN

Education:

A.S. in Business (1978)
INDIANA UNIVERSITY • KOKOMO, IN

Airline-sponsored workshops and seminars

✔ Robin's Objective is short and specific.
✔ Her Qualifications demonstrate superior career performance.
✔ Languages and international travel are important for her new position.

JOHN BARCLAY   2 Militia Way ■ Charleston, SC 29407 ■ 803/ 555-6294

Summary of Qualifications:

- USPGA-certified golf teaching professional.
- Successful experience in commissioned sales of golf instruction.
- Strong background in program assessment, development, and implementation.
- Outstanding interpersonal and motivational skills with students at all levels.

Employment Highlights:

HEAD TEACHING PRO
Pinewoods Golf Club ■ Charleston, SC   1989 to present

- Personally maintain a capacity schedule of lessons on a commissioned basis.
- Generate a core of repeat students through expansion of instructional programs.
- Participate in intra-club promotions to increase membership and participation.
- Spearheaded 4 teams to Divisional wins and advancement within the League.
- Network with manufacturers of athletic equipment and clothing.
- Select quality equipment and clothing for sale in the pro shop.

CO-HEAD TEACHING PRO
Tall Grass Golf & Country Club ■ City, State   1987 to 1989

ASSISTANT TEACHING PRO
Idlewild Country Club ■ City, State   Summers 1985 and 1986

Golf Achievements:

No. 1 Ranking ■ Mid-Atlantic Amateur Golf Association   1987

Winner ■ Mid-Atlantic Sectional Amateur Golf Championships   1986

Winner ■ South Carolina Amateur Golf Championships   1985

Education:

A.S. in Business   1987
Allen University ■ Columbia, SC

✔ John's resume stresses all the facets of his profession, e.g., teaching, program
  development, sales, marketing, and personal performance.
✔ It is easy to scan because of his consistent use of boxes.

GRAPHIC DESIGNER (Desktop Publishing)

DESIRABLE

Macintosh II Graphic Designer and Typesetter. Full knowledge of Desktop Publishing and most Mac-compatible graphic software including:

ANDREA BARRON
15-C Willow Avenue
Greenwich, CT 06830
203/ 555-2995

ALDUS PAGEMAKER • QUARK XPRESS • LETRASET READY SET GO • ADOBE ILLUSTRATOR • MICROSOFT WORD • ALDUS POWER POINT • LETRASET IMAGE STUDIO • CLARIS MACDRAW AND MACPAINT • ETC.

WORK EXPERIENCE

SNAP IMAGES (audiovisual)
724 Madison Avenue
New York City

KR PLUS (design studio)
210, rue d'Alsace
92300 Levallois, FRANCE

ALCATEL N.V. (communications)
75015 Paris, FRANCE

CAP INFORMATIQUE (computers)
164, bd Victor Hugo
75008 Paris, FRANCE

EDUCATION

NORTHWESTERN UNIVERSITY
BS in Communications – 1987

5/89 to present

Full-time graphic artist for a highly-regarded New York design firm.

11/87 to 3/89

Freelancing computer graphic artist for various French companies in a variety of capacities including:

- Design & production of promotional publications, tariffs, international magazines, etc.

- Production of graphic images including logos, stylized maps, and hi-tech illustrations.

- Creation of 35mm high resolution slides (knowledge of Honeywell Slidewriter and PICT software.)

✔ Andrea's resume showcases her graphic design expertise.
✔ Graphics and bold type attract attention to the most important information.
✔ The overall presentation is interesting because of its asymmetry.

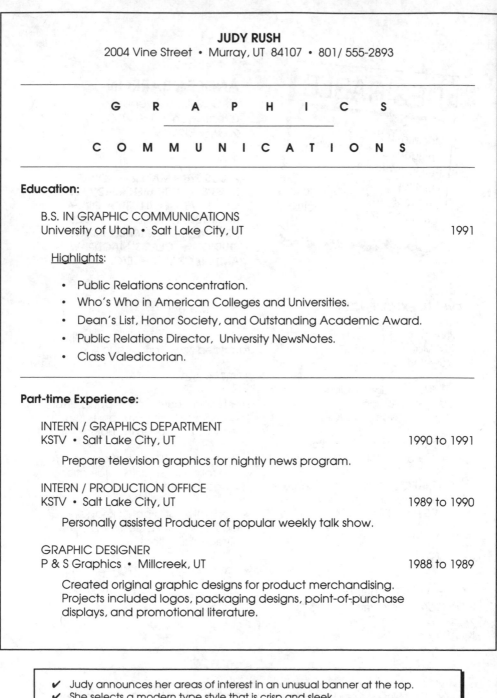

JUDY RUSH
2004 Vine Street • Murray, UT 84107 • 801/ 555-2893

G R A P H I C S

C O M M U N I C A T I O N S

Education:

B.S. IN GRAPHIC COMMUNICATIONS
University of Utah • Salt Lake City, UT   1991

Highlights:

- Public Relations concentration.
- Who's Who in American Colleges and Universities.
- Dean's List, Honor Society, and Outstanding Academic Award.
- Public Relations Director, University NewsNotes.
- Class Valedictorian.

Part-time Experience:

INTERN / GRAPHICS DEPARTMENT
KSTV • Salt Lake City, UT   1990 to 1991

   Prepare television graphics for nightly news program.

INTERN / PRODUCTION OFFICE
KSTV • Salt Lake City, UT   1989 to 1990

   Personally assisted Producer of popular weekly talk show.

GRAPHIC DESIGNER
P & S Graphics • Millcreek, UT   1988 to 1989

   Created original graphic designs for product merchandising.
   Projects included logos, packaging designs, point-of-purchase
   displays, and promotional literature.

✔ Judy announces her areas of interest in an unusual banner at the top.
✔ She selects a modern type style that is crisp and sleek.
✔ Her Education is presented first since all of her experience is part-time.

GRAPHIC DESIGNER (Free-lance)

LLOYD BARROWS

409-H Broadway
Fargo, ND 58102

701/ 555-9603

QUALIFICATIONS:

- Master of Fine Arts majoring in Graphic Design.
- Proven ability to understand client concerns and meet deadlines.
- Accomplished at interacting with clients and production personnel.
- Expert at integrating design, production, sales, and marketing considerations.
- Manage large-scale graphic promotion projects and remain within budget.

PROFESSIONAL EXPERIENCE:

Free-lance Designer (1989 to present)
CRANE GRAPHICS • Fargo, ND

- Supervise design projects including direct mailers, trade show graphics, mast-heads, slides, catalogs, and newsletters from concept through final production.

- Expert at layout, design, type specification, copy fitting, paste-up, procurement of photographs, and supervision of final printing.

- Key accounts include Moorhead Publishing, Harrington Office Systems, High Sky Publishing Company, DataSend Information Services, and University Press.

Art Director (1985 to 1989)
ENGLEWOOD ADVERTISING AGENCY • Moorhead, ND

- Directed Graphic Arts staff in the creation of hard-hitting advertisements for trade journals and glossy magazines. Agency won numerous design awards.

Assistant Art Director (1983 to 1985)
NOYES CORPORATION • West Fargo, ND

EDUCATION:

MFA in Graphic Design (1983)
BFA in Graphic Design (1981)
TRENT SCHOOL OF DESIGN • Fargo, ND

- ✔ Lloyd's use of half-lines is understated, yet sophisticated.
- ✔ His Qualifications establish him as a seasoned, competent professional.
- ✔ Professional Experience includes specific projects, skills, and clients.

BRIAN REYNOLDS

124 Hickory Ridge Road
Karns, TN 37921

Residence: 615/ 555-2754
Business: 615/ 555-8000

OBJECTIVE:

Concierge for a large, metropolitan hotel.

EDUCATION:

Bachelor of Arts in Hotel Management
DAVID LIPSCOMB UNIVERSITY • Nashville, TN   **1991**

Concentration in Public Relations • American Marketing Association • Men's
Tennis Team • Financed 100% of education.

RELATED EXPERIENCE:

Concierge
SHERATON HOTEL • Knoxville, TN   **May 1990 to present**

- Successfully performed all responsibilities related to this position including
  staff coordination, customer service, and public relations.

- Closely collaborated with all departments to ensure smooth hotel operations
  and the implementation of special programs.

- Received outstanding weekly performance evaluations in the areas of job
  knowledge, dependability, resourcefulness, and overall professionalism.

- Performed as **Host at General Curtin's Pub (Jul 1990 to Aug 1990)**.

Assistant Functions Coordinator
PROSPECT PLACE INN • Oak Ridge, TN   **May 1989 to May 1990**

- Supported Functions Manager in all areas of planning, scheduling, and
  supervising small and large group functions.

- Assumed responsibilities of Food and Beverage Supervisor during his absence.
  Hired and scheduled food and beverage employees. Organized, scheduled,
  and serviced banquets.

Night Manager
HIGH POINT RESTAURANT • Alcoa, TN   **May 1988 to May 1989**
CHILHOWEE CAFE • Maryville, TN   **May 1987 to May 1988**

✔ Brian's Objective is targeted toward a very specific position.
✔ He presents his Education first as a "prequalifier" for an industry position.
✔ Brian explains his 2 current positions and only lists others to avoid repetition.

NANCY STEVENS

Interior Decorator

89 Lyme Road ✱ Topeka, KS 66605 ✱ 913/ 555-6547

PROFILE:

✱ *Bachelor of Science in Fine Arts (Washburn University) — specialized in interior and landscape design.*

✱ *Design coursework at Embry-Penta Interior Design School.*

✱ *More than a decade of experience consulting with residential and business clients on design projects involving space planning, color selection, painting, lighting, and accents.*

✱ *Proficient in quickly translating customer requirements into pleasing interior decorating schemes. Received numerous awards in home interior design.*

✱ *Ability to tastefully utilize a wide variety of styles including traditional, contemporary, modern, Western, and Far Eastern styles.*

✱ *Expert in managing multiple projects and meeting deadline and budget constraints.*

✱ *Maintain a philosophy of providing the ultimate in customer service.*

✱ *Highly adept in sales, marketing, and promotion.*

✱ *Client List / Portfolio available upon request* ✱

✔ Nancy decorates her resume with graphics and a "dressy" type style.
✔ Adequate spacing keeps her resume easy to read.
✔ Nancy's experience is general, but is supported by her client list and portfolio.

G
B

Introducing

~ GENA BRILEY ~

For over fifteen years Gena Briley has provided a wide variety of tasteful interior design services to commercial and residential clients worldwide. She has remodeled skyscraper lobbys and foyers, corporate offices, work areas, retail businesses, hotels, municipal buildings, hospitals, homes, condominiums, and financial institutions. *Each client receives the utmost in personal attention and is guaranteed satisfaction!*

Gena's hallmark is the ability to combine highly creative design with thorough technical expertise. This combination allows her to successfully and efficiently manage the many critical aspects of a design project so that quality is assured and time requirements are met. From concept through completion, Gena is masterful in using color, lighting, and accents to create a pleasing environment. The scope of her projects includes space planning, renovation, window and wall treatments, textiles, furniture, and accessories. She specializes in unique design problems and their solutions. *No design project is too complex, too difficult, or too large for Gena.*

Gena is affiliated with numerous critically-acclaimed local, national, and international interior design professionals and works very closely with leading art galleries. *Gina can also provide her clients with original art, antiques, and decorative accents.*

Portfolio and presentation boards
are available upon request.

P.O. BOX 2855 ~ Lincoln, NE 68505 ~ 402/ 555-3025

✔ Interior design is a personal service, so Gina's personalized approach to her alternative resume is appropriate.
✔ Her resume can effectively be used to attract new clients or a new position.

INTERIOR DESIGNER (Free-lance)

CHARLTON DESIGNS

Lois Charlton • 4703 Market Street • Philadelphia, PA 19108 • 215/ 555-4550

INTERIOR DESIGNER specializing in residential spaces

A living space is a reflection of one's inner story, easier told in color and texture than words.

EDUCATION:

Fashion Institute of Technology • A.A. IN APPLIED DESIGN (1988)

School of Visual Arts • B.A. IN PSYCHOLOGY (1980)

DESIGN EXPERIENCE:

Collaborated with other designers on space planning, decorating, drafting, model-making.
Quentin Baker • Vieira Associates Inc. • Amos Stein, Designer.

Free-lance interior designer with corporate and individual clients
A child's bedroom to accommodate toys, an activity center, and sleep space for friends • A
contemporary office for the female president of a marketing firm • A loft bedroom for a teenager
• A designer's studio maximizing north light.

Hands-on experience in decoration, including upholstery and slipcovers, drapery and curtains,
wood finishing, refinishing and painting, needlepoint and rug making.

Work with artists by researching ideas, assisting in fabrication, and hanging shows.

PUBLISHING EXPERIENCE:

Publisher, *Design News* newsletter

Contributor, *Marketing Now!* magazine

SPECIAL MENTION:

Designed and executed decoration of apartment featured on "Lifestyles" television program.

Scale model of greenhouse room included in the "Horticultural '90" annual exhibit.

MEMBERSHIPS:

American Society of Free-lance Designers

Society for Historic Preservation

✔ As a free-lancer, Lois creates her resume on her own company letterhead.
✔ To establish a personal tone, she shares her philosophy of design.
✔ Her resume demonstrates competence in numerous areas of design.

S · L

10 Admiral Fitzroy Lane
Newport, Rhode Island 02840
401/ 555-3545

STEPHANIE LUNDGREN

EXPERIENCE

~ **Designer / Metalsmith**
STEPHANIE LUNDGREN DESIGNS, INC.
Newport, RI (1985 to present)
14k gold, sterling silver jewelry

~ **Metalsmith**
MERRICK JEWELERS
Providence, RI (1978 to 1985)
Sterling silver, 14k gold jewelry

~ **Potter / Metalsmith**
TREASURE TROVE
Newport, RI (1983 to 1985)
Porcelain, sterling silver

~ **Fine Arts Teacher**
PROVIDENCE PUBLIC SCHOOLS
Providence, RI (1979 to 1985)

~ **Pottery Instructor**
CONTINUING EDUCATION PROGRAM
Cranston, RI (1981 to 1983)

~ **Studio Arts Teacher**
PROVIDENCE HIGH SCHOOL
Providence, RI (1977 to 1978)

EDUCATION

~ **Bachelor of Arts cum laude (Studio Art)**
STATE UNIVERSITY OF NEW YORK
New Paltz, NY (1976)

~ **Stone Setting (Instructor: Ned Ames)**
PROVIDENCE CRAFTS CENTER
Providence, RI (1987)

~ **Metalsmithing, Ceramics**
WENTWORTH MUSEUM SCHOOL
Providence, RI (1986)

~ **Jewelry**
TREMBLAY SCHOOL OF CRAFTS
Pawtucket, RI (1985)

STEPHANIE LUNDGREN

TRADE SHOWS

~ Jewelry Buyers Market
New York, NY (1989 to 1991)
Newport, RI (1990)

~ Gift Show
International Crafts Division
New York, NY (1987 to 1991)

GALLERIES

~ Hyde Art Museum
Newport, RI (1989, 1991)
Artful Crafts II & III Exhibits

~ Gallery of Decorations
Pawtucket, RI (1991)
Featured Artist

~ The Art Spectrum
Newport, RI (1985 to present)
Juried Exhibitor

~ Society of Arts and Crafts
Providence, RI (1988 to 1990)
Juried Exhibitor

~ Newport Art Association
Newport, RI (1989, 1990, 1991)
A Show of Hands (Juried)

~ Truman Boutique
Newport, RI (1990, 1991)
One Person Show

~ Artisans Gallery
Providence, RI (1989)
Five Artists Exhibition (Juried)

~ Bearce Gallery
Newport, RI (1989 to present)
10 Jewelers Exhibition (Juried, May & June 1989)

PROFESSIONAL ASSOCIATIONS

~ Society of Arts and Crafts
Providence, RI (1987 to present)

~ National Crafts Council
New York, NY (1982 to present)

~ Society of Goldsmiths
Providence, RI (1983 to present)

~ Moderne Museum of Art
New York, NY (1986 to present)

~ Arts Umbrella
Providence, RI (1988 to present)

~ American Arts Foundation
New York, NY (1980 to present)

References and portfolio available upon request

✔ Stephanie's resume is 2 pages to accommodate her impressive professional career, but it is easy to scan because of centered section headings, lines dividing sections, and the selection of a delicate type style.

RICHARD POVIS
134 Rockford Road
Crystal, MN 55428
612/ 555-9892

EXPERIENCE

Free-Lance Trumpet Soloist   **1986 to present**

Promote personal career through negotiating and securing concert engagements. Direct programming, scheduling, advertisement, and all aspects of production. Hire and supervise assistants.

Contract Musician   **1986 to present**
MINNEAPOLIS SYMPHONY ORCHESTRA   MINNEAPOLIS , MN
ST. PAUL BALLET ORCHESTRA   ST. PAUL, MN

Instructor / Trumpet, Flugelhorn, Chamber Music   **1983 to present**
ROLAND LEWIS MUSIC SCHOOL   FRIDLEY, MN

Provide individualized and group instruction for students of a broad range of age and abilities. Research instructional materials and methods. Implement motivational techniques. Plan and organize musical performances.

Recruiter   **1988 to 1990**
BAYBERRY MUSIC SCHOOL / Admissions Office   GOLDEN VALLEY, MN

Conducted formal interviews and auditions with prospective candidates for admission. Submitted written evaluations to Admissions Committee members outlining impressions and recommendations regarding each candidate. Frequently established long-term relationships with promising students.

EDUCATION

Master of Music   **1986**
MINNESOTA CONSERVATORY OF MUSIC   MINNEAPOLIS, MN

Bachelor of Arts in Music Theory   **1984**
CONCORDIA COLLEGE   ST. PAUL, MN

✔ Richard stresses diverse aspects of his free-lance music career, e.g., technical, marketing, production, business, teaching, and mentoring.
✔ Section headings are an attractive, but subtle graphic element.

PHOTOGRAPHER

Photography
Video
Multi-media

ALICIA HUGO

328 Taft Street • New Orleans, LA 70130 • 504/ 555-8844

Experience:

Free-lance Photographer   **1985 to present**

Perform technical and operational functions to develop and maintain a free-lance photography business specializing in industrial, architectural, and wedding photography.

Proficient at sales and marketing, contract negotiation, client needs assessment, scheduling and delivery of service, vendor relations, staff recruitment and supervision, trouble-shooting, and customer service.

Established a local reputation as a high-quality, cost-effective alternative to major studios.

Highlights:

- Sophisticated corporate multi-media presentations
- Commercial marketing communications projects
- Video memories of special events
- Photo shoots for business and V.I.P. portfolios
- Stills for real estate and architectural purposes

Training:

Advanced Photography Degree   **1984**
METAIRIE SCHOOL OF PHOTOGRAPHY

Comprehensive Photography Certificate   **1983**
BONNEBEL SCHOOL OF PHOTOGRAPHY

References:

References and Portfolio available

✔ Alicia's resume format displays a photographer's talent for visual composition.
✔ She emphasizes her specialty areas in the upper left corner.
✔ Alicia stresses both technical and business competence.

K • S • M • A

~ JEAN LONBORG ~

"The Future is Now"

As KSMA's Program Director, Jean is responsible for round-the-clock live radio programming — music, promotions, news, and sports. She is the final judge and jury of station standards.

Jean began her career as a D.J. at USC's college station when women D.J.'s were unknown. She developed a loyal following and introduced a new musical sound to the west coast, New Age Jazz. Her personal style and knowledge of music soon caught the attention of KSMA, where she signed on as a part-time D.J. upon graduation.

Her popularity continued to grow and soon she had a full-time shift. Since 1986 she has been Program Director and host of the longest running new music show on radio.

Jean's contributions to securing KSMA's stature as a nationwide leader in creative programming are evident. Her awards are:

- 1991 MusArt P.D. of the Year

- 1988 & 1990 Davis Awards for best P.D.

- 1987 "People's Choice" recognition as most creative P.D.

P
H
O
T
O

H
E
R
E

KSMA Radio • 1600 Wilshire Boulevard • Santa Monica, CA 90406 • 213/ 555-6000

✔ Jean's resume is a promo sheet on her station's letterhead.
✔ It combines a background narrative with current industry achievements.
✔ As a broadcast professional, a photo is a plus.

RESTAURANT MANAGER

PAUL MUSTO
107 Strobel Road
Trumbull, CT 06611
203/ 555-3701

Objective

Restaurant Manager with a growing national chain. Willing to relocate.

Professional Experience

PAPA GINO'S   Bridgeport, CT
General Manager   **1988 to present**

Manage all operations of this highly successful Italian restaurant with annual sales exceeding $3.5M. Oversee personnel, finance, food preparation, purchasing, marketing, customer service, maintenance, and security.

- Coordinated all details of restaurant opening.
- Received Store of the Month Award during sixth month of operation.
- Within two years vaulted restaurant to top 8 of 550 in overall profitability.
- Selected by top management to participate in national management meetings.

LA MIA CUCINA   Trumbull, CT
Assistant Manager   **1985 to 1988**
Host/Waiter   **1983 to 1985**

Education

POST COLLEGE   Waterbury, CT
A.S. in Business Administration   **1983**

IN-SERVICE TRAINING
Restaurant Management, Time Management, Goal Setting

References

Available upon request

✔ Paul's Objective includes a major selling point, willingness to relocate.
✔ His job description highlights achievements with bullets.
✔ In-service training is directly related to his management career.

ANITA MARIE WAYANS
16-F Long Wharf • Boston, MA 02109 • 617/ 555-9813

T A L E N T   A G E N T

P R O D U C T I O N   C O O R D I N A T O R

Experience:

MORRIS MODELING AGENCY   **BOSTON, MA**
Director of New Model Development   **1989 to present**

Oversee all aspects of career development for 50 male and female models:

- Travel nationwide to interview and evaluate prospective talent.
- Supervise and critique photographic sessions.
- Teach modeling business practices classes.
- Strategize promotional programs for individual models.
- Handle model-client contract negotiations and relationships.
- Train new booking agents.

GORCHEV PHOTOGRAPHY STUDIO   **BOSTON, MA**
Production Coordinator   **1987 to 1989**

Planned and supervised all aspects of shoots for commercial photo studio:

- Bid, budgeted, and coordinated jobs.
- Casted and contracted talent.
- Scouted locations.
- Arranged for sets, props, backdrops, permits, and related necessities.

Education:

BRYANT-PARKS MODELING SCHOOL   **BOSTON, MA**
Video Commercials, Photo and Print Projection   **1987**

✔ Anita achieves a strong presentation by using bold capitals frequently.
✔ Her top heading echoes her 2 career positions.
✔ She keeps job descriptions short and to the point.

TELEVISION DIRECTOR

DIRK TARREYTON

21 Hyacinth Avenue
Winter Park, FL 32751

407/ 555-5470

PROFESSIONAL EXPERIENCE

WORL-TV

Assistant Director (1990 to present). Working on *The Ancient Traditions*, a series of 36 half-hour lectures covering the span of Eastern civilization. (The first 12 shows were illustrated with art supplied through The Far East Art Museum.) Analyze scripts and plan shots to illustrate specific points in lectures. Supervise the transfer of art to tape at Contraves Studios. Edit to fill gaps in shows partially assembled.

FREE-LANCE

Director (1988 to 1990). Orlando International Airport, Gatorland Zoo, Maitland Residential Community, Ben White Raceway, Florida Hospital, Silver Pines Country Club, University of Central Florida, Orlando Science Center, US Naval Training Center.

Production Support (1986 to 1988). Transamerica Insurance, HBO, Seaworld, Orlando Highway Authority, Orlando Tourist Center, Blue Lake Productions, Walt Disney Studios.

SUNBURST STUDIOS - Orlando, FL

Director (1984 to 1986). Assisted clients in defining production goals and establishing budgets. Produced and directed in-the-studio and on-location drama and comedy series. Hired and supervised freelance staff, booked facilities and equipment, and supervised equipment maintenance.

Production Assistant (1982 to 1984)
Intern (1981 to 1982)

EDUCATION

MERCY COLLEGE - Dobbs Ferry, NY
M.A. in Applied Media (1981)
B.S. in Communications (1978)

CONTINUING EDUCATION - Playwriting, Videotape Postproduction, ENG/EFP

LIFE MEMBER - National Academy of Television Arts & Sciences

> ✔ Dirk organizes his career into three phases.
> ✔ His experience encompasses technical, operational, and client services.
> ✔ Dirk lists major free-lance assignments to strengthen his credentials.

SUSAN GRIMES
447 Apache Street
Tulsa, OK 74151
918/ 555-4033

EXPERIENCE

Executive Producer   **1987 to present**
KSCR - SCRABBLE TELEVISION   **TULSA, OK**

Originated and successfully promote *new concept, interactive, cable TV Scrabble* program to prospective advertisers and viewing audience.

- Direct all marketing, managerial, and operational functions.
- Supervise large technical crew during videotaping of programs.
- Produce commercials, design sets and promotional aids.
- Recruit, train, and supervise technical staff and performers.
- Write and edit scripts.

Studio Manager   **1984 to 1987**
GEARY PHOTOGRAPHY STUDIO   **SAPULPA, OK**

Managed technical and operational activities for *large volume photographic studio* specializing in corporate advertising.

- Devised, implemented, and managed an efficient workflow system.
- Developed job quotations for key accounts including Phillips Petroleum.
- Provided excellent customer service which contributed to sales growth.
- Supervised purchasing, accounting, and inventory control functions.
- Coordinated vendors, props, locations, and stylist services for shoots.
- Personally scouted locations.

Associate Producer   **1982 to 1984**
MILLER ADVERTISING AGENCY   **TULSA, OK**

Account Executive   **1980 to 1982**
KBTL RADIO   **BARTLESVILLE, OK**

EDUCATION

AS in Communications   **1980**
NORTHEASTERN STATE UNIVERSITY   **TAHLEQUAH, OK**

✔ Susan combines narrative and bulleted sentences to ease scanning.
✔ Italics emphasize the most important information for the reader.
✔ She lists earlier positions to show career growth and versatility.

THEATRICAL DIRECTOR

FRANK MONTE
1006-C Garcia Canyon Road
Dona Ana, NM 88032
505/ 555-0071

EDUCATION:

BACHELOR OF ARTS IN DRAMA
New Mexico State University • Las Cruces, NM (1990)

THEATRICAL EXPERIENCE:

DIRECTORIAL EXPERIENCE:

N.M.S.U. Drama Department

"Driving Miss Daisy" (1990) • Director
"The Boys in the Band" (1989) • Assistant Director
"Love Letters" (1988) • Assistant Director

Children's Theatre

"Hansel & Gretel" (1986) • Assistant Director

STAGE MANAGEMENT EXPERIENCE:

N.M.S.U. Drama Department

"Wait Until Dark" (1986) • Stage Manager

TECHNICAL EXPERIENCE:

N.M.S.U. Drama Department

"Private Lives" (1988) • Master Electrician
The Shakespeare Festival (1988) • Sound Engineer
"The Dining Room" (1987) • Shift Crew Chief
Women's Drama Festival (1987) • Construction and Lights

Spectrum Players

"I Do, I Do" (1986) • Spot Operator
"Mame" (1986) • Flys
"Gypsy" (1986) • Spot Operator

✔ Frank organizes his theatrical experience into 3 professional sub-categories.
✔ He demonstrates experience in varied types of productions.
✔ His list of credits can be discussed more fully in an interview.

CHARLENE BERGAMINI

305 Red Bluff Road • Pasadena, TX 77501   713/ 555-2861

Education / Training:

Certificate - Cruise Counselor
CRUISE LINE INTERNATIONAL ASSOCIATION (CLIA)   1990

Associate Degree in Travel & Tourism Business Management
TEXAS SOUTHERN UNIVERSITY • Houston, TX   1988

- Automated Airline Reservations (SABRE)
- Internship at Travel Unlimited - Houston, TX

Certificate - Travel Agent Training Program
PASADENA COMMUNITY COLLEGE • Pasadena, TX   1986

Professional Experience:

Cruise Sales Agent
ISLAND CRUISES, INC. • Houston, TX   1990 to present
CARIBBEAN CRUISELINE • Pearland, TX   1988 to 1990

Travel Consultant
HOUSTON TRAVEL SERVICE • Houston, TX   1987 to 1988

Travel Counselor
ADVENTURE VACATIONS • Pasadena, TX   1986 to 1987

Reservations Agent
HOSKINS TRAVEL AGENCY • Dickinson, TX   1986

Organizations:

American Organization of Travel Consultants
Around-the-World Adventures

References available upon request

✔ Charlene presents Education first because it is a "prequalifier" in her industry.
✔ She omits job descriptions because her duties are well-known.
✔ Membership in professional organizations shows an interest in career growth.

WRITER

THOMAS RITTER
1023 Glebe Road
Arlington, VA 22210
703/ 555-0888

Objective:

FEATURE WRITER / REPORTER

Highlights:

- GUBERNATORIAL CAMPAIGNS - published political essays and human interest features.

- PREPARED AN INVESTIGATIVE REPORT for television broadcast which demonstrated abuse of state gun law.

- PUBLISHED NUMEROUS EDITORIALS nationally.

- WROTE, CO-PRODUCED AND TAPED a sports satire for marketing to regional television stations.

- PUBLISHED BIOGRAPHY of local entrepreneur.

Employment:

Free-lance Writer (1988 to present)

Writer / Reporter (1986 to 1988)
THE WASHINGTON POST • Washington, DC

Education:

M.S. in Journalism (1986)
DEPAUL UNIVERSITY • Chicago, IL

B.S. in English (1984)
ELMHURST COLLEGE • Elmhurst, IL

Portfolio and references available on request

✔ Thomas' Objective allows him flexibility in pursuing 2 types of positions.
✔ His Highlights section demonstrates his writing versatility, and he uses smalll capitals to further emphasize diverse assignments.

MS. JACKIE NORTON
47 Andover Road
Stoneham, MA 02180
617/ 555-0237

SUMMARY

Writer/Project Manager

Marketing communications and public relations for diverse industries. Projects include brochures • newsletters • documentation • press kits • data sheets • advertisements • advertorials • speeches • feature articles.

EXPERIENCE

Senior Writer / Consultant   **1987 to present**
EMPIRE COMMUNICATIONS SERVICES   TEWKSBURY, MA

Direct creative operations of communications company from project concept through final production for clients in biomedical firms.

Corporate Communications Manager   **1985 to 1987**
BIOGEN, INC.   CAMBRIDGE, MA

Planned and implemented domestic and international communications programs to promote and reinforce product and company image.

Marketing Communications Coordinator   **1983 to 1985**
NOWTEK, INC.   BOSTON, MA

Promoted text-retrieval software to trade and consumer press, and managed production of marketing and sales literature.

EDUCATION

Bachelor of Arts / Communications   **1983**
BOSTON UNIVERSITY   BOSTON, MA

References and portfolio available upon request

✔ Jackie precedes her name with "MS." to alleviate gender confusion.
✔ Her Summary incorporates her career objective and areas of expertise.
✔ Jackie mentions her portfolio because it is a necessity in her field.

Computer Science and Engineering 6

The Mystery of Technology

Our lives are impacted daily by the knowledge and skill of computer science and engineering professionals. Rapid advances in areas as simple as home appliances and toys and as complex as telecommunications, biomedicine, aeronautics, transportation, and energy, are a benefit to us all and a direct result of your competence.

Yet, it is extremely difficult to translate your accomplishments onto paper because for most non-technical people, what you do and how you do it remains a mystery.

Eliminate The Jargon

Keep in mind that in most cases, a non-technical Human Resources professional will be the first to screen your resume. Therefore, the major challenge is to write your resume in such a way that it stresses your technical know-how, but is understood by both technical and non-technical personnel. You can include pertinent technical terms, but try to eliminate all jargon related to either your specialty or company.

Education Is A Major Credential

In many cases, your college degree will be both an important "prequalifier" and a signal to the prospective reader as to your field of interest, so you should begin with your

Education section. Include major projects and specialized coursework. Even an A.S. degree is significant when combined with continuing education courses.

However, if your work experience or company is much more impressive than your education, begin with that information first.

If appropriate, it is advisable to include a special Computer section to list the specific hardware, software, programming languages, and operating systems with which you are familiar. Or, you can highlight these same elements in capital letters within your job descriptions. Don't forget to include the popular computer software programs with which you are familiar, such as word processing, spreadsheets, and database management. They may seem elementary to you, but they're a plus to your prospective employer.

What Does Your Company Do?

With such a proliferation of industries, both manufacturing and high tech, and continuing mergers and buy-outs, it is impossible to keep up-to-date on the status of companies. Yesterday's baby food manufacturer is today's biotech engineering firm. Therefore, it's a good idea to explain what your company does, as such an explanation clarifies your own position. One short sentence describing size, products, annual sales, or parent company is appropriate. We have included many examples in this chapter.

Stress Technical and Non-Technical Skills

Some computer science and engineering positions require technical competence only. Others require technical expertise as well as management and interpersonal skills. Think of all your non-technical responsibilities, such as project management or customer support. Identify and present specific achievements requiring organization, coordination, liaison, and troubleshooting.

Technical Action Verbs

The following technical action verbs for computer science and engineering professionals can be used in addition to the comprehensive list found in Chapter 1:

Analyze	Diagnose	Maintain	Research
Assemble	Draft	Model	Resolve
Calculate	Document	Modify	Service
Configure	Evaluate	Modernize	Support
Construct	Fabricate	Mold	Test
Convert	Generate	Mount	Train
Customize	Implement	Perform	Transfer
Debug	Install	Program	Troubleshoot
Design	Integrate	Quantify	Update
Devise	Load	Repair	Verify

APPLICATIONS ENGINEER

ERNEST DOGGETT
3205 Hamilton Road
Whitehall, OH 43213
614/ 555-3991

Summary:

Computer Applications Engineer specializing in computer graphics • Versatile in utilizing PC's and VAX applications • Extensive customer support experience in software applications development, pre- and post-sales technical consultation, installations, and troubleshooting • Solid writing, research, and presentation skills • Strong background in project management and staff supervision • Graduate degree candidate in computer science • Degreed in physics.

Experience:

Applications Engineer • DIGITEX COMPANY • Columbus, OH (1988 to present)
($40M manufacturer of electronic publishing systems)

- Major contributor to development of interface between company VAX system and IBM to broaden applications, resulting in growth of worldwide customer base.
- Install, support, enhance, and troubleshoot customized Graphics systems.
- Collaborate with R&D and Sales in applications development and sales efforts.
- Introduced electronic bulletin board to help field engineers maintain systems.
- Integrated company application software to increase versatility across industries.

Data Processing Manager • WESSON COMPANY • Springfield, OH (1985 to 1988)
($12M environmental consulting firm)

- Customized software for data analysis, accounting, and budgeting operations.
- Managed a staff of 7 computer programmers and 2 computer operators.
- Researched, designed, and operated an IBM System 36.

Education:

M.S. Candidate in Computer Science • OHIO STATE UNIVERSITY • Columbus, OH
(Completed 44 credits in C, PASCAL, OPERATING SYSTEMS, and MIS)

B.S. in Physics • FRANKLIN UNIVERSITY • Columbus, OH (1985)

- ✔ Ernest condenses his experience in a Summary section at the top of his resume.
- ✔ Company descriptions under his titles enhance his professional image.
- ✔ Since Ernest is a candidate in Computer Science, he lists completed courses.

HELEN MIASMA

127 Dale Street, Roseville, MN 55113   612/ 555-3922

EDUCATION

1980   Minneapolis College of Art & Design   Minneapolis, MN
BACHELOR OF ARCHITECTURE

REGISTRATION

1980   Minnesota Board of Registration of Architects

EXPERIENCE

1987 - present   Melanson, Smythe & Grimes, Inc.   St. Paul, MN
ASSOCIATE & HEAD DESIGNER

- Project Manager – $40M retail project
  Sherman Appliance Center – Roseville, MN

- Project Manager – $12M, 28-unit office complex
  One Bayberry Place – Eau Claire, WI

- Head Designer/Project Manager – $31M medical complex
  VA Medical Center – Minneapolis, MN

1983 - 1987   Showplace Architects   St. Paul, MN
PARTNER & DIRECTOR OF DESIGN

- Co-founded small firm specializing in design/build of turnkey theater facilities.

- Created and coordinated a design and construction team.

1980 - 1983   Dickinson Design, Inc.   Minneapolis, MN
ARCHITECT

- Extensive design background encompassing site, landscape, building, interior, and graphic design.

- Experienced in numerous building types including office, bank, mall, retail, theater, medical, and residential.

- Received 1983 AIA design award for office complex.

✔ Helen's field needs to show creativity, so she uses a stylish heading and format.
✔ Because a degree is so important in her field, she starts with Education first.
✔ She lists her AIA award to strengthen her image of competency.

COMPUTER DESIGN ENGINEER

MAURICE REILLY
210 Draper Street
Palo Alto, CA 94302
415/ 555-4142

EXPERIENCE: **Computer Design Engineer** **1991 to present**
ATALAN CONTROL DEVICES San Jose, CA

Designed embedded systems for Process Control applications; coordinated integration of hardware and software.

Wrote firmware for Motorola 680x0 microprocessors.

Devised algorithm for accelerating I/O.

Completed Course on Advanced Data Telecommunications.

COMPUTERS:

Hardware: Entire line of Intel and Motorola microprocessors. Knowledge of all popular buses including VME.

Software: Forth, Assembler, C, Fortran, APL, UNIX, DOS.

EDUCATION: **M.S. in Chemical Engineering** **1991**
B.S. in Computer Engineering **1990**
STANFORD UNIVERSITY Palo Alto, CA

Computer Architecture	Bus & I/O Design
Embedded Computer Systems	Systems Integration
Digital Signal Processing	Telecommunications
Digital & Analog Circuitry Design	Process Control Systems

Designed a Motorola 68010 microprocessor-based laser diode nephelometer.

Simulated a network controller for coordinating activities between Remote Terminal Units in a SCADA system.

Researched data telecommunications design for enabling systems to be remotely controlled.

Designed a PAL-based system for controlling processes during Liquid Chromatography.

Interfaced an Intel 80286 microprocessor with a hardened Temperature Control Ssytem.

✔ Maurice's use of bold type highlights degrees and accomplishments.
✔ Because of his very specific field, a Computers section is a must.
✔ Maurice is relatively new to the field, so he also emphasizes his education.

ANGELA SINCLAIR
149 Wilder Road
Caldwell, ID 83605
208/ 555-4038

SUMMARY OF QUALIFICATIONS:

- 8+ years experience in technical services and project management.
- Expertise in coordinating work activities of a multi-disciplinary team.
- Proven ability to problem-solve and meet deadlines.
- Proficiency in developing and implementing effective training programs.
- Excellent oral and written communication skills.

PROFESSIONAL EXPERIENCE:

Computer Installation Director
LEFEBURE COMPANY • Boise, ID   1984 to present

Direct the installation and support of minicomputer-based banking systems.

- Formulate specifications for custom software, prepare specifications sheets for programmers, design input screens, and develop installation workplans.
- Coordinate activities of field engineers, programmers, and bank personnel.
- Design and conduct comprehensive end-user training classes.
- Troubleshoot system problems.
- Deliver pre- and post-sale marketing presentations.

Project Manager
BIOGEN RESEARCH CORPORATION • Nampa, ID   1983 to 1984

Directed a million-dollar project for computerizing a $47M genetics research company.

- Oversaw team of 4 software/hardware engineers in the research, selection, installation, and testing of a computer modeling and data analysis system.
- Maintained records of 10,000+ genetic testing results.
- Generated data analysis reports for laboratory managers.

EDUCATION:

Bachelor of Science in Computer Science
SEATTLE UNIVERSITY • Seattle, WA   1983

✔ Angela utilizes a Summary section to quickly highlight her qualifications.
✔ She provides a company description in italics to enhance her status.
✔ Short bulleted statements are easier to read than long narrative paragraphs.

EDWARD SHAUNNESSEY
1289 East 88th Avenue
Thornton, CO 80229
303/ 555-8136

SUMMARY:

Expert in the installation and troubleshooting of a wide area networks (WAN) and local area networks (LAN) • Proven ability to communicate with technical and non-technical users • Demonstrated skill in meeting deadlines within demanding environments • Consistently recognized by management for superior performance, management skills, and problem-solving ability.

PROFESSIONAL EXPERIENCE:

ELCON TRANSDUCER COMPANY   DENVER, CO
MANAGER OF COMPUTER OPERATIONS   **1987 to present**

Supervise six Computer Operators in the operation and maintenance of two IBM 36 Series mainframe computers and on-line IMS system supporting 825 users. *Assume responsibilities of Manager of Operations as needed.*

- Ensure proper and efficient operation of on-line IMS production and test system, analysis of its performance, optimization, and implementation of restart and recovery procedures to insure hardware utilization at maximum capacity and to minimize loss of production time to users.
- Developed tracking system for training of operations personnel.
- Assisted Corporate Training Manager in creation of Operations Manual.
- Conduct orientation tours of computer room for new company employees.

DATAVOX TELECOMM INTERNATIONAL   COMMERCE CITY, CO
PROJECT ENGINEER   **1984 to 1987**

Supervised staff of three in the operation of a large local area computer network.

- Proficient in the installation and repair of all peripherals connected to the network including terminals, modems, printers, and multiplexers.
- Coordinated the installation of a gateway to outside information services.

EDUCATION:

REGIS COLLEGE   DENVER, CO
B.S. IN ELECTRICAL ENGINEERING   **1984**

✔ Edward presents his skills in a Summary section at the beginning of his resume.
✔ He describes his overall duties in a short paragraph and uses bullets to highlight important skills.

DRAFTER (Entry level)

DARLENE HYLAND

29 Magnolia Street
Bondurant, IA 50035
515/ 555-6287

OBJECTIVE:

DRAFTING POSITION

EDUCATION:

Certificate of Completion • 720-hour drafting course
ROSS TECHNICAL SCHOOL • Ames, IA   May 1991
G.P.A.: 4.0 • Scored 93% on Spatial Visualization Exam.

Coursework:

Module I:	Introduction to Drafting	(120 hours)
Module II:	Basic Drafting Skills	(150 hours)
Module III	Machine/Assembly Drawing	(120 hours)
Module IV:	Electronic Drafting	(210 hours)
Module V:	Computer Aided Drafting	(120 hours)

Planning to pursue A.S. in Engineering.

SKILLS:

Strong organizational skills   Task oriented
Self-motivated and efficient   Ability to learn quickly

EXPERIENCE:

Interior Decorator • Des Moines, IA   1989 to present

REFERENCES:

Available upon request

✔ Darlene is trying to change fields from interior decorating to drafting, so she presents her Education first and her Experience last.
✔ She highlights her 720-hour certificate and her intention to pursue Engineering.

RAMESH AGARWAL
207 Lutton Drive
Houston, TX 77002
713/ 555-9741

EDUCATION:

UNIVERSITY OF TEXAS • Galveston, TX
Bachelor of Science in Electrical Engineering   **1985**

IN-HOUSE COURSES
Bipolar Characterization, CMOS Characterization, Semiconductor Manufacturing Operations, Contamination Control, Wet Etch Station Operation, OSHA Hazards, Chemical Safety, Circuit Design-ASTAP

IEEE Member

EMPLOYMENT:

UNITROL CORP. • Houston, TX
Electrical Engineer   **1992 to present**

TEXAS INSTRUMENTS • Houston, TX
Senior Engineer   **1990 to 1992**
Associate Engineer   **1988 to 1990**
Engineer   **1985 to 1988**

EXPERIENCE:

- **4 Bipolar Wafer Processes, including:**

  - Electrical testing of product
  - Program automatic electrical testers
  - Monitor process line electrical parameters
  - Circuit analysis
  - Monitor and analyze test yields
  - Insure timely customer shipments

- **128K CMOS SRAM**
- **144K CMOS SRAM**

  - Generate documentation
  - Circuit design and analysis
  - Hardware characterization
  - Failure analysis
  - Program electrical testers
  - Customer liaison

✔ Ramesh segments his career history into three easy-to-read sections.
✔ He begins with Education as this specialized field requires a degree.
✔ Employment and Experience sections condense all of his job functions.

ENGINEERING TECHNICIAN

MICHAEL PARSIGIAN
193 Spring Valley Road
Boulder City, NV 89005
702/ 555-3022

Experience:

PRUITT TESTING LABORATORIES • Henderson, NV

Engineering Technician (1985 to present)

Support in the preparation for manufacturing of high reliability products for space applications totalling $3M in annual sales. Receive excellent performance evaluations.

- Review customer engineering drawings for compliance with company's capabilities and recommend approval or rejection of job orders.
- Translate customer drawings into company test procedures: reference spec numbers, work stations, and MIL standards.
- Assist customers with special applications and cross referencing part numbers.
- Request Sample Department to build and test product: evaluate data to determine best range of samples to ship to customer.
- Generate price & delivery quotes: review price & quote history and QC clauses.
- Review and approve Purchase Order: research stock inventory and direct Assembly Supervisor to build estimated yield.
- Monitor assembly and test procedures to expedite on-time shipping.
- Resolve all customer questions, problems, and returns.
- Utilize H.P. terminals connected to company computer banks.
- Familiar with Textronix curve tracers, H.P. capacitance bridges, and A.T.E., etc.
- First and only technician to complete the computerization of a comprehensive tracking system addressing testing, assembly, inventory, and costing.

Electrical Test Worker (1980 to 1985)

- Implemented testing of semi-conductor devices for space program.
- Devised efficient workflow procedures.

Education:

NORTHROP UNIVERSITY • Los Angeles, CA
A.S. in Electrical Engineering (1981)

✔ Michael only has an A.S., so he lists his Experience first and his Education last.
✔ He includes a short job description in italics to enhance his image.
✔ His use of short, bulleted statements makes his resume inviting to read.

ENVIRONMENTAL ENGINEER

BARBARA ANDREADIS
4029 Bristol Street
Santa Ana, CA 92703
714/ 555-2049

EDUCATION:

COLORADO COLLEGE   COLORADO SPRINGS, CO
B.S. in Environmental Engineering   **1984**

TRAINING:

Particulate Monitoring Training
Remedial Action Training
Right-To-Know Training
Hazardous Materials Training

EXPERIENCE:

E.R. MOHN CONSULTANTS, INC.   IRVINE, CA
Environmental Engineer   **1988 to present**
Assist in negotiations on behalf of a resource recovery authority for provision of transfer station, hauling, and landfill services to support the operation of a 3,000 ton per day resource recovery facility. Quantified the cost of providing such services during start-up and first three years of commercial operation.

Researched and authored a technical and financial feasibility report for a 700 ton per day resource recovery project in Santa Rosa. Prepared life-cycle costs and cash flow projections in order to evaluate the financial feasibility of the project. Provided regulatory comment on major project contracts.

Participated in acceptance tests as part of the environmental engineering team at an 850 ton per day resource recovery facility in Sacramento.

Provided technical support to the construction oversight of a 2,050 ton per day resource recovery facility. Involved with site inspections, invoice approvals, and progress report preparation. Assisted in air sampling efforts at various hazardous waste sites in support of feasibility studies and remedial action plans.

WESTON ASSOCIATES   COSTA MESA, CA
Environmental Engineer   **1984 to 1988**
Assisted in the development of smoke plume emission monitoring guidelines for the steel-making industry. Devised and implemented testing procedures for EPA-funded projects.

✔ Barbara lists her degree first, in bold, because it is crucial in her field.
✔ She presents a Training section next because it quickly demonstrates her skills.
✔ Mention of the size of recovery facilities plus EPA funding elevates her position.

FACILITIES ENGINEER

ARTHUR KINNISON

254 Comstock Road
Cranston, RI 02910

Home: 401/ 555-9837
Business: 401/ 555-2000

OBJECTIVE: Senior Position in Facilities Management requiring both in-depth experience and a strong background in engineering and construction.

PROFESSIONAL EXPERIENCE:

HAMILTON SHIPBUILDING   WARWICK, RI
1M square foot multi-site facility staffing 4,500 employees and housing offices, labs, clean rooms, computer areas, and a prototype fabrication plant within 37 buildings.

Supervisor of Facilities Engineering (1986 to present)
Direct staff of 3 in the planning, design, construction, maintenance, and troubleshooting of all plumbing, electrical, water treatment, HVAC, and pollution control systems.

Facilities Engineer (1979 to 1986)
Solely responsible for all functions described above. Wide range of expertise eliminated the need for all outside engineering consultants.

RALSTON ENVIRONMENTAL DESIGN COMPANY   PROVIDENCE, RI
Consulting engineering firm specializing in HVAC design.

Project Engineer (1975 to 1979)

EDUCATION:

UNIVERSITY OF RHODE ISLAND   KINGSTON, RI
B.S. in Mechanical Engineering (1975)

CONTINUING EDUCATION:
Carrier Air Conditioning – Technical Development Program
Johnson Controls Supervisors School – Milwaukee, WI
Trane Energy Conservation Seminars
Cleaver-Brooks Boiler School – Harrisburg, PA

FACILITIES ENGINEER (continued)

LICENSES:

Rhode Island Department of Public Safety
Refrigeration Technician No. 002681
Refrigeration Contractor No. 00537
Building Construction Supervisor No. 002377

ACHIEVEMENTS:

- Designed and supervised the construction of more than 450 HVAC systems, process cooling systems, chillers, and scrubbers.

- Standardized equipment attrition.

- Provided maintenance staff with expertise in limiting selection of equipment, thereby facilitating quick and efficient repair.

- Standardized inventory and systems controls in order to reduce stock requirements.

- Established program of annual inspections with in-house personnel and service contractors.

- Installed emergency back-up and override systems to eliminate/reduce downtime and prevent "panic" repairs.

- Compiled reserve of rebuilt equipment taken from obsolete systems in anticipation of emergency cooling needs and for use in non-funded installations.

- Implemented remote diagnostics on inaccessible systems with reduction/elimination of downtime.

- Interfaced potential problem conditions into main security systems to facilitate immediate response.

REFERENCES:

Available upon request

✔ Arthur's Objective is long because he is trying to combine 2 disciplines.
✔ He lists Continuing Education courses which are specific to his field.
✔ Licenses are important so they are placed at the top of his second page.

FIELD SERVICE ENGINEER

BRIAN COLLINS
18 Pierce Lane
Fremont, CA 94536
415/ 555-2941

EDUCATION:

ITT TECHNICAL INSTITUTE   **Oakland, CA**
A.S. in Electronics Technology   **1980**

Coursework included DC and AC Networks, Electronic Circuits, Electronic Instruments, Digital Computers, Digital and Analog Control Circuits, Data Transmission, Microprocessor Software.

Pursuing Bachelors degree in Electrical Engineering.

EXPERIENCE:

ABCON DIAGNOSTICS   **Richmond, CA**
Field Service Engineer   **1989 to present**

Install, maintain, and repair optical scientific examination equipment including scanning electron microscopes, XRD diffraction systems, and mass spectroscopy systems. Regularly troubleshoot problems via telephone with engineering staff. Territory encompasses entire state of California.

PICTOGRAFIX CORPORATION   **Milpitas, CA**
Field Service Representative   **1986 to 1989**

Installed, maintained, and repaired manufacturing equipment for the photolithographics industry. Interacted extensively with engineers and equipment operators. Serviced a national territory.

GREENE TECHNOLOGIES, INC.   **Hayward, CA**
Field Service Engineer   **1985 to 1986**

Installed, serviced, and tested laser-guided surface flaw inspection equipment for assuring quality of rigid magnetic media used in the manufacture of both hard and floppy computer disks. Also serviced in-house inspection machines, tested products pre-shipment, and assisted with R&D projects.

SENSOTEK CORPORATION   **San Jose, CA**
Electronics Technician   **1984 to 1985**

Mounted components onto printed circuit boards, performed mechanical assembly, and tested system.

✔ Although Brian only has an A.S. degree, he still begins with Education because his coursework shows a high degree of proficiency and he can immediately cite, in bold italics, his pursuit of an Electrical Engineering degree.

RAYMOND BAUER
189 Scott Road
Mount Lebanon, PA 15228
412/ 555-3958

EDUCATION:

Bachelor of Science in Mechanical Engineering
DUQUESNE UNIVERSITY • Pittsburgh, PA   1989

coursework:

Computer-Aided Design (Computervision CAD system), FOR-TRAN, Machine Design, Analysis and Design of Thermal Fluid Systems, Statistics for Engineers.

projects:

Designed and fabricated a positioning/restraining device for use in x-raying infants at a local general hospital.

Planning to pursue graduate engineering studies.

EXPERIENCE:

Industrial Engineer / Methods & Process
ELTEK CORPORATION • Pittsburgh, PA   1989 to present

- Devise methods for the manufacture of multi-layer board assemblies for military applications.
- Review and analyze product drawings, technical data, product specifications and samples.
- Establish operation sequence, workplace layout, machines, equipment, tooling, and processes required to fabricate, machine, assemble and process the product according to government/military specifications.
- Establish manufacturing work patterns requiring low labor costs while maintaining high production schedules.
- Assist engineering team in designing tooling.
- Incorporate appropriate changes into manufacturing processes as needed.
- Provide floor support to 80 highly skilled assemblers.
- Acquired in-depth knowledge of procedures required in handling electrostatic sensitive devices.

Manufacturer's Assistant in Rod Pultrusion
DEE MANUFACTURING • Dormont, PA   Summer 1988

- Wrote Operation Manual for rod pultrusion machine.
- Collected data and performed analysis of data to maximize efficiency of rod pultrusion machine.

✔ Since Raymond only had one full-time job, he begins with his Education.
✔ He communicates highly technical knowledge in coursework and projects.
✔ He highlights his graduate engineering pursuits to increase his professionalism.

MANUFACTURING ENGINEER

KYLE JAMISON
1507 W. Highland Street
Pasadena, TX 77501
713/ 555-2306

Education:

B.S. in Mechanical Engineering   **1985**
TEXAS SOUTHERN UNIVERSITY   HOUSTON, TX

Experience:

Manufacturing Engineer   **1987 to present**
FRIGITEK CRYOGENICS   HOUSTON, TX

- **Vendor Liaison** – provide engineering support and integration with critical vendors throughout both pre-production and established production; convey and follow-up on corrective action.

- **Material Review Board Member** – provide technical input on vendor and in-house discrepancies; define and implement rework and corrective action.

- **Material/Assembly Process** – define and document critical material processing including both in-house and vendor-related efforts.

- **Tooling** – define and coordinate the design and procurement of new tools; maintain and improve existing tools.

- **Assembly Documentation** – generate the production of new assembly procedure and work orders; maintain existing documentation.

- **Failure Analysis** – conduct methodical F.A. and follow-up including documentation of findings and implementation of corrective action.

- **Test Equipment** – provide production engineering support in the design of new test equipment; assist in the maintenance of existing equipment.

- **Producibility** – provide value engineering on both new and existing products resulting in significant cost reduction and quality improvements; initiate, define, evaluate and document new or alternate methods and technology.

Mechanical Engineer   **1985 to 1987**
BROWN-JENKINS MANUFACTURING COMPANY   HOUSTON, TX

- Supported 30 production floor personnel by troubleshooting test equipment.

- Oversaw production operations of electronic test stations designed out-of-house.

- Supervised 2 tool makers in the construction of a variety of manufacturing tools.

✔ Using bold type, Kyle segments his recent experience into 8 important areas to make it easier for the reader to evaluate his skills.
✔ The first area, Vendor Liaison, shows his ability to communicate with people.

ANTHONY GIORDANO
312 Layton Road
Oak Creek, WI 53154
414/ 555-3036

EDUCATION:

ILLINOIS INSTITUTE OF TECHNOLOGY   Chicago, IL
Bachelor of Science in Mechanical Engineering   1985

EXPERIENCE:

LOADSTAR INTERNATIONAL   Milwuakee, WI
Manufacturing Engineering Manager   1989 to present

Manage the manufacture of weighing and batching systems, representing $18M in annual sales. Lead a group of 3 supervisors and 65 hourly production staff. Direct manufacturing engineers supporting the load transducer and strain gage areas.

- Increased transducer output 62% in first twelve months.
- Increased manufacturing efficiency by 24% through improved labor utilization.
- Reduced manufacturing losses by 19%.
- Resolved major producibility issues impacting production output.
- Received *Managerial Award* in May 1990 for outstanding leadership.

JERGUSON PUMP COMPANY   Racine, WI
Lead Manufacturing Engineer   1985 to 1989

Supervised 17 toolmakers at a pump manufacturing company with $35M in annual sales. Supported new product introduction into Manufacturing by assessing producibility, and selecting proper capital equipment, tooling, and methods.

- Modernized the machine shop through the implementation of CNC machining equipment resulting in reduced costs and shorter lead times.
- Developed and implemented a comprehensive manufacturing plan leading to the timely shipment of 100 large, nuclear-rated pumps worth $5M.
- Spearheaded the department's "Producibility Team" leading to the resolution of more than 35 long-standing producibility problems.
- Implemented a department-wide manufacturing methods procedure that greatly improved the quality of manufacturing documentation.

✔ Anthony's job descriptions present impressive figures and percentages, which enhance his achievements.
✔ He highlights his Managerial Award in italics.

MARINE ENGINEER

JOHN KOWOLSKI
255-C Thompsons Bridge Road
Talleyville, DE 19803
302/ 555-4601

QUALIFICATIONS:

- 10+ years of experience as Licensed Engineering Officer directing the maintenance, troubleshooting, and repair of ship systems including HVAC, machinery, electrical systems, plumbing, structural components, water treatment, and plant automation.
- 3 years of experience as a Treatment Plant Operator performing effluent testing for pH and chlorine residual and maintaining all equipment.
- Identified and remediated conditions requiring repair and improvement.
- Trained, assigned, supervised, motivated, and evaluated engineers and staff.
- Maintained work history on systems and machinery to evaluate efficiencies.
- Planned and implemented safety meetings with all personnel.
- Prepared for annual Coast Guard inspections.
- Consistently maintained standards for efficiency, safety, and cost effectiveness.

EXPERIENCE:

Licensed Operating Engineer   **1984 to present**
RYKER COMPANY   Wilmington, DE

Licensed Treatment Plant Operator   **1981 to 1984**
WILMINGTON GENERATION PLANT   New Castle, DE

EDUCATION:

Bachelor of Science in Marine Engineering   **1981**
DELAWARE MARITIME ACADEMY   New Castle, DE

LICENSES:

First Assistant Engineer Diesel – Unlimited Horsepower
Third Assistant Engineer Steam – Unlimited Horsepower
Delaware Operating License Grade 2 – Waste Water Treatment Systems

---

✔ John condenses 10+ years experience into one prominent Qualifications section placed at the top of his resume.
✔ He lists his Licenses because they are important to his field.

MECHANICAL ENGINEER

DAVID ENSOR
13 Coolidge Street
Kansas City, MO 64155
816/ 555-0499

MECHANICAL ENGINEER

Education:

B.S. in Mechanical Engineering Technology   1991
DEVRY INSTITUTE OF TECHNOLOGY • Kansas City, MO

> *Coursework*: Fluid Mechanics, Advanced Thermodynamics, Heat Transfer, Vibrations, Automatic Controls, Machine Design III, FORTRAN.

A.A.S. in Mechanical Design Technology   1989
DEVRY INSTITUTE OF TECHNOLOGY • Kansas City, MO

> *Coursework:* Strength of Materials, Thermodynamics, Mechanism Design, Manufacturing Processes, Mechanical Drafting, Tooling, Production, Machine Design, Hydraulics and Pneumatics, BASIC.

> *Project:* Designed a log splitter encompassing a computer analysis of structure and a complete analysis of hydraulic systems, beam deflection, and fatigue.

Planning to pursue studies in electronic engineering and business.

Computer Skills:

Hardware: APPLE, DEC VAX, IBM 43-41 (CAD), Impres 600 (CAD)

Software: P-FRAME

Languages: BASIC, FORTRAN

Experience:

Mechanical Designer • ENTEK DESIGN • Kansas City, MO   1989 to present

- Designed structural frame for high speed robotic operations for textile clothing industry project. Components included jigs and fixtures, cams, linkages, belt drives, and planetary gear boxes.
- Gained familiarity with geometric tolerancing.
- Participated in Design Board meetings.

✔ David's degree qualifies him for a higher-level position, so he signals his desire by placing his career goal in the upper right corner.
✔ He highlights important coursework, projects, and computer skills.

MIS MANAGER

SANDRA GOLLON
27 Hotton Pond Road
Brookline, MA 02146
617/ 555-7672

OBJECTIVE: Senior MIS position encompassing analysis and programming

EXPERIENCE:

LOTUS DEVELOPMENT COMPANY
Principal Information Systems Specialist (1991 to present)
Senior Programmer/Analyst (1990 to 1991)
Programmer/Analyst (1988 to 1990)

DIGITAL EQUIPMENT CORPORATION
Program Data Coordinator (1983 to 1988)

EDUCATION:

BOSTON UNIVERSITY   **MS in MIS (1988)**   **BSBA in MIS (1983)**

PROJECTS:

- Led team for new release of *customer administrative training system.*

- Provided support for *direct marketing database* system maintenance.

- Collected, defined, and implemented *standards for MIS training systems.*

- *Managed three programmers* in the Customer Administrative Services Center.

- Generated *product reporting and storage system graphs* for the Business Center.

- Handled programming, analysis, and report generation for *customer surveys.*

COMPUTER SKILLS:

- DCL
- COBOL
- Rdb
- EDT
- FMS
- TDMS
- DTR
- CMS
- Decforms
- C

✔ Sandra's Objective states the level, field, and breadth of position desired.
✔ She uses capitals, bold, and italics to highlight important information.
✔ Projects and Computer sections summarize pertinent accomplishments/skills.

GARY HUDSON
283 Lincoln Way
Charlotte, NC 28209
704/ 555-8506

EDUCATION:

Bachelor of Science in Nuclear Engineering (1981)
LEHIGH UNIVERSITY • Bethlehem, PA

COMPUTERS:

Hardware:	IBM-PC, IBM 3090
Software:	LOTUS 1-2-3, MATHCAD, dBASE, WORDPERFECT
Languages:	FORTRAN, BASIC

EXPERIENCE:

Nuclear Engineer
UNITED ENGINEERS AND CONSTRUCTORS • Huntersville, NC

> **ALARA Consultant at Maguire Nuclear Power Station** (1985 to present)

Support Health Physics at this multi-unit power facility. This position requires in-depth knowledge of nuclear systems, NRC and federal regulations, dose and radwaste reduction techniques, sensitivity to human factors and management skills.

- Improve the Health Physics procedures and integrate them with high dose maintenance and inspection procedures.

- Act as liaison between Health Physics and station procedures management.

- Minimize excessive radwaste generation and establish procedures to both monitor its production and prevent mixing of high and low level waste.

Gary Hudson   page 2

> **PP & G Nuclear Power Station Engineering Project** (1981 to 1985)

- In Fortran, developed a program which estimates normal operational activity levels in a containment and identifies unsafe levels of pressure boundary leakage, taking into account aerosol removal mechanisms such as plateout, gravitational settling, diffusiophoretic removal on fan coolers, and filtration units.

- Controlled quality, accuracy, costs, and scheduling of radiological design analyses. Wrote and submitted report to Plant Management.

- Performed design verification and ALARA reviews for radwaste storage facilities.

- Created a Fortran program to develop Zones and track post-accident doses to operators performing post-accident mitigating functions inside Plant Buildings.

- Calculated all effluent radiation monitor set points.

- Calculated plant site radiation doses due to liquid and gaseous effluent releases.

- Analyzed radiological consequences of postulated accidents including control room habitability, and post-accident access.

- Performed shielding analyses of direct and scattered gamma radiation.

- Calculated dose sustained by equipment in support of mechanical and electrical equipment qualification.

- Performed calculations supporting the preparation of the Offsite Dose Calculation Manual and the Appendix I Report.

REFERENCES:

Available upon request

- ✔ Gary's engineering degree is very important, so he presents it first.
- ✔ He next shows his well-rounded Computer expertise.
- ✔ Bulleted sentences quickly convey Gary's vast experience.

PLASTICS ENGINEER

MARIANNE HENDERSON
130-C Briar Wood Estates
Marietta, GA 30060
404/ 555-3867

SUMMARY

Plastics Engineer with excellent management potential • Extensive hands-on experience in the design, development, selection, manufacturing, and testing of graphitic components. Expert in the use of computer-aided design and computer-aided manufacturing systems.

EXPERIENCE

BOEING MILITARY AIRPLANE COMPANY • Wichita, KS
Plastics Engineer (1988 to present)

- Provide expertise in plastics design, processing, and materials selection requiring interaction with R&D, Technical Support Staff, and Manufacturing department.

- Train and supervise new engineers in the implementation of physical test suites for evaluation of helicopter rotor blades.

- Use CAD system in the design of fuselage housings requiring expertise in mechanical drawing, dimensioning, and tolerances.

- Evaluate, select, and test graphite components for strength, durability, weatherabilty, and cyclic mechanical and heat stress.

- Perform and supervise in-depth failure analysis of helicopter blades. Highly knowledge-able in the use of photomicrographic examination techniques.

- Streamlined and optimized design and production of an airplane control system compo-nent which resulted in greatly improved performance and a 45% reduction in cost.

EDUCATION

WORCESTER POLYTECHNIC UNIVERSITY • Worcester, MA
Bachelor of Science - Plastics Engineering (1988)

✔ Marianne's Summary states her readiness to move into management.
✔ Company name recognition followed by a detailed description of a wide range of technical and supervisory accomplishments are strong credentials.

PROGRAMMER / ANALYST

JAMES VISHAY
1504 Cass Avenue
Clarendon Hills, IL 60514
312/ 555-6144

MAJOR QUALIFICATIONS:

- 10+ years of successful experience as a computer programmer/analyst.

- Expert knowledge of FORTRAN, COBOL, and ASSEMBLEY languages on mini-computers and mainframe computers made by IBM, DEC, and PRIME.

- Strong background developing, testing, and documenting software.

PROFESSIONAL EXPERIENCE:

DELCO TURBINE ENGINE COMPANY   CHICAGO, IL
Senior Programmer / Analyst   **1989 to present**

Project leader for MRP projects. Knowledge of DEC PDP-11 Series computers.

- Developed a program that automated the inputting of manufacturing data. Analyzed information on the distribution tape, devised appropriate data structures, and created FORTRAN program modules.

- Directed staff of three in the conversion of a manual inventorying system to a computerized FORTRAN system.

- Analyzed and documented system flow of a FORTRAN tape library system.

AMERICAN AUTO PARTS CORPORATION   EVANSTON, IL
Programmer / Analyst   **1987 to 1989**

Conducted programming and research projects for a manufacturer of automotive parts. Programmed in ASSEMBLER on an IBM 3600 system.

- Modified and updated portions of a report-generating program which monitored work-in-progress of automotive parts manufacture.

- Designed, programmed, and documented a report generating program which tracked distribution of automotive parts.

- Researched the ability of an IBM 3600 system to network with peripherals made by DEC and PRIME.

JAMES VISHAY   page 2

CABLEVISION OF AMERICA, INC.   CHICAGO, IL
Programmer / Analyst   **1985 to 1987**

Modified, organized, and coordinated software services for company's customer billing system. Knowledgeable of the Prime 750 computer.

- Developed COBOL routines to efficiently perform billing procedures for a customer database of more than 1 million records.
- Devised procedures to import and export data to a WANG VS system.
- Wrote a set of test programs verifying integrity of data.
- Provided customer support.

UNIVERSAL MEDICAL SYSTEMS, INC.   SKOKIE, IL
Software Programmer   **1983 to 1985**

Developed, debugged, and documented software for a hospital patient records system. Programmed in FORTRAN and ASSEMBLER.

ACCU-TUNE SENSOR CORPORATION   DOWNERS GROVE, IL
Programmer   **1981 to 1983**

EDUCATION:

INDIANA UNIVERSITY NORTHWEST   GARY, IN
B.S. in Computer Science   **1981**

✔ A Major Qualifications section at the beginning of James' resume highlights his 10 years of experience and quickly shows his knowledge of computers.
✔ Short descriptions in italics reinforce his experience with computers.

QUALITY CONTROL MANAGER

KEVIN BISHOP
1993 Petrovitsky Road
Renton, WA 98055
206/ 555-2004

OBJECTIVE: Technical Manager within a medium-sized high tech company

EXPERIENCE: TESTRONICS • Bellevue, WA
($5M manufacturer of surge generators and ESD simulators)

Quality Control Manager (1987 to present). Direct the planning, scheduling, and operation of five key technical areas: Quality Control Engineering, Process Control Engineering, Quality Assurance, Testing, and Incoming Inspection.

- Hire, train, and manage 8-person staff including supervisors, engineers, inspectors, and technicians.

- Closely collaborate with Engineers, Production Staff, and Top Management to insure accurate, timely and cost effective production and shipping of product.

- Established initial organization of all four Quality Control areas. Developed documentation methods and testing procedures.

- Utilize computer to generate reports, quality control and test schedules, and accounting ledgers.

- Contribute to engineering design of products.

- Implemented conversion from monthly to weekly shipping schedule which improved company cash flow.

Previous positions (1981 to 1987) included **Assistant QC Manager, QC Engineer, and Test Technician.**

EDUCATION: B.S. IN ELECTRICAL ENGINEERING (1981)
Seattle University • Seattle, WA

AFFILIATIONS: American Society of Quality Control Engineers

✔ Kevin states his exact job requirements in his Objective.
✔ He lists, but does not describe, previous positions to avoid repetition.
✔ The Affiliations section supports Kevin's degree of professionalism.

MELANIE WELCH
1467 Salem Street
Lexington, MA 02173
617/ 555-0299

EDUCATION

B.S. Mechanical Engineering
University of Massachusetts – Amherst, MA   1984

PROFESSIONAL EXPERIENCE

Regional Sales Manager
GCA Corporation – Bedford, MA   1988 to present

Sell environmental monitoring instruments and data acquisition equipment to the process industry, manufacturing plants, the military, and governmental agencies.

- Developed and manage a network of manufacturer's representatives in the northeastern US responsible for $1M in annual sales.

- Increased sales 200% in the southeastern and southwestern US territories during a three year period.

- Established company products in the regulations of several states' air quality programs.

- Conduct numerous large-group sales presentations and training seminars for company representatives, engineering personnel, and governmental agency officials.

- Designed several successful IBM-PC and APPLE MACINTOSH-based software programs including direct-mail marketing campaigns, sales & marketing forecasts, sales/lead tracking systems, quotation status reports, and advertising media analyses.

- Familiar with most aspects of microcomputing including word processing, database, desktop publishing, networking, and telecommunications.

Melanie Welch *page 2*

National Sales Engineer
BLH Electronics – Waltham, MA   1986 to 1988

Sold load cell transducers, strain gages, force measurement instrumentation, and weighing & batching systems to Measurement & Control engineers.

- Attracted large-volume OEM accounts by discovering new and innovative applications for existing product line.

- Collaborated closely with Engineering to provide support for new product development.

- Familiar with materials testing, metrology, and a wide variety of metal-working processes.

Sales Engineer
Mil-Mar Company – Woburn, MA   1984 to 1986

Sold complete systems for the storage and handling of chemical process fluids for manufacturer's representative operating in eastern MA and southern NH. Equipment included automated filtration systems, chemical-duty pumps, heat exchangers, tanks, and liquid-level controllers.

- Familiar with the food and chemical processing industries, the pulp and paper industry, and architectural & engineering (A/E) firms.

PERSONAL

Married; no children. Willing to travel and consider relocation.

Tournament tennis player. Chairperson, Lexington Newcomer's Club.

✔ Melanie's stylish format conveys a sense of energy, a key trait for salespeople.
✔ She uses numbers and percentages to punctuate her sales achievements.
✔ Competitiveness and sociability are key traits shown in her Personal section.

SYSTEMS APPLICATION PROGRAMMER

ROBERT ARMAND

128 Thibeau Place
Metairie, LA 70004

Residence: 504/ 555-2837
Business: 504/ 555-3700

EXPERIENCE

COMPU-AID ENGINEERING SYSTEMS   NEW ORLEANS, LA

Systems Applications Programmer (1989 to present)

Successfully perform a wide variety of evaluation, programming, and service activities to support the financial and manufacturing operations at the corporate and divisional levels. Report to the Vice President of Technical Services.

Research customer applications on-site, evaluate and select CAE/CAD hardware, evaluate and improve internal technical services, develop and revise software, trouble-shoot internal and customer problems, and provide internal and customer training.

Programmer (1987 to 1989)

Researched, analyzed, coded, debugged, and implemented new and existing programs written in FORTRAN 77 on a PRIME system.

Resolved customer and internal inquiries systems, assisted in the installation of both hardware (MINI VAX, IBM PC's) and software (PRAXA–UNITRONIX) for the accounting and manufacturing departments, generated codes to produce customized reports, documented procedures, and provided training and technical support.

COMPUTERS

HARDWARE

PRIME, IBM, DEC VAX. Terminals, peripherals, modems.

LANGUAGES AND OPERATING SYSTEMS

FORTRAN, C, COBOL, PRIMOS, MS-DOS, VMS

EDUCATION

LOYOLA UNIVERSITY   NEW ORLEANS, LA

B.S. in Computer Science (1987)

✔ Robert begins with his Experience section rather than Education to stress his high-level employment at his present company.
✔ Computer-related data is highlighted in bold, capital letters for emphasis.

SYSTEMS DEVELOPMENT MANAGER

ARNOLD DRANETZ
422 Swatling Road
Latham, NY 12110
518/ 555-4921

PROFESSIONAL EXPERIENCE

COMPUTER TRANSACTIONS CORPORATION • Albany, NY   1981 to present
($12M manufacturer of transaction hardware and software • 3 divisions • 250 employees)
Manager / Systems Development (1988 to present)
Manager / Computer Systems and Services (1981 to 1988)

Accomplishments:

- Spearhead the successful development of company's transaction services business from start-up to consistent profitability for 14 years, the primary source of cash flow for the company.
- Created high volume, quick response on-line transaction processing systems and services including: check authorization, credit authorization, electronic mail distribution, time reporting system, and EFT transaction system.
- Designed, developed, implemented, and managed host systems and computer centers. Concurrently managed field service department, with responsibility for total operating budgets and staff of 40.
- Direct R&D department consisting of 8 software engineers, 1 electrical engineer, 1 mechanical engineer, and 3 support staff. Objectives include the completion of the LINK product line (family of transaction terminals for the POS and credit card environment) and the design of new host software systems.
- Achieved the successful transfer of transaction services to a new Chicago division, consolidating both human and technical resources to realize significant cost savings.

Computer Engineer • WEATHER SYSTEMS, INC. • Troy, NY   1975 to 1981

EDUCATION / TRAINING

UNION COLLEGE • Schenectady, NY   1975
M.S. in Applied Mathematics

RENSSELAER POLYTECHNIC INSTITUTE • Troy, NY   1973
B.S. in Mathematics

Knowledge of 14 computer languages and 20 computer systems.

✔ Arnold utilizes specific figures liberally to emphasize his responsibilities.
✔ He lists very specific Accomplishments with a minimum of technical jargon.
✔ Arnold highlights computer proficiency in a separate line under Education.

TECHNICAL INSTRUCTOR

JAMES FIELDING

206 Linwood Avenue
Ridgewood, NJ 07451

201/ 555-8824

EXPERIENCE   HEWLETT-PACKARD CORPORATION   PARAMUS, NJ

May 87
to
Present

Senior Technical Instructor

Develop, update, and present classes on hardware repair and operating system maintenance for Field Service Representatives and Systems Analysts. Create new courses and audio/visual aids for new devices. Assist in the development of audio/visual self-study courses for dissemination to field support personnel. Initiate and teach mutual training programs for technical and sales staffs.

Assist the Education Manager in the overall operation of the Education Department including scheduling classes and labs, maintaining lab equipment, maintaining systems spares inventory and logistical transfers, preparation and reconciliation of annual and quarterly budget, and review and implementation of department policy. Direct Instructors and Associate Instructors on the implementation of department policies and course development.

HONEYWELL CORPORATION   TEANECK, NJ

Oct 83
to
May 87

Field Service Engineer

Installed, repaired, and performed preventative maintenance on various system and peripheral hardware. Maintained operating systems for proper functioning and performed necessary system generation parameter changes. Performed pre-installation surveys to assist customers in preparing and maintaining a proper computer system environment.

JAMES FIELDING PAGE 2

EDUCATION	RUTGERS UNIVERSITY	NEWARK, NJ

Jun 83 **Bachelor of Engineering Technology**

Major: Computer Technology. Strong Liberal Arts background.

Coursework: PASCAL, COBOL, FORTRAN on VAX 11/780 system

BASIC, 8086 ASSEMBLER, C using IBM-PC & CORVUS Filesharing Network.

CPU architecture, design, and related courses.

Data Base Management, Operating Systems, and Data Communications.

PROFESSIONAL SEMINARS

Time Management

Understanding Employee Relations

Psychology in Management

Matsushita H7000 Series PC Repair

RELATED ACTIVITIES

Presenter at Computer Industry Seminars conducted at local vocational high schools.

Small business computer and educational consultant.

Elected member of local School Board. Appointed to Capital Improvements and Policy Committees.

✔ James' format highlights the names of his prominent employers.
✔ He augments his degree with a list of highly technical coursework and professional seminars.

ROGER SKINNER
367 Larchmont Drive
South Bend, IN 46624
219/ 555-0482

SUMMARY OF QUALIFICATIONS:

- Successful experience providing technical support for a high tech manufacturer.
- Outstanding product knowledge with demonstrated training skills.
- Proven ability to troubleshoot and resolve complex customer problems.
- Solid record of contributions through improved departmental procedures.
- Strong supervisory capability.

PROFESSIONAL EXPERIENCE:

Technical Support Engineer • DARIAN COMPANY • Elkhart, IN   1988 to present
($118M in annual sales of high-vacuum pumps)

Administer Technical Support Services for a worldwide industrial customer base. Cited by Technical Support Manager for technical expertise, outstanding customer service orientation, and ability to assess procedural weaknesses and implement effective solutions.

Highlights:

- Developed appropriate resources to efficiently identify and resolve equipment problems and maintain system operations for customers, resulting in improved customer relations.
- Trained, supervised, and evaluated an in-house Technical Service Specialist and provided technical direction/support to field staff.
- Assisted in the areas of sales & marketing support, engineering, quality assurance, sales forecasting, budget planning, and quotation preparation.
- Prepared service procedures and trained servicemen. Reduced servicing costs by providing accurate technical assistance via telephone.

EDUCATION:

Bachelor of Science in Industrial Engineering
INDIANA UNIVERSITY • Fort Wayne, IN   1988

✔ A Summary of Qualifications section quickly highlights Roger's skills.
✔ A brief company description in parentheses elevate his professional stature.
✔ The bulleted Highlights section is an easy-to-read way to present information.

DANIEL FONTAINE
818 22nd Street
New York, NY 10019
212/ 555-4192

QUALIFICATIONS:

- **15+ years telecommunications consulting experience**

  Proficient in the design, documentation, installation, modification, and trouble-shooting of sophisticated workload management systems. Expert at assessing customer need and designing effective solutions. Knowledge of hardware, software, peripherals, UNIX, C, PC, DOS, switch technology, and communications interfaces.

- **Strong sales and customer service orientation**

  Manage complex hardware and software support services for multiple processor sites. Participate in sales presentations and contract negotiations.

- **Effective training skills**

  Design and present comprehensive training programs for all levels of staff and management. Proficient in conducting needs assessments and developing programs. Expert in technical, customer service, and administrative areas.

- **Solid management record**

  Trained, scheduled, and supervised diverse employee populations in administrative and technical areas. Compiled annual budget, oversaw $450,000 in inventory, and handled $350,000 in monthly billing.

EXPERIENCE:

TELETEK ASSOCIATES • New York, NY
Senior Consultant — 1990 to present
Consultant — 1986 to 1990

TACONIC TELEPHONE • Pittsfield, MA
Staff Manager / Asst. Staff Manager — 1980 to 1986

EDUCATION:

SPRINGFIELD COLLEGE • Springfield, MA
B.S. in Math — 1980

✔ Daniel's Qualifications section identifies, highlights, and describes four strong functional areas which relate to his entire career in telecommunications.
✔ He lists, but does not describe, job titles to avoid repetition.

TELECOMMUNICATIONS TECHNICIAN

RONALD BAMBERG

592 Durant Road
Brandon, FL 33511

Residence: 813/ 555-4774
Business: 813/ 555-6060

EDUCATION

UNIVERSITY OF SOUTH FLORIDA   TAMPA, FL

Bachelor of Science in Management   **Candidate**
Concentration in Management Information Systems. Minor in Computer
Science.

COMPUTER TRAINING INSTITUTE   TAMPA, FL

Diploma   **1987**
Analog Electronics, Digital Electronics, Microprocessor Technology.

COMPUTERS

HARDWARE
_____

DEC 10; PDP 11; VAX 11/730, 11/750, 11/780, 11/785
AT&T PC's 6300, 6350, 6386/UNIX
AT&T 3B2 310, 400, 500

LANGUAGES AND OPERATING SYSTEMS
_____

COBOL, PASCAL, C, MS-DOS, VAX/VMS, UNIX

SOFTWARE
_____

Multiple communications, spreadsheets, word processing, editors,
compilers, data base managers.

EXPERIENCE

NOVATEL CORPORATION   TEMPLE TERRACE, FL
_____
($1M developer of telephone call accounting software)

Lead Telecommunications Technician   **1988 to present**

- Assemble hardware including printers, memory, modems, IO's.
- Repair defective components at the board level.
- Provide 24-hour service capability for hardware-related problems.

Ronald Bamberg   **Page 2**

EXPERIENCE
(continued)   **Systems Administrator**   **1988 to present**

- Perform diagnostics to maintain integrity of system.
- Tune system to meet requirements of current software.
- Test and troubleshoot current software and UNIX O/S system.
- Collaborate with programmers on major software enhancements.
- Customize existing programs and directories.
- Provide 24-hour on-line service capability for software problems.
- Set up user log-ins.
- Provide security measures.
- Load supportive software and UNIX operating systems.

National Trainer   **1988 to present**

- Train end-users and in-house technicians using highly standard-ized OJT program.
- Train AT&T sales staff on joint sales/marketing techniques.
- Write technical documentation for end-users and technical staff.

VICEROY CORPORATION   LAKELAND, FL

Computer Operator   **1986 to 1988**

- Performed diversified computer operations in a timesharing/ batch environment.
- Monitored systems operations and responded to maintain efficient performance.

MILITARY   UNITED STATES ARMY   **1982 to 1986**

(Honorable Discharge)

REFERENCES   AVAILABLE UPON REQUEST

✔ Ronald's combined B.S. candidacy and computer training diploma are his primary qualifications.
✔ He cites 3 job titles at Novatel because he performs these duties simultaneously.

Education 7

To Resume Or Not To Resume

Most educational institutions require you to complete an application form and submit transcripts and letters of recommendation with the application. A resume is often viewed as extraneous. However, it is highly recommended that you send a resume with each application as the resume fosters your professional image and enhances the importance of your credentials. It is also easier for a reader to scan a resume than an application form.

Educators Wear Many Hats

The profession of education encompasses teaching, administration, coaching, training, counseling, and research. Obviously, no two resumes used in the field will stress the same qualifications. Yet, education as a whole is a very "credential-oriented" profession, and two particular credentials are crucial for all educators to stress on their resumes - namely, college degree and areas of certification within your own state. You probably won't land a job without both.

Because Education is so credential-oriented, sometimes it is very difficult to decide whether to open your resume with your Education or Experience section. It's easier if you're affiliated with a prestigious educational or professional institution since you want to stress that association, but usually, it's a judgment call.

Beyond Your Job Description

Think of education and one quickly thinks "classrooms, students, books, tests." Yet, you know your real scope of expertise. Let the reader know too. When writing your resume, think beyond the classroom - to program development, system-wide committees, professional memberships, town-wide organizations, continuing education courses, publications, presentations, leadership roles, teaching honors, administrative responsibilities, parent recognition, student awards, extra-curricular activites - in short, the myriad of involvements which account for your excellence as an educator.

Covering all these areas might even require two pages, but there are some easy ways to include all your important information without scaring the reader away:

- Write a *concise* Objective indicating position and grade level desired.
- Concentrate on your *achievements*; outline or omit your general duties.
- Use horizontal lines and prominent headings to *segment* your sections.

Toot Your Own Horn

If you're an educator who has difficulty assessing or believing your own value, try to overcome your modesty on your resume. Sometimes consulting with a colleague or friend can help you identify special accomplishments which you take for granted, but that a prospective employer might view as unique.

Include A Personal Section

Since most careers in education are heavily involved with interpersonal relationships, it is appropriate for you to include a Personal section and describe leadership roles, special skills, interests, and even family background. This information provides insight into your individuality and enhances your candidacy.

Burn Out

An unfortunate by-product of a career in education is burn out; therefore, there exist numerous educators at all levels who frequently consider a career change. Two challenges exist for educators contemplating a career change - deciding on the new career and designing a resume to facilitate the change.

The first challenge can readily be solved, though it requires time, effort, assistance, often a financial investment, and a healthy dose of self-confidence, patience, determination, energy, and optimism. You might start by consulting with a career counselor or successful career changer who can recommend relevant books, articles, workshops, networks, or re-training internship programs.

To help you with the second challenge, several samples of resumes for career changes are included in this chapter of resumes which are indexed by job title.

ART TEACHER (Graphic Arts)

KATHERINE FLEMING   92 Elmwood Terrace ■ Irvine, CA 92720 ■ 714/ 555-5211

EXPERIENCE:

Graphic Arts Instructor (1982 to present)
IRVINE PUBLIC SCHOOLS • Irvine, CA

Developed and expanded a junior high school curriculum into a creative program which introduces students to a wide variety of artistic experiences and encourages the exploration of art-related occupations.

- Initiated the popular "ART P.M." after-school enrichment program for talented students. Visit artist studios, galleries, museums, and art schools. Conduct workshops to explore unusual mediums. Brainstorm ideas and problems.

- Supervise the in-house student production of a yearbook and literary magazine. Utilize skills in photography, layout, writing, typesetting, printing, binding, advertising, sales, and distribution.

- Conducted student contest, "California Architecture in the Year 2000."

- Serve on Computer Committee - develop units to incorporate the use of computers in graphic design; wrote grant to receive used Macintosh equipment.

- Coordinate with teachers on school projects, e.g., logos, murals, set designs.

Guest Instructor (1984 to 1988)
CALIFORNIA TECHNICAL SCHOOL OF DESIGN • Newport Beach, CA

Art Editor & Book Designer (1986 to 1988)
LAKEWOOD PUBLISHING CO. • Newport Beach, CA

Education:

Master of Creative Arts in Learning (1982)
UNIVERSITY OF SOUTHERN CALIFORNIA • San Diego, CA

Bachelor of Fine Arts (1980)
BOSTON UNIVERSITY • Boston, MA

✔ Katherine 's resume stresses her success in promoting enriching art activities outside the classroom.
✔ Her resume reflects subtle and attractive graphic touches, e.g. lines, boxes.

ART TEACHER (Studio Arts)

TRACEY ARROYO

95 Hightower Lane
Irving Park, IL 60641

Telephone: 312/ 555-6221
Messages: 312/ 555-9678

EDUCATION

UNIVERSITY OF CHICAGO • GRADUATE SCHOOL OF ART   1980 to 1982
Master of Fine Arts Degree Program

UNIVERSITY OF CHICAGO • GRADUATE SCHOOL OF ART   1975
Master of Fine Arts / Painting

LOYOLA UNIVERSITY   1973
Bachelor of Fine Arts

ART TEACHING

JUNIOR HIGH SCHOOL and HIGH SCHOOL • Elsdon, IL   1976 to present
Head of Teaching Team.

SUMMER SCHOOL PROGRAM • Elsdon, IL   1981 to 1985
Grades 2 through 5.

CHICAGO COLLEGE OF ART • Chicago, IL   Evenings, 1978 to 1981
Painting and Drawing Instructor.

ELSDON HIGH SCHOOL • Elsdon, IL   1973 to 1975
Studio Art Teacher.

PROFESSIONAL MEMBERSHIPS

National Art Education Association • Museum of Higher Arts

Chicago Arts Council • Chicago Museum Corporate Lending Program

COMMITTEES

CHAIRMAN, ART CURRICULUM COMMITTEE   Present

MEMBER, ART EVALUATION COMMITTEE   1988 to present

MEMBER, ARTS CURRICULUM TASK FORCE   1984 to 1987

ART TEACHER (continued)

ARTS ADMINISTRATION

CHAIRMAN, IRVING PARK ARTS COUNCIL   1988 to present

HEAD OF TEACHING TEAM, Junior High School, Elsdon, IL   1982 to present

DIRECTOR, KIDS' ART PROGRAM, Elsdon, IL   1977 to 1982

CREATOR AND DIRECTOR of the following programs: 1974 to 1976

- Youth Center Art Program, Irving Park, IL
- Irving Park Community Arts Center
- Senior Citizen Art Workshop, Chicago, IL

AWARDS AND SCHOLARSHIPS

1985 Recipient of EDCO Grant for graphics art curriculum design

1983 Nominee for Chicago Alliance for Arts Education • Outstanding Teacher Award

1982 Jurors Award • Stahlmeyer Gallery

The Best of Show Award • Chicago Arts Council

The Best in Category Award • Chicago Arts Council

Four Year Full Tuition Scholarship • Loyola University

Two Year Full Tuition Teaching/Research Assistantship • University of Chicago

EXHIBITS   (partial listing)

The Fullbright Art Gallery • Chicago, IL

The Hyde Museum • Chicago, IL

The Fine Art Gallery • Chicago, IL

✔ Tracey establishes herself as both an art teacher and artist.
✔ Her numerous awards and exhibits reflect positively on her school system.
✔ She places special attention on the graphic presentation of her resume.

ASSISTANT SUPERINTENDENT

Confidential Resume

of

STEPHEN BOSTWICK

23 Oceanside Drive
Warwick, RI 02887

Residence: 401/ 555-9823
Office: 401/ 555-2200

EXPERIENCE:

Assistant Superintendent of Schools (K-12)
Warwick, RI   1984 to present
(2,800 suburban student enrollment • 275 professional and paraprofessional staff • $14M budget)

Highlights:

MAJOR CONTRIBUTOR TO POLICY / BUDGET PLANNING AND ADMINISTRATION

PERSONNEL ADMINISTRATION *(Recruitment, Supervision, and Evaluation)*

PROGRAM DEVELOPMENT *(School and Community)*

CURRICULUM DEVELOPMENT *(Model Programs)*

STAFF DEVELOPMENT

Coordinator of Secondary Education
Warwick, RI   1975 to 1984

Senior Supervisor in Education
RHODE ISLAND DEPARTMENT OF EDUCATION   1970 to 1975

Research Associate
RHODE ISLAND EDUCATIONAL CENTER FOR CURRICULUM DESIGN   1968 to 1970

EDUCATION:

Post-graduate work in Curriculum and Instruction (27 credits)
PROVIDENCE COLLEGE   1983 to 1986

Master of Arts in Government
PROVIDENCE COLLEGE   1971

Bachelor of Arts in Education
PROVIDENCE COLLEGE   1968

Stephen Bostwick

CERTIFICATIONS:

RI Certificate: Superintendent / Assistant Superintendent (K-12), Principal (7-12).

CONSULTING POSITIONS:

- Public Schools of Providence, RI
- Scholastic Editorial Advisory Board
- NEA Center for the Study of Curriculum
- Providence Education Center
- Excellence in Education Program for Rhode Island State Schools

STAFF DEVELOPMENT ACTIVITIES:

Legal Issues in Education	Simulations in the Classroom
Performance Objectives	Value Clarification and Problem Solving
Social Studies in Open Space High Schools	Opening the Elementary Classroom
Performance Objectives in the Social Studies Classroom	Mainstreaming
Team Teaching and the Individualization of Instruction	Career Planning
Basic Principles of Curriculum Development and Evaluation	Skills Improvement
Interdisciplinary Learning Packages	Current Trends in Curriculum
Individual Behavioral Objectives for IEP's	Curriculum Mapping

PROFESSIONAL AFFILIATIONS:

President, School Executives Association	Life Member, NEA
Association of School Administrators	Association for Curriculum Development
National Association of Elementary Principals	Mu Lambda Kappa

References available upon request

✔ Stephen patterns his resume after a Curriculum Vitae and omits explanations.
✔ He lists key administrative areas - personnel, budgets, programs, curriculum.
✔ At his career level, a 2-page resume is appropriate and necessary.

COACH

PETER VESPA

Business Address

Basketball Office, UMass
Amherst, MA
413/ 555-0900

Home Address

2-A Townhouse Apartments
Sunderland, MA 01375
413/ 555-8245

EDUCATION:

Clarkson University   **Potsdam, NY**
MASTER OF SCIENCE IN SPORT MANAGEMENT   1985
Collegiate athletic administration and program management.

Colgate University   **Hamilton, NY**
BACHELOR OF ARTS   1983
History major; certified to teach geography.

EXPERIENCE:

Assistant Basketball Coach   **1985 to present**
UNIVERSITY OF MASSACHUSETTS   AMHERST, MA
Recruit and coach on the varsity level.

- Coordinated scouting materials and team.
- Coached defensive play aspect of varsity practices and games.
- Recruited throughout New England.
- Organized prospect visits to university.
- Managed components of walk-on program.
- Performed game day defensive adjustments and substitutions.

NCAA Baseball Playoff Coordinator   **Summer 1987**

Assistant Baseball Coach   **Summer 1986**
UNIVERSITY OF MASSACHUSETTS   AMHERST, MA
Performed daily coaching in defensive aspects of the varsity team and
participated extensively in scouting throughout New England.

Assistant Basketball Coach   **Summer 1985**
UNIVERSITY OF MASSACHUSETTS   AMHERST, MA
Organized and managed scouting reports and overnight trips.

ACTIVITIES:

*Four year starter and letter winner in basketball and baseball
Patterson Memorial Award winner for spirit and sportsmanship
President, Pi Eta Kappa Fraternity
Numerous professional speaking engagements*

✔ Peter's degree is a strong credential, so he lists Education first.
✔ He describes only his full-time position.
✔ His activities are from college, but are still relevant to his coaching career.

COMPUTER TECHNOLOGY TEACHER

TINA LOWRY
23 Freeport Extension
Livingston, MS 39202
601/ 555-8325

EDUCATION:

Candidate • **Master of Science in Computer Technology** • Jackson State University
Completed coursework: Computers and Education, Integrating Computers into the Elementary Curriculum, Using LOGO in the Classroom, Using BASIC in the Classroom, Computer Graphics, Computers in Writing, Research in Special Education.

Master of Science in Special Education • Our Lady of Holy Cross College   1988

Bachelor of Science in Elementary Education • University of New Orleans   1986

Continuing Education Coursework (29 credits) includes Cognitive Mapping and Augmentation, Diagnosing Special Needs in the Pre-School Child, Meeting the Special Needs of All Learners, Language Acquisition, The Emotionally Disturbed Child, Individual Intelligence Testing, Managerial Psychology, Behavior Controls in the Classroom.

CERTIFICATIONS:

Generic Special Teacher, Teacher of School Age Children with Moderate Special Needs

Pursuing certification in Computer Technology in Elementary Education.

EXPERIENCE:

Special Education Teacher • Westland Public Schools   1988 - present

Establish and implement the goals, methods, and curriculum of a self-contained classroom serving the needs of up to 17 cognitively delayed students aged 8-13. Provide language-based focus incorporating academic, cognitive, and pre-vocational training as well as affective education. Supervise an assistant teacher and student teachers. *Program has served as model for other school systems.*

Introduced the computer as a critical learning tool for both regular and special education students. Develop and adapt educational software, teach workshops to staff and parents, and actively participate on Computer Curriculum Committee. *Program has served as a model for other school systems.*

Consult with teachers and parents regarding the mainstreaming of special needs students and the adaptation of regular curriculum for grades K-6. Chair special education team meetings and develop computerized goals for students participating in substantially separate programs.

✔ Tina's Education and Certification sections announce a new career direction.
✔ She lists specific courses to emphasize her recent knowledge.
✔ In italics, she highlights the model special ed. programs she developed.

COUNSELOR

JAMES ARSENAULT
24 Providence Street
Fort Douglas, UT 84113
801 / 555-2438

SUMMARY OF QUALIFICATIONS:

- Master of Education in Counseling.
- Utah Certification in Counseling and Teaching.
- Teaching and counseling experience in diverse educational and business settings.
- Strong training and background in career development testing and programming.

EXPERIENCE (1983 to present):

Counseling

- **Career Information Center, Foothill High School.** Managed the evaluation and classification of career materials. Conducted career exploration courses.
- **Counseling Center, University of Utah.** Developed the Career Planning Office. Provided personal, academic and vocational testing and counseling.
- **Murray Community College.** Provided personal, academic, and vocational counseling to special needs students displaying academic and personal problems.
- **Private Practice.** Developed and conducted a variety of vocational testing, counseling, and stress management.
- **OrgPro, Inc.** Designed management behavior programs for a consulting firm.

Teaching

- **Murray Community College.** Instructor - Family Dynamics
- **University of Utah.** Continuing Education Instructor - Sociology
- **Foothill High School.** Teacher - Dyslexic and Dysgraphic Students

EDUCATION:

Master of Education in Counseling (1985)
BRIGHAM YOUNG UNIVERSITY

Bachelor of Arts in Psychology (1983)
BRIGHAM YOUNG UNIVERSITY

✔ James' summary qualifies him for either counseling or teaching positions.
✔ He focuses on the range of his experience rather than the time periods.
✔ More detailed information can be discussed in an interview.

DEVELOPMENTAL EDUCATOR

PRISCILLA GIDDINGS
833 Old Lyme Road
Wells, ME 04090
207/ 555-2467

Education:

BS - Human Services and Early Intervention Specialist
KEENE STATE COLLEGE • Keene, NH   *May, 1988*
Dean's List, Teaching Assistant, State Certification

Professional Experience:

Developmental Educator.
EARLY INTERVENTION PROGRAM • Portland, ME   *1988 to present*

- Plan and direct small group developmental toddler and sensory motor programs.
- Provide individual child-oriented therapy and parent support and education.
- Coordinate services with DSS, area hospitals, and community agencies.
- Provide educational assessments and team representation for evaluations.
- Administer educational diagnostic and screening evaluations.

Practicum Intern.
PARENTS AND TOTS PROGRAM • Wells, ME   *Fall, 1987*
CENTER FOR DISABLED CHILDREN • Wells, ME   *Fall, 1985 and 1986*

Student Teacher.
ALMA EUSTIS MEMORIAL SCHOOL • Ogunquit, ME   *Winter, 1988*
PINE WOODS SCHOOL • Kittery, ME   *Fall, 1988*
MORSE SCHOOL • Wells, ME   *Spring, 1987*

Other Work Experience:

Supervisor - Special Projects • WELLS RECREATION DEPT. • Wells, ME   *Summer, 1987*

Recreation Leader • WELLS RECREATION DEPT. • Wells, ME   *Summers, 1985 and 1986*

Supervisor • BABY JAMES TOY STORE • Portland, ME   *Part-time, 1982 to 1984*

✔ Priscilla's Education section encompasses degree, honors, and certification.
✔ She describes her most current position and lists practicums and related work experience which support her career.

EARLY CHILDHOOD TEACHER (Bachelor's Degree)

ROSE HIGHLAND
432-A Canyon View Road
North Little Rock, AR 72114
501 / 555-8659

EDUCATION

degree:

B.S. in Early Childhood Education
UNIVERSITY OF ARKANSAS   1989

activities:

American Association for Childhood Education
Financed 100% of college education.

graduate coursework:

Young Children's Impulse Control, Keys to Developing a
Successful Language Arts Curriculum

EXPERIENCE

work experience:

Nursery Supervisor
PLAY NURSERY • Little Rock, AR   5/89 to present
Initiated a new nursery program within a large health club
facility servicing 14 infants and children. Selected and
ordered equipment; recruited, trained, and supervised
childcare staff; designed play space; developed activities
programs; and publicized program to the membership.

Head Teacher
REED CHILDREN'S CENTER • Asher, AR   1/88 to 5/89
Planned and supervised educational units, arts & crafts
projects, and field trips for 12 multi-cultural four year olds.
Supervised an assistant teacher and part-time high school
student. Conducted parent conferences.

student teaching:

NILES AMERICAN SCHOOL • Greece   10/87 to 12/87

PARK SCHOOL • Little Rock, AR   9/87 to 10/87

TOP NURSERY SCHOOL • Levy, AR   9/86 to 12/86

References available upon request

✔ Rose utilizes markers in the left margin to emphasize credentials and effectively
  differentiate between paid experience and student teaching.
✔ She cites unique teaching and program development experience.

EARLY CHILDHOOD TEACHER (Entry-level)

SANDRA MILES
12 Valley Street • Monroeville, PA • 15146
412/ 555-2399

OBJECTIVE:

Early Childhood Teacher (K-2)

EDUCATION:

DUQUESNE UNIVERSITY   PITTSBURGH, PA
B.S. in Early Childhood Education   **1991**

CONTINUING EDUCATION
**Teaching Strategies and Curriculum Development for Young Children,
Whole Language Approach, Effective Speaking & Human Relations   1991**

CERTIFICATIONS:

Elementary Education (K-2) - Pending; CPR; Advanced Life Saving

TEACHING EXPERIENCE:

TURTLE LANE HOUSE   SIOUX FALLS
Student Teacher / Pre-school   **Spring 1991**

Plan and implemented curriculum for 12 children ages 2 through 4. Integrated
music, art, math, social studies, language, literature, and socialization activities
to promote learning and foster self-esteem. Conducted parent conferences and
provided suggestions to remedy learning/behavioral problems.

RELATED EXPERIENCE:

YEAR 2000 MUSEUM / CHILDREN'S MUSEUM   AVALON, PA
Computer Learning Coordinator   **1990**

HAMPSHIRE MUSEUM / HAMLINE UNIVERSITY   BRENTWOOD, PA
Assistant Conservator   **1989**

EXTENSIVE TRAVEL THROUGHOUT EUROPE.

REFERENCES: Available upon request

✔ Sandra is a recent graduate who presents her necessary credentials clearly.
✔ Her certifications in CPR and Life Savings are important in her field.
✔ She includes related experience which is both relevant and interesting.

EARLY CHILDHOOD TEACHER (Master's Degree)

CHRISTINA OLMOS
67 Sierra Trail
Hatch, NM 87937
505/ 555-1928

EDUCATION

Master of Education
NEW MEXICO STATE UNIVERSITY   1980

Bachelor of Science in Elementary Education
NEW MEXICO STATE UNIVERSITY   1978

28 post-graduate credits in Education

CERTIFICATION

Elementary Education (K-8)   Elementary Principal (K-8)

TEACHING EXPERIENCE

Early Childhood Education Teacher
EARLY EDUCATION CENTER, ALBUQUERQUE, NM   1984 to present

Plan and implement a comprehensive enrichment program to meet the social, recreational, cultural, and educational needs of groups of culturally diverse preschoolers. Present in-depth orientation program to parents and interested citizens outlining history, funding, goals, objectives, and activities.

Grade 1 Teacher / Self-contained Classroom
PARKER SCHOOL, HATCH, NM   1982 to 1984

Instructed and assessed small groups in reading, language arts and mathematics. Participated in special education meetings and parent conferences.

Kg Teacher / Team Approach
PARKER SCHOOL, HATCH, NM   1978 to 1982

Introduced children to their first formal learning experience. Trained student teachers.

References available upon request

✔ Christina's master's degree sets her apart from the competition.
✔ She includes teaching positions that support her specialization.
✔ Her section headings are centered to emphasize each important area.

ELEMENTARY TEACHER (Bachelor's Degree)

BARRY CATALDO
378 Cliff Drive
Stamford, CT 06904
203/ 555-3433

OBJECTIVE: Elementary Education Teacher

EDUCATION: FAIRFIELD UNIVERSITY   FAIRFIELD, CT

Jun 85   **Bachelor of Science in Education cum laude**
Major: Elementary Education   Minor: Mathematics

EXPERIENCE: NORWALK ELEMENTARY SCHOOL   NORWALK, CT

Jan 87
to
present

Grade Five Teacher
- Wrote and implemented Math curriculum.
- Designed Student Council program.
- Presented materials to School Committee.
- Conducted meetings with professional colleagues.
- Representative to state Teachers Association convention.
- Authored monthly parent newsletter.

HARTSHORN SCHOOL   STAMFORD, CT

Sep 85
to
Jun 86

Grade Six Teacher
- Taught Math, Science, Geography.
- Organized school athletic programs.
- Implemented extra-curricular activities.

NORWALK NORTH YMCA   NORWALK, CT

Jan 84
to
Aug 85

Program Director
- Oversaw daily functioning of after school daycare program.
- Supervised staff of summer daycare programs.
- Coordinated overall management of 125 children in program.

REFERENCES FURNISHED UPON REQUEST.

✔ Barry emphasizes teaching duties beyond his daily routine.
✔ His resume is particularly easy to read because of the attractive use of lines, capitals, bold, bullets, white space, and abbreviated months.

PHILIP BAGLEY
18 Hunters Pond Road
Derry, NH 03038
603/ 555-0294

OBJECTIVE: Elementary Teacher, Grades 1-8

EDUCATION:

RIVIER COLLEGE   NASHUA, NH
B.S. in Elementary Education with honors   December 1991
Minor in Psychology. Teaching practicums, grades 5-7.

CONTINUING EDUCATION
Math Their Way, Whole Language, Computer Lab, Behavior Reinforcement
Planning to pursue graduate studies in Education

CERTIFICATIONS:

NEW HAMPSHIRE Certification in Elementary Education (1-8) - Pending

EXPERIENCE:

OAKWOOD SCHOOL   DERRY, NH
Student Teacher - Grade 4   Fall 1991

Implemented all aspects of the academic curriculum in math, science, and language arts. Planned and taught thematic units to small groups and the whole class on creative writing, reptiles, and the use of computers. Incorporated computer and art activities into the curriculum. Reinforced learning activities for special education students. Participated in parent-teacher conferences and PTO functions.

Earned outstanding evaluations for all areas of teaching performance.

TENDER TOTS CENTER   DEERFIELD, NH
Head Teacher - Pre-school   part-time, 1990 to 1991

Planned and taught a structured, experiential pre-school program promoting readiness activities, appropriate social interaction, and the development of positive self-esteem. Interacted daily with parents to provide feedback on each child's progress and welfare.

References available upon request

- ✔ Philip's resume is typical and appropriate for a new teacher.
- ✔ His two teaching experiences eliminate the need to describe Practicums .
- ✔ In italics, he emphasizes excellent performance evaluations.

ELEMENTARY TEACHER (Master's Degree)

BRENDA FORD
7 Grapevine Lane
Mount Airy, OH 45239
513/ 555-9983

EDUCATION

graduate:

MA Elementary Education
OBERLIN COLLEGE • GRADUATE SCHOOL OF EDUCATION

undergraduate:

BA Economics
KENT STATE UNIVERSITY

PROFESSIONAL HIGHLIGHTS

experience:

Elementary Teacher/Grades 4-6
OAKLEY PUBLIC SCHOOLS • Oakley, OH (6 years)

Elementary Tutor/Grades 2-5
OAKLEY PUBLIC SCHOOLS • Oakley, OH (12+ years)
(Math instruction for underachievers)

Instructor
TATE JUNIOR COLLEGE • Glenmary, OH (current)
("Pre-school Learning Activities")

Educational Consultant
EDUCATOR'S ASSISTANT • Mount Airy, OH (6 years)
(Assist pre-school teachers to select readiness materials)

committees:

Ways and Means Committee Chairman
PARENT TEACHERS BOARD • Oakley, OH (12+ years)

Co-Chairman
CURRICULUM COMMITTEE • Walsh College (current)

presentations:

Adult Education
("Developmental Stages of Pre-schoolers")

References available upon request

✔ Brenda's resume is in outline form to accompany her application.
✔ She notes her experiences in number of years to achieve greater impact and avoid repetition of dates when jobs and activities overlap in time.

ELEMENTARY TEACHER (Post-graduate Studies)

THEODORE MYJEWSKI
9 Buchnell Circle • San Antonio, TX • 78205
521/ 555-6753

EDUCATION:

UNIVERSITY OF TEXAS • Austin, TX
31 post graduate credits in curriculum design, computers, gifted education

RICE UNIVERSITY • GRADUATE SCHOOL OF EDUCATION • Houston, TX
M.Ed Elementary Education

UNIVERSITY OF HOUSTON • Houston, TX
B.A. Sociology

TEACHING EXPERIENCE:

SAM HOUSTON SCHOOL • San Antonio, TX (1989)
Coordinator, San Antonio Bicentennial Celebration

Supervised and organized fourth and fifth graders in researching town history, conducting interviews with residents, and compiling results. Planned and led field trips. Facilitated writing and production of Bicentennial Program for school and parents.

SAM HOUSTON SCHOOL • San Antonio, TX (Spring 1989)
Teaching Assistant, grade 5

Participated in Community Problem Solving Grant for Gifted and Talented Students. Collaborated with teacher and students in brainstorming, researching, and analyzing the problem of teen drug abuse in the local community.

SAN ANTONIO ZOOLOGICAL SOCIETY • San Antonio, TX (1989)
Guide

Conducted tours for elementary school classes describing animal life, stressing conservation, and nurturing respect for the animal kingdom.

RIVER BEND SCHOOL • Austin, TX (1985 to 1988)
Computer Teacher, grade 6

Assisted children with self-designed computer program (GeoDraw) that draws their homes and other public buildings on a town map used to create a giant school mural.

RIVER BEND SCHOOL • Austin, TX (1982 to 1985)
Substitute Teacher, grade 4

COMMUNITY SERVICE:

TOWN MEETING MEMBER • San Antonio, TX (1985 to present)

SCHOOL COMMITTEE MEMBER • San Antonio, TX (1969 to 1985)

PARENT TEACHER BOARDS • San Antonio, TX (1973 to 1985)

GRADUATE SCHOOL COURSEWORK:

Using Computers in the Classroom	The Real Cause of Low Achievement
Advanced Teaching Methods and Materials	Computer Literacy for Educators
Creating a Computer Educational Environment	Computers and Language
Math Instruction — The Middler Method	Literature for Children
Development of Creative Writing Curriculum	Advanced Curriculum for the Gifted

REFERENCES:

Available upon request

✔ Theodore has a diverse background in teaching, coursework, and community service which deserves a 2-page resume.
✔ His sections are well-segmented to aid scanning.

LOUISA CASTRO
2113 Crystal Avenue
Throggs Neck, NY 10465
212/ 555-8589

SUMMARY

ESL Administrator - Masters Degree with twenty years of specialized experience in **multi-cultural education**. Areas of expertise include:

- Bilingual Education
- Mentoring
- Cooperative Learning
- At-risk Students
- Cross-cultural Issues
- Circular Migrants
- Cultural Equity
- Managing Change
- Community Outreach

EXPERIENCE

STATE OF NEW YORK REGENTS
Co-Director - Project ESL   **1991 to present**
Assist Greater Melville area to restructure curricula and organize programs to enhance learning for all students, particularly those at-risk.

Administrative Highlights:

- Interview school personnel to identify sites for project participation.
- Implement an integrated ESL program in three schools.
- Consult on needs assessments/program implementation.
- Research and design training sessions and workshops.
- Conduct focus groups and annual institutes.
- Submit grant proposals and annual reports to U.S. Dept. of Education.

SYOSSET PUBLIC SCHOOLS   SYOSSET, NY
ESL Coordinator   **1985 to 1991**
Bilingual Specialist   **1980 to 1985**
ESL Teacher   **1975 to 1980**

EDUCATION

UNIVERSITY OF SANTIAGO   SANTIAGO, CHILE
Bachelor of Arts - English as a Second Language   **1975**

✔ Louisa's Summary allows the reader to quickly scan her specialty areas.
✔ She describes only her current achivements as an administrator, but still lists prior positions in teaching as they are the foundation for her present career.

FREDERICK JULIANO

168 Forest Street
Wakefield, MA 01880
617/ 555-2984

SUMMARY

BS Degree in Education with concentration in bilingual education • Fluency in Italian derived from language immersion programs, travel, and residence abroad • Solid foreign language teaching and tutoring experience • PGA-certified golf teaching professional • State and national men's fencing ranking and winner of several international tournaments • Former fencing coach and ski instructor.

TEACHING EXPERIENCE

Private Language Instructor and Tutor   **1989 to present**

Provide Italian language instruction to students at all academic levels. Custom design programs to emphasize strong verbal skills. Curriculum encompasses Italian magazines, cassettes, role playing, and original material.

Italian Teacher
Mario Sciortino School • Medford, MA   **1985 to 1989**

Taught Italian (grades 6-8) and Spanish (grade 7) in classes of eight to fifteen students. Emphasized language learning through oral and written means.

Golf Instructor
Bousquet Country Club • Stoneham, MA   **1986 to present**

Provide group and individual instruction to teenagers and adults at all levels of proficiency. Lead all special competitive events and coach teams.

EDUCATION

Bachelor of Science in Education / Concentration in Bilingual Education
Bennett College • Greensboro, NC   **1985**

Certificates from foreign language immersion programs.

✔ Frederick's diverse background is immediately apparent in his summary.
✔ He is an unusual educator whose personal background is as interesting to the reader as his teaching career.

GUIDANCE COUNSELOR

DIANE LEE
45 Lipton Drive
Grand Rapids, MI 49501
616/ 555-6759

OBJECTIVE: Guidance Counselor (grades 7-12)

CERTIFICATION: Guidance Counselor (grades K-12)

EDUCATION: **MA in Educational Counseling**
AQUINAS COLLEGE • Grand Rapids, MI   1991

- *Coursework* - Alcohol & Drug Abuse, Psychological Testing, Family Counseling, Adult Development, School Counseling, and Clinical Practice.

- *Internship* - Phelps High School, Dutton, MI
Assisted students with personal and academic decision-making. Attended guidance meetings and team evaluations. Taught Career Counseling classes.

BS in Psychology
UNIVERSITY OF MICHIGAN • Ann Arbor, MI   1984

- *Community Practicum:* Provided academic, personal, and leisuretime counseling to juvenile offenders.

EMPLOYMENT: **Substitute Counselor** • KINGMAN HIGH SCHOOL.
Grand Rapids, MI   Spring 1989
Assumed counseling caseload of freshman and sophmore students. Assisted with academic, vocational, and personal issues.

Manager • SOUTHKENT HUMAN SERVICES, INC.
Southkent, MI   1986 to 1989
Directed community living programs for retarded and emotionally disturbed residents. Supervised, trained, and evaluated counseling staff. Wrote and implemented teaching plans. Provided crisis intervention and liaison to families.

Manager • VALLEYWOOD STREET CENTER, INC.
Godwin, MI   1984 to 1986
Directed community living programs for retarded adults. Developed innovative public relations through the coordination and integration of services. Selected, supervised, and evaluated counseling staff. Liaison to community agencies.

- ✔ Diane's Objective targets her for a Secondary Guidance position.
- ✔ As a recent graduate, her coursework and internship are both important.
- ✔ Diane's closely-related work experience substantially boosts her candidacy.

GUIDANCE DIRECTOR

GREGORY STARNES
89 Yellow Creek Road
Roswell, GA 30075
404/ 555-7279

EXPERIENCE:

ADAMS SCHOOL FOR LEARNING DISABLED   ROSWELL, GA
Director of Guidance & Placement Services   **1985 to present**

> Established initial guidance program and currently administer all facets for a student body of 220 from grades 5 through post-graduate. Developed curriculum guides, grading policy, record maintenance procedures, graduation criteria, competency testing curriculum & evaluation instruments, and student counseling programs.

> Evaluate collegiate and secondary school special education services. Coordinate nationwide college visitation program. Design and maintain database of post-secondary program information for student and community utilization.

> Implemented national testing programs for special education students. Presented findings of a statistical study of culturally-biased SAT scores and presented results to the state Association of College Admissions Counselors.

Language Arts Supervisor   **1983 to 1985**
Math & Language Arts Teacher   **1981 to 1983**

EDUCATION:

M.Ed in Guidance & Counseling cum laude   **1987**
EMORY UNIVERSITY   ATLANTA, GA
Kappa Kappa Tau, Graduate Education Council, College Accreditation Team

B.A. in English magna cum laude   **1980**
KENNESAW STATE COLLEGE   MARIETTA, GA
Who's Who in American Colleges and Universities

ASSOCIATIONS:

Association of College Admission Counselors   AHSSPPE

Learning Disabilities Advisory Council   Association of Secondary Educators

---

> ✔ Gregory elaborates on achievements in his current job as an administrator and lists former teaching positions to show career growth.
> ✔ He cites academic honors which are impressive.

JOSEPH SKILLINGS
276 Beacon Park Drive
Bennington, NE 68007
402/ 555-2212

EDUCATION:

Candidate • **Ed.D in Curriculum and Instruction** • Creighton University

Ed.M in Secondary Reading • Creighton University   *1985*

B.A. in Elementary Education • Bellvue College   *1980*

EXPERIENCE:

Bellvue Public Schools
HEAD TEACHER • English Department   *1985 to present*
ENGLISH AND READING TEACHER • Grades 6 & 7   *1985 to present*
TEACHER • Grade 5   *1982 to 1985*

Barton's English School, France
LANGUAGE ARTS TEACHER • Grades 5 - 9   *1980 to 1982*

ACHIEVEMENTS:

- Administered a secondary English department including scheduling, staffing, testing programs, faculty meetings, budget, curriculum, and student placements.

- Introduced system-wide programs in developmental reading and summer reading. Established goals, methods, curriculum, materials, and staffing requirements.

- Researched and recommended developmental vocabulary series for grades 6 - 9.

- Assisted in the incorporation of Basic Skills Testing Program system-wide.

- Coordinated the Junior National Honor Society selection and induction process.

- Fostered student participation in the Scholastic Junior Reading Contest.

- Formed and headed student literature club.

- Received award for sustained superior performance as a teacher.

- President of the Bennington Chapter of the Nebraska Teachers Association.

✔ Joseph's candidacy for an Ed.D is his key credential, so he states it first.
✔ His long association with the Bellvue Schools is embellished in a list of major achievements derived from all his years of teaching.

HEALTH / PHYSICAL EDUCATION TEACHER

MARY GORMLEY

78-C Harborside Drive
Dupont, SC 29407
803/ 555-3186

EDUCATION:

B.A.- HEALTH / PHYSICAL EDUCATION • COLLEGE of Charleston   1982

CERTIFICATIONS:

SOUTH CAROLINA TEACHING CERTIFICATE: Health / Physical Education (K-12)

RED CROSS CERTIFICATION: Water Safety Instructor • Advanced First Aid Instructor

TEACHING:

CHARLESTON GIRLS' PREP SCHOOL • Charleston, SC

Life Science - grade 6	1986 to present
Earth Science - grade 7	1986 to present
Physical Education - grades 2 to 9	1982 to 1986

CHEERLEADING COACHING:

DUPONT REGIONAL HIGH SCHOOL • Dupont, SC   1982 to present
Develop routines, coach practices, and lead performances for grades 10 to 12. Coach football, soccer, and basketball. Coordinated High School cheerleading activities at the 1987 Peanut Bowl as well as the 1988 Regional High School Super Bowl.

CHEERLEADING JUDGING:

SOUTHERN HIGH SCHOOL COMPETITION	1989 to 1991
REGIONAL PREP SCHOOLS CHEERLEADING COMPETITION	1988
CAROLINAS CHEERLEADING COMPETITION	1988 to 1989

WATER SAFETY:

WATERFRONT DIRECTOR • Camp Tomahawk   1985 to present
Directed the testing, categorizing, instruction, and re-evaluation of swimmers.

LIFEGUARD/WATER SAFETY INSTRUCTOR • SC Park Commission   1980 to 1982

✔ Mary's resume goes beyond classroom duties and presents Mary as an educator involved in numerous activities related to her specialization.
✔ Her various activities set her apart from other candidates in the field.

INTERN / ADMINISTRATOR

LAURA BUCHANAN

223 Brandywine Drive
Arlington, VA 22210
703/ 555-7844

SUMMARY:

- Ed.D candidate in Policy, Planning, and Administration.
- M.S. in Educational Administration; M.S. in Special Education.
- Nine years of successful public school administrative experience.
- Thirteen years of distinguished public school teaching.
- Proven ability to provide effective leadership in policy, curriculum, and administration.

EDUCATION:

VIRGINIA COMMONWEALTH UNIVERSITY — GRAD. SCHOOL OF EDUC.   RICHMOND, VA
Ed.D in Policy, Planning, and Administration   **Candidate**

UNIVERSITY OF RICHMOND   RICHMOND, VA
MS in Educational Administration   **1986**

VIRGINIA UNION UNIVERSITY   RICHMOND, VA
MS in Special Education   **1981**

VIRGINIA UNION UNIVERSITY   RICHMOND, VA
BS in Elementary Education - cum laude   **1976**

EXPERIENCE:

TUCKAHOE PUBLIC SCHOOLS   TUCKAHOE, VA
Intern - Administrator   **1990 to present**

Selected to this unique administrative position on the basis of merit. Perform administrative functions including building operations, staff scheduling & supervision, curriculum development, parent conferences, student discipline, and report writing. Participate in all administrative meetings to determine and review system-wide policy. Assume overall responsibility for school in absence of Principals. Member of town-wide Strategic Planning Committee.

Head Teacher   **1982 to 1990**

Performed all building-level administrative duties as assigned by Principal. Gained an overview of budgeting, programming, and evaluation. Assumed authority for building in Principal's absence. Selected as Outstanding Teacher by School Committee. Commended by Director of the Inservice Training Project of the NFIE for evaluation, editing, and revision of an inservice training manual.

Chapter 6 Pilot Program Teacher   **1989 to 1990**

Recognized by School Committee and Superintendent of Schools for effectiveness as a teacher in the Wonderkids' Reading Program; presented program to annual conference of the state Reading Association.

Grade 2-5 Teacher   **1978 to 1990**

Consistently cited by administrators and parents for teaching proficiency at all elementary grades and with academic underachievers. Actively involved in system-wide committees, curriculum development, and professional associations.

CERTIFICATIONS:

Elementary Education (K-8)   Superintendent

Reading Specialist (K-12)   Supervisor/Director, Elementary Principal

ASSOCIATIONS:

National Society for Supervision and Curriculum Development, Coalition of Educational Leaders, National Educational Association

COMMITTEES:

Superintendent's Council, School Improvement Council, Text-Selection, In-Service

✔ Laura summarizes her impressive credentials immediately.
✔ She segments each important section with horizontal lines.
✔ Laura's resume reflects her career track into Educational Administration.

LIBRARIAN

JANET VICKERS
3 Logan Street
Ogden, UT 84401
801 / 555-9753

EXPERIENCE:

WEBER STATE COLLEGE

Suburban Campus Library (85,000 volumes • 425 periodical titles • 9 staff members)

Chief Librarian (1989 to present)

Serials/Reference Librarian (1983 to 1989)

Trainee (1981 to 1983)

HIGHLIGHTS:

- Direct the daily operations of a campus library.
- Determine policies and procedures, explore technological applications, and plan future directions.
- Hire, train, supervise, and evaluate full-time professional and support staff.
- Administer $350,000 annual budget; recommend funding levels and allocations.
- Plan and provide user services including computer literature searches.
- Oversee collection development for reference and serials collections.
- Prepare proposals, reports and statistical analyses.
- Communicate with book publishers.
- Supervise cataloguing of microfiche and processing of interlibrary loan requests.

EDUCATION:

UTAH STATE UNIVERSITY
Master of Science in Library and Information Science (1984)

UTAH STATE UNIVERSITY
Bachelor of Arts in English (1981)

✔ Janet's brief description of the library is very informative to the reader.
✔ Since her present duties are far more sophisticated than those earlier in her career, she describes only current highlights.

PHYSICAL EDUCATION TEACHER

VIVIAN PARNELL
43-G Rancho Ocho Drive
Camarillo, CA 93010
818/ 555-4936

OBJECTIVE: Physical Education Teacher/Coach (7-12)

EXPERIENCE:

Physical Education Instructor • Foy High School • Foy, CA   1987 to present
   Plan and supervise open gym activities for students grades 9-12.

Physical Education Teacher • Malibu School District • Malibu, CA   1985 to 1987
   Planned and taught K-9 physical education courses in 4 schools.

Team Coach • Foy High School • Foy, CA   1986 to present
   Varsity soccer, field hockey, girls basketball

Assistant Director • Camp Moonbeam • Malibu, CA   Summers, 1985 to present
   Plan and manage activities, budgeting, and staffing for 150+ youngsters ages 4 to 15.
   Supervise and evaluate counseling staff, resolve camper discipline problems, confer with
   parents, and coordinate special events including overnights.

EDUCATION:

B.S. in Physical Education • Northrop University   1985

   • DOUBLE MAJOR in Teaching and Sports Medicine.
   • PRESIDENT of the Physical Education Club.
   • SECRETARY of the Student Activities Committee.
   • VARSITY TEAMS: Soccer, Field Hockey, Basketball.

TRAINING:

Student Teacher • Agoura Public Schools   Spring, 1985
   Planned and conducted Physical Education, Health, and Sports Medicine classes at both the
   middle school and high school.

Student Intern • Milton Hospital   Fall, 1984
   Assisted patients in the rehabilitation of acute and chronic sports-related injuries.

CERTIFICATIONS:

Secondary Physical Education (5-12); Advanced Life Saving; CPR; First Aid.

✔ Vivian's Objective is well supported by both experience and training.
✔ The reader can easily scan Vivian's highlights in bold print.
✔ When Vivian adds her next position, she can omit her Training section.

ANDREA KOWALSKI
12 Appleton Street
Washington, DC 20002
202/ 555-9070

SUMMARY

More than ten years of administrative/teaching experience including positions as Principal and Professional Development Coordinator. *Strengths in:*

- Curriculum Design
- Needs Assessment
- Staff Development
- Program Development
- Special Education
- Budgeting

EXPERIENCE

THOMAS EDISON SCHOOL   ALEXANDRIA, VA
Principal   **1990 to present**

- Provide administrative leadership to a 400-student private school (K-12) leading to the successful maintenance of state accreditation.
- Oversee curriculum development, staff recruitment and evaluation, parent programs, budgeting, and special education team meetings.
- Introduced numerous innovative educational/social awareness programs.

BELMONT PUBLIC SCHOOLS   BELMONT, VA
Principal - Day Elementary School   **1987 to 1990**

- Oversaw daily operations of a 600-student public elementary school (K-6).
- Redesigned school-wide programs promoting intradisciplinary teaching.
- Facilitated staff acceptance of a new performance evaluation instrument.

Professional Development Coordinator   **1985 to 1987**

- Developed a system-wide, long-term staff development plan, budget, and assessment instrument adopted by the School Committee.

Teacher (Grades 6-8)   **1983 to 1985**

EDUCATION

AMERICAN UNIVERSITY   WASHINGTON, D.C.
M.Ed - Administration   **1987**
B.S. - Elementary Education   **1983**

✔ Andrea's short Summary incorporates much valuable, scannable information-length of career, areas of experience, job titles, and professional strengths.
✔ She describes all administrative positions because of varied achievements.

SCIENCE TEACHER

BERTRAM SCOGGINS
16 Old Mill Road
Chattanooga, TN 37401
615/ 555-0842

OBJECTIVE: Science Teacher (Grades 5-9)

SUMMARY:

- 12+ years as a creative teacher of Chemistry and Biology.
- Create student-centered learning environment through use of innovative techniques.
- Lifelong interest in aviation; active both as an instructor and participant.

ACCOMPLISHMENTS:

- Secured a $4,500 grant from the National Science Foundation to develop a study for students to explore caves and other geological areas in the Shenandoah Valley. The student data was incorporated into the Department's formal report on mapping surveys.
- Designed and implemented an Urban/Suburban Exchange Program which utilized the city as a learning environment. Areas of study included the Aquarium, Airport, and the design of the Transit Authority.
- Developed numerous system-wide curriculum units including Cell Reproduction and Division.
- Coordinated internship programs and supervised 4 student teachers per semester.
- Created audio/visual materials utilizing underwater photography.
- Cited by the U.S. Flight Instructors Association for outstanding instruction and training.

EDUCATION:

FISK UNIVERSITY
Master of Education (1987)

CARSON-NEWMAN COLLEGE
Bachelor of Science in Education (1979)

EMPLOYMENT:

PUBLIC SCHOOLS OF CHATTANOOGA, TN
Science Teacher (1979 to present)

✔ Short dividing lines segment Bertram's credentials into scannable sections .
✔ His Summary presents a very unique side of a science teacher.
✔ His accomplishments surpass the classroom setting.

SOCIAL STUDIES TEACHER

Albert Washburn

890 Maple Street • Sherman, SD 57060 • 605/ 555-7774

Objective

Social Studies Teacher (3-8)

Education

M.A. in SOCIAL STUDIES • Augsburg College • Minneapolis, MN	1983
B.A. in EDUCATION • Bethel College • Minneapolis, MN	1980

Certifications

SOUTH DAKOTA Certification • History, Language Arts - Grades K through 12.

Experience

BRIAR SCHOOL • Sioux Falls, SD	1987 to present
PUBLIC SCHOOLS • Sioux Falls, SD	1980 to 1987

Teach social studies and language arts within self-contained classrooms of fifth and sixth graders. Specialize in integrating creative arts and enrichment activities into the curriculum. Participated in private school accreditation process through the development of a student council and the evaluation of the school sports program. Collaborated with state recreational officials to design and implement field trip curricula.

NATIVE AMERICAN ESL Program • Sioux Falls, SD   1987 to present

Teach English as a Second Language to native American residents.

References available upon request

✔ Albert achieves a contemporary look to his resume through the use of modern lettering and centered headings.
✔ He divides information into short, scannable segments.

SPECIAL NEEDS EDUCATOR

HENRY LARKIN
466 Buckhead Lane
Norcross, GA 30071
404/ 555-3527

EDUCATION:

Ed.M in Special Education • Emory University (1987)

B.A. in Psychology • Oglethorpe University (1985)

EMPLOYMENT:

Medical Educator • Hosmer Hospital (1987 to present)

Therapeutic Recreation Director • St. Francis Hospital (1985 to 1987)

EXPERIENCE:

Special Education

- Developed educational programs for hospitalized children with severe head injuries. Performed diagnostic assessments, identification of learning styles and compensatory strategies, and curriculum development. Consulted to public school systems to insure implementation of appropriate classroom settings and teaching approaches upon student discharge from hospital.

- Taught multi-handicapped children in a self-contained classroom. Closely collaborated with staff of three therapy departments in order to successfully integrate individual therapy goals into the educational program.

Computer Consultant

- Researched and adapted hardware and software for special education programs.

- Collaborated with the Teachers Software Company in the development of word processing software appropriate for special education programs.

Presentations

- "New educational techniques for head-injured children ." - ACCH.

- "Computers as educational tools for children with severe head injuries." - Child Development School, Emory University.

✔ Henry's primary credentials are his degrees, so Education is presented first.
✔ He divides his experience into three key areas of expertise.
✔ Henry's resume saves space by avoiding needless repetition .

SPECIAL EDUCATION PROFESSOR

Curriculum Vitae
of

ABBIDEE FRASER

79 Painted Gate Circle
Houston, TX 77002

Residence: 713/ 555-7848
Office: 713/ 555-2591

SUMMARY

20+ years college teaching and administrative experience • Graduate and undergraduate courses related to reading/language and learning problems • Academic and advisory committees • Program development and implementation • Consultant and writer.

EXPERIENCE

Professor
Department of Special Education
HOUSTON BAPTIST UNIVERSITY

1988 to present

Associate Professor
Department of Education
HOUSTON BAPTIST UNIVERSITY

1982 to 1988

Adjunct Faculty
Department of Special Education
UNIVERSITY OF HOUSTON

1977 to 1982

Elementary and Reading Teacher
Franklin Public Schools
FRANKLIN, TX

1975 to 1977

EDUCATION

ED.D in Reading/Language
TEXAS SOUTHERN UNIVERSITY

1981

ED.M in Reading
TEXAS SOUTHERN UNIVERSITY

1974

B.S. in Elementary Education
SOUTHWEST TEXAS STATE UNIVERSITY

1972

Abbidee Fraser   Page 2

AWARDS

Distinguished Educator Award
HOUSTON BAPTIST UNIVERSITY   1982

CONSULTING POSITIONS

Inservice Program on Multi-sensory Approaches for the L.D. Child
Houston Bureau of Education   1989

Inservice Program on Psychometric Testing
Houston Public Schools   1987

COMMITTEES

Acting Chairperson, Department of Special Education

Acting Coordinator of Teacher Education

Chairperson, Undergraduate Special Education Curriculum Committee

Graduate Special Education Curriculum Committee

PROFESSIONAL AFFILIATIONS

American Association of College Professors   Association for Exceptional Children

International Reading Association   Council for LD Children

Epsilon Pi Gamma   Kappa Kappa Mu   Pi Gamma Delta

PUBLICATIONS

List of publications available upon request

✔ Abbidee includes key credentials, e.g., experience and education, on page
   one and supporting experience on page two of her curriculum vitae.
✔ She includes publications as a separate document because of their length.

SPECIAL SERVICES ADMINISTRATOR

JEANETTE REED
732 Arlington Heights Road
Nutley, NJ 07110
201/ 555-7836

PROGRAM ADMINISTRATION

Professional Experience:

ADAMS PUBLIC SCHOOLS • NUTLEY, NJ
(Suburban public school system • Student population of 3,200)

Director for Special Services (1989 to present). Plan, develop, and administer a wide variety of special service programs including Adult Continuing Education, Senior Citizens' Education, Summer School, School Attendance/Census, Pupil Transportation, Data Processing, and Out-of-System Tuition Reimbursement. *Report directly to the Superintendent of Schools.*

Highlights:

- Expanded Adult Education and Summer School course offerings. Conducted community needs assessments, recruited instructors, publicized programs, and oversaw scheduling, contracts, and registration.
- Chaired Superintendent's Advisory Council and Summer School Committee.
- Established Senior Citizens' Education Program with Council on Aging.
- Developed out-of-system tuition reimbursement policy and coordinated student application and evaluation process prior to acceptance.

Systemwide Coordinator / ESL Teacher (1985 to 1989). Designed, taught, and coordinated English as a Second Language curriculum for grades K-6. Organized social events for the Newark Residents Secondary Language Program.

Education:

LA SALLE UNIVERSITY
Bachelor of Arts with honors (1984)

References: Available upon request

✔ Jeanette's general heading is a useful alternative to a specific job objective.
✔ She concentrates on her present employment rather than previous experience, and balances a general job description with specific achievements.

CAREER CHANGE (Elementary Principal)

WESLEY WHITMAN
89 Cogshall Road
Hamden, CT 06514

Residence: 203/ 555-7438   Business: 203/ 555-2905

QUALIFICATIONS:

- 17 years administering programs, personnel, budgets, schedules, and facilities.
- 5 years as Board Member and Past President of a Municipal Retirement Fund.
- Masters Degree with post-graduate coursework in administration and finance.
- 8 years leadership in professional and community organizations.

ADMINISTRATIVE EXPERIENCE:

- President of a 34-member Administrators Association for four years. Negotiated contracts and participated in resolving labor disputes.
- President of the Cityside Municipal Retirement Fund. Doubled assets as a direct result of the implementation of successful investment strategies.
- Provided strong leadership, training, and evaluation for a staff of 37. Developed and maintained a $900K annual budget. Promoted community relations programs.
- Principal of the first public school to accommodate a multiple-handicapped population. Instituted innovative special education curricula.
- Chaired a systemwide Arts Program. Developed school committee policies, job specifications, parent newsletters, and teacher handbooks.

EDUCATION:

Master of Education • Trinity College (1978)

Bachelor of Science • Fairfield University (1974)

EMPLOYMENT:

Administrator • Public Schools of New Haven, CT (1974 to present)

✔ Wesley emphasizes his entire range of administrative experience rather than his lengthy tenure in a public school system.
✔ Specific facts and figures augment the description of his achievements.

CAREER CHANGE (College Dean)

EVELYN O'DONNELL
1767 Massachusetts Avenue
Lexington, MA 02173
617/ 555-1359

EXPERIENCE:

Dean • MARSDEN JUNIOR COLLEGE

Administrator • MEDFORD PUBLIC SCHOOLS

ACCOMPLISHMENTS:

- **Administration**

  Supervised and coordinated academic programs, staff of 28, and student activities at Marsden Junior College during a rapid period of expansion. Administered all facets of programs and developed budgets in excess of $3M for maintenance and operation of Medford Public Schools. Revised educational and building specs for a $18M, 3100-pupil high school.

- **Program Development**

  Implemented the concepts of open-spaced classrooms, independent study, and field study. Promoted a model county-wide tutorial exchange program with Harvard College. Designed special education, vocational education, and bi-lingual education programs.

  Instituted the use of computers in education for scheduling, attendance, grade reporting, test analysis, computer education, and time-sharing in the industry's infancy.

- **Personnel Training**

  Interviewed, selected, and evaluated professional staff of 225. Fostered staff development through in-service seminars. Facilitated contract negotiations.

  Directed and developed jobs for a bi-lingual career program. Provided ongoing counseling.

- **Public Relations**

  Initiated parent, student, teacher organizations. Introduced dynamic community outreach programs. Published brochures and articles promoting a positive school image.

EDUCATION:

38 Credits • ADVANCED GRADUATE STUDY

Master of Arts • HARVARD COLLEGE

Bachelor of Arts • HARVARD COLLEGE

✔ Evelyn's resume reflects her experience in four key administrative areas.
✔ She presents her credentials in terms of accomplishments rather than duties.
✔ Evelyn omits dates from her resume to avoid age discrimination.

CAREER CHANGE (Counselor)

MYRNA WOODS   16 Prospect Park • La Jolla, CA 92037 • 619/ 555-1278

PROFESSIONAL EXPERIENCE:

RESUMES PLUS - La Jolla, CA   *part-time, 1988 - present*
Director. Founded career planning service offering testing, counseling, interview practice, and resume preparation. Establish professional networks. Deliver presentations to universities, institutions, and professional organizations.

SAN DIEGO PUBLIC SCHOOLS - San Diego, CA   *1980 - present*
Guidance Counselor / Grades K-12. Assisted students with academic, vocational, and personal decision-making. Supervised staff in the implementation of special needs programs. Consulted to students, parents, and staff. Chaired team meetings. Administered psychological evaluations and wrote detailed assessments.

COUNCIL FOR CHILDREN - San Diego, CA   *part-time, 1985 -1988*
Board Member. Formulated community needs assessment. Supervised personnel search committee. Established systemwide reporting policy for child abuse cases. Developed and presented workshops to area professionals.

SUMMERFIELD MEMORIAL HOSPITAL - Santa Barbara, CA   *1975 - 1980*
Psychologist. Supervised staff in testing procedures and data collection for a clinic testing the effects of medication on learning disabled children. Represented clinic at national conferences.

EDUCATION:

MA IN EDUCATION - Pepperdine University   *1979*

M.ED IN COUNSELING - Stanford University   *1977*

BA IN PSYCHOLOGY - San Diego State College   *1975*

PRESENTATIONS:

Creating an Effective Resume   *Perspectives on Parenting*

Combating Child Abuse and Neglect   *Workshop on Parent and Family Counseling*

PUBLICATIONS:

Woods, M. The five resume-preparation questions most frequently asked by women changing careers. *Career Directions,* Vol. X, Fall, 1989.

Woods, M. Forming a single parent group: one counselor's experience. *Parent Counseling Association of Southern California Journal,* Vol. 1. Fall, 1976.

✔ Myrna has already begun her career change part-time.
✔ Her resume seeks to establish her as a competent professional with strong business, educational, presentation, and publication credentials.

CAREER CHANGE (Foreign Language Instructor)

RUDOLF SCHRANK
45-3 Farnum Street ■ Chicago, IL 60613 ■ 312/ 555-6694

Profile:

Born and educated in Europe, I continue to travel worldwide. I am fascinated by varied cultures, comfortable among diverse populations, and fluent in German, English, and French. This unique background enhances my adaptability and creativity.

My love of people and languages led me to a career as a foreign language instructor, where I found great satisfaction in developing creative curricula and motivating students to reach their goals and acquire new skills and insights. My high energy level and thirst for challenge served as a catalyst for initiating a business enterprise and seriously pursuing sailing, parachuting, and photography.

Highlights:

FOREIGN LANGUAGE INSTRUCTOR • *Oak Park High School* • Chicago, IL   1980 to present

- Teach German and French at all grade levels in multi-racial community.
- Received "Outstanding Educator in America" award.
- Year-long sabbatical in France to research and photograph French culture.
- Sailing Club Advisor / Instructor; Tennis Coach.
- Coordinate and chaperone annual student immersion travel to Europe.

TRANSLATOR • *Hyperion Corporation* • Chicago, IL	1984 to 1990
INSTRUCTOR • *European Language Institute* • Chicago, IL	1980 to 1984
MANAGER • *Illinois Parks Commission*	1980 to 1982
OWNER • *Edelweiss Bakery* • Chicago, IL	1976 to 1980

Education:

CAGS • *University of Chicago* • Chicago, IL	1984
MASTER OF EDUCATION • *Roosevelt University* • Chicago, IL	1979
BACHELOR OF ARTS • *Von Dreiz University* • Salzburg, Austria	1977

References:

Personal and professional references available upon request.

✔ Rudolf's Profile acquaints the reader with his personal side.
✔ He highlights teaching, administrative, and business enterprises so that his future career options are numerous.

CAREER CHANGE (Teacher A)

ANNEMARIE MANZI   1803 Canarsie Avenue ■ Brighton, NY 11235 ■ 718/ 555-0265

Qualifications:

- Innovative and competent professional with a successful performance record.
- Demonstrated capability managing simultaneous projects and meeting deadlines.
- Quick thinker who can master new concepts rapidly and convey them to others.
- Adept at researching, organizing, reporting, and presenting information.
- Skilled at teaching, counseling, and motivating.
- Extensive travel and residence abroad - working knowledge of Italian.
- Comfortable relating to people with diverse backgrounds.

Achievements:

- Planned and coordinated innovative curricula.
- Devised assignments, experiments, and test instruments to facilitate learning.
- Addressed different learning styles and levels.
- Organized enrichment trips to enhance curriculum.
- Program Chairperson for several professional organizations.
- Directed a community fund raising committee for several years.

Education:

Master of Science
NEW YORK UNIVERSITY • New York, NY   1987

Bachelor of Arts
NEW YORK UNIVERSITY • New York, NY   1983

Employment Highlights:

Teacher
BETSY ROSS SCHOOL • Brighton, NY   1987 to 1990
HOPMAN SCHOOL • Brooklyn, NY   1983 to 1987

✔ Annemarie stresses competencies and achievements acquired as a teacher
which will be useful in a different career.
✔ Short, bulleted sentences contribute to an easy-to-read presentation.

CAREER CHANGE (Teacher B)

NORA GAYNOR
473 Quarton Road • Birmingham, MI • 313/ 555-3826

SUMMARY

Energetic teacher with strong interest in international relations • Fluent in Thai, Vietnamese, and French • Extensive independent travel and study in France and Southeast Asia • Comfortable relating to people of diverse cultures and ages.

EDUCATION

Bachelor of Arts in Asian Studies   1990
MICHIGAN STATE UNIVERSITY   ANN ARBOR, MI

- GPA: 4.0. Coursework included Political Horizons in Southeast Asia, Challenges in American Foreign Policy, and International Politics.

- Phi Gamma Mu Scholastic Honorary. Valedictorian.

- Student Representative - Int'l. Society for the Study of Southeast Asia.

INTERNATIONAL EXPERIENCE

Independent Travel/Language Immersion (Summers, 1988-present)
VIETNAM, THAILAND, CAMBODIA, FRANCE, SWITZERLAND

WORK EXPERIENCE

Asian Language Teacher/Curriculum Developer (K-6)   1990 to present
JACKSON STREET SCHOOL   WESTLAND, MI

Teaching Assistant - English as a Second Language   1990 to present
ADULT EDUCATION PROGRAM   BIRMINGHAM, MI

Private Tutor - Intermediate French   1988 to 1990

ACTIVITIES

Fund Raiser / Jr. Member of Policy Committee
AMNESTY INTERNATIONAL

Host for Foreign V.I.P's
INTERNATIONAL SOCIETY FOR THE STUDY OF SOUTHEAST ASIA

Guest Speaker - Cultural Diversity
AREA SCHOOLS AND UNIVERSITIES

✔ Nora's format pleases graphically and aids the reader in locating sections.
✔ Her Summary stresses important credentials necessary for her career switch.
✔ The Activities section contains information directly related to her new field.

Finance and Banking 8

A Very Conservative Industry

Money is a powerful force in our society. All too often it becomes our singular focus because it so totally symbolizes achievement, power, security, freedom, and love. Yet, despite our obsession with finding new and innovative strategies to multiply or save our money, financial institutions remain our most conservative. They, and the people they employ, must be perceived as conservative to earn the public's trust.

To compete within such a conservative industry, your resume must project conservatism in both content and presentation. Keep it simple, straightforward, and serious.

Project A Stable Career Path

In Finance and Banking, the majority of professionals build a stable career path starting with college. If you're like most, you probably majored in accounting, economics, finance, or business. You probably held a typical entry-level position as a Junior Accountant, Bookkeeper, Teller, or Management Trainee. And, you probably continue to progress in a fairly straight career direction within similar institutions.

Since stability is so highly valued, it makes sense to demonstrate your solid career track by listing each step along the way. However, to avoid repetition, it is not necessary to *describe* each junior position or routine duty. Stress only higher level functions.

Degrees, Licenses and Certifications Are Crucial

In Finance and Banking, certain educational and training credentials, e.g., C.P.A., C.M.A., Registered Agent, instantly validate your ability to perform competently and legally within your specialization. Even a very strong college G.P.A. in your major field is noteworthy. Therefore, as a form of "prequalification," it is appropriate to present your Education and/or Certification sections before your Experience section.

Computers Are Here To Stay

Computers have revolutionized Finance and Banking. Just think of electronic spread-sheets, ATM's, and Financial Information Systems. If you are a recent graduate, it is likely that you are already familiar with popular hardware and software relevant to your area of specialization. If not, it is advisable that you rapidly become familiar.

Because computers are now an integral part of the industry, it is important to emphasize your computer expertise on your resume. This can be effectively accomplished either within the body of your job descriptions or in a separate Computer Skills section.

Can Your Achievements Be Measured?

No one can dispute the vital function that you, as a Finance and Banking professional play in the day-to-day operation of a company or institution. Technical expertise, attention to detail, analytical skill, and the ability to integrate and problem-solve are essential. Yet, the results of your efforts are often difficult to measure, and even more disheartening, your duties are frequently perceived as routine and repetitive.

Even so, you can still identify and explain certain important achievements without disclosing confidential company facts and figures. For instance:

- Did you implement, upgrade, or automate systems?

- Did you streamline workflow?

- Did you reduce backlogs?

- Did you recruit, hire, train, motivate, schedule, or evaluate staff?

- Did you write procedural manuals?

- Did you develop or expand a client base or client services?

- Did you consolidate operations?

- Did you perform special projects?

ACCOUNTANT – ENTRY LEVEL

DOUGLAS RAPP
14 Hemlock Road
Grandville, MI 49418
616/ 555-0241

OBJECTIVE: Entry-level Accountant

EDUCATION: AQUINAS COLLEGE
B.S.B.A. 1991

major: Accounting

projects: Student Marketing Association Team Projects

- Established a computer system for accounting, inventory, and pricing for a "mom and pop" grocer.

- Established a cash accounting system to address all A/R and A/P needs for the Student Marketing Association.

activities: Varsity Swim Team, Golf Team

CERTIFICATION: C.P.A. EXAM – results pending

EMPLOYMENT: H.R. BLOCK, INC.
Tax Accountant p.t., 1990 to 1991

Consult with clients and prepare their small business and personal tax returns using a PC computer system.

DOWN THE AISLE AGAIN p.t., 1990 to 1991
Junior Accountant

Performed G/L accounting for this boutique specializing in preowned bridal clothing. Developed monthly and end-of-year financial statements and monthly sales & inventory reports. Converted from cash to accrual accounting system.

SUMMER EMPLOYMENT included Camp Waterfront Director.

References available upon request.

✔ A new graduate, Douglas begins with his Education rather than part time jobs.
✔ His Certification section is crucial to establish his career path.
✔ Douglas' Summer Employment shows leadership potential.

DONNA CHIESA
171-B Hazelwood Apartments
Cary, NC 27511

Residence: 919/ 555-3822   *Business:* 919/ 555-3400

PROFESSIONAL EXPERIENCE:

WARREN FURNITURE CORPORATION   RALEIGH, NC

A/P Supervisor   1989 to present
A/P Asst. Supervisor   1987 to 1989
Hire, train, supervise, and evaluate a staff of 15 in the preparation of 138,000 invoices annually for 271 store locations in 43 states.

- Reduced backlog of invoices by half within nine months.
- Significantly streamlined workflow by reorganizing staff assignments.
- Upgraded control procedures resulting in a perfect audit.
- Computerized tracking system for inter-departmental documentation.
- Assisted MIS team to computerize quarterly reporting.

Tax Accounting Assistant   1984 to 1987
Computed quarterly and annual payroll, sales, and use tax for all stores.

DREXEL STATIONERS   RALEIGH, NC

Bookkeeper   1982 to 1984

EDUCATION:

ST. AUGUSTINE'S COLLEGE   RALEIGH, NC

Associates Degree in Accounting   1984

References available upon request

✔ Donna's job titles in bold demonstrate a steady career growth since college.
✔ Her current job description incorporates impressive figures in the introductory sentence and specific achievements highlighted with bullets.

ACCOUNTING SUPERVISOR

FREDERICK PRICE
3 Amberlight Drive
Monona, WI 53716

Residence: 608/ 555-4299   *Business:* 608/ 555-8990

PROFESSIONAL EXPERIENCE:

ASSOCIATED FREIGHTWAYS • Madison, WI
Accounting Supervisor (1990 to present)

Manage Payroll, A/P, A/R, Billing and Freight operations for $95M international firm.

* Recruit, train, supervise, and evaluate clerical staff of ten.
* Direct cash flow activities for domestic operations.
* Oversee sales tax collection in all states to comply with regulations.
* Upgraded software for A/P operations.

DUNKIRK MEDICAL SUPPLIES • Madison, WI
Accountant (1987 to 1990)

Supported the Domestic Controller on closings, budgeting, and tax reporting.

* Handled closing activities, financial statement preparation and analysis for three domestic subsidiaries. Prepared the annual plan and quarterly forecasts of same.
* Monitored and reported on capital expenditure activities for 11 locations to determine asset category, useful life, and depreciation expenses.
* Prepared weekly sales reports utilized by management as a projection tool.
* Assisted in the design and implementation of computerized A/R system.

WHITING BANK • Middleton, WI
Payroll Accountant (1985 to 1987)

EDUCATION:

EDGEWOOD COLLEGE • Madison, WI
M.B.A. Candidate

LAKELAND COLLEGE • Sheboygan, WI
B.A. in Accounting (1986)

Computer Training: dBase, Peachtree Accounting, Lotus 1-2-3

✔ Strong action verbs emphasize Frederick's current supervisory level.
✔ A key strength is his familiarity with computerized systems in both positions.
✔ MBA candidacy and computer training enhance Frederick's Education.

ASSET-BASED FIELD EXAMINER

RHONDA VILLARI
37 Richland Street
Turner, KS 66106

Residence: 913/ 555-3781   *Business:* 913/ 555-3000

EXPERIENCE: **Asset-Based Field Examiner**
SUBURBAN NATIONAL BANK
Kansas City, KS   1990 to present

Conduct field audits of current and prospective $5M - $50M commercial customers. Evaluate and report on financial condition and collateral through reviews of A/R, A/P, inventory, and general accounting procedures.

Consistently receive commendations for quality of work. Recommended for management position.

Accounting Assistant
HASTINGS CLOTHING WAREHOUSE
Kansas City, KS   part-time, 1989 to 1990

Performed general accounting duties including asset and liability analysis and inventory and depreciation analysis.

EDUCATION: **Bachelor of Science**
KANSAS STATE UNIVERSITY
Manhattan, KS   1990

Finance Major with concentration in Accounting.

coursework: Managerial Accounting, Cost Accounting, Investments, Financial Management, International Banking

honors: Dean's List (8 semesters)
Student Accounting Society

Planning to pursue an MBA in Finance part-time.

References available upon request

✔ Rhonda uses italics throughout her resume to emphasize key points.
✔ She elaborates on her Education because her job history is short.
✔ As an alternative to citing her G.P.A., Rhonda notes Dean's List achievements.

GEORGE HUGHES
1332-H Columbia Court
Houston, TX 77023
713/ 555-4507

OBJECTIVE: Assistant Actuary leading to Associate and Fellow in the Society of Actuaries

EDUCATION: **Bachelor of Arts in Economics** **1988**
TEXAS A&M UNIVERSITY GALVESTON, TX

Concentration: Finance. G.P.A.: 3.6

Enrolled for 100 Exam in Calculus and Linear Algebra.

COURSEWORK: Financial Analysis, Statistics, Econometrics, Public Finance, Corporate Finance, Accounting, Personal Finance, Investments.

EXPERIENCE: **Research Economist** **1990 to present**
TEXAS DEPARTMENT OF COMMERCE HOUSTON, TX

- Analyzed labor statistical reports from service industries throughout Texas to determine breakdown of age and gender.
- Generated monthly employment, hour and earning estimates based on survey results.
- Contacted employers to verify statistics and complete reports.
- Trained newly hired economists.
- Utilized SPSS, a demographics program for the IBM-PC.

Account Controller / Securities **1988 to 1990**
EMBARCADERO BANK HOUSTON, TX

- Provided custodian financial services to fund investments.
- Controlled and administered the portfolio's assets.
- Processed liabilities and income for daily security investment transactions.
- Worked with money managers to resolve account problems.

✔ George's Objective is a statement of the formal career path in his field.
✔ His Degree, Exam, and Coursework substantiate his Objective.
✔ His current position describes research, training, and computer experience.

KATHERINE MALLOY
8 Hawley Circle
Bartonville, IL 61607

Residence: 309/ 555-2355   *Business:* 309/ 555-6065

PROFESSIONAL EXPERIENCE:

HARDY COMMERCIAL BANKS • Peoria, IL

Assistant Treasurer/ Bank Officer (1991 to present)
Direct operations and customer service activities at this full-service bank.
Achieved #1 standing in customer satisfaction and fund retention in 1991.

- Oversee operation of ATM networks.
- Review loan applications for submission to Board of Directors.
- Function as Manager at all branches as needed.

Mortgage Originator (1987 to 1991)
Prepared mortgage applications for submission to secondary markets.

- Interviewed, qualified, and advised customers.
- Compiled and verified appropriate documentation.
- Provided liaison between bank and other financial institutions.

PEORIA PEOPLE'S BANK • Peoria Heights, IL

Management Trainee (1986 to 1987)
Branch operations including balancing procedures, business development, customer relations, product knowledge, and personnel management.

Senior Customer Service Representative (1985 to 1986)
Customer Service Representative (1984 to 1985)

EDUCATION:

AMERICAN INSTITUTE OF BANKING   1989
Commercial Loans, ATM services, Personal Investments

BRADLEY UNIVERSITY   1981 to 1984
Business Coursework - 90 credits

✔ Katherine distinguishes herself from all other bank managers by emphasizing in italics her substantial achievement in her current position.
✔ Management Training and other courses compensate for her lack of Degree.

ASSISTANT CONTROLLER

DREW VICKERY

59 Muddy River Road
Etna, PA 15223
412/ 555-8883

EDUCATION:

UNIVERSITY OF PITTSBURGH • Pittsburgh, PA
Certificate in Accountancy in progress (6 courses completed)

THIEL COLLEGE • Greenville, PA
B.S. in Business Administration (1985)

EMPLOYMENT:

1991 - present MEDICAL EQUIPMENT COMPANY • Pittsburgh, PA
Assistant Controller - For medical equipment distributor. Perform collections, payroll, note and depreciation schedules, and inter-company accounting. Maintain general ledgers on IBM AS/400. Reconcile accounts and bank statements and prepare sales and payroll taxes.

1989 - 1991 MKS ELECTRONICS • Berkeley Hills, PA
Accounting Manager - For small electronics firm. Oversaw general ledger, trial balance, and preparation of financial reports including balance sheet and income statement. Maintained depreciation and fixed asset schedules. Processed payroll from time cards to payroll tax reports. Assisted and supervised accounting clerk with accounts payable and accounts receivable work.

1986 - 1989 BRILLIANCE MANUFACTURING COMPANY • Crafton, PA
Bookkeeper - Reported directly to the Controller of medium-size clothing manufacturer. Handled accounts payable, accounts receivable, journal entries, trial balance, and general ledger work processed on a computerized system. Calculated employee time cards and prepared payroll data. Processed labor and material for open cost book and prepared work-in-process summary.

REFERENCES:

Available upon request

✔ Drew presents Education first because he is earning his Certificate.
✔ He capitalizes company names to highlight his diverse work environments.
✔ Dates are prominent in the left margin to emphasize employment continuity.

AUDIT MANAGER

ERNEST LABETTE, CPA
18 Town Way
Peabody, MA 01960
508/ 555-7434

EDUCATION:	BABSON GRADUATE SCHOOL OF BUSINESS

EDUCATION: BABSON GRADUATE SCHOOL OF BUSINESS
                      MBA in Finance   1988

                      • Internship at Bank of New England

                      BRANDEIS UNIVERSITY
                      BA in Accounting   1986

EXPERIENCE: ARTHUR ANDERSEN COMPANY

                      Audit Manager – Small Business Division   **1991 to present**

Handle audit engagements and develop client relationships in the emerging small business market. Client emphasis in service industries. Received performance-based promotion.

Provide special services to clients including:

• development of accounting and management controls

• research of technical accounting issues

• coordination of services in connection with client transactions

• guidance in complying with financial reporting requirements

Also supervise and train staff, contribute to staffing decisions, and direct budgeting and billing arrangements for engagements.

Audit Senior – General Audit Dept.   **1988 to 1991**

Member of the audit staff of both SEC and large privately held corporation engagements. Client base mainly in high tech R&D. Received extensive training in audit procedures, researching technical issues, and in financial reporting requirements.

REFERENCES: Available upon request

    ✔ CPA following Ernest's name immediately establishes his credentials.
    ✔ His degrees from prestigious schools strengthen his candidacy.
    ✔ Ernest stresses Client Services before his management functions.

AUDIT SUPERVISOR

LORRAINE BARREAU
81 Franklin Street
Shreveport, LA 71102
504/ 555-2276

EDUCATION:

LOUISIANA STATE UNIVERSITY • Shreveport, LA
Masters of Business Administration (1987)

- Concentration in Finance.
- Overall G.P.A.: 3.8.
- Coursework included Security Analysis and Portfolio Construction, Money and Capital Markets, Corporate Finance, Personal Finance, Financial Management, Investments.

OUR LADY OF HOLY CROSS COLLEGE • New Orleans, LA
Bachelor of Arts in Finance *with honor* (1985)

PROFESSIONAL EXPERIENCE:

HOLMES BANK AND TRUST
INTERNAL AUDITING DEPARTMENT • Bossier City, LA

Senior Audit Supervisor (1991 to present)

- Examine and evaluate bank operations to assess the level of compliance with regulatory policies and management's procedures and directives.
- Plan and implement audits of bank branches.
- Consult with operating managers to determine audit needs and to plan for new information systems development.
- Supervise and evaluate the performance of 6 audit staffers. Assign and schedule work, direct staff with regard to audit procedures, and review audit reports.

Audit Supervisor (1989 to 1991)

- Investigated the operations of all bank-wide functions including analyze the degree of management control and the effectiveness of established procedures.
- Presented final audit reports and defended recommendations to bank management.
- Trained and supervised new audit staff.

Senior Auditor (1988 to 1989)
Staff Auditor (1987 to 1988)

✔ Although Lorraine's audit experience is substantial, she still presents her Education first, as it establishes the appropriate professional credentials for her field.
✔ To avoid repetition she does not describe her two earliest positions.

BANK MANAGER

ALBERT COREY
177 Old Orchard Road
Mallory, TN 38109

Residence: 901/ 555-8874   *Business:* 901/ 555-2020

Summary of Qualifications:

- Progressive management experience in banking operations.
- Knowledge of alternative loan structures, payment schedules, and business development.
- Proven ability to initiate successful training programs and motivate staff.
- Solid organization, communication, and problem-solving skills.
- Strong customer service orientation.

Professional Experience:

RIVERSIDE BANK • Riverside, TN

Branch Manager (1988 to present). Supervise and maintain administrative control over Department Managers and branch staff in order to sustain profitability and growth for a full-service commercial bank.

- Establish and maintain branch budgets.
- Evaluate and approve all major financial transactions.
- Review and approve consumer credit.
- Solicit new business opportunities including "cross-selling" of products.

Assistant Branch Manager (1986 to 1988)

MALE STOP • Memphis, TN
HAPPY DAYS CARD SHOP • Memphis, TN
Retail Management Positions (1980 to 1986)

Education/Training:

AMERICAN INSTITUTE OF BANKING
Principles of Lending, Bank Management, Commercial Law, Selling Skills

DE SOTO HIGH SCHOOL
Diploma *(College Curriculum)*

✔ Albert's Summary stresses skills appropriate for other management jobs.
✔ He de-emphasizes prior retail experience by omitting job descriptions.
✔ Banking courses and H.S. diploma compensate for his lack of a degree.

BILLING MANAGER

MARJORIE HOWLAND
393 Claypool Road
Middletown, IN 47356
317/ 555-2585

AREAS OF EXPERTISE

Billing • **Accounts Receivable** • **Credit and Collections** • **Payroll**

PROFESSIONAL EXPERIENCE

Billing Manager
SQUEAKY KLEEN CORPORATION • Muncie, IN   1988 to present
(National commercial cleaning service franchise with $300M in annual sales)

- Direct 10 Supervisors with ultimate responsibility for the processing of 11,000 weekly invoices by 26 Billing Clerks.

- Closely coordinate with Payroll, A/R, and Credit departments as well as company CEO.

- Provide troubleshooting of accounts via telephone and personal contact.

- Assisted in the conversion from a manual to on-line billing system.

- Streamlined billing procedures resulting in a substantial increase in company revenues.

Payroll Manager
HIGHLAND MEDICAL OFFICES • Selma, IN   1985 to 1988
(Five-physician, 3-office medical practice)

- Supervised staff of 5 in Payroll, Billing, A/R, and Credit and Collections functions.

- Converted the Payroll and A/R functions to computer.

- Wrote procedures manuals to document Payroll, A/R, and Billing.

Office Manager
LYNN MEDICAL OFFICES • Lynn, IN   1980 to 1985

EDUCATION

B.S. in Business Administration   1985
ANDERSON UNIVERSITY • Anderson, IN

✔ Marjorie's Areas of Expertise section both summarizes her current proficiencies and allows her to seek a new position in any of these areas.
✔ Company descriptions clarify the scope of her responsibilities.

BOOKKEEPER

MARIE OLNEY
17 Clifford Court
McLean, VA 22101
703/ 555-0338

EXPERIENCE:

Bookkeeper
PROCOMM INDUSTRIES
Arlington, VA   1987 to present

Perform computerized bookkeeping functions for a division of 70 employees.

Oversee A/P, A/R, payroll, inventory, expenses, cash reconciliations, petty cash, collections, and cost control.

Expert in Lotus 1-2-3

Train and supervise junior staff.

Payroll Assistant
BRITT PUMP MANUFACTURING
Shirlington, VA   1985 to 1987

Collected and assembled bi-monthly payroll information for 1500 employees.

Generated payroll reports.

Assisted in preparing federal tax reports on computer.

Consulted with employees on benefit plans.

EDUCATION:

A.S. in Accounting   1984
STRAYER COLLEGE
Washington, DC

Computer Science Courses   1985
ARLINGTON COMMUNITY COLLEGE
Arlington, VA

REFERENCES: Available upon request

✔ Marie uses several effective techniques to avoid a sparse-looking resume: large left margins; job title, company name, city and state all on separate lines; and a closing statement about references.

C.F.O.

NATHAN WOHL, C.P.A.

2455 Hillsdale Avenue
Cambrian Park, CA 95124

Residence: 408/ 555-4056
Office: 408/ 555-7030

1987 - present

INFOCOMP CORPORATION   Santa Clara, CA
(International computer consulting organization with $75M annual revenues)

CFO / Controller. Oversee financial, planning, information systems, and tax compliance activities. Member of the Executive Committee which formulates financial, operating, and administrative policy.

Finance

- Upgraded the accounting department including personnel, job descriptions and financial controls to meet the requirements of a growing organization.

- Improved collections through the development of a receivables performance measurement system to which project managers are held accountable.

- Developed cash management techniques with banks to optimize the utilization of free cash against revolving debt or temporary investments.

- Directed the integration of an acquired software organization.

Planning

- Developed PC-based techniques in tax planning and budget planning.

Information Systems

- Directed the formulation of the company's systems strategy.

- Established an information system that provides world-wide accounting and performance information and a comprehensive database for marketing.

1985 - 1987

CAPITAL CORPORATION   San Jose, CA
(Venture capital firm specializing in $10-20M high-tech investments)

Controller. Administered the financial operations of its wholly-owned investments and participated in the development of a joint venture plan.

1983 - 1985

ALPERT & MARLEY, CPA's   Cupertino, CA
Senior Auditor / Staff Auditor.

1982

SANTA CLARA UNIVERSITY   Santa Clara, CA
M.S. - Financial Management

1980

MENLO COLLEGE   Atherton, CA
B.S.B.A. - Accounting

✔ Nathan omits section headings and uses a horizontal line to segment sections.
✔ He organizes his current position into major functions in the left margin.
✔ Company descriptions provide the reader with a frame of reference.

DOROTHY SPECK, C.P.A.

27 Dupont Drive
Shaker Heights, OH 44120   216/ 555-2149

EMPLOYMENT:

Manager - Corporate Practice Group
Tax Department
Big Six Accounting Firm • Cleveland, OH   1990 to present

Tax Manager in 142-member tax department of a big six CPA firm:

- Co-manage the 32-person Corporate Practice Group which specializes in the taxation and tax planning for corporations and sole proprietorships.

- Wrote comprehensive practice manual for payroll taxation practice.

- Implement efficient tax return preparation techniques; developed training programs and department-wide quality control systems.

Vice President, Taxation
Cuyahoga Accountancy • Garfield Heights, OH   1985 to 1990

Tax Principal of a 22-member local CPA firm:

- Directed corporate tax preparation, consulting, and research.

- Developed and expanded range of client services.

- Specialized in unique engagements requiring innovative problem-solving.

- Prepared tax information letters for corporate clients.

- Provided in-house tax training, quality control, and internal workflow systems.

Senior Accountant / Staff Accountant
Bailey and Jones • South Euclid, OH   1980 - 1985

EDUCATION:

Master of Science in Taxation
Case Western Reserve University • Cleveland, OH   1988

Bachelor of Science in Accountancy
University of Cincinnati • Cincinnati, OH   1980

✔ Dorothy ensures confidentiality by omitting the name of her current firm.
✔ She stresses impressive job titles and degrees in bold.
✔ She begins her most senior positions with an italicized summary description.

CONTROLLER

HERBERT STILES
43 Grant Avenue
South Burlington, VT 05401
802/ 555-7321

EXPERIENCE:

ASA COMPUTER CORPORATION • Essex Junction, VT   1990 to present
Controller

- Established line of credit used in financing working capital requirements.
- Implemented departmental budget vs. actual reporting system.
- Consolidated branch accounting operations resulting in staff reduction.
- Improved P.C.-based general ledger and A/P software to improve reporting.
- Maximized tax benefits of company re-organization.

CHAMPLAIN MANUFACTURING • Burlington, VT   1987 to 1990
Manager - Corporate Accounting

- Reduced personnel turnover through a departmental re-organization.
- Reduced time to complete monthly close of general ledger by 14%.
- Ensured compliance with tax law revisions.
- Project leader for the conversion of A/R software.
- Established a Cost Accounting System to track profitability of 450 products.

VAIL RESEARCH AND DEVELOPMENT CORP. • Burlington, VT   1985 to 1987
Senior Audit Supervisor

CHITTENDEN FINANCIAL SERVICES • Winooski, VT   1982 to 1985
Staff Auditor

EDUCATION:

TRINITY COLLEGE OF VERMONT • Burlington, VT
Master of Business Administration (1990)

UNIVERSITY OF VERMONT • Burlington, VT
Bachelor of Science in Accounting (1981)

ACCREDITATIONS:

CMA, CPA

✔ Herbert capitalizes company names to stress varied work environments.
✔ Each bulleted sentence describes a specific achievement.
✔ Accreditations are important credentials that merit a separate section.

CREDIT ANALYST

PAULA NICHOLSON
9 Damon Road
Agawam, MA 01001

Residence: 413/ 555-4144   Business: 413/ 555-1800

EDUCATION:

SPRINGFIELD COLLEGE   SPRINGFIELD, MA
MBA / Finance   **1990**

HAMPSHIRE COLLEGE   AMHERST, MA
BS / Accounting   **1986**

PROFESSIONAL EXPERIENCE:

SPRINGFIELD COMMERCIAL BANK   SPRINGFIELD, MA
Credit Analyst   **1991 to present**

- Analyzed financial statements of major corporations, large domestic and international banks, investment companies and broker/dealers to evaluate credit quality for commercial lending decisions.
- Prepared Credit Approval Summaries on client's financial position in light of current economic conditions and future business outlook.
- Established foreign exchange credit lines for international clients at capital market locations based upon their creditworthiness.
- Monitored audit status reports for 12 divisions to ensure compliance.
- Reviewed overdraft reports to safeguard the Bank's position against potential losses.

Portfolio Accountant   **1989 to 1991**

- Supervised daily accounting operations, weekly reconciliation of accounts, and administration of client relationships for 32 domestic mutual funds.
- Controlled daily pricing of funds, coordinated audit process with external auditors, and prepared management reports.

COOPER INDUSTRIES   HOLYOKE, MA
Accountant   **1986 to 1989**

✔ Paula makes the subjective decision to present her Education first, and for greater emphasis sets the section off with horizontal dividing lines.
✔ Her entry-level Accountant position is no longer important to describe.

EQUITY ANALYST INTERN

RHONDA DIETRICH
2337 Causeway Boulevard
Bronx, NY 10462
212/ 555-6662

EDUCATION:

B.S.B.A. in Finance   **1989**
UNION COLLEGE SCHOOL OF MANAGEMENT

EXPERIENCE:

Equity Analyst Intern   **1991 to present**
MANNHEIM INVESTMENTS GMBH – Frankfurt, Germany

Perform financial and market analyses of individual publicly listed German companies and their respective industries; present results and make investment recommendations. Produce an international market news service, an up-to-date source of information on the German market, and the variables which affect it, for all overseas equity branches.

Assistant to Vice President   **1989 to 1991**
PRUDENTIAL-BACHE SECURITIES – New York City, NY

Formulated and maintained a large client data base. Researched key industries and developed a direct mail marketing campaign targeting those industries for potential expansion of broker's client base. Created reference manual of sales materials for use by brokers. Independently studied products and investment strategies.

Market Researcher   **Summer 1989**
CITY ISLAND BANK – Bronx, NY

Developed and administered survey to solicit customer satisfaction information for use in future planning by local bank. Analyzed and presented results to President.

Student Marketing Coordinator   **part time, 1988 to 1989**
NATIONAL MANAGEMENT ORGANIZATION OF STUDENTS

Coordinated a staff of 7 in the marketing of business internship programs to executive decision-makers of top U.S. companies. Negotiated contracts, created marketing literature, and planned public relations activities. Personally established new accounts and functioned as corporate liaison. Conducted board and staff meetings.

LANGUAGES:

Fluent in German and French

✔ Rhonda limits her job descriptions to four lines to invite scanning.
✔ Summer and part-time employment are valuable business experiences.
✔ Foreign languages are an important asset to list for international business.

RICHARD LEE
505 Florence Street
Branwood, SC 29610
803/ 555-9034

PROFESSIONAL EXPERIENCE:

PERMA-FORM BOX COMPANY   GREENVILLE, SC
($25M manufacturer of corrugated cardboard products)

Director of Finance and Administration	**1991 to present**
Controller	**1987 to 1991**
Senior Accountant	**1983 to 1987**

PROFESSIONAL HIGHLIGHTS:

- Direct the daily operations of Accounting, Data Processing, Personnel, Customer Service, Credit, Purchasing, and Shipping. *Report to Executive Vice President.*

- Established policies and procedures for newly created MIS Department. *Automated accounting function and implemented computerized MRP system.*

- Participate in strategic planning decisions. *Enhance production operations through the continuous phase-out of unprofitable lines.*

- Analyzed and recommended budget and staffing needs based on sales projections. *Centralized the accounting function and redistributed personnel.*

- Prepared financial statements including SEC filings and corporate income tax returns. *Handled cash management function.*

- Managed corporate-wide health, liability, and property insurance programs. Reduced insurance premiums by eliminating duplicate coverage. *Researched alternative health insurance programs and implemented third-party administrator resulting in $300K savings.*

- Administered personnel and benefits programs. *Terminated defined benefits plan and implemented 401K plan.*

EDUCATION:

FURMAN UNIVERSITY   GREENVILLE, SC
   B.S. in Accounting   **1983**

✔ Richard's resume condenses many years of experience onto one page.
✔ He summarizes duties and emphasizes key elements in italics.
✔ Richard's Education is of lesser importance so he presents it last.

FINANCIAL ANALYST

PROFESSIONAL OVERVIEW

BRUCE HAGOPIAN
2004 King Avenue
Billings, MT 59101
406/ 555-3776

I am seeking a Financial Analyst position within a small professional services environment which will build on my training and experience in accounting and computerized business systems. I have acquired a broad range of accounting experience and am eager to utilize it in a higher level accounting function. Ideally, a new position will offer professional challenge and an opportunity to grow even further within the field.

I hold an AAS in Accounting and have completed a Certificate in Business Systems at the Microcomputer Systems Educational Schools. Throughout my career I have proven myself a dedicated and loyal professional who is well-organized, detail-oriented, and successful at getting the job done independently. I am able to learn quickly, keep current through professional publications, and enjoy the stimulation of new challenges.

Highlights:

- 8+ years broad-based accounting experience.

- Positions encompassing payroll, banking, G/L, A/R, A/P, credit & collections.

- Diverse industry exposure — banking, advertising, health care, retail.

- Knowledge of computerized systems for business and accounting functions.

- Ability to quickly analyze and understand "the total business picture."

- Strong mathematical aptitude and analytical skills.

- Facility in posting and reconciling general ledger through trial balance.

- Experience in processing end-of-the-month accruals and depreciations.

- Knowledge of automated payroll systems and cost control systems.

✔ Bruce's alternative resume sparks the reader's interest and also de-emphasizes any career drawbacks, such as gaps in employment.
✔ Specific positions, companies, and dates can be supplied at an interview.

FINANCIAL CONSULTANT

LAWRENCE HEMPHILL
279 Spring Valley Road
Pine Hills, FL 32808

Residence: 407/ 555-0366   *Business:* 407/ 555-8080

SUMMARY:

Licensed full-service financial broker • Strong background in accounting, finance, and sales & marketing • Solid experience planning and managing diversified portfolios for small companies and upper income individuals • Proven ability to perform financial analysis of listed and OTC equities.

PROFESSIONAL EXPERIENCE:

KALE & LEACHMAN, BROKERS   ORLANDO, FL
FINANCIAL CONSULTANT   **1987 to present**

- Manage diversified portfolios of 200 small business owners and senior level executives. Assist clients to formulate financial objectives; conduct asset reviews; and design and implement investment strategies.
- Prospect new clients through lead generation and follow-up. Personally established more than 100 new accounts. Ranked first out of 10 in sales during 1989, generating $200K in commissions.

EMPIRE BROKERAGE CORPORATION   TAFT, FL
ACCOUNT EXECUTIVE   **1984 to 1987**

- Personally increased client base from zero to 210 accounts.
- Taught college-accredited brokerage course which emphasized product knowledge and sales skills.
- Appointed to Sales Club for generating $100K in commissions during first year.
- Completed **Executive Trainee Program (1983 to 1984)**.

EDUCATION:

ROLLINS COLLEGE   WINTER PARK, FL
B.A. IN FINANCE   **1983**

✔ Lawrence's Summary encompasses key credentials from both positions.
✔ Job descriptions incorporate important figures to substantiate achievements.
✔ Executive Training is listed, but not described, to save space.

FINANCIAL SERVICES MANAGER

PETER HEMENYA
52 Lawson Road
Guild, NH 03754
603/ 555-6478

OBJECTIVE

Financial Services Manager with a large retail bank

EMPLOYMENT

Financial Services Manager	**1990 to present**
UNION SAVINGS BANK	GUILD, NH
Manager / Assistant Manager	**1988 to 1990**
Sales / Service Representative	**1986 to 1988**
CAPITAL SAVINGS BANK (SBLI Department)	EXETER, NH
Assistant Manager	**1983 to 1986**
PATRIOT SAVINGS BANK	EXETER, NH

ACHIEVEMENTS

- Spearheaded branch to #1 in customer satisfaction and fund retention.

- During an acquisition, integrated bank personnel, services, and deposits.

- Oversaw the opening of bank branch - implemented personnel and QC policies.

- Grew bank portfolio to $35M in insurance policies/$17M in retirement plans.

- Initiated community outreach programs to promote bank's products/services.

EDUCATION

B.S. in Business Administration (Finance)	**1983**
NEW ENGLAND COLLEGE	HENNIKER, NH

✔ Peter's format is modern, crisp, functional, and exceptionally easy to read.
✔ His Objective is precise and supported by his highlighted job titles.
✔ To avoid repetition he combines key achievements from his whole career.

KRISTIN BLOUNT

19-D Gross Pointe Apartments • Bellevue, IL 61604   309/ 555-5021

EDUCATION:

BACHELOR OF SCIENCE IN ACCOUNTANCY • Bradley University   1988

TRAINING SEMINARS in International Finance, Business Writing   1990

COMPUTER EXPERIENCE:

Hardware: IBM PC, HP VECTRA, PRIME 9950, IBM SYSTEMS 36

Software: Lotus 1-2-3, Pre-Audit, Accounting Plus, MS Word

EMPLOYMENT:

SHAW INTERNATIONAL BANK • PEORIA, IL

International Accountant (1991 to present). Analyze foreign loans, foreign exchange and money market transactions. Investigate and analyze prior period accrual adjustments. Perform monthly yield analysis and prepare financial statement comments. Prepare monthly closing adjustments for three entities. Prepare reports on foreign exposure, liquidity review, financial statements and management reports on foreign loan profitability.

HANRAHAN ACCOUNTANTS, INC. • PEORIA, IL

Staff Accountant (1990 to 1991). Compiled and analyzed client records, verified supporting documentation, and prepared accounting and auditing work papers. Analyzed balance sheet and income statements to determine validity and accuracy. Assisted in the preparation of financial statements. Prepared corporate, partnership, and individual tax returns.

BOYD TRUCK BODY CORPORATION • East PEORIA, IL

Accounting Assistant (1988 to 1990). Managed all A/R and A/P functions, reconciled monthly bank statements, and prepared weekly payroll checks. Compiled data required by independent accountant for tax reports and financial statements. Rectified account problems.

References available upon request.

✔ Kristin considers her Education and Computer Experience key credentials, so presents those sections first.
✔ She inserts her employment dates in each paragraph to de-emphasize them.

DAVID SHURTLEFF

6 Thomas Smith Road • Carrboro, NC 27510   919/ 555-2997

EDUCATION:

MBA / International Economics   1990
UNIVERSITY OF NORTH CAROLINA • Chapel Hill, NC

BA / Finance   1987
WAKE FOREST UNIVERSITY • Winston-Salem, NC

EXPERIENCE:

Internal Auditor   1990 - present
GRAPHI-SOFT CORPORATION • Research Triangle Park, NC
(International software manufacturer • $ 250M annual sales)

- Plan, direct, and perform financial statement and operational audits of domestic and foreign subsidiaries. Specialize in international divisions.
- Prepare reports recommending accounting control improvements for review and implementation by top corporate executives and divisional management.
- Assist external auditors in performing their year-end audits.

Contract Administrator   1988 - 1990
DURCON INDUSTRIES • Durham, NC

- Administered international sales contracts up to $1M including preparation of invoices, identification of export/import regulations, arrangement of customs inspections, authorization of shipment releases, and customer relations.
- Automated document tracking system to expedite contract administration.

Audit Trainee   1987 - 1988
KLINE, GOLD, & PIERCE, CPA'S • Chapel Hill, NC

COMPUTER SKILLS:

Languages: BASIC, FORTRAN, PASCAL, C.
Software: Lotus 1-2-3, G/L Plus, dBase.
Hardware: IBM-PC, IBM System 36.

LANGUAGE SKILLS:

Fluent in reading, writing, and speaking German and Russian.

✔ David's resume is a well-balanced presentation of Education, Experience, Computer Skills, and Language Skills in order of importance to his career.
✔ He emphasizes his international experience wherever appropriate.

INVESTMENT BROKER

JONATHAN LEVINE
1168 Nakoma Road
Madison, WI 53703
608/ 555-2668

EXPERIENCE:

TURNER ASSOCIATES • Middleton, WI   1991 to present
CREIGHTON-DEWAR INVESTMENTS • Madison, WI   1987 to 1991

Investment Broker
Gained solid record for devising marketing strategies, securing new business, servicing and expanding existing accounts, and generating revenues.

- Developed a new client base of 375+ high net worth individuals.
- Achieved #3 ranking in production for experienced broker sales class.
- Consistently generated revenues with an average of 5+ new sales daily.
- Advised clients on portfolio structure, financial markets, and individual risk tolerance.
- Expedited daily stock trades by communicating timely information.
- Researched and recommended 150+ publicly traded companies.
- Planned and executed direct mail marketing programs.
- Recruited and trained 6 new brokers, generating $450,000 in revenues.
- NASD Series 7 and 63 licensed.

UNITED UNDERWRITERS • Hilldale, WI   1985 to 1987

Sales Representative
Sold insurance to local retail customers primarily through cold-calling.

EDUCATION:

MARQUETTE UNIVERSITY • Milwaukee, WI   1985

B.A. in Finance

References available upon request

✔ Jonathan combines simiilar positions at two companies to avoid repetition.
✔ He limits the explanation of his earlier position because it was entry-level.
✔ Jonathan includes facts and figures in his achievements for emphasis.

JUNIOR ACCOUNTANT

NINA KREIBICH
883 Jefferson Avenue
Gorder, UT 84403
801/ 555-2154

EDUCATION:

Bachelor of Arts in Accounting   **1990**
WEBER STATE COLLEGE   OGDEN, UT

RESULTS PENDING FROM C.P.A. EXAM

Anticipate part-time graduate studies.

COURSEWORK:

Auditing, Cost Accounting, Advanced Accounting, Taxation Corporate Finance, Business Evaluation, Computer Accounting

EXPERIENCE:

Junior Accountant   **1990 to present**
CARSON PRODUCTS, INC.   OGDEN, UT

Assist in accounting functions for a small manufacturing firm:

- Payroll Preparation and Processing
- Accounts Payable, Accounts Receivable
- Posting to General Ledger
- Tax Filing
- Preparation of records for outside auditor
- Month end closings and trial balances

Payroll Accountant   **p.t., 1989 to 1990**
KRIEG SHOES   NORTH OGDEN, UT

Utilized Lotus 1-2-3 in the preparation of payroll records for a retail chain with three branches.

Payroll Clerk   **p.t., 1988 to 1989**
HILL REHABILITATION HOSPITAL   ROY, UT

Processed bi-weekly payroll for up to 450 health care personnel.

REFERENCES:

Personal and professional references available upon request

✔ Nina has held only one full-time position since graduation, so her Education and Coursework sections are appropriate to present first.
✔ The C.P.A. Exam and graduate school plans establish her career track.

LOAN ADMINISTRATOR

VICTORIA TENG

1733 Chambersburg Road
Huber Heights, OH 45424

Residence: 513/ 555-9118   *Business:* 513/ 555-0666

PROFESSIONAL EXPERIENCE

Loan Administrator   **1990 to present**
KITTYHAWK BANK   DAYTON, OH
(Full-service commercial bank staffing 125+ employees at main office and 5 branches)

Administer $400M loan portfolio comprised of commercial, residential, construction, home equity
and consumer loans and reserve credit. Supervise staff of 18 Lending Supervisors, Processors and
Servicers, and support personnel. Direct efforts to establish networks within secondary loan market.
Supported in the software conversion for servicing mortgages resulting in increased revenues.
Under consideration for promotion to Assistant Vice President.

Bank Officer   **1986 to 1990**
DEPOSITOR'S TRUST   NORTHRIDGE, OH
(Full-service community bank staffing 50 employees at main office and 3 branches)

Performed personnel and credit management functions for all branches including staffing, payroll/
benefits administration, loan processing, and collections procedures. Revised personnel manual and
general procedural manual. Represented bank at professional and community public relations
functions. Reported directly to the President and assumed responsibility for total bank operation in
his absence. Maintained positive working relationship with Board of Directors.

Prior positions (1980 to 1986) included **Assistant Treasurer, Head Teller, Teller.**

EDUCATION

A.S. Degree in Finance   **1989**
UNIVERSITY OF DAYTON   DAYTON, OH

Certificate of Achievement   **1986 to present**
DAYTON INSTITUTE OF BANKING EDUCATION   DAYTON, OH

Personnel Management, Human Relations in Business, Principles of Management, Effective
Business Writing, Personal Money Management, Introduction to Savings Association Business,
Mortgage Loan Servicing, Real Estate Principles, Secondary Mortgage Market, and Compliance.

✔ Victoria's job descriptions convey a breadth of banking experience.
✔ She notes an impending promotion to boost her candidacy.
✔ Victoria supports her career growth with ongoing banking education.

LOAN MANAGER

CHARLES TIBBETS
24 Appian Way
Little Rock, AR 72201

Residence: 501/ 555-7044   Business: 501/ 555-2300

EXPERIENCE: GILLIAM BANK & TRUST • Little Rock, AR
(6-branch, publicly-owned thrift institution • Assets of $425M)

Construction Lending Manager   **1990 to present**
Plan and direct construction lending activities with sensitivity toward
shifting market conditions, the need for flexibility in tailoring loan
programs, and the value of loan quality over loan volume. Demonstrate
the ability to attract and retain both loan and deposit accounts. Consistently maintain a loan portfolio requiring few workout problems, even
in depressed markets.

- Established construction lending function as a stand-alone profit
  center for Bank.

- Grew Construction Lending Group into a 10-person Department.

- Personally managed $18M portfolio and collected origination fees of
  $325M in 1990.

- Contributed to $35.4M in loan growth in 1991, a 16% increase over
  1990.

- Actively participated in net commercial loan growth of $6.5M for 1991
  while providing sound management of an existing portfolio of $23M
  ($19M advanced).

Retail Lending Product Manager   **1988 to 1990**
Personally spearheaded the establishment of the Bank's Equity Line of
Credit resulting in the advancement of $4.75M within one year. With the
addition of Representatives and Credit Line Underwriters, the Bank has
advanced $53M.

Assistant Treasurer   **1986 to 1988**
Management Trainee   **1983 to 1986**

EDUCATION: FLORIDA ATLANTIC UNIVERSITY • Boca Raton, FL
B.A. in Economics   **1983**

MEMBERSHIPS: Commercial Bank Association, Retail Credit Roundtable, Banking Managers Association

---

✔ Charles' current job description effectively incorporates his banking philosophy with his specific achievements.
✔ His list of memberships demonstrates his commitment to the banking field.

LOAN OFFICER

EVELYN TURKANIS
907 Pierremont Road
Shreveport, LA 71102

Residence: 318/ 555-2117   *Business:* 318/ 555-6000

EXPERIENCE: NORTON BANK   SHREVEPORT, LA
                     Loan Officer - Media Business   **1989 to present**

- **Generated $40M+ in loan commitments** from twelve national clients acquiring cable television systems and radio stations in various stages from construction to MSO's. Manage all phases of the analysis of the financial package, on-site evaluation of properties and market, and preliminary and final structuring of the deal. Negotiate and troubleshoot with corporate presidents, senior bank managers, and attorneys.

- **Cited by Manager for exceeding standards** in business development, administration, maintaining credit quality, and personal development. Secured ten new clients and greatly improved communications with one unresponsive client. Doubled actual gross profits over forecasted goal in F.Y. '90. Exceeded gross profit goal for F.Y. '91.

- **Selected to complete numerous special projects**. Utilized Lotus 1-2-3 to create database of referral sources. Researched and reported on telephone industry as prospective loan market. Interviewed applicants for Loan Officer Development Program. Assisted senior lenders in writing annual reviews of clients.

Credit Analyst   **1987 to 1989**

- **Reviewed Bank's commercial portfolio annually** including Fortune 500 companies. Analyzed each company's financial condition, assessing its market place and business risk. Presented recommendations to senior management.

- **Volunteered for company-supported activities.** United Way, Chamber of Commerce, Aerobics Leader.

EDUCATION: SOUTHERN METHODIST UNIVERSITY   DALLAS, TX
                     Bachelor of Arts in Finance   **1986**

- Concentration in Economics and Banking

✔ Evelyn identifies major areas of achievement while at Norton Bank.
✔ Her descriptions are comprehensive and include pertinent figures.
✔ Volunteer activities show company loyalty and community involvement.

MORTGAGE UNDERWRITER

LUCILLE FIGUEROA
1024 Van Buren Boulevard
Catonsville, MD 21228

Residence: 301/ 555-2933   *Business:* 301/ 555-7880

PROFESSIONAL EXPERIENCE:

Mortgage Underwriter
PEOPLE'S BANK • Baltimore, MD   1989 to present

- Originate and review mortgage applications.
- Possess sign-off authority for loans up to $350K.
- Portfolio loans and sell loans on the secondary market to FNMA and FHLMC.
- Provide liaison between credit union and secondary markets and mortgage insurance companies regarding current regulations and procedures.
- Implement QA through the review of 80% of loans following closings.
- Train new mortgage originators.

Branch Manager
NATIONAL UNIBANK • Ruxton, MD   1986 to 1989

- Managed an 18-person main office.
- Trained and evaluated branch personnel.
- Underwrote mortgage and consumer loans up to $125K.
- Assumed responsibility for branch loans in the absence of loan officer.
- Controlled cash flow with daily limits up to $275K.

Assistant Branch Manager
Branch Supervisor / Head Teller
WOLCOTT TRUST • Parkville, MD   1982 to 1986

EDUCATION:

A.S. in Banking Studies
AMERICAN INSTITUTE OF BANKING   1986

CERTIFICATIONS:

Licensed Agent
SAVINGS BANK LIFE INSURANCE (SBLI)

Notary Public

References available upon request

- ✔ Lucille's resume demonstrates a direct career path in banking.
- ✔ She omits job descriptions of earlier positions to avoid repetition.
- ✔ Certifications are important credentials in the banking industry.

NORMAN HOBBS
18 Cunimisset Road
Warwick, RI 02886
401/ 555-2098

PROFESSIONAL EXPERIENCE:

SENTRY BANK • Warwick, RI
Note Teller / Commercial Loan Department (1991 to present)
Administer all requisite procedures and paperwork related to notes, guaranties, collateral, and renewals. Research and resolve inquiries and requests from lenders, branches, and customers.

Senior Customer Service Representative (1988 to 1991)
Provided quality customer service with emphasis on recognizing customer needs. Assumed responsibility for processing transactions, problem resolution, cross-selling bank services, controlling cash supply, maintaining security requirements, assisting in staff scheduling and monitoring, maintaining ATM's, and preparing reports.

FIDELITY BANK & TRUST • Pawtucket, RI
Assistant Branch Manager (1986 to 1988)
Assisted in day-to-day operations encompassing personnel, customer service, security, purchasing and recordkeeping. Aided in the reorganization of the branch office resulting in the tripling of anticipated volume. Built the NOW Account Department from 0 to 6,500 accounts. Established cost-effective inventory control system.

FEDERATED BANKS OF RHODE ISLAND • Providence, RI
Customer Service Representative (1985 to 1986)
Contacted customers via telephone to assist in rectifying problems related to late payments.

Head Teller / Teller (1983 to 1985)

PROFESSIONAL COURSEWORK:

CAPE COD COMMUNITY COLLEGE
A.S. in Business (1983)

AMERICAN INSTITUTE OF BANKING
Branch Management, NOW accounts, Commercial Lending, Collections

---

References available upon request

✔ Norman's job descriptions reflect his breadth of banking experience in lending, customer service, and operations.
✔ American Institute of Banking courses support that experience.

PAYROLL MANAGER

SHEILA RAPUCCI
56 Winship Court
Norwalk, CT 06853
203/ 555-0026

EXPERIENCE:

STOP & SHOP CORPORATION
(34-store grocery chain • $750M sales • 8,000 employees)

Payroll Manager (1985 to present)
Plan and manage daily operations of the Central Payroll Department. Interact with top management groups up to the C.E.O. Member of Payroll Task Forces. *Received numerous Corporate Performance Awards.*

Highlights:

• Guarantee the accuracy, integrity, and maintenance of payroll information through the incorporation of changes in company policies and tax laws.

• Insure the timely deposit of withholding taxes for each payroll according to government regulation schedules.

• Effectively process and maintain the integrity of special, more complex payroll disbursements.

• Trained and supported payroll staff at store locations in the conversion from a manual to a computerized system.

• Monitor external payroll processing vendor.

• Recommend enhancements to PC system.

Assistant Payroll Manager (1980 to 1985)

TRAINING:

POST COLLEGE

A.S. in Business Administration (1979)

ORGANIZATIONS: National Payroll Managers Association

References available upon request

✔ Sheila describes her employer to emphasize her responsibilities.
✔ She highlights Awards within the opening paragraph to spark interest.
✔ Sheila explains only her current position to avoid repetition.

DOROTHY HELMS
104 Locke Drive
Twin Lake, FL 33604
813/ 555-8344

EXPERIENCE:	ARMSTRONG MANUFACTURING **Regional Credit Manager**	TAMPA, FL **1989 to present**

- Portfolio management, credit and documentation.
- Average commitment of $175,000 with limit to $800,000.
- Debt collections, litigation, and re-marketing.
- Collateral evaluation procedures.
- Lines of credit on vendor accounts.

EDGEWATER COMPANIES **Senior Credit Analyst**	BRANDON, FL **1987 to 1989**

- Financing transaction review up to $1.5 million.
- Credit and documentation analysts supervision.
- Credit authority of $75,000.
- Debt collections and funding process.

TRI-CON MEDICAL DEVICES COMPANY **Inventory Analyst**	DOVER, FL **1983 to 1987**

- Cost analysis and purchasing control policy.
- Invoice/receivable processing and formatting.

EDUCATION:	UNIVERSITY OF SOUTH FLORIDA **Master of Business Administration**	TAMPA, FL **1983**

UNIVERSITY OF SOUTH FLORIDA **Bachelor of Science in Accounting**	SARASOTA, FL **1981**

References available upon request

- ✔ Dorothy briefly describes her scope of responsibilities because she assumes the reader will understand the basics of her positions.
- ✔ The readability of this format is achieved through bullets, lines, and spacing.

REGISTERED REPRESENTATIVE

NANCY KRAEMER

447 Q Street
Ralston, NE 68127
508/ 555-6809

EDUCATION:

UNION COLLEGE • Lincoln, NE
B.S.B.A. in Finance (1986)

LIFE UNDERWRITERS TRAINING COUNCIL
Personal and Business Insurance, Financial Planning

CREDENTIALS:

Registered Life, Property, and Casualty Agent (Multi-lines)

National Association of Securities Dealers (Series 6 & 63)

National Association of Life Underwriters (Omaha Chapter)

EXPERIENCE:

MUTUAL OF OMAHA INSURANCE COMPANY • Omaha, NE
Registered Representative (1989 to present)

Fully licensed for the sale and service of traditional and equity-based insurance products, fixed and variable annuities, mutual funds, and property and casualty coverage for personal and business markets.

Employ cold canvassing skills to establish new accounts among business owners and upper income home owners.

Recognized within top 10% of company for sales production. Earned National Sales Performance Award.

HOPEDALE PUBLISHING • Omaha, NE
Telemarketing Representative (1985 to 1989)

Consistently exceeded quotas on telemarketing calls and sales of new sports magazine for women.

✔ Nancy presents key qualifications, Training and Credentials, first.
✔ Her job description covers product lines, sales techniques, and achievements.
✔ She describes only relevant sales achievements from her entry-level position.

SENIOR ACCOUNTANT (Private)

JEFFREY PINE
306 Larchmont Street
Buckhead, GA 30625
404/ 555-8002

EDUCATION:	**B.S. in Accountancy**	**1984**
	EMORY UNIVERSITY	ATLANTA, GA

EXPERIENCE:	**Senior Accountant**	**1990 to present**
	MEDI-SCAN PRODUCTS	NORCROSS, GA
	(Medical imaging equipment company)	

- Prepare G/L including fixed assets and depreciation.
- Assist in production of the yearly budget.
- Prepare monthly receivable aging report.
- Prepare monthly financial statement and cash flow summary.
- Perform job cost accounting.
- Support auditors during year end audit.
- Prepare monthly review of budget to actual figures.
- Prepare and post all standard journal entries.
- Report directly to the V.P. of Finance and Administration.

General Accountant	**1988 to 1990**
Payroll Supervisor	**1984 to 1988**
NAPCO AUTOMOTIVE CORPORATION	MARIETTA, GA
(Manufacturer of plastic molded parts)	

- Processed bi-weekly payroll for 175 employees.
- Assisted in the automation of A/P and G/L.
- Designed reports in Lotus 1-2-3 and ACCPAC software.
- Audited employee travel expense reports.
- Reconciled G/L accounts.
- Awarded company's Outstanding Service recognition.

REFERENCES: Available upon request.

✔ Jeffrey succinctly lists all areas of responsibility.
✔ He identifies his Manager to demonstrate his stature within the organization.
✔ He lists his Award last so the reader will close with a strong impression.

SENIOR ACCOUNTANT (Public)

PHYLLIS CLARKSON
4205-K Connecticut Avenue
Washington, DC 20015
202/ 555-7792

OBJECTIVE: Senior Accountant position in the field of public accounting.

EDUCATION:

YALE UNIVERSITY   **New Haven, CT**
B.S. Degree in Business Administration   **1987**

Concentration: Accounting
Member of Honorary Accounting Society
Cumulative GPA: 3.92

Successfully passed all parts of uniform C.P.A. Exam

EMPLOYMENT:

HARPER & THAMES, CPA's   **Washington, DC**
Senior Accountant   **1989 to present**

Supervise staff accountants in the audit, review, and compilation of financial statements for small businesses. Prepare individual, corporate, and trust tax returns. Closely coordinate timing of engagements with clients and staff. Assist clients in improving the internal controls within their accounting systems.

POE ACCOUNTING COMPANY   **Washington, DC**
Staff Accountant   **1987 to 1989**

Independently performed test work in a variety of audit areas. Worked closely with client personnel at appropriate levels in order to coordinate the completion of assigned tasks. Developed communication and planning skills necessary to meet audit timetables for completion. Used word processing and computing software in preparation of audit work papers.

YALE UNIVERSITY - Controller's Office   **New Haven, CT**
Billing Assistant   **Summer 1986**

Assisted in the preparation and processing of payments and pre-registration of students for the fall semester.

✔ Phyllis' Objective is concise and specific.
✔ Her Education section contains impressive achievements related to her field.
✔ Job descriptions cite both technical expertise and client interaction.

TAX ACCOUNTANT (Entry-level)

LENA KANE

18 State Street   Maplewood, MN 55109 • 612/ 555-1893

OBJECTIVE: Tax Accountant in public accounting.

CERTIFICATION: Passed practice portion of C.P.A. exam.

EXPERIENCE: **Staff Accountant**
Davis-Griggs Accountants
St. Paul, MN   1990 to present

Perform a full range of corporate tax preparation functions including partnership, corporation, fiduciary, and payroll quarterly reports. Prepare client work papers and input data into computer for analysis. Perform on-site auditing of corporate ledgers.

Independent Personal Income Tax Preparer
Midway, MN   1989 to present

Junior Accountant
IANELLA ACCOUNTING, INC.
Roseville, MN   1988 to 1990

Prepared bank reconciliations and payroll quarterly reports. Performed client work papers and input data into computer for analysis.

EDUCATION: **Bachelor of Science in Accountancy**
MACALESTER COLLEGE
St. Paul, MN   1988

**COMPUTER
SKILLS:**   **Hardware** • HP, TI, DEC, Prime, IBM-PC

Software • Lotus 1-2-3, Pre-audit, AccPac, MS Word

✔ Lena's stylistic heading differentiates her resume from others.
✔ Her two current positions do not conflict because her private tax practice caters to individual clients as opposed to corporate clients.

TAX ACCOUNTANT (Senior)

MARY ARINELLO
36 Mountain Drive
Coburg, OR 97401
503/ 555-4449

SUMMARY: Diversified experience in Accounting and Tax Return Preparation with emphasis on payroll, financial statements and depreciation. Background includes positions as *Staff Accountant* and *Tax Manager* for a subsidiary of a major high-tech company, and *Senior Tax Accountant* for a multi-state consulting firm.

SKILLS: **Accounting:** Maintain records, prepare payroll and related reports, advise and review accounting operations of district offices, assist in the implementation of computerized records, supervise large staffs, and prepare financial statements.

Tax: Prepare federal and state tax returns for divisions and subsidiaries, compute tax depreciation with conversions, account for deferred tax provisions, teach tax preparation.

Computers: Lotus 1-2-3, Symphony, and Accounting Plus.

EXPERIENCE: HOUSTON ENGINEERING • Eugene, OR
Senior Tax Accountant (1987 to present)

Prepare federal and state income tax returns for multi-state consulting firm and subsidiaries. Oversee fixed asset accounting, property tax returns, sales tax returns, profit sharing plan, and other employee benefit returns.

NEURO-GENE CORPORATION • Eugene, OR
Tax Manager (1985 to 1987)
Tax Accountant (1984 to 1985)
Staff Accountant (1981 to 1984)

EDUCATION: PACIFIC LUTHERAN UNIVERSITY • Tacoma, WA
B.S. in Business Administration (1980)

References available upon request

✔ Mary uses lines to divide her resume into short sections for easy reading.
✔ The prominent headings in the left margin guide the reader to each section.
✔ She describes only her present position to avoid repetition.

KENNETH SHORE
990 Remington Road
Elm Grove, WI 53122
414/ 555-2803

EXPERIENCE

SHIPLEY CORPORATION   **Milwaukee, WI**
$20M supplier of electronics products

Vice President of Administration and Finance   **1989 to present**

- Direct the implementation of all financial and administrative policies, procedures, controls and financial reporting requirements.

- Implement and comply with financing arrangements under a secured revolving
line of credit and acquisition debt.

- Instituted a tracking system of cash flow requirements and inventory needs.

- Established a personnel program of consistent and fair policies, procedures
and practices.

- Coordinate all year-end audit work with external auditors.

BAXTER INDUSTRIES   **Milwaukee, WI**
$8B diversified, multi-national corporation

Group Controller   **1987 to 1989**

- Assisted Group Officer and Controller's Department as the financial liaison
between six Divisions with aggregate sales exceeding $800M.

- Reviewed operating performances, inventory control systems, capital expenditures, plant relocations, and acquisitions and divestitures.

- Participated in formulating Divisional long- and short-term strategies to
insure the achievement of product group and corporate goals.

- Division responsibility included Consumer Product Group; Venture Capital
and Financing Group; and Specialty Consumer Group.

KENNETH SHORE   **PAGE 2**

Senior Auditor   **1985 to 1987**

- In-charge auditor on Division audits, both domestic and international.

- Documented areas of internal control strengths and weaknesses.

- Reviewed, revised, and implemented audit programs for both financial and operational audits of Divisions and Corporate office.

- Performed year-end audit work at selected Divisions.

SHANE & JABLONSKI ACCOUNTANTS   **Brookfield, WI**

Senior Auditor   **1983 to 1985**
Staff Auditor   **1981 to 1983**

- Performed audits of financial statements for diversified client base.

- Prepared management letters documenting actions to improve internal controls for presentation to corporate officers.

EDUCATION

UNIVERSITY OF WISCONSIN   **Milwaukee, WI**
Master of Science in Taxation   **1986**

UNIVERSITY OF WISCONSIN   **Green Bay, WI**
Bachelor of Science in Accounting   **1981**

CERTIFIED PUBLIC ACCOUNTANT

MEMBERSHIPS

National Society of CPA's, American Association of Accounting Executives

---

References available upon request

✔ Kenneth's impressive experience as a finance executive merits 2 pages.
✔ The spacing, dividing lines, and use of bullets allow for easy scanning.
✔ Kenneth's company descriptions provide a framework for his accomplishments.

SUSAN BEKINS
1007-E 102nd Avenue
Parkrose, OR 97220

Residence: 503/ 555-9962   *Business:* 503/ 555-2300

PROFESSIONAL EXPERIENCE:

PORTLAND PEOPLE'S BANK

Vice President / Community Banking • Portland, OR   1990 to present
Direct business development, customer service, and operational activities at five branches in order to maintain Bank superiority in the marketplace.

- Develop and implement local marketing strategies.
- Establish goals, budgets, and procedures.
- Expand business relationships with retail and commercial customers.
- Function as a specialist for consumer investment products.
- Plan manpower needs and recruit and train staff.

Community Business Development Officer • Oak Grove, OR 1987 to 1990
Serviced existing customers and prospected among the business community.

- Exceeded sales goals of banking products including employee benefits programs, investment vehicles, and cash management services.
- Established network of contacts among Controllers, Human Resources Managers, Presidents, and Vice Presidents.

Previous positions — Branch Manager and Customer Service Representative

---

EDUCATION:

REED COLLEGE
Bachelor of Science in Management   1985

AMERICAN INSTITUTE OF BANKING   1986 to present
Commercial Lending, Business Development, Consumer Investing

References available upon request

✔ Susan's job titles signify steady career growth at the bank.
✔ Her emphasis on Business Development and Customer Service instead of only Operations will allow her to seek employment outside of banking.

V.P. OPERATIONS

FRANKLIN CARUTHERS
202 Chestnut Street
Merion Station, PA 19066

Residence: 215/555-2707   *Business:* 215/555-6000

PROFESSIONAL EXPERIENCE:

LIBERTY BANK & TRUST • Philadelphia, PA

Vice President of Operations (1990 to present). Manage operations supporting more than $10B in sales of deposit products. Develop annual budgets and long-term strategic plans. *Report to the Executive Vice President.*

Achievements:

- Developed new products including Certificates of Deposit, Money Market Deposit Account, Individual Retirement Account, Market Rate Checking, Tax Free Market Rate Checking, CD Backed Line of Credit, and Zero Coupon CD's.

- Developed new markets including E.F. Hutton, American Express International Bank, and International Development Bank CIGNA Companies, and Prudential-Bache.

Assistant Vice President of Operations (1987 to 1990). Developed operational strategies to support the implementation of a Certificate of Deposit program. *Reported to the Senior V.P.*

Achievements:

- Designed, developed and implemented an in-house Certificate of Deposit computer system with a capacity of more than $15B in sales.

- Provided operational support to E.F. Hutton broker network. Planned and implemented marketing presentations to major banks and S&L's.

- Generated $22M in fee income by servicing the E.F. Hutton Certificate of Deposit Program.

- Ensured compliance with all state and federal banking regulations.

- Increased in-house awareness of the Bank's Deposit Program through Focus Groups.

Previous positions – **Senior Banking Officer** (1987), **Banking Officer** (1986 to 1987).

EDUCATION:

BOSTON UNIVERSITY
Bachelor of Science in Business Administration (1986)

✔ Franklin begins each job description with an overall scope of responsibilities.
✔ His Achievements headings organize and emphasize accomplishments.
✔ Franklin identifies his Managers to demonstrate his senior level.

V.P. REPORTING

SHERYL TRASK
33 Garrison Way
Cranford, NJ 07016

Residence: 201/ 555-9224   *Business:* 201/ 555-3434

PROFESSIONAL EXPERIENCE:

V.P. of Financial Reporting
SMYTHE LABORATORIES — Union, NJ   1988 to present
($125M testing laboratory • 1,500 employees • 12 states)

Prepare, analyze, and present monthly financial statements and summaries that accurately reflect the company's results of operation and financial position. Oversee billing and collections activities. Prepare annual report for review by independent public accounting firm. Collaborate with clients to ensure coordination with their internal financial systems.

- Reduced billing cycle from 8 to 3 days.
- Reduced work cycle for preparation of financial statements from 17 to 12 days.
- Reduced DOS from 45 to 29 days through aggressive collection procedures.

Chief Accountant
SAN-DOZ CORPORATION — Kearny, NJ   1985 to 1988
(Chemical manufacturing firm • 1,200 employees • 5 national/international divisions)

Supervised A/P, Payroll, and Travel Expenditures. Prepared comprehensive monthly consolidated corporate financial statements for Controller.

Payroll Supervisor
JAYCO ENGINEERING — Newark, NJ   1982 to 1985
(R&D firm • 700 employees)

Oversaw the processing of weekly payroll checks.

EDUCATION:

Bachelor of Science in Accountancy
FAIRLEIGH DICKINSON UNIVERSITY — Madison, NJ   1981

Continuing Education - Financial Reporting, Cash Management, Staff Management

---

References available upon request

✔ Sheryl provides more information about her current position because it is at the management level.
✔ Her Continuing Education lists only higher-level finance and business courses.

Health Care 9

The Changing Face Of Health Care

Health Care is a constantly changing industry, influenced like none other by shifts in economy, technology, population, environment, and social mores.

It is continually shaped by astounding medical breakthroughs, ever-more sophisticated equipment, quality assurance priorities, patient satisfaction concerns, and overriding budgetary constraints. Health care is now a bona fide business.

The Diversity Of Health Care Professionals

The fast-paced evolution in health care has spawned new and exciting directions for health care professionals. In addition to assuming vital roles as clinicians, technicians, researchers, academicians, and instructors, you are also excelling as administrators, analysts, marketeers, and technologists.

To meet the industry's complexities, it is unlikely that you can fulfill your specialty without an understanding of, or expertise in, other areas. It is, therefore, imperative that your resume demonstrate your many proficiencies, your enthusiasm for keeping abreast of trends, and your flexibility in upgrading and expanding your skills.

Consider A Curriculum Vitae

A Curriculum Vitae (C.V.) is a simple-to-draft style of resume which is used extensively in the health care profession. A C.V. lists, but does not explain, your credentials.
It is usually organized in chronological order and assumes that the reader understands
your profession and does not need elaboration. Typical sections in a C.V. are:

- *Education*

- *Training*

- *Licenses*

- *Honors*

- *Internships*

- *Employment*

- *Awards*

- *Publications*

- *Conferences*

- *Presentations*

- *Affiliations*

For your convenience, we have included several examples of C.V.'s in this chapter.

Recommendations Are Crucial

Health Care is a "life and death" profession. There is very little margin for error in
performance. Therefore, recommendations endorsing your competency from supervisors, department heads, or professors are extremely influential in this highly
competitive field. Even in instances when you are not required to submit letters of
reference with your application, you might consider doing so.

A Conservative Approach

When composing your resume, you need to acknowledge the serious nature of the
health care industry by adopting a very conservative approach. A straightforward
format with simple lettering on traditional bond paper is advisable. Project an image
of someone who can indeed be trusted to make "life and death" decisions.

CASE MANAGER

JOEL SCHENCK
909 Concord Way
Denton, ID 83704
208/ 555-2116

CASE MANAGER

PROFESSIONAL EXPERIENCE:

CARVER ELDER CARE COMPANY   BOISE, ID
Supervisor of Case Managers   **1989 to Present**
Case Manager   **1987 to 1989**

- Hire, train, and evaluate case managers.
- Implement agency policies and government regulations.
- Monitor service and budget activities.
- Centralize and optimize use of client information.
- Manage client assessment development and implementation.
- Provide liaison among community resources.
- Prepare and deliver presentations.

WESTSIDE HOSPITAL   WESTSIDE, ID
Therapist   **1986 to 1987**

- Developed individual care plans and provided crisis management.
- Coordinated treatment plans with community specialists.
- Presented cases for discussion by medical personnel.

JUMP START PROJECT   BORAH, ID
Head Teacher   **1984 to 1986**

- Developed and supervised three special educational programs.
- Trained, scheduled, and supervised staff.
- Co-managed client cases and personally directed client cases.
- Administered all operations in absence of Program Supervisor.

EDUCATION:

BOISE STATE UNIVERSITY   BOISE, ID
Bachelor of Arts in Psychology   **1984**

Planning to pursue Master's degree in Health Care Administration.

- ✔ Joel's resume traces a typical career path in human services administration.
- ✔ He includes management responsibilities in non-management positions.
- ✔ He emphasizes his intention to progress further in management.

BARBARA HOPE

2476 Park Avenue
New York, NY 10021

Residence: 212/ 555-5904
Business: 212/ 555-0000

SUMMARY:

Experienced manager accustomed to total P&L responsibility • Ability to identify and resolve significant control weaknesses and develop effective policies and procedures • Proficient in devising and implementing sophisticated computer systems for business applications • Strong background in contract administration • Outstanding analysis, communication, negotiation, coordination, and troubleshooting skills.

EXPERIENCE:

Chief Executive Officer (1987 to present)
Wheels for Kids Program • New York, NY

Plan and direct procedural and fiscal operations for this special needs transportation program. Directed contract administration and operational planning in start-up phase.

- Administer major contracts in excess of $4M with Fortune 500 companies. Provide technical assistance and consultation to the New York City Transportation Planning Review Board in the development of transportation corridors.

- Supervise 10 managers with ultimate responsibility for 50 administrative staff, 180 support personnel and 160 vehicles. Utilize Federal Express driver training program. Company has remained non-union and enjoys low employee turnover.

- Implement a state-of-the-art computerized system to administer complex maintenance, reservations, scheduling, dispatch, and personnel functions.

- Developed initial specifications for vehicle modifications. Continually test new transportation products to maintain high quality and cost-effective equipment.

- Appointed Director to numerous professional and community Boards.

Administrator (1984 to 1987)
New York City Center for Transportation Research • New York, NY

EDUCATION:

BA / MBA (1984)
Colgate University • Hamilton, NY

✔ Barbara's quick rise to CEO is accentuated by her powerful Summary and Experience sections which summarize competencies and accomplishments.
✔ Her joint BA and MBA further validate her credentials.

NORMAN BERKOWITZ
44 Calvert Springs Road
Crestline Heights, AL 35203
205/ 555-9312

SUMMARY:

M.B.A. in Health Care Administration • More than 10 years successful experience in Fiscal Reporting and Finance • Proficient at health care cost reporting and reimbursement, general accounting, and budgets / forecasts • In-depth knowledge of state and federal regulations pertaining to health care reimbursement.

PROFESSIONAL EXPERIENCE:

HOMEWOOD HOSPITAL   HOMEWOOD , AL
CHIEF FINANCIAL OFFICER   **1986 to present**

Oversee the entire financial operation of a 280-bed general hospital with a $76M annual operating budget. Supervise all required reporting functions. Handle Research Grant Administration, Construction Management, Corporate Development, Financial Planning, Materials Management, and Utilization Management.

Achievements:

• Coordinated the corporate restructuring of hospital.

• Initiated successful appeal to Health Care Plus Provider Reimbursement Board resulting in $650K in additional reimbursement.

• Implemented a Utilization Management Program which substantially reduced the average length of hospital stay.

• Negotiated MIS contract resulting in $350K cost savings to hospital.

• Completed $3.2M Critical Care unit construction under budget.

CALVIN HANES MEMORIAL HOSPITAL   BIRMINGHAM, AL
GENERAL ACCOUNTING MANAGER / Senior Mgmt. Team   **1980 to 1986**

EDUCATION:

EMORY UNIVERSITY   ATLANTA, GA
M.B.A. IN HEALTH CARE ADMINISTRATION   **1985**
B.S. IN BUSINESS ADMINISTRATION   **1979**

✔ A prospective employer can scan Norman's Summary section and quickly determine whether he has the appropriate qualifications.
✔ The Accounting Manager position can be discussed in an interview.

CHIROPRACTIC PHYSICIAN

ELIZABETH CUNNINGHAM
Chiropractic Physician

239-D Franklin Street
Houston, TX 77039

Residence: 713/ 555-9569
Office: 713/ 555-2010

EDUCATION

Doctor of Chiropractic
Diplomate National Board of Chiropractic Examiners   **1984**
SOUTHWESTERN CHIROPRACTIC COLLEGE   HOUSTON, TX

Master of Science in Sport Management   **1981**
BAYLOR UNIVERSITY   WACO, TX

Bachelor of Science in Physical Education   **1979**
BAYLOR UNIVERSITY   WACO, TX

CERTIFICATIONS

CERTIFIED CHIROPRACTIC SPORTS PHYSICIAN

PROFESSIONAL EXPERIENCE

Co-Director   **1986 to present**
JOHNSON CHIROPRACTIC CENTER   HOUSTON, TX

Assistant Director   **1984 to 1986**
ELMWOOD CHIROPRACTIC CLINIC   HOUSTON, TX

SPORTS AFFILIATIONS

Chiropractic Physician

U. S. NATIONAL WOMEN'S LACROSSE CHAMPIONSHIPS - HOUSTON, TX (1991)
INTERNATIONAL GAMES, III - NICE, FRANCE (1990)
ASIAN ATHLETIC CHAMPIONSHIPS - SINGAPORE (1989)
AMERICAN WOMEN'S FIELD HOCKEY MATCHES - AMHERST, MA (1989)
PROFESSIONAL WOMEN'S SOFTBALL TOUR - PALM BEACH, FL (1988)

CHIROPRACTIC PHYSICIAN (continued)

Emergency Medical Team Coordinator

NEW YORK CITY MARATHON (1989)
U.S. / RUSSIA GYMNASTICS COMPETITION (1988)
WORLD BICYCLING RACES (1987)

PRESENTATIONS

Sports Injuries Related to the Knee   **1991**
NATIONAL CHIROPRACTIC INSTITUTE   WASHINGTON, DC

Preventing Shin Splints in Runners   **1990**
U.S. RUNNER'S ASSOCIATION   HOUSTON, TX

Origin of Tennis Elbow   **1987**
CHICAGO CHIROPRACTIC COLLEGE   CHICAGO, IL

Evaluation of Aerobics Exercises   **1987**
ALVIN MOORE CHIROPRACTIC COLLEGE   DETROIT, MI

PUBLICATIONS

List of publications upon request

MEMBERSHIPS

NATIONAL SPORTS INJURIES COUNCIL
FOUNDATION FOR CHIROPRACTIC EDUCATION AND RESEARCH
AMERICAN CHIROPRACTIC ASSOCIATION
TEXAS STATE CHIROPRACTIC SOCIETY

Professional and personal references available

✔ Elizabeth presents her professional background in a traditional curriculum
   vitae which lists, but does not explain, her major credentials.
✔ Sections appear in the order of importance for her field.

CLINICAL DIRECTOR

AMANDA GRISWOLD

37 Highbank Road • Sweetwater, FL 33144   305/ 555-7702

PROFESSIONAL EXPERIENCE:

HUMANA HOSPITAL • Miami, FL
Clinical Director of Specialty Nursing (1987 to present)
Head Nurse / ICU-CCU (1980 to 1987)
Staff Nurse / ICU-CCU (1977 to 1980)

Coordinate all nursing activities on specialty services of 350-bed teaching hospital. Provide liaison between Head Nurses and V.P. of Medical Services. Assume role of Associate Director of Nursing. *Cited for excellence in leadership and clinical skills.*

Highlights:

- Hire, schedule, and evaluate 75 nursing and ancillary staff.
- Plan, implement, and monitor $4M+ budget.
- Research, select, and coordinate purchase of all major equipment.
- Establish nursing policies, procedures, standards, and QA programs.
- CHAIRPERSON - Policy and Safety Committees.
- MEMBER - Emergency Action Plan and Nursing Executives Committees.
- Directed the opening of a new cardiac unit. Purchased $220K in equipment, developed policy, procedures, and standards of care, and trained staff.
- Directed the $145K reconstruction of a new medical-surgical unit as a joint venture with a physician-run surgical practice.
- Directed the $200K renovation of the ICU; supervised the design and construction and the purchase of new equipment.
- Directed Pediatric renovation; purchased $175K patient monitoring system.
- Coordinated new computerized central patient registration system.

EDUCATION:

FLORIDA INTERNATIONAL UNIVERSITY • Miami, FL
MS in Nursing Management (1980)
BS in Nursing (1976)

✔ Amanda condenses a lengthy career onto one page by listing each position, but only explaining her current one, since it is most relevant.
✔ She identifies staff, budget, purchasing, program, and facility responsibilities.

CLINICAL INFORMATION SPECIALIST

MARTIN MINOOSIAN
23 Candle Hill Drive
E. Lansing, MI 48823
517/ 555-9653

PROFESSIONAL EXPERIENCE

Clinical Information Specialist
MEDI-FORMS CORPORATION • Lansing, MI   1988 to present

- Coordinate hardware and software installations for client medical facilities, including needs assessment, specification writing and quality assurance.
- Design and conduct client-specific training and education programs.
- Provide on-going client support, education and system performance evaluations.
- Train newly-hired information specialists.
- Assist marketing staff with product demonstrations.

Health Record Manager
JOSIAH JAMISON MEMORIAL HOSPITAL • E. Lansing, MI   1985 to 1988

- Administered health record activities of the Outpatient Health Program.
- Assisted in the automation of an information retrieval system.
- Served as Chairperson of the Standards Committee.
- Identified staffing and capital equipment needs for annual budget.

Medical Record Supervisor
FRANDOR CONTINUING CARE FACILITY • Frandor, MI   1981 to 1985

- Designed new Medical Record Department - purchased supplies and equipment, developed filing system, and integrated clinic records.
- Instituted departmental job descriptions, policies and procedures, and forms.
- Complied with licensing and accreditation standards of patient care.
- Conducted utilization review and quality assurance studies.
- Recruited and trained administrative staff.

EDUCATION

BS in Health Record Administration (with honors)
BUTLER UNIVERSITY • Indianapolis, IN   1981

Clinical Placements within a hospital, medical center, and HMO.

References available upon request

✔ Martin's current position incorporates his knowledge of health care information systems, facilities, and operations.
✔ Each position describes duties in order of importance to his career growth.

DOLORES RODRIGUEZ, RN, CCRN, C.S.
2-I Blandford Street
Des Plaines, IL 60016
312/ 555-7774

EDUCATION

Master of Science
UNIVERSITY OF ILLINOIS • Chicago, IL   1987
Critical care and teaching within the Clinical Nurse Specialist Program

Bachelor of Science in Nursing
JUDSON COLLEGE • Elgin, IL   1983

EXPERIENCE

Critical Care Clinical Specialist / Nursing Education and Research
HOLY FAMILY HOSPITAL • Des Plaines, IL   1989 to present

- Provide consultation to nursing staff in ICU, CCU, and Telemetry.
- Develop interdisciplinary continuing education programs.
- Supervise hospital operations on weekends and holidays.
- Develop competency-based critical care orientation.
- Provide direct care to patients and families requiring specialized intervention.
- Preceptor to graduate nursing students.
- Develop and teach CCRN review course.

Critical Care Education Coordinator / Education, Research and Development
LUTHERAN GENERAL HOSPITAL • Park Ridge, IL   1986 to 1989

Medical Critical Care Staff / Charge Nurse
COOK COUNTY UNIVERSITY HOSPITAL • Chicago, IL   1984 to 1986

ACTIVITIES

Consultant for Cardiovascular Support Groups • Advanced Life Support Instructor •
Professional Education Task Force of AMA • Nurse Expert Witness • Guest Host, "Medical
Issues" television program • Published author • Leadership role in numerous professional
organizations • Elected to Delta Delta Gamma.

✔ Dolores' certifications follow her name and do not need a special section.
✔ To avoid repetition, Dolores describes only her current position.
✔ Her impressive professional activities merit a special section.

CLINICAL NURSE SPECIALIST (Gerontology)

BETH HARRIS, RN, MS

3692 Leandro Drive, SW
North Miami, FL 33161

Residence: 305/ 555-8177   *Office:* 305/ 555-3000

OBJECTIVE

Gerontological Clinical Nurse Specialist

EDUCATION

Master of Science / Concentration in Gerontological Nursing
LONG ISLAND UNIVERSITY • Southampton, NY   1989
Thesis: *"Memory loss in the elderly in long-term care."*
Research Assistant: Edited geriatrics chapter in nursing text.

Bachelor of Science in Nursing
IONA COLLEGE • New Rochelle, NY   1985

EXPERIENCE

Geriatric Clinical Nurse Specialist
DADE COUNTY HOSPITAL • Miami, FL   1989 to present
(100 bed teaching hospital with geriatric population exceeding 50% of patient census)

Assess, develop, implement, and monitor interventions to meet educational needs of the
hospital nursing staff who provide geriatric care.

Education:

- Plan, implement, and evaluate orientation / educational programs.
  CPR, Falls Prevention, Memory Loss
- Initiate / coordinate clinical conferences.
  Incontinence, Medications, Depression
- Act as Preceptor to college nursing students.
- Report on findings of current geriatric research.

Beth Harris, RN, MS   Page 2

Collaboration:

- Collaborate with nurse managers and staff to assess clinical learning needs.
- Support hospital departments in providing educational conferences /programs.
- Facilitate ongoing medical treatment plans for geriatric patients.
- Assist social workers and continuing care coordinators with discharge planning.

Consultation:

- Act as a resource to unit staff for implementation of the nursing process.
- Assist staff in implementing creative approaches to solving clinical problems.
- Promote effective communication between nursing staff and health services.
- Nursing Representative on Geriatric Care Review Team.

Nursing Service Activities:

- Support in the revision of nursing hospital policy and procedure.
- Participate on numerous nursing department and hospital committees:
  Nursing QA, Nursing Care Evaluation, Product Evaluation, Ethics Committee, Elderly Task Force, Outreach to the Elderly Committee
- Participate in activities which promote professional growth:
  Geriatric Grand Rounds
  Conferences - Geriatric Assessment, Geriatric Oncology, Vision Impairment in the Elderly, Aging in America, Uniqueness of the Geriatric Client
  Guest Speaker on "Helping the Elderly Patient Cope With Loss"
  Member of Florida Nurses Association, American Nurses Association, Gerontology Society of America, and American Geriatrics Society

Staff Nurse / General Medical Unit
MIAMI BEACH GENERAL HOSPITAL • Miami Beach, FL   1985 to 1989
(Primary population of geriatric patients)

Charge nurse responsible for the supervision of registered nurses, nursing assistants, and student nurses in the care of general medical patients with acute/chronic illnesses.

- Coordinated discharge planning.
- Member of Advisory Board for Nursing Education.
- Floor Presentation Coordinator for General Medical Nursing Grand Rounds.
- Speaker at Charge Workshop – General Medical Nursing Service.

✔ Beth's 2-page resume is easy to read because of section dividers and bullets.
✔ Her four main function headings, Education, Collaboration, Consultation, and Nursing Services organize the numerous duties of her current position.

ROSE SCHARLACH

3 Bishop Pond Road • Kenner, LA 70062

EDUCATION:

Master of Science in Medical-Surgical Nursing
LOYOLA UNIVERSITY • New Orleans, LA   1984

Bachelor of Science in Nursing
DILLARD UNIVERSITY • New Orleans, LA   1980

EXPERIENCE:

Surgical Staff Nurse
ATKINS-DICKINSON HOSPITAL • Harahan, LA   1990 to present
Provide post-operative care for 14-bed intensive care unit and 18-bed discharge unit.
Perform discharge teaching and participate in patient research studies.

Surgical Critical Care Nurse
ST. REGIS HOSPITAL • Jefferson, LA   1985 to 1990
Provided post-operative care to cardiac and general surgical critical care patients.

Instructor/Critical Care Nursing
XAVIER HOSPITAL • Metairie, LA   1983 to 1985
Planned and implemented educational programs including orientation, in-service
education, and continuing education. Participated on numerous hospital committees.

Critical Care Staff Nurse
CHARITY HOSPITAL • New Orleans, LA   1980 to 1983

TEACHING:

Basic Coronary Care • Cardiac Care Patient Discharge • Cardiac Life Support

MEMBERSHIPS:

American Nurses Association • Council of Clinical Nurse Specialists
State Nurses Association • Nurse Expert Witness Committee
American Association of Critical Care Nurses • Society of Nurse Educators

---

✔ Rose's resume stresses clinical, instructional, and membership experiences.
✔ She includes only a brief overview of each position because she assumes the
reader is familiar with the specific duties of her positions.

CHARLES MADANI
18 Fulton Street
Glendale, MO 63122
314/ 555-9003

CLINICAL VIROLOGIST

Professional Experience:

Senior Technologist

ARGOS LABORATORIES • Florissant, MO   1989 to present
(Small clinical laboratory servicing private physicians)

Train and supervise technologists in sophisticated laboratory procedures to diagnose a wide range of diseases and infections including venereal disease, AIDS, and Rubella. Troubleshoot equipment, provide client test interpretation, perform computerized data entry and editing, and implement inventory control and quality assurance programs.

Responsible for total department in supervisor's absence.

Medical Technologist

JEFFERSON MEMORIAL HOSPITAL • Hazelwood, MO   1985 to 1989
(Pathology, Immunology, and Chemistry Departments)

Performed all standard testing procedures for blood and tissue samples. Established QC procedures, ordered and evaluated new products, and trained new technologists. Participated in extensive training program for new antibody screening product.

Education/Training:

Medical Technology Certification
KIRKWOOD HOSPITAL • Kirkwood, MO   1985

Bachelor of Arts in Chemistry
ROCKHURST COLLEGE • Kansas City, MO   1983

National Chemistry Academy Achievement Award

Continuing Education Workshops: Virology, Chlamydia, Connective Tissue Disease, Monoclonal Antibodies

---

References available upon request

✔ Charles' Objective is extremely straightforward and specific.
✔ His descriptions of the labs help the reader understand his background.
✔ Charles stresses both technical and management responsibilities.

DENTIST

Curriculum Vitae

BARRY ROSEN
561 Silver Lake Road
Hampton, WI 53218

Residence: 414/555-2758   *Office: 414/555-0888*

EXPERIENCE:

1990 to present
Periodontal Associate
EASY CARE DENTAL CLINIC
Milwaukee, WI

EDUCATION:

1988
Doctor of Dental Medicine
MARQUETTE UNIVERSITY SCHOOL OF DENTAL MEDICINE
Milwaukee, WI

1982
Combined BS/MS in Anatomy
EDGEWOOD COLLEGE SCHOOL OF MEDICINE
Madison, WI

TRAINING:

1984 to 1988
Dental Assistant
DENTAL OFFICES OF H. ARONSON
Madison, WI

1988
Oral Pathology Lab Instructor
MARQUETTE UNIVERSITY SCHOOL OF DENTAL MEDICINE
Milwaukee, WI

1987 to 1989
Research Fellow - J. Jones, PhD, DMD
MARQUETTE UNIVERSITY SCHOOL OF DENTAL MEDICINE
Milwaukee, WI

1987 to 1989
Clinical Assistant - Palate Graft Clinic
MARQUETTE UNIVERSITY SCHOOL OF DENTAL MEDICINE
Milwaukee, WI

✔ Barry's C.V. is an outline to establish basic Education and Training credentials.
✔ As a new dentist, Barry's Experience section is understandably short.
✔ Background specifics are commonly discussed in an interview.

EDUCATIONAL NURSING SPECIALIST

FRANCESCA CAPUTO, R.N., B.S.N.

---

92 Irvington Drive • Lowry, CO 80230   303/ 555-4687

EDUCATION:

REGIS COLLEGE   DENVER, CO
M.Ed. • Instructional Enrichment and Development for the Adult   **1987**
Focus on Educational Assessment, Learning and Teaching Styles, Topics in Education.

BETH-EL COLLEGE OF NURSING   COLORADO SPRINGS, CO
B.S. Nursing   **1983**
Emphasis on Psychology, Sociology, and Education.

NEWMAN MEMORIAL HOSPITAL SCHOOL OF NURSING   LAKEWOOD, CO
Diploma in Nursing   **1980**

EXPERIENCE:

MOUNT URIS HOSPITAL   DENVER, CO
Educational Specialist / Nursing QA Coordinator   **1987 to present**

- Chairperson, Nursing Quality Assurance Committee
- General Nursing and Unit Orientation (Self-learning modules)
- Continuing Education Coordinator
- Advanced Cardiac Life Saving Instructor

RADBURN GENERAL HOSPITAL   COLORADO SPRINGS, CO
Nursing Education Coordinator   **1984 to 1987**

- Surgical Rehab, Diabetes, AIDS Educator
- Inservices, Staff Development, and Continuing Education
- Clinical Preceptor – Beth-El Senior Nursing Students

PROFESSIONAL ACTIVITIES:

Guest Speaker for Nursing Leadership / Management Course

Researcher on effectiveness of self-learning module instruction

Researcher on implication of AIDS for the medical profession

Secretary, Regional Council for Inservice Hospital Educators

Member, Nursing Quality Assurance Network

✔ Francesca immediately establishes her clinical and instructional credentials.
✔ She lists very specific programs which she has coordinated.
✔ Her activities are important because they are directly related to her career.

EXECUTIVE DIRECTOR

ALVIN PIKE
307 Villa Nuevo Drive
Stanfield, AZ 85272

602/ 555-2116

OBJECTIVE:

EXECUTIVE DIRECTOR for a large rehabilitation facility.

PROFESSIONAL HIGHLIGHTS:

GREATER PHOENIX REHABILITATION CENTER   PHOENIX, AZ
(Rehabilitation hospital providing physical, occupational, and emotional therapy to inpatients and outpatients recovering from organic or accident-induced trauma)

Director of Physical Therapy Services (1989 to present)
Established and developed a new-concept physical therapy outpatient program. Surveyed market areas and referral base; determined staff, equipment, and budget needs; devised distribution system; implemented billing operations; formulated policies and procedures. Currently manage $400K budget and staff of 11 in servicing 200 patients annually.

This successful program generated $1M in gross patient revenues in FY '90, a tenfold growth since its inception. Consult to other health care facilities regarding the program.

SOUTHWEST COMMUNITY HOSPITALS, INC.   TUCSON, AZ
(Health system comprised of 3 community hospitals and an ambulatory care facility)

Administrative Director for Physical Therapy (1986 to 1989)
Controlled a $700K budget and directed administrative operations of a 35-person department. Developed, monitored and updated policies and procedures; reviewed, evaluated and reported the quality, safety and appropriateness of services; collaborated with top management regarding departmental operations.

Successfully facilitated a smooth audit by the state regulatory commission.

TEMPE HOSPITAL   TEMPE, AZ
Chief Physical Therapist (1982 to 1986)
Staff Physical Therapist (1980 to 1982)

EDUCATION:

SOUTHWESTERN COLLEGE GRADUATE SCHOOL   PHOENIX, AZ
MBA Candidate

UNIVERSITY OF ARIZONA   TUCSON, AZ
BS in Health Care Management cum laude (1984)
AS in Physical Therapy (1980)

✔ Alvin highlights his Objective in capital letters for emphasis.
✔ He includes important facts and figures to strengthen his candidacy.
✔ He accents his most important achievements in italics.

FAMILY NURSE PRACTITIONER

SHARON PAPPALARDO, RNC, FNP
72 Sebastion Way
Urbandale, IA 50322
515/ 555-3644

EDUCATION:

M.S. in Nursing / Family Nurse Practitioner   **1983**
DRAKE UNIVERSITY   DES MOINES, IA

B.S. in Nursing   **1981**
MARYCREST COLLEGE   DAVENPORT, IA

CERTIFICATIONS:

License, Registered Nurse – Iowa

Certificate, Family Nurse Practitioner – American Nursing Association

---

PROFESSIONAL EXPERIENCE:

Family Nurse Practitioner   **1989 to present**
MIDWEST FAMILY HEALTH SERVICES   WEST DES MOINES, IA

In a collaborative primary-care practice with emphasis on women's health care, provide physical assessment and management of adults with common and chronic illnesses. Develop nutritional regimens, and provide counseling in nutrition and preventive health care. Counsel on family planning and AIDS prevention.

Family Nurse Practitioner - Primary Care   **1985 to 1989**
Family Nurse Practitioner - Emergency Care   **1983 to 1985**
BROADLAWNS HOSPITAL   DES MOINES, IA

In a collaborative primary-care practice in internal medicine, provided physical assessment, health care management, teaching, and counseling for a diverse population with common and chronic illnesses. Coordinated community services for and monitored home-care and geriatric patients. Coordinated emergency code chart protocol system for health center. Led wellness and stress-management seminars for patients. Precepted graduate Nurse Practitioner student. Co-taught college graduate clinical practicum in assessment and diagnosis.

✔ Sharon accentuates her certifications by listing them after her name.
✔ To avoid repetition, she combines two positions at the same clinic.
✔ Sharon's resume is easy to read because of its spacing and separation lines.

FAMILY PRACTITIONER

ARTHUR DAVIS, MD

Residence
989 Fremont Street
San Bernardino, CA 92403
805/ 555-9241

Office
2 Harbrace Center
San Bernardino, CA 92403
805/ 555-0440

EDUCATION:

1984	**Doctor of Medicine** COLUMBIA SCHOOL OF MEDICINE • NEW YORK, NY
1979	**Bachelor of Science in Biology** *magna cum laude* UNIVERSITY OF CALIFORNIA • IRVINE, CA

MEDICAL LICENSES:

CALIFORNIA AND NEW YORK

MEDICAL BOARDS:

1985	Diplomate of National Board of Medical Examiners

TRAINING:

1984 to 1985	**Rotating Internship in Family Practice** LOS ANGELES COUNTY HOSPITAL • Los Angeles, CA

EXPERIENCE:

1990 to present	**Staff Physician** REED OUT-PATIENT CLINIC • San Bernardino, CA
1989 to present	**Private Practitioner** SHERWOOD HEALTH CENTER • San Bernardino, CA
1985 to present	**School Physician** SAN BERNARDINO HIGH SCHOOL • San Bernardino, CA

PUBLICATIONS:

Davis, Arthur. "Healthwatch" *Weekly column appearing in two local newspapers.* Current.

Davis, Arthur. "Childhood vaccinations." *U.S. Journal of Medicine*, Vol. IV, No. 6, January 1987, pp. 178-179.

✔ Arthur utilizes a standard Curriculum Vitae to simply list his credentials.
✔ For convenience, he furnishes his office address and telephone number.
✔ Arthur includes a short list of publications in the body of his C.V.

HEALTH CARE ADMINISTRATOR

ROBERTA HAYES
18 Thorndike Street
Columbia, SC 29203
803/ 555-3179

SUMMARY:

M.B.A. in Health Care Administration with 15+ years progressive experience as a health systems specialist • Able to assess and improve health care systems • Expert in researching and interpreting policies, regulations, and laws • Proficient in patient advocacy, staff training and development, and public relations functions.

PROFESSIONAL EXPERIENCE:

RICHLAND MEMORIAL HOSPITAL, Columbia, SC
Patient Representative Officer (1987 - present)

Identify and resolve critical care patient problems requiring mediation with all levels of staff. Classify cases necessitating risk management and QA review. Generate reports establishing complaint trends with proposals for improvement. Conduct and analyze annual *Patient Satisfaction Study* for review by senior management.

Plan and implement the *"Professional Performance"* training program for all hospital employees to increase employee sensitivity to patients' needs.

Member, Patient Advocacy Committee, Health Consumer Advisory Board, Ambulatory Patient Care Council, and Community Health Education Commission.

HARTSFIELD HOSPITAL, Forest Acres, SC
Night Administrator (1982 - 1987)

Directed all hospital operations including coordination of professional and administrative staff; interpretation and application of hospital policy, federal regulations, and state law; and collaboration with state and federal agencies, political representatives, public safety departments, health care facilities, legal representatives, and patients and their families.

Received letters of commendation from hospital management for outstanding performance in dealing with emergency situations. Twice received Superior Performance Award.

Roberta Hayes   *page 2*

Assistant Medical Administrative Manager (1975 - 1982)

Supported in the management of key functions to insure the efficient operation of Medical Administrative Services. Conducted system reviews to monitor the effectiveness of internal programs; wrote administrative policies as well as cost containment proposals; functioned as liaison to legal staff and advocate to patients; scheduled and trained medical administrative personnel; supported the computerization of a patient records system.

EDUCATION:

CLEMSON UNIVERSITY, Clemson, SC
MBA in Health Care Administration (1975)
Bachelor of Science in Sociology (1973)

CONTINUING EDUCATION
Health Care QA, Public Relations, Risk Management, Patient Advocacy

AFFILIATIONS:

Member of Governing Body, The People's Home • South Carolina Association of Health Care Administrators • South Carolina Society of Patient Advocates

PUBLICATIONS:

Hayes, Roberta. "Identifying 5 major risk factors in managing critical care patients." *American Journal of Health Care Administration*, Vol. XI, No. 6, March 1990, pp. 23-26.

Hayes, Roberta. "Patient satisfaction: the key to success." *Patient News*, Spring 1989.

REFERENCES:

Available upon request

✔ Roberta's Summary helps the reader to quickly understand her key qualifications without reading through her 2-page resume.
✔ She draws attention to the letters of commendation and awards in italics.

BARBARA WILKISON
809-A Cliffside Apartments
Belle Meade, TN 37205
615/ 555-8931

SUMMARY OF QUALIFICATIONS:

Master of Science in Psychology with solid background in training, program development, public relations, and consulting within diverse health care environments • Strong interest in developing and marketing Employee Assistance Programs and Management Training Programs to industry • Demonstrated skill in writing, presenting, research, and supervision.

PROFESSIONAL EXPERIENCE:

COORDINATOR OF EDUCATION	1987 to present
Middle Tennessee Family Health Institute	Nashville, TN

(Large private, non-profit nutritional care and education agency)

- Train and supervise ten regional educators in the design, development, and implementation of quality education programs for clients and professionals.
- Direct public relations activities including media broadcasts, community outreach programs, and consultation to school systems.
- Create and maintain educational materials for 25,000 clients annually.
- Guest lecturer at numerous area colleges and professional organizations.

CONSULTANT	1989 to present
Nashville Family Planning Center	Nashville, TN

- Consult in the research, design, and marketing of a family planning program.

THERAPIST	1985 to 1987
Rutherford County Hospital	Murfreesboro, TN

- Provided clinical support for a caseload of 25 teenagers requiring prenatal services.
- Co-facilitated support groups and provided training to hospital staff and social workers.
- Chairman of "Safe Sex" Task Force to develop educational programs for teens.

EDUCATION:

MASTER OF ARTS IN PSYCHOLOGY	1985
BACHELOR OF ARTS IN EDUCATION	1983
Memphis State University	Memphis, TN

✔ Barbara's Summary not only includes her areas of accomplishment, but incorporates a career interest in the industry which is supported by her credentials.
✔ She highlights positions rather than institutions because of this interest.

LABORATORY TECHNOLOGIST

DONNA ORTIZ
1889 Dewhurst Avenue
Newark, NJ 07105

Residence: 201/ 555-8427   *Business:* 201/ 555-3700

OBJECTIVE:

Senior position as a Licensed Clinical Laboratory Technologist / Manager

EXPERIENCE:

Laboratory Technologist / Manager (1985 to present)
SENTRY CLINICAL LABORATORIES • Nutley, NJ
(Large independent clinical laboratory)

- Supervise 15 technicians in all phases of laboratory operation in order to ensure quality and efficiency. Schedule, train, and evaluate personnel.

- Establish standards for testing times and mechanisms for work flow. Develop, monitor, and revise written operational procedures.

- Participate on Methodology and QA Committees. Provide liaison to hospital administration, physicians, nurses, and ancillary personnel.

- Plan and present monthly inservice education seminars.

- Keep current on technical and research developments within the field.

- Administer personnel records and payroll data.

- Previous positions: **Senior Technician** (1982 to 1985) and **Technician** (1980 to 1982).

TECHNICAL COURSEWORK:

Chemistry, Biology, Methodology, Hematology, and Bloodbanking.

LICENSE:

Clinical Laboratory Technologist – Department of Health, Education, and Welfare

REFERENCES:

Available upon request

- ✔ Donna's Objective establishes her management level career goal.
- ✔ She describes only her current position because it supports her goal.
- ✔ Technical Coursework and Licenses further validate her credentials.

MANAGEMENT CONSULTANT

Confidential Resume

of

FAITH GALLO

57 Bleeker Street   Residence: 212/ 555-3578
New York, NY 10014   Business: 212/ 555-0900

Summary of Qualifications:

Master's Degree with concentration in Health Care Administration ■ Successful experience in health care planning and management consultation ■ Solid working relationship with local health care institutions and provider agencies ■ Knowledge of state needs assessment methods and government agency policies ■ Strong communication, negotiation, and presentation skills ■ Experienced with computer applications.

Professional Experience:

Health Care Management Consultant
AMERICAN HEALTH CARE CONSULTANTS ■ New York, NY   1989 to present

Scope of responsibilities:

- **Strategic plan development** encompassing environmental assessment, data base development, evaluation of strategic business units and directions, and implementation plans.

- **Market research, feasibility studies, and business planning** for both existing programs and new business development.

- **Master facility planning** involving programming, project definition, and architectural oversight.

- **Financial analysis** including capital needs assessment, pricing, and reimbursement.

- **Merger and affiliation studies** pertaining to joint venturing between hospitals, physicians, and other health care facilities.

- **Certificate of Need** preparation and defense.

- **Oral and written presentations** to boards, committees, and physicians.

MANAGEMENT CONSULTANT (continued)

Faith Gallo   **Page 2**

Senior Program Analyst / Determination of Need (DON) Program
NEWARK PUBLIC HEALTH DEPARTMENT ■ Newark, NJ   1987 to 1989

Scope of responsibilities:

- **Review and analysis of a large volume of DON applications** involving new construction and renovation; new technology and equipment; acute care, long-term care, and specialty care programs.
- **Task Force Chairperson** for developing geriatric psychiatric guidelines.
- **Oral and written presentations** to the state Public Health Council.

Senior Contracts Administrator
NEWARK ENVIRONMENTAL PROTECTION DEPARTMENT ■ Newark, NJ   1986 to 1987

Contracts Administrator
MEDIGENICS CORPORATION ■ Clinton Hill, NJ   1985 to 1986

Office Manager - Executive Offices
CURTIS HEALTH CLINIC ■ Nutley, NJ   1983 to 1985

Education:

MPA in Health Care Administration
NEW YORK UNIVERSITY ■ New York, NY   1988
(Sigma Nu National Honor Society)

BA in Sociology
DREW UNIVERSITY ■ Madison, NJ   1983

Activities:

American Public Health Association • The Society for Hospital Planning and Marketing • Women's Association of Health Care Professionals • American Council of Health Care Executives • National Association for Retarded Adults (Board of Directors) • Special Olympics (Program Chairman) • American Red Cross (Volunteer)

✔ Faith's concern about confidentiality is emphasized at the top of her resume.
✔ Her Scope of Responsibilities sections cluster and organize her major duties.
✔ Two pages are easy to scan because of adequate spacing in all sections.

NURSING STUDENT

WANDA GERVAIS
31 Hurlburt Street • Baton Rouge, LA 70821
504/ 555-4558

OBJECTIVE: Staff nursing position in a large teaching hospital.

EDUCATION:

Sep 1988   **Louisiana College School of Nursing**
to   Pineville, LA
Jun 1991   **Diploma in Nursing**

Sep 1984   **Merrydale High School**
to   Merrydale, LA
Jun 1988   **Diploma**

HONORS: Nursing Honor Society (3 years)

CERTIFICATIONS: CPR, Basic Life Support, Red Cross First Aid

WORK EXPERIENCE:

Nov 1990   **Baker Medical Offices (Orthopedic Medicine)**
to   Baker, LA
present   **Medical Assistant**

SCHOOL ACTIVITIES:

Sep 1990   **Louisiana College School of Nursing**
to   - Resident Assistant
Jun 1991   - Policies and Procedures Committee

Sep 1989   - Class Rep to Nursing Staff Board
to   - Freshman Advisor
Jun 1990   - Admissions Office Student Tour Guide

Sep 1988   - Class Secretary
to   - Yearbook Photographer
Jun 1989   - Dormitory Council

✔ Wanda's Objective demonstrates a clear career path.
✔ As a student, Wanda emphasizes Education and School Activities.
✔ She abbreviates months and uses small type to de-emphasize dates.

NURSING SUPERVISOR

ANNE BAGLEY, RN
153 Red Bridge Road
Lewiston, ME 04240
207/ 555-8944

EXPERIENCE

Nursing Supervisor • PINEWOODS NURSING COMMUNITY
Lewiston, ME   1989 to present

- Supervise 90-bed continuing care nursing facility during 7AM-3PM shift.
- Direct patient care, frequently involving critical situations.
- Provide in-service training, orientation, and supervision of nurses and aides.
- Plan and implement patient care and develop discharge plans.

Registered Nurse • LAWRENCE MEMORIAL HOSPITAL
Auburn, ME   1985 to 1989

- Provided nursing care on 54-bed cardiac floor.
- Experienced in primary nursing, one-on-one nursing, and charge responsibilities.
- Taught in-service training courses on CPR, cardiac resuscitation, and medications.

Nurses Aide • AUBURN REHABILITATION FACILITY
Auburn, ME   1983 to 1985

- Maintained personal hygiene and safety of diverse patient caseloads.
- Experienced with pediatric and adult rehabilitation populations.

EDUCATION

Associate Degree in Nursing Science • WESTBROOK JUNIOR COLLEGE
Portland, ME   1983

LICENSES

Maine RN License. Certified in CPR, Advanced Life Support, and Red Cross First Aid.

References available upon request

✔ Anne's resume is concise, but comprehensive.
✔ She describes all relevant caseloads, teaching, and supervising activities.
✔ Important Licenses are also detailed.

OPTICIAN

LEONARD PAINE
901 Siphon Road
Chubbuck, ID 83201
208/ 555-3002

Objective:

Licensed optician in private practice or retail service.

Education:

IDAHO STATE UNIVERSITY • Pocatello, ID
Bachelor of Science Degree in Biology 1988

Certifications:

IDAHO / AMERICAN BOARDS OF OPTICIANRY
Certification as Dispensing Optician 1985

Experience:

BARRY RICHARDSON, O.D. • Pocatello, ID

Optician **1988 to present**
Assistant Optician **1985 to 1988**

Perform all functions of a licensed optician for a private practice:

- Annually service more than 1,500 patients of all ages with a variety of optical disorders including cataracts.

- Assist patients in selecting and dispensing frames.

- Measure pupillary distance and bifocal heights.

- Edge and tint both plastic and glass lenses as well as bifocals.

- Resolve patient discomfiture; follow up on contact lens users.

References:

Available upon request

✔ Leonard's resume is easy to scan because of section dividers.
✔ His Objective allows him flexibility in terms of his next company.
✔ His job description demonstrates his experience in all aspects of opticianry.

OSTEOPATH

NANCY EGLESTON, D.O.

Residence
106 Forest Street
Olneyville, RI 02909
401/ 555-0837

Office
18 Main Street
Providence, RI 02903
401/ 555-7770

EDUCATION:

1985   **Doctor of Osteopathic Medicine and Surgery**
RHODE ISLAND COLLEGE OF OSTEOPATHIC MEDICINE

1981   **Bachelor of Science**
PROVIDENCE COLLEGE

LICENSES:

RHODE ISLAND AND NEW YORK

BOARDS:

1986   Diplomate, National Board of Osteopathic Medical Examiners

---

TRAINING:

1985 to 1986   **A.O.A.-Approved Internship**
PROVIDENCE HOSPITAL • Providence, RI

EXPERIENCE:

1986 to present   **Private Practitioner**
FULTON MEDICAL GROUP • Cranston, RI

1987 to 1989   **Attending Physician / Outpatient Department**
CRANSTON OSTEOPATHIC HOSPITAL • Cranston, RI

OSTEOPATH (continued)

1988 to present	**Medical Director** HISPANIC COMMUNITY HEALTH PROGRAM • Fall River, MA
1988 to present	**Medical Director** RHODE ISLAND COUNCIL ON AGING • Providence, RI
1985 to 1986	**Physician** WORLD HEALTH ORGANIZATION • New York, NY
1985 to 1986	**Volunteer Physician** WORLD WIDE MEDICAL PROGRAM • Malawi, East Africa

TEACHING:

1991	**Dermatology Instructor** RHODE ISLAND COLLEGE OF OSTEOPATHIC MEDICINE
1990	**Adjunct Clinical Faculty** RHODE ISLAND COLLEGE OF OSTEOPATHIC MEDICINE
1990	**Course Director / Medical Studies** RHODE ISLAND COLLEGE OF OSTEOPATHIC MEDICINE
1989	**Volunteer Lecturer / Medical Careers** PROVIDENCE YMCA

PRESENTATIONS:

1991	**American Academy of Dermatology**
1990	**Medical Society Leadership Conference**
1989	**American Osteopathic National Conference**

OSTEOPATH (continued)

MEMBERSHIPS:

AMERICAN OSTEOPATHIC ASSOCIATION
RHODE ISLAND MEDICAL SOCIETY
RHODE ISLAND OSTEOPATHIC SOCIETY
AMERICAN COLLEGE OF OSTEOPATHIC PRACTITIONERS
AMERICAN MEDICAL WRITERS ASSOCIATION

PUBLICATIONS:

Egleston, Nancy. "The Pediatric Caseload in Osteopathic Medicine." *Journal of the American Osteopathic Association.* February, 1991. Vol. XX, No. 3, pp. 271-275.

Egleston, Nancy. "Current Trends in Osteopathic Medicine." *Osteopathic News.* April, 1987. Vol. XII, No. 6, pp. 347-352.

WRITING ACTIVITIES:

Book Reviewer for the *American Medical Writers Association Awards (1989, 1990).*

Multiple Book Reviews and Letters to the Editor in *Journal of the American Osteopathic Association.*

Multiple Free-lance Articles and Interviews published in a variety of newspapers and magazines nationwide.

REFERENCES:

Personal and professional references available.

✔ Nancy is in private practice and not currently seeking a job, so her Curriculum Vitae will function as a professional credential.
✔ Three pages is scannable because of section dividers and large headings.

PHLEBOTOMIST

TINA DEARBORN
1773 Chimney Rock Road
Bellaire, TX 77401
713/ 555-2074

SUMMARY: Experienced phlebotomist, knowledgeable about hospital procedures, skilled at specimen processing, and adept at dealing with a wide range of patient populations.

EDUCATION:

Certificate in Medical Assisting	**1985**
HOUSTON MEDICAL INSTITUTE	HOUSTON, TX

Liberal Arts Coursework	**1984**
TEXAS SOUTHERN UNIVERSITY	HOUSTON, TX

Diploma - College Prep Curriculum	**1983**
FRESNO HIGH SCHOOL	FRESNO, TX

EXPERIENCE:

Phlebotomist	**1990 to present**
RINDGE MEDICAL LABS	BELLAIRE, TX

Perform a wide range of laboratory functions including venipunctures, planting throat cultures, urine dipsticks, and specimen processing. Maintain accurate patient logs and files. Member of the QA Team to insure quality and error-free work.

Phlebotomist	**1988 to 1990**
JEFFERSON DAVIS HOSPITAL	HOUSTON, TX

Performed morning rounds on all floors including the Nursery and Emergency Room. Assisted in codes, outpatient drawing, and some specimen processing.

Phlebotomist	**1986 to 1988**
TEXAS MEDICAL CENTER	HOUSTON, TX

Performed a high volume of daily venipunctures and entered data into computer. Processed specimens and assisted with rounds.

Phlebotomist	**Internship 1985**
SPARKS MEDICAL CLINIC	PASADENA, TX

REFERENCES: Available upon request

✔ Tina's Summary stresses important credentials in her field.
✔ With no college degree, Tina includes all other education.
✔ She shows progressive career growth in her job descriptions.

PROJECT MANAGER

ANDREW SIMONESCU

3447 Rotunda Drive
Burlington, MA 01803

Residence: 617/ 555-2729
Business: 617/ 555-4000

EXPERIENCE: LAHEY CLINIC (LC)   BURLINGTON, MA

Project Manager	**1990 to present**

Direct research, analysis, evaluation, and implementation of new LC programs. Develop workplans, investigate trends, design and conduct feasibility studies, and generate cost / benefit assessments. Prepare operating proposals and recommendations to senior management.

- Analyzed current area dialysis services and technologies.
- Managed pilot study of computer-assisted radiation program.
- Evaluated alternatives to hospitalization for pediatric patients.
- Drafted recommendations for child care center for DMP employees.

TEXAS INSTRUMENTS – HEALTH SYSTEMS DIV.   ACTON, MA

Marketing Coordinator	**1988 to 1990**
Sales Support Administrator	**1987 to 1988**

Supported the sale of a major hospital information system. Managed company relationships with software vendors. Consulted on product positioning, pricing strategy, and market analysis. Planned and implemented marketing programs including trade shows, collateral materials, journal articles, press releases, direct mail, and demos.

NEW ENGLAND DEACONESS HOSPITAL   BOSTON, MA

Research Assistant	**1985 to 1987**

EDUCATION: UNIVERSITY OF MASSACHUSETTS   AMHERST, MA

MBA in Health Care Administration	**1987**

UNIVERSITY OF MICHIGAN   DEARBORN, MI

Bachelor of Arts summa cum laude	**1984**

✔ Andrew's resume highlights well-known health care institutions.
✔ He emphasizes his current position by opening with general statements of responsibility, and then highlights specific achievements with bullets.

PSYCHIATRIST

Curriculum Vitae

of

MARSHA BRAVERMAN, MD
2033 Alameda Avenue
Lakewood, CO 80215

Home: 303/ 555-2998   *Office: 303/ 555-7070*   *Hospital: 303*/ 555-7000

EDUCATION:

1970   Board Certified in Psychiatry

1965   **Doctor of Medicine**
                UNIVERSITY OF DENVER SCHOOL OF MEDICINE

1960   **Bachelor of Arts**
                STANFORD UNIVERSITY

MEDICAL LICENSES:

                CALIFORNIA
                COLORADO

TRAINING:

1967 - 1968   **Resident in Psychiatry**
                BETHESDA HOSPITAL • Cherry Hills Village, CO

1966 - 1967   **Resident in Psychiatry**
                ARVADA MENTAL HEALTH CENTER • Arvada, CO

1964 - 1965   **Intern**
                DENVER GENERAL HOSPITAL • Denver, CO

PSYCHIATRIST (continued)

PROFESSIONAL EXPERIENCE:

1988 - present	**Consulting Psychiatrist** COLORADO STATE PRISON • Sheridan, CO
1988 - present	**Part-time Private Practice** ARVADA MENTAL HEALTH CENTER • Arvada, CO
1980 - present	**Courtesy Staff** BETHESDA HOSPITAL • Cherry Hills Village, CO
1980 - 1988	**Chief of Outpatient Psychiatry Department** SWEDISH HOSPITAL • Englewood, CO
1980 - 1988	**Clinical Instructor in Psychiatry** UNIVERSITY OF DENVER • Denver, CO
1975 - 1980	**Staff Psychiatrist** DENVER GENERAL HOSPITAL • Denver, CO
1970 - 1975	**Staff Psychiatrist** ST. ANTHONY HOSPITAL • Federal Heights, CO

PROFESSIONAL ORGANIZATIONS:

AMERICAN PSYCHIATRIC ASSOCIATION

COLORADO PSYCHIATRIC ASSOCIATION

AMERICAN ASSOCIATION FOR FORENSIC PSYCHIATRY

CALIFORNIIA MEDICAL SOCIETY

✔ For convenience, Marsha lists three telephone numbers.
✔ Her C.V. traces her career from Education to Professional standing.
✔ Explanations of each position are not necessary on a C.V.

REGIONAL ADMINISTRATOR

DOROTHY ROSS

179 Tremont Street
Castleton, IN 46250

Residence: 317/ 555-3609
Business: 317/ 555-2159

EXPERIENCE:

VISITING CARE CORPORATION INDIANAPOLIS, IN

Regional Administrator **1989 to present**

Establish new staff-assisted home dialysis programs. Hire, train, and manage large technical and administrative staffs; select, order, and warehouse equipment; initiate and implement comprehensive marketing campaigns. Assume total P&L responsibility.

- Ranked as highest region in company in revenue growth in FY '90.
- Consistently operate at a 23% profit margin with no employee turn-over.
- Currently establishing two local dialysis clinics.

CARE SERVICES OF AMERICA CHICAGO, IL

QA Manager - Dialysis Services Division **1987 to 1989**

Administered QA Programs for 300 outpatient facilities providing three million treatments annually. Supervised QA analysts and all clerical personnel; conducted site visits and evaluated pertinent data to insure compliance with regulations; facilitated the annual re-certification process for each facility.

- Maintained a 95%+ annual rate of re-certifications.
- Established computerized data base of 23,000 patients.
- Maintained a low rate of incident reports related to risk management.

STAFF NURSE POSITIONS **1980 to 1987**

EDUCATION:

ST. XAVIER COLLEGE CHICAGO, IL

BS in Organizational Behavior **1983**
AS in Business Administration **1981**
Nursing Diploma **1979**

✔ Dorothy's resume reflects her successful leap from nursing into management.
✔ She describes staffs, programs, and facilities under her direction.
✔ She combines prior nursing positions under one heading to save space.

REGISTERED DIETICIAN

VINCENT MARTINI, R.D.
15 Wildwood Road
Dunaire, GA 30030
404/ 555-9248

Professional Experience:

DOCTOR'S MEMORIAL HOSPITAL
Food Production Manager

ATLANTA, GA
1989 to present

Manage the day-to-day line operation of food production for patient, cafeteria, and extended services use exceeding 4,000 meals per day.

- Oversee standardized meal preparation and develop modified menus.
- Hire, train, supervise, and evaluate a staff of 53 food production employees.
- Implement stringent quality assurance programs and sanitary procedures.
- Monitor a large capital operating budget and prepare annual budget reports.
- Train and supervise dietetic interns.

HOLY FAMILY HOSPITAL
Clinical Dietitian

ATLANTA, GA
1987 to 1989

Managed the primary nutritional care for a diverse patient population.

- Established departmental policies and procedures.
- Initiated quality assurance program.
- Supervised staff of dietitians, diet technicians, and food services employees.
- Conducted community classes and educational programs.
- Provided educational services for outpatient population.
- Participated in discharge planning rounds.

GEORGIA REGIONAL HOSPITAL
Dietetic Intern

PANTHERSVILLE, GA
1986

DEKALB COUNTY DAY CARE CENTERS
Nutritionist

DECATUR, GA

1985 to 1986

Education:

CLARK ATLANTA UNIVERSITY
Bachelor of Science in Nutrition

ATLANTA, GA
1985

✔ Vincent introduces current jobs with a short general statement of responsibility, then follows up with specific duties related to staffing, programs, and budgets.
✔ Hospitals and job titles are easy to scan because of bold and capitals.

DENISE GRADY, R.N.

441 Winn Street • Laurel, MT 59044   406/ 555-0822

HIGHLIGHTS:

Licensed R.N. with 14+ years critical care nursing • BSN candidate • Progressive charge responsibility • Proficient at staff training, precepting, and supervision • Participation on professional committees • Distinguished service award.

NURSING SKILLS:

- Assessment and observation for post-anesthesia complications.
- Administration of critical care medications and ordered medications.
- Cardiac monitoring, care of the ventilator-dependent patient, and those with arterial and Swanz-Ganz catheter.
- Charge duties, time scheduling, and staff evaluation.
- Pre- and post-operative patient teaching.
- Venipuncture in pre- and post-operative patients.
- Coordination and implementation of care of one-day surgical patients.
- Identification of cardiac arrythmias.
- Intravenous therapy.
- Liaison between hospital, agencies, and community resources.
- Support of dying patients and family members.
- Chairperson of Nursing QA Committee.
- Preceptor for University Advanced Life Support Program.
- Recipient of hospital award for distinguished professional service.

EMPLOYMENT:

HEALTH SERVICES, INC. • Billings, MT
Head Nurse / Recovery Room (1988 to present)
Assistant Head Nurse / ICU (1982 to 1988)
Staff Nurse / Emergency Room (1978 to 1982)

EDUCATION:

EASTERN MONTANA COLLEGE
Bachelor of Science in Nursing Candidate

ST. VINCENT SCHOOL OF NURSING
Diploma (1977)

✔ Denise emphasizes key credentials in her Highlights section.
✔ She itemizes all of her nursing skills to avoid repetition from job to job.
✔ She groups all of her positions together since they occurred in one hospital.

REGISTERED NURSE (Emergency Care)

ROBERT WYETH, R.N.

4 Patriot Place • St. Albans, WV 25177   304/ 555-3811

EXPERIENCE:

- REGISTERED NURSE with expertise in pre-hospital and in-hospital emergency care.

- ADMINISTRATIVE RESPONSIBILITY for Level II Emergency Room.

- DIVERSE PATIENT CARE - Code 99 management, IV therapy, ambulance transport.

- RESEARCH, DEVELOPMENT, AND DESIGN of specialized treatment units.

- INSERVICE INSTRUCTOR - EMT and critical care nursing re-certification.

- COMMITTEE MEMBERSHIP - Emergency Services, Nursing QA.

- COMMUNITY SERVICES - Emergency Medical Services Advisory Boards.

- CERTIFICATIONS - RN, CEN, EMT-A.

- TRAINING - Air / Sea Rescue, Med Flight.

EMPLOYMENT:

KANAWHA COUNTY HOSPITAL • Charleston, WV
Head Nurse / Emergency Room (1987 to present)
Charge Nurse / Emergency Room (1983 to 1987)

EMORY EMERGENCY AMBULANCE SERVICE • Dunbar, WV
Emergency Medical Technician (1978 to 1983)

EDUCATION:

MARSHALL UNIVERSITY
Bachelor of Science in Nursing Candidate

CHARLESTON COLLEGE OF NURSING
Associate of Science in Nursing (1977)

✔ Robert's nursing credentials are impressive as grouped under Experience.
✔ Use of capitals further emphasizes important activities under Experience.
✔ Robert can explain details of the Employment section during his interview.

REGISTERED NURSE (Psychiatric Care)

JUANITA WEEKS, R.N.
8239-J First Avenue
Dishman, WA 99213
509/ 555-3667

Education:

GONZAGA UNIVERSITY • Spokane, WA
Bachelor of Science Degree in Nursing   1988

Clinical Placements in community mental health, school health, medical-surgical, and pediatrics.

Continuing Education Units in Nurse's Role in Medical Emergencies, Group Dynamics, The Psychiatric Patient, and Case Management.

Experience:

VA HOSPITAL • Spokane, WA   1988 to present

Staff Nurse / Inpatient Psychiatric Unit

As part of a multi-disciplinary management team, provide primary nursing care on a 15-bed adolescent psychiatric unit. Hospitalizations range from three to six weeks. Presenting problems include depression, hostility, and sociopathy primarily resulting from the effects of long-term substance abuse and dysfunctional family units.

- Perform nursing assessments, devise nursing care plans, and coordinate discharge planning.
- Compile rating scales to assess progress of patients and effectiveness of medications and other therapies both in-hospital and at-home.
- Perform charge nurse responsibilities during weekend shifts.

BRIGGS NURSING HOME • Garland, WA   Summers 1986 to 1988
Nurses Aide

Organizations:

American Nurses Association

Washington Nurses Association

✔ Juanita is in her first job, so she presents her Education section first.
✔ Her diverse Clinical Placements will allow her to pursue various nursing areas.
✔ By following her name with R.N., she does not need a section for Licenses.

LILLIAN FONG
306 Dumbarton Road
Lakeside, VA 23228
804/ 555-4448

PROFESSIONAL EXPERIENCE:

ST. MARY'S HOSPITAL   RICHMOND, VA

Senior Staff Nurse - Pediatric Clinic   **1989 to present**

Coordinate care for patients and their families from admission to discharge. Provide direct care through daily contact on unit, and indirect care by coordinating and directing patient goals through a team approach with other staff members including doctors, psychologists, and social workers.

Supervisor - Ambulatory Care   **1982 to 1989**

Supervised head nurses and nurse practitioners with ultimate responsibility for 75 medical and administrative personnel. Assumed responsibility for entire hospital operations one weekend per month. Recruited, trained, scheduled, and supervised a volunteer staff of college students pursuing medical careers. *Planned and managed department budget of $800,000.*

Recruited, staffed, and supervised medical/ and administrative staff at two new community walk-in centers. Developed staff roles and training methods; provided ongoing troubleshooting in all areas of staff operations.

Other Nursing Positions

- *Henrico Doctor's Hospital* (1979 to 1982)
- *St. Luke's Hospital* (1975 to 1979)

EDUCATION:

VIRGINIA COMMONWEALTH UNIVERSITY   RICHMOND, VA
Bachelor of Science in Nursing   **1974**

Continuing Education • Time Management, Proposal Review, Needs Assessment, Program Evaluation, Planning and Administration, Quality Assurance, Nursing Management.

✔ Because Lillian is a manager, she presents her overall scope of responsibilities for each position, rather than the details.
✔ Continuing Education courses compensate for lack of a graduate degree.

CHRISTINE DEMPSEY
177 Lowell Road
Hudson, NH 03051
603/ 555-2765

OBJECTIVE: Director of Social Services / Employee Assistance Programs

EXPERIENCE:

NASHUA MEMORIAL HOSPITAL • Nashua, NH
Director of Social Services (1989 to present)

Manage discharge planning activities for 275 patients monthly at a general hospital specializing in medical-surgical services. Significantly lowered rate of discharge delays through efficient high risk screening. Reduced number of inappropriate hospital admissions through pro-active marketing of services to private office physicians.

Initiated and directed numerous employee assistance programs including medical screening, emotional counseling, and fitness activities.

ST. JOSEPHS HOSPITAL • Nashua, NH
Supervisor of Social Services (1985 to 1989)

Planned and implemented policies, procedures, standards, and budgets for a new social services department in a 375-bed teaching hospital specializing in trauma and rehabilitation. Spearheaded departmental growth to 16 staff members providing comprehensive clinical social work services to patients and families, many coping with catastrophic illness or accidents.

Non-medical staff representative to Trauma Counseling Committee.

MILFORD HOSPITAL • Milford, NH
Social Worker - Substance Abuse Unit (1983 to 1985)

EDUCATION:

RIVIER COLLEGE • Nashua, NH
MS in Social Work (1985)

NEW ENGLAND COLLEGE • Henniker, NH
BS in Liberal Arts (1983)

✔ Christine uses double lines to emphasize her Objective because she is seeking to make a career change from human services to industry.
✔ She supports this planned transition with related experience in her current job.

SOCIAL WORKER (Case Manager)

JAMES FUSCO

168 Locust Street • Sparks, NV 89431   702/ 555-8111

EDUCATION:

University of Nevada • Las Vegas, NV
Bachelor of Science in Social Work (1985)

Planning to pursue a Master's Degree in Social Work.

EXPERIENCE:

- Experienced with client populations including elderly, juvenile offenders, substance abusers, teenage parents, and the emotionally disturbed.

- Conducted comprehensive client assessments encompassing emotional, social, vocational, developmental, financial, and legal factors.

- As part of an interdisciplinary clinical team, developed, wrote, monitored, and modified client treatment plans.

- Prepared and presented cases to institutional committees.

- Provided crisis intervention and acted as a liaison to service providers and community agencies.

- Wrote reports and maintained case records and pertinent documentation.

- Participated in client education and discharge planning.

- Performed field and home visitations, court observations, and background investigations.

EMPLOYMENT:

Kings Row Mental Health Center • Reno, NV
Case Manager (1988 to present)

Sun Valley Clinic • Sun Valley, NV
Staff Social Worker (1985 to 1988)

✔ James' Education is his primary credential, particularly his MSW plans.
✔ His Experience section describes the breadth of his social work exposure, and allows him to avoid repeating duties under each position he has held.

SOCIAL WORKER (Forensic)

GINA YERRA, LICSW
228 Longview Terrace
Bloomington, MN 55420
612/ 555-3366

EDUCATION:

Expert Witness Training   1989
MOUNT SINAI STATE HOSPITAL   MINNEAPOLIS, MN
(12-week course providing training in determining diagnosis of mental illness, need for psychiatric hospitalization, and prediction of dangerousness and violence)

Master of Social Work   1987
HAMLINE UNIVERSITY   ST. PAUL, MN
(Coursework in Diagnosis & Treatment, Adult Psychopathology, and Therapeutic Group Work)

Bachelor of Arts in Human Development   1985
CARLETON COLLEGE   NORTHFIELD, MN

PROFESSIONAL EXPERIENCE:

Clinical Forensic Social Worker   1989 to present
DEACONESS STATE HOSPITAL FOR WOMEN   MINNEAPOLIS, MN

Perform assessments, psychotherapy, crisis intervention, and case management for a population of violent, mentally ill female adults referred from prisons, courts, and state hospitals. Function as an expert witness in court: testify as to diagnosis of mental illness, need for psychiatric hospitalization, and prediction of dangerousness and violence. Assume responsibility for unit in Supervisor's absence.

Mental Health Counselor   1987 to 1989
CHRISTIAN COMFORT HOUSE   EDINA, MN

Implemented mileu treatment for 8 female residents exhibiting chronic psychiatric disorders. Provided short-term counseling and continuity of treatment implemented by each client's primary therapist and administered appropriate crisis interventions to ensure the safety and well-being of clients. Managed all aspects of 3 client cases including recordkeeping, reports, scheduling of team meetings, and coordinating other agency and community services.

Social Worker Intern   1985 to 1987
ST. PAUL DISTRICT COURT CLINIC   ST. PAUL, MN

✔ Gina begins with her key qualifications: specialized training and education.
✔ She describes her training program to further validate her credentials.
✔ Her internship at a court clinic relates to her current forensic specialty.

SOCIAL WORKER (Private Practice)

MARVIN FRANKEL, L.I.C.S.W., B.C.D.

29 Eustis Street • St. Matthews, KY 40207 • 502/ 555-2861

CURRICULUM VITAE

SUMMARY

Licensed Clinical Social Worker with 10+ years of private practice in the diagnosis and treatment of family and / or work-related issues • Implement treatment plans involving crisis intervention, short term therapy, or intermittent treatment • Utilize a behavioral approach to reach treatment goals • Collaborate with other professional and community organizations • Professional consultant, trainer, supervisor.

EDUCATION

Master of Social Work   **1980**
BELLARMINE COLLEGE   LOUISVILLE, KY

Bachelor of Arts   **1978**
UNIVERSITY OF CINCINNATI   CINCINNATI, OH

CERTIFICATE PROGRAMS   **1980 to present**
Marital Therapy, Substance Abuse, The Family Dynamic, Group Therapy, Work Stressors

---

EXPERIENCE

Private Practice   **1986 to present**

Clinical Social Worker   **1984 to 1986**
FIELDS VILLAGE COUNSELING CLINIC   ST. MATTHEWS, KY

Clinical Social Worker   **1980 to 1984**
HUMANA HOSPITAL   LOUISVILLE, KY

AFFILIATIONS

Social Work Referral Service • National Association of Social Workers • American Academy of Clinical Social Workers • American Society of Training and Development

---

✔ Marvin's C.V. is somewhat atypical because it begins with a Summary which describes his breadth of social work experience.
✔ Marvin's Certificate Programs and Affiliations are integral to his profession.

SOCIAL WORKER (Psychiatric)

MARK SPRAGUE
Ph.D, L.I.C.S.W., B.C.D.
77 North Meridian Road
Turley, OK 74156
405/ 555-1138

Professional Experience:

Clinical Social Worker - Department of Psychiatry
HILLCREST HOSPITAL • Tulsa, OK   1980 to present
(University of Tulsa-affiliated teaching hospital)

Maintain clinical social work caseload encompassing client treatment, professional supervision, and consultation. Actively participate in professional associations and activities which contribute to the growth of clinical social work as a profession.

Scope of activities:

• Caseload of individuals, couples, groups, and families
• Treatment of severe character and personality disorders
• Specialist in phobia and panic disorders
• Supervisor of MSW candidates and colleagues
• Leadership role in professional organizations and conferences
• Contributor to numerous professional journals

Doctoral Clinical Resident
CITY OF FAITH HOSPITAL • Tulsa, OK   1978 to 1980
(Department of Psychiatry and Department of Social Work)

Clinical Social Worker
CHILDREN'S MEDICAL CENTER • Tulsa, OK   1975 to 1978
(Early Intervention Team for Developmentally Delayed Pre-schoolers)

Education:

Ph.D in Clinical Social Work
UNIVERSITY OF TULSA • Tulsa, OK   1980

Master of Social Work
UNIVERSITY OF TULSA • Tulsa, OK   1975

Bachelor of Science in Psychology
UNIVERSITY OF TULSA • Tulsa, OK   1973

✔ Mark distinguishes himself by listing degrees and licenses under his name.
✔ His Scope of Activities are presented in short, pertinent phrases.
✔ Mark presents only the basics of early work experience to avoid repetition.

SPEECH - LANGUAGE PATHOLOGIST

ANDREA SEIBERT
283 Bristol Way
Milton, MA 02186   617/ 555-2383

OBJECTIVE: SPEECH-LANGUAGE PATHOLOGIST in health care setting

EDUCATION:

> BOSTON UNIVERSITY   BOSTON, MA
> **Master of Science (1988)**
>
> CURRY COLLEGE   MILTON, MA
> **Bachelor of Science (1986)**

CERTIFICATIONS:

> American Speech and Hearing Association (1988)

EXPERIENCE:

> MASSACHUSETTS GENERAL HOSPITAL   BOSTON, MA
> Speech, Hearing, and Language Clinic
>
> **Speech-Language Pathologist** (1988 to present)
>
> Provide diagnostic, therapeutic, and associated counseling services within an urban teaching hospital clinical setting. Service infants, children, and adults presenting chronic articulation, fluency, language, voice, and neurological deficits.
>
> - Provide out-patient, inpatient, and short-term rehabilitation therapy.
>
> - Design and implement parent training programs for early child language stimulation.
>
> - Co-direct weekly pre-school therapeutic language groups.
>
> - Collaborate with in-house Child Development Center, Neuropsychology Department, Otolaryngology Department, Cranio-Facial Team, and Rehabilitation Medicine.
>
> - Consult with special educators in area school systems.
>
> NEW ENGLAND REHABILITATION CENTER   WOBURN, MA
> **Intern (1987)**
>
> BOSTON UNIVERSITY SPEECH AND HEARING CENTER   BOSTON, MA
> **Intern (1987)**

✔ Andrea's concise, specific Objective is emphasized in capital letters.
✔ Her Education and Certifications are key qualifications, presented first.
✔ Andrea describes diagnostic, therapeutic, and counseling proficiencies.

SURGEON

Curriculum Vitae

of

EDWARD RAUSCH, M.D.
3812 Troy Avenue
Beech Grove, IN 46107
317/ 555-0419

EDUCATION:

1970	M.D., Purdue University Medical School

TRAINING:

1970 - 1971	Rotating Internship Winona Memorial Hospital, Indianapolis, IN
1971 - 1972	First Year Surgical Resident Humana Hospital, Indianapolis, IN
1972 - 1975	Second Year, Third Year and Chief Resident Humana Hospital, Indianapolis, IN
1975	General Surgical Fellow St. Vincent Hospital, Indianapolis, IN
1975 - 1976	Fellow in Cardiac Surgery St. Vincent Hospital, Indianapolis, IN

CERTIFICATION:

1976	Certified by American Board of Surgery
1978	Registered by Indiana Board of Registration

FELLOW:

1979	American College of Surgeons

Edward Rausch, M.D.   **Page 2**

**TEACHING
APPOINTMENTS:**

    1981 - present   Indiana University School of Medicine, Indianapolis, IN

**HOSPITAL
APPOINTMENTS:**

    1976 - present   Humana Hospital, Indianapolis, IN
                                     Department of Surgery Chairman (1983- 1985)
                                     Executive Committee (1985 - 1989)
                                     Associate Chief of Surgery (1989 - 1991)

    1976 - 1980   Methodist Hospital, Indianapolis, IN

    1976 - 1987   St. Francis Hospital, Indianapolis, IN

MEMBERSHIPS:

                                 American Medical Association

                                 Marion County Medical Society

                                 Indianapolis Medical Society

                                 Indianapolis Chapter - American College of Surgeons

                                 Indiana Regional Surgical Society

✔ Edward's conservative C.V. sparingly uses bold only for name and headings.
✔ Experience is in chronological, rather than reverse chronological order to allow the reader to easily trace his career path.

ULTRASONOGRAPHER

JANICE DRAPER
21 Franconia Drive
Rose Hill, VA 24281
703/ 555-3307

OBJECTIVE:

Ultrasonographer specializing in abdomen, small parts, and vascular. ARDMS eligible.

EDUCATION:

ULTRASOUND DIAGNOSTIC SCHOOL • ARLINGTON, VA

Certificate of Completion - Echocardiography (1990)

Certificate of Completion - Sonography Program (1990)
Program covers the physical principles of ultrasound, medical terminology, tomographic anatomy, physiology, pathology, scanning protocols, and medical ethics.

EXPERIENCE:

ARLINGTON GENERAL HOSPITAL • ARLINGTON, VA
RADIOLOGY DEPARTMENT
Ultrasonographer (1990 - present)

- Perform diagnostic ultrasound procedures and interpret sonograms.

- Perform emergency examinations in intensive care unit.

- Operate diagnostic ultrasound equipment and identify malfunctioning equipment.

- Assist physicians with percutaneous puncture, mass biopsy, transrectal ultrasound of the prostate.

- Review pathology, surgical, and delivery reports to follow patient progress and provide a means of validating the accuracy of ultrasound examinations.

MEMBERSHIPS:

THE SOCIETY OF DIAGNOSTIC MEDICAL SONOGRAPHERS

✔ Janice's Objective denotes her profession, specializations, and proficiency.
✔ She describes her certificate program, as it is a major qualification in her field.
✔ Janice's use of bullets breaks up the description of her duties for easier reading.

Human Resources 10

Human Resources Is A Catalyst

Human Resources Administration is no longer the ugly stepsister of the business world, no longer just the keeper of time cards and records. It has come into its own as an important and influential arm of the corporate world, a conduit for fostering motivation and productivity in the workforce. As Human Resources professionals, you are attuned to society's changing lifestyles, values, and laws in order to advocate both the needs of the organization and the individual. You must demonstrate a thorough understanding of both to be effective in your jobs.

Demonstrate A Career Path

As society becomes more sophisticated, its complexity is reflected in corporations, and ultimately, in Human Resources departments. As a Human Resources professional, you now have a choice. Gain breadth as a generalist or depth as a specialist. Whichever path you choose, it is critical to demonstrate on your resume both your career direction and your expertise.

Use an Objective (or an Alternative to an Objective found in samples in Chapter 3 – Special Career Situations) to signal your career path at the beginning of your resume.

If you are a generalist, try to mention within your job description as many different Human Resources functions for which you have been responsible. Conversely, if you are a specialist, emphasize your comprehensive knowledge and experience in your specialty. The following catagories are some of the many diverse specialties that now fall under the Human Resources umbrella:

- Recruitment and Placement

- Training and Development

- Compensation and Benefits

- Performance Appraisal

- Career Management

- Employee Assistance

- Employee Relations

- Labor Relations

- Health, Safety, and Security

Communication Is Your Top Priority

To function as an effective Human Resources professional it is likely that you now require specialized education and training. Yet, never forget that your primary attribute is still your "people" skills – your ability to relate, negotiate, problem-solve, and function as a liaison within the organization.

So, in addition to competence in your special area of Human Resources, your resume also needs to reflect your strong interpersonal and communication skills. While it is difficult to quantify these skills, you can describe the types of staff, projects, and problems for which you are responsible. You should also claim credit for positive results which you achieved.

Many Paths Lead To a Human Resources Career

As the resumes in this chapter demonstrate, there is no typical career path for Human Resources professionals. Some of you began as administrative staff, many of you obtained undergraduate and/or graduate degrees in the field, while others entered from human services or academic careers.

Since only the end result is important – your effectiveness in relating to people and competently discharging your duties within the organization, no one career path is superior. Therefore, emphasize your current achievements and skills, and avoid repeating descriptions or presenting unrelated background information.

BENEFITS ADMINISTRATOR

MARTHA RAINIER
1857 N.E. Eighth Street
Bellevue, WA 98004
206/ 555-4927

EXPERIENCE:

ALDUS CORPORATION • Seattle, WA
Benefits Administrator (1990 to present)
Human Resources Coordinator (1988 to 1990)
Records Supervisor (1987 to 1988)

HIGHLIGHTS:

- Administer medical insurance, life insurance, pensions, disability insurance, leaves of absence, and anniversaries for up to 2,500 exempt and non-exempt employees.
- Recruited, trained, and supervise staff of five in records maintenance activities.
- Generate E.E.O reports, turnover analyses, and unemployment status reports.
- Designed procedural training manual for Human Resource Managers.
- Redesigned a professional leave program to promote interaction with HR Managers.
- Process unemployment claims and represent company at protest hearings.
- Assisted in designing a performance review form.
- Conduct industry-wide wage and salary surveys.
- Fully converted life insurance coverage to a new carrier.
- Created a system for tracking unemployment rates.
- Chairperson, Corporate Health Committee.

EDUCATION:

UNIVERSITY OF WASHINGTON • Seattle, WA
Certificate in Human Resources Management (1987)
Bachelor of Arts in Psychology (1986)

✔ Martha uses horizontal lines to segment her resume into easy-to-read sections.
✔ She lists all her job titles in one company to show career growth.
✔ To avoid repetition, Martha summarizes her experience under Highlights.

JOHN PARMENTER
293 Sparhawk Road
Ridgeland, MS 39157

Residence: 601/ 555-8421   Business: 601/ 555-6767

Professional Experience:

GASTON DEPARTMENT STORES • Jackson, MS

Benefits Manager (1987 to present)

Negotiate and administer all employee benefits plans including life insurance, accidental d&d, 401K plans, accident for travel, long- and short-term disability, savings through credit union, and health care.

- Collaborate closely with third party administrators to ensure compliance.
- Conduct employee orientation sessions and exit interviews.
- Fully administer in-house short-term disability plan.
- Facilitate the resolution of workers compensation claims.
- Track employee sick and vacation hours.
- Assist Operations Manager in all other human resources functions.

FULTON MANUFACTURING • Clinton, MS

Office Manager (1985 to 1987)

- Initiated efficient office systems and performed full-charge bookkeeping functions.
- Directed customer relations and provided troubleshooting of problems.
- Functioned as liaison between bankers, attorneys, and owners.

Education:

BELHAVEN COLLEGE • Jackson, MS

Human Resources Management, Benefits Administration, Communication, Interviewing Skills, Personal Finances (1985 to 1987)

✔ John introduces his current position with a general description, then bullets specific areas of responsibility for emphasis.
✔ He lists coursework related to his field to compensate for his lack of degree.

COMPENSATION & BENEFITS SPECIALIST

BARBARA ENTWHISTLE

413 Lone Oak Road
Mendota Heights, MN 55050

Residence: 612/ 555-2952
Business: 612/ 555-4050

EDUCATION:

Certification Candidate
AMERICAN COMPENSATION ASSOCIATION

M.B.A. Candidate – Human Resources Management
HAMLINE UNIVERSITY

B.S. in Business Management
AUGSBURG COLLEGE (1984)

PROFESSIONAL EXPERIENCE:

Compensation & Benefits Specialist
TRI-MARK INDUSTRIES • St. Paul, MN (1988 to present)

Highlights:

- Modified exempt and non-exempt salary structure to promote equitable compensation company-wide and position company competitively in the marketplace. Conducted surveys and benchmark pricing to establish new structure. Presented compensation seminars.

- Evaluated new positions and re-evaluated certain existing jobs to determine appropriate salary levels. Co-developed performance appraisal system and supervised its implementation to insure ongoing compliance with salary administration program.

- Facilitated the transition to a new insurance company in order to acquire cost-effective benefits. Researched and negotiated with firms.

- Managed HRIS software, user training, and security programs. Developed quantitative computer reports to enhance departmental productivity.

- Prepared and presented departmental budgets.

- Established new HMO, Stock Purchase, and 401K programs.

Personnel Representative
NORTH LAKES SAVINGS BANK • Roseville, MN (1986 to 1988)
DESMOND MEDICAL SYSTEMS • Minneapolis, MN (1984 to 1986)

✔ Barbara opens with impressive credentials in her Education section.
✔ She highlights major achievements in her current position.
✔ To avoid repetition, she lists, but does not describe, earlier positions.

CHRISTOPHER WILCOX
156 Pueblo Peak Road
Los Alamos, NM 87544
505/ 555-2059

Summary:
- M.S. in Counseling with a specialty in work/family dysfunctions.
- Proven ability to assess company need and develop appropriate programs.
- Well-developed presentation, training, and supervision skills.
- Demonstrated effectiveness interacting with staff and management.

Highlights:

SANTA FE DRUG TREATMENT PROGRAM	1990 to present
INDIAN COUNCIL OF NEW MEXICO	1988 to 1990

- Provide individual and family counseling to staff and management.
- Deliver stress management workshops company-wide.
- Explore client issues re: employment, self-esteem, and relationships.
- Supervised peer counselors in case management and counseling techniques.
- Collaborate with community agencies for appropriate referrals and services.
- Lectured in the areas of alcoholism and family dynamics.
- Authored several articles on topics related to human development.

DRISCOLL APOTHECARIES   1986 to 1988

- Directed personnel activities for $8M drug store chain.
- Updated Employee Policies Manual.
- Facilitated conflict resolution for full- and part-time staff.

PERSONNEL BOARD, TOWN OF LOS ALAMOS   1986 to present

- Selected to 3-person Board which screened, interviewed, and recommended placements for town-wide paid and volunteer positions.

Education:

COLLEGE OF SANTA FE
Master of Science in Counseling   1986

KANSAS WESLEYAN UNIVERSITY
Bachelor of Arts in Psychology   1984

Memberships:

AMERICAN PSYCHOLOGICAL ASSOCIATION
NATIONAL SOCIETY FOR HUMAN RESOURCES PROFESSIONALS

✔ Christopher's resume presents a career change into Employee Assistance by identifying his key credentials for the field in the Summary section.
✔ The Highlights section omits job titles and concentrates only on specific duties.

THERESA HERSCOTT
482 Hickman Road
Windsor Heights, IA 50311
515/ 555-9404

PROFESSIONAL EXPERIENCE:

CONTROLONICS INDUSTRIES   DES MOINES, IA

Employment Specialist – Corporate Headquarters   **1990 to present**

- Administered programs to meet company's temporary employee needs. Negotiated terms and conditions of a national contract with an outside agency. Made
  hiring decisions, conducted performance reviews, and recommended salary changes
  for 40 employees. *Annual charge backs totalled $500K.*
- Coordinated the recruiting and hiring function for Marketing Division.
- Researched and compared job-posting programs in preparation for establishing
  company's first job-posting program for 1,000 non-exempt employees.
- Designed and implemented an on-campus recruiting program. Conducted 300 on-
  campus interviews and presented management with top candidates.

Senior Recruiter – Marketing Division   **1986 to 1990**

- Screened and interviewed applicants for professional and executive positions.
- Designed ad copy and brochures for recruitment purposes.
- Counseled company employees about new positions as they became available.
- Initiated employee-referral program to increase quality referrals.

Recruiter – Administration   **1984 to 1986**

EDUCATION:

IOWA STATE UNIVERSITY   AMES, IA
B.S. in Human Resources Management   **1984**

References available upon request

✔ Theresa's resume shows a straight career path in HR within one company.
✔ To avoid repetition, she omits explanation of her position as a Recruiter.
✔ Her B.S. in HRM is at the end because of her strong work experience.

PETER FREITAS
17 Fordham Road
Osceola, IN 46561
219/ 555-0347

OBJECTIVE: Human Resources Generalist

EMPLOYMENT: **Human Resources Administrator**   **1987 to present**
               NOVACOMM CORPORATION   Elkhart, IN
               ($6M telecommunications equipment maker)

               Human Resources Administrator   **1985 to 1987**
               NET TECH COMPANY   Mishawaka, IN
               ($8M network software developer)

               Human Resources Assistant   **1982 to 1985**
               ASCOT METAL STAMPING   South Bend, IN
               ($3M parts fabricator)

HIGHLIGHTS: • Developed position descriptions

               • Administered employee benefit programs

               • Recruited all entry level and administrative personnel

               • Interviewed prospective job candidates

               • Designed employment advertisements

               • Directed corporate relocation program

               • Facilitated employee relations programs

               • Coordinated personnel policy administration

               • Researched wage and salary information

               • Initiated employee communication announcements

               • Identified external training sources

EDUCATION: **Certificate in Human Resources Management**   **1982**
               UNIVERSITY OF INDIANAPOLIS   INDIANAPOLIS, IN

REFERENCES: Available upon request

✔ Peter's concise Objective establishes his career direction.
✔ He briefly describes his employers to shows his diverse experience.
✔ Peter lists all positions, but combines data in his Highlights to avoid repetition.

MARC SHORTER

Human Resources Consultant

1774 St. Charles Road
Elmhurst, IL 60126
312/ 555-3054

EXPERIENCE:

Human Resources Consultant 1985 to present

Provide HR consultation to small, emerging, and established organizations in diverse fields including banking, publishing, software development, and education.

Strong record of innovative achievement in all HR areas including recruitment, benefits analysis & design, employee relations, training & supervision, career development, outplacement, policies and procedures, legal compliance, change management, cultural diversity, and dispute mediation.

Clients include *Apple Computer* and *Houghton Mifflin*.

Director of Human Resources 1982 to 1985
BANK OF CHICAGO Chicago, IL

Manager of Personnel Administration & Training 1980 to 1982
Personnel Administrator 1978 to 1980
DE PAUL UNIVERSITY Chicago, IL

EDUCATION:

B.A. in Human Resources Management 1978
NORTHERN ILLINOIS UNIVERSITY De Kalb, IL

PROFESSIONAL ACTIVITIES:

- Member, Illinois Task Force on state and federal legal compliance issues.

- Instructor, Personnel Management - Northern Illinois University.

- Chair, Membership Committee - Greater Illinois Human Resources Association.

✔ Marc's resume is designed as a promotional piece for his consulting business because of the heading and the emphasis on consulting achievements.
✔ Other information is listed to validate his credentials in the HR consulting field.

HUMAN RESOURCES MANAGER (Health Care)

FRANCINE CIULLA
60 Decatur Road
Scottdale, GA 30079
404/ 555-2394

AREAS OF EXPERTISE:

- Personnel Administration
- Program Development
- Labor Relations
- HR Information Systems

PROFESSIONAL EXPERIENCE:

GEORGIA REGIONAL HOSPITAL
Human Resources Manager

Atlanta, GA
1986 to present

- Manage a 5-person staff servicing 900 union and non-union employees.
- Oversee hospital payroll expenditures in excess of $12M.
- Formulate and administer all policies regarding recruitment, hours, wages, and conditions of employment for exempt and non-exempt employees.
- Provide training to department heads regarding fair and equitable administration of employee policies.
- Implemented a Human Resources Information System (HRIS).
- Represent management position during collective bargaining process.
- Analyze current programs and personnel in order to plan for future trends.
- Created hospital policy handbook and related documentation.
- Perform Quality Control of employee programs and practices.
- Keep current on all state and federal labor, safety, and health laws.

V.A. HOSPITAL
Human Resources Administrator

Atlanta, GA
1980 to 1986

EDUCATION:

B.S. in Human Resources Management
AGNES SCOTT COLLEGE

1980
Decatur, GA

✔ Francine describes her Areas of Expertise in lieu of an Objective.
✔ Specific figures and accomplishments strengthen her job description.
✔ To avoid repetition, she lists, but does not describe her earliest position.

HUMAN RESOURCES MANAGER (High Tech)

SUSAN BOYER   618 Old Leeds Road, Birmingham, AL 35223 ■ 205/ 555-3119

Summary:

- Experienced Human Resources Manager.
- Expert in employee relations, performance management, compensation and benefits administration, conflict resolution, policy development, affirmative action, training and development, and safety.
- In-depth knowledge of changing regulations, policies, and procedures pertinent to all aspects of HR management.
- Able to introduce organizational change with sensitivity toward the needs of the individual as well as the organization.

Achievements:

- Member of Senior Management Staff instrumental in assessing organizational need and developing policies and procedures.
- Introduced objective, accurate, and constructive performance appraisals in conformity with corporate policy and legal requirements.
- Facilitated the smooth adaptation by management and staff to new corporate policy, procedure, and culture following company merger.
- Introduced an on-line HRIS program.
- Delivered multi-media presentations to communicate changes in corporate policy.
- Planned and conducted diverse management training programs.
- Developed and monitored salary plans for exempt and non-exempt personnel.

Employment:

HUMAN RESOURCES MANAGER	NeuroTech • Birmingham, AL	1989 to present
ASST. HUMAN RESOURCES MANAGER	Dade Insurance • Bessemer, AL	1985 to 1989
PERSONNEL ADMINISTRATOR	Miro Finishing • Tuscaloosa, AL	1983 to 1985

Education:

BS in HR Management	University of Alabama – Birmingham	1985
AS in Business	University of Alabama – Tuscaloosa	1983

✔ Susan's Summary is a general description of her credentials as an HR Manager.
✔ Her Achievements are specific and span her entire career.
✔ To avoid repetition, she omits descriptions of each position.

HUMAN RESOURCES MANAGER (Manufacturing)

BETTY MCGEE
5892 El Camino Real
San Carlos, CA 94070
408 / 555-5363

OBJECTIVE: Human Resources Manager

EXPERIENCE:

Human Resources Manager **LASER OPTICS CORP.** **1990 - present**

Created and manage total Human Resources function for $20 million optical manufacturer with 500 exempt and non-exempt multicultural employees in 3 locations.

Highlights:

- **Benefits -** Research and upgrade broad cost-effective benefits packages to match organizational needs and industry competitiveness.

- **Recruitment -** Insititute creative multi-pronged recruitment program including in-house campaigns, national advertising campaigns, and job fairs.

- **Compensation/Performance -** Designed a complete wage & salary structure and formal performance review process.

- **Employee Relations -** Recognized as a hands-on manager with an Open Door policy and record of achieving "win-win" solutions.

- **Training & Development -** Pro-active in arranging in-house training for all staff. Monitored employee performance and fostered promotions.

- **HRIS -** Assessed corporate needs, researched and interviewed software firms, selected system, and facilitated the smooth conversion.

- **Downsizing -** Designed a severance package, supported managers in handling psychological needs of employees, and expedited paperwork.

- **Compliance -** Maintain knowledge of changing labor and safety regulations, and implement policies, training, and advisory committees.

Personnel Administrator **ALTEC OPTICS, INC.** **1987 - 1990**

EDUCATION:

Bachelor of Arts **COLLEGE OF NOTRE DAME** **1987**

✔ Betty's Highlight section conveys the breadth of his HR experience.
✔ Her job as a Personnel Administrator is more junior and needs no explanation.
✔ Betty saves space by listing company and college data on single lines.

CARRIE MUNSON

Human Resources

279 Gleason Street
Danvers, MA 01923

Residence: 508/ 555-4723
Business: 508/ 555-8000

EXPERIENCE: MAGNETRONICS R&D COMPANY • Cambridge, MA

1979 - present **Human Resources Manager.** Selected to establish new HR Department in response to company expansion.

Develop and direct all HR activities to meet the continuing needs of an evolving high tech organization. Participate in strategic and management planning sessions. Function in coaching/problem-solving role on issues of employee relations, employee development, and organizational concepts.

- Initiate wage and salary structures, benefit packages, EEO procedures, and employee relations programs.
- Recruit, train and manage HR staff including administrator, recruiter, and secretary.
- Establish recruitment and hiring function for all employees including the development and promotion of company image.
- Update HR policies and procedures based on extensive research of similar organizations.
- Coordinate in-house training courses.

1976 - 1979 **Personnel Assistant.** Performed a variety of cross-functional tasks to support corporate goals and objectives.

- Performed personnel recruitment and coordination.
- Oversaw facilities and space planning.
- Purchased equipment and supplies.
- Managed administrative support services.

EDUCATION: SPECIALIZED EDUCATION in Personnel Administration, HR Strategies, Interviewing Techniques, Wage and Salary Administration, Time Management, Needs Assessments.

1976 SALEM STATE COLLEGE • Salem, MA
A.A. in Human Resources Management

✔ Carrie uses an HR heading under her name in lieu of an Objective.
✔ Dates listed prominently in the left margin stress her years in the field.
✔ She combines narrative and bulleted statements to ease reading.

ORGANIZATIONAL CONSULTANT

LISA CHANG
18 Azalea Lane
Carrboro, NC 27510
919/ 555-0081

AREAS OF EXPERTISE:

- Organizational Consultation
- Training and Facilitation
- Management Development
- Employee Relations

QUALIFICATIONS:

- 10+ years as an internal and external Organizational Consultant specializing in health care and human services organizations.

- Comprehensive training experience within the areas of human relations, behavioral skills, management training, and organizational awareness.

- Training and facilitation with culturally diverse groups.

- Varied experience in crisis management, problem-solving, and negotiating in an "employee relations" role.

- Outstanding teaching and writing skills.

- Experienced in developing a Human Resources Information System (HRIS).

PROFESSIONAL EXPERIENCE:

Independent Organizational Consultant	**1981 to present**
Employee Relations Specialist REX HOSPITAL	**1975 to 1981** RALEIGH, NC
Special Education Teacher DURHAM SCHOOL DEPARTMENT	**1973 to 1975** DURHAM, NC

EDUCATION:

M.S. in Industrial Psychology	**1986**
B.S. in Special Education UNIVERSITY OF NORTH CAROLINA	**1973** CHAPEL HILL, NC

- ✔ Lisa's resume combines both general and specific areas of expertise, and is used to gain new clients or a new job.
- ✔ Her Experience and Education sections show her successful career change.

RECRUITER (Agency)

HAROLD SHERWOOD

53 Mockingbird Lane
New Castle, DE 19720

Residence: 302/ 555-2638
Business: 302/ 555-6066

OBJECTIVE: Corporate Recruiter

AREAS OF EXPERTISE:

PLANNING/
RESEARCH
- Expert at collaborating with management to determine hiring needs.
- Adept at locating resources to target qualified candidates.
- Proficient at uncovering channels to effectively reach key people.

RECRUITING
- Successful recruitment of talent for corporate staffing at all levels.
- Productive networking to maintain and expand base of contacts.
- Effective creation of recruitment advertisements.
- Solid telephone and resume pre-screening of interviewees.

INTERVIEWING/
SCREENING
- Skillful evaluation, assessment, and selection of candidates.
- Expert interviewing skills for effective transfer of information.
- Accomplished problem-solving ability from first interview to hire.

COMMUNICATION/
NEGOTIATION
- Diplomatic and tactful; skilled in effective and positive interaction.
- Proficient in negotiation and persuasive reasoning.
- Adept at establishing dialogue and developing rapport.
- Intent listener; able to discern needs and uncover important data.
- Expert at representing candidates and client companies effectively.

EMPLOYMENT:

RECRUITER (1987 to present)
Sales World, Wilmington, DE

RECRUITER (1984 to 1987)
Administrative Recruiters, Wilmington, DE

EDUCATION:

B.S. IN HUMAN RESOURCES MANAGEMENT (1984)
Ramapo College, Mahwah, NJ

- ✔ Harold's stylistic heading commands attention.
- ✔ His Objective establishes his specific career goal.
- ✔ He divides his experience into key functions to support his Objective.

LINDA GHELLI
1201 Second Avenue
New York, NY 10009
212/ 555-5977

EXPERIENCE:	**Senior Recruiter**	**1991 to present**
Recruiter	**1989 to 1991**
PAN AM WORLD AIRLINES	NEW YORK, NY

Organize and coordinate recruitment for reservationist and flight attendant positions. Represent airline in recruiting programs at high schools, colleges, and career fairs. Provide liaison between airline and candidates in resolving problems and communicating information. Closely collaborate with corporate headquarters to update procedures and trouble-shoot problems.

Screen and process letters of application; interview walk-in candidates; conduct preliminary evaluations; schedule panel interviews and fitness testing; arrange background investigations; verify applications and evaluation results.

Train and supervise newly hired recruiters.

Recruiter – Sales Staff	**1987 to 1989**
WILKINS DEPARTMENT STORES	WASHINGTON, DC

Screened resumes, pre-qualified candidates via telephone, and selected applicants for interview. Conducted initial personal interviews and recommended candidates for subsequent interviews with department managers.

EDUCATION:	**B.S. in Human Resources Management**	**Candidate**
COLLEGE FOR HUMAN SERVICES	NEW YORK, NY
A.S. in Psychology	**1987**
CAPITOL COLLEGE	LAUREL, MD

References available upon request

✔ Linda lists current job titles before the prominent company to show growth.
✔ To ease reading, she uses semi-colons to separate short job descriptions.
✔ She lists her degree status as "Candidate" because she has not yet graduated.

TRAINING COORDINATOR (Banking)

JEFFREY HEGSTROM
460 Monmouth Road
Worthington, OH 43085   614/ 555-2004

EXPERIENCE:

BANK ONE   COLUMBUS, OH
Training Coordinator   **1988 to present**
Assistant Training Coordinator   **1985 to 1988**

- Research, design, and implement staff development programs for orientation, training, continuing education, and community relations purposes.

- Programs encompass organizational management, adult learner principles, motivating and improving employee productivity, and comprehensive training on new bank products and services.

- Collaborate with department heads to determine current departmental procedures and to assess present and future staff development needs.

- Participate on Task Forces and Committees to keep current on the organization.

- Create self-paced training modules and job task analysis manuals.

- Generated a proposal on the cost-effectiveness of expanding the Continuing Education Department vs. contracting outside trainers.

- Coordinate with public relations staff to market continuing education courses to finance and banking professionals within the community.

AMERICAN BANKING ASSOCIATION
Advisory Board – Curriculum Development   **1990 to present**

EDUCATION:

UNIVERSITY OF CINCINNATI   CINCINNATI, OH
B.S. in Human Resources Management   **1985**
Concentration in Training

References available upon request

✔ Jeffrey's two most current job positions show growth within his company.
✔ He lists an Advisory Board position related to his field as an added credential.
✔ Jeffrey specifies his concentration in Training as part of his degree.

TRAINING COORDINATOR (Entry-level)

DIANA KEATING   38 Briar Cliff Road, Brentwood, TN 37027 ■ 615/ 555-6598

....

Qualifications:

- Experience in Training and Development within various organizations.
- Solid record of achievement in program design, implementation, and evaluation.
- Demonstrated skill organizing, coordinating, and motivating groups.
- Excellent communication, organization, and problem-solving skills.

Achievements:

- Active ASTD member and frequent contributor to *Training News*.
- Recruited, trained, coordinated, and motivated Advisory Committee members.
- Trained and supervised staff in the production of training materials.
- Member of regional Task Force on career development and training.
- Designed and conducted staff training on interview and recruitment techniques.
- Redesigned orientation package and conducted orientation programs.
- Chaired Program Evaluation / Needs Assessment Teams.
- Guest lecturer at Belmont College and David Lipscomb University.

Employment:

ADMINISTRATIVE COORDINATOR	AIDS Action Committee	1990 to present
COMMUNITY LIAISON	Department of Social Services	1987 to 1990
ADMINISTRATIVE ASSISTANT	American Red Cross	1985 to 1987

Education:

BS in Sociology	Fisk University	1985

References:

Available upon request

✔ Diana combines many unusual design elements, e.g., dotted underline heading, boxes instead of bullets, three columns for Employment and Education information, and omits narrative.

TRAINING COORDINATOR (Entry-level)

WALTER FENG

2049 Bergen Street • Newark, NJ 07102   201/ 555-3688

SUMMARY:

Educational & professional credentials encompassing training, research, writing:

- Master of Science in Training & Development.
- Bachelor of Arts in English.
- Certificate in Technical Writing.
- Knowledge of Chinese and ESL training.
- Experience in desktop publishing.

ACCOMPLISHMENTS:

- *Awarded Master of Science in Training & Development at Drew University.*
  Successfully completed ASTD-accredited degree program including a 275-hour
  internship at Hoffmann LaRoche and Schering-Plough Corp. Member, ASTD.

- *Created numerous Training Programs.*
  "Welcoming Diversity," a bilingual employee handbook
  "Bridging Differences between Chinese and American Culture"
  "Employing Training" classes to ensure federal compliance
  Case study materials for telemarketing skills course

- *Utilized writing and desktop publishing skills in high tech environment.*
  Generated newsletters, brochures, technical notes, ads, forms, and manuals to meet
  the needs of a growing firm.

EMPLOYMENT:

Technical Writer	CYBER CORPORATION	1985 to present

EDUCATION:

MS in Training & Development	DREW UNIVERSITY	1990
Certificate in Technical Writing	BLOOMFIELD COLLEGE	1985
BA in English	SETON HALL UNIVERSITY	1984

✔ Walter's Summary stresses his key credentials for a career change to Training
& Development: Education and Technical Writing background.
✔ He utilizes an attractive graphic style to reflect his creative field.

GREGG VON KAMP

Human Resource Administration

662-C Pontiac Avenue
Cranston, RI 02910

Residence: 401/ 555-2096
Business: 401/ 555-0884

EDUCATION:	**B.A. in Human Resources Administration**	**1990**
	QUINNIPIAC COLLEGE	Hamden, CT

- G.P.A.: 3.6
- Admissions Office Tour Guide
- Residence Assistant

Planning to pursue an M.B.A. in Human Resource Management.

EXPERIENCE:	**Training Coordinator**	**1990 to present**
	RHODE ISLAND DEPT. OF REVENUES	Providence, RI

Coordinate all aspects of 30 annual training programs for staff of state-funded tax education hotlines throughout the state. Consistently cited by participants for excellence in overall organization.

Highlights:

- Plan and execute agenda, logistics, collateral materials, and registration procedures.

- Locate, interview, and hire tax experts to participate in training.

- Provide on-site support in telephone skills during trainings.

- Prepare, compile, and analyze needs assessments and evaluation instruments.

- Provide ongoing liaison between Department and offices.

AFFILIATIONS: American Society of Training and Development

Rhode Island Human Resources Association

Volunteer - Rhode Island Association for Retarded Citizens

✔ Gregg uses a heading under his name instead of an Objective.
✔ He opens with his Education because he is planning graduate studies and his professional career is relatively short.

TRAINING COORDINATOR (Health Care)

ROBERTA LAMBERT
273 Wilton Road
Lauderhill, FL 33313
305/ 555-7068

PROFESSIONAL EXPERIENCE:

Training Coordinator   1991 to present
DADE DEPT. OF SOCIAL SERVICES – PROJECT FUTURE   MIAMI, FL

- Train and supervise five regional educators in the design, development, and implementation of quality AIDS education programs.

- Direct public relations activities including media broadcasts, community outreach programs, and consultation to school systems.

- Guest lecturer at local universities and professional organizations.

Marketing Consultant – Training Programs   1988 to 1991
FRANKLIN HEALTH CONSULTANTS   HOLLYWOOD, FL

- Developed successful marketing strategies to promote Employee Assistance Programs and Management Training Programs within the health care industry.

- Wrote curriculum for diverse programs including management training, assertiveness training, stress management, managing diversity, and AIDS education.

- Provided in-service training on presentation skills.

Therapist   1984 to 1988
MIAMI HEALTH CLINIC   MIAMI, FL

- Provided individual, family, and group counseling to alcohol abusers.

- Successfully recruited, trained, and coordinated large staff of volunteers.

- Established Project Recovery in conjunction with Alcoholics Anonymous.

EDUCATION:

Certificate in Human Resources Management   1988
COLLEGE OF BOCA RATON   BOCA RATON, FL

B.S. in Clinical Psychology   1984
FLORIDA INTERNATIONAL UNIVERSITY   MIAMI, FL

✔ Roberta's resume reflects her successful career change in 1988.
✔ She lists her Human Resources Management Certificate before her B.S. degree because it is more relevant to her current field.

JILL NEWCOMB
1369 Glenbrook drive
Garland, TX 75040
214/ 555-9012

SUMMARY:

10+ years management experience in Training with proven ability to:

- Launch the *Total Quality Management* process.

- Build *Employee Involvement* as the key strategy in quality improvement.

- Engineer *"Manage By Prevention"* transition in the workplace.

- Train and facilitate *Quality Improvement Teams.*

- Create a climate of *results-oriented participation* and *customer focus.*

- Guide *organizational change strategies .*

EXPERIENCE:

SOUTHWESTERN BELL – Dallas Offices
Director of Training and Development (1989 to present)

Provide training for 3,000 employees, with $2M budget and 30 reporting employees.

- Implemented Service Quality process with 50%+ increase in client satisfaction.

- Retained 100% top rated employees in turbulent industry.

- Decreased required training time by 35%.

- Increased training productivity by 45%.

- Initiated employee skill audit to mitigate "Workforce 2000" challenges.

- Controlled costs using process improvement to reduce rework 15% to date.

JILL NEWCOMB

Director of Quality Process (1985 to 1989)

Launched "Total Quality Management" process aligned with business goals.

- Participated in strategic planning process with corporate officers.

- Pioneered Quality Process group which provided training, team facilitation and customer satisfaction measurements company-wide.

- Created employee involvement process in cooperation with Labor Relations.

Manager of Human Resources Development (1983 to 1985)

Human Resources Generalist (1980 to 1983)

EDUCATION:

UNIVERSITY OF DALLAS
M.Ed in Organization and Human Resources Development (1983)

SOUTHERN METHODIST UNIVERSITY
B.A. in Psychology (1980)

PROFESSIONAL SERVICE:

Memberships:

- American Society for Quality Control
- American Society for Training and Development
- National Society for Performance and Instruction

Conference Presentations:

- ASTD - "Coaching Technical Experts as Instructors" (1989)
- NSPI - "Using Internal Consulting Skills for Customer Service" (1991)

✔ Jill's impressive career at a prestigious company merits a 2-page resume.
✔ She uses horizontal lines to segment her information into scannable sections.
✔ Jill uses italics to emphasize key phrases throughout her resume.

Law and Security 11

Follow the Letter of the Law

Law is a practical, precise, logical science. Although the field of law is constantly evolving in response to changes in society, the very nature of the legal process renders progress slow and methodical. The legal profession remains very conservative, and within it, certain basic skills are highly valued – the ability to organize; to communicate both verbally and in writing; to attend to details; to follow through in a timely manner; and to research, analyze, reason, and problem-solve.

In addition, legal practitioners, law enforcement officers, and security officials are charged with the responsibility of safeguarding the lives and property of others. They are expected to respect and defend the law. Sound judgment, maturity, and seriousness of purpose are called for.

Your resume needs to reflect these qualities both in presentation and content. It is, therefore, advisable to adopt a conservative approach to resume-writing to match the traditional "culture" of the law and security professions. Present your facts in a clear, precise manner. Select a simple type style. Print your resume on white paper. Write your cover letter on matching printed letterhead. And pay special attention to proof-reading.

Are You a Generalist or a Specialist?

Due to the complexity of the law and the litigiousness of society, many legal practitioners choose to become expert in a specific legal area. For instance, you may specialize in corporate law, real estate law, immigration law, etc. Or, you may choose to remain a generalist. In either case, this type of information should be clearly communicated in your Objective and within the body of your resume.

Consider A Curriculum Vitae

Attorneys, like physicians and professors, are a group of professionals who traditionally prepare Curriculum Vitae's instead of resumes. A Curriculum Vitae is a brief outline of your career. It lists, in order of importance, key credentials such as Degrees, Licenses, Positions, Memberships, Conferences, and Publications. Descriptions and details are purposely omitted and are discussed later, during the interview.

Emphasize Degrees, Licenses, and Certificates

The legal profession requires its practitioners to meet rigorous standards. Whether you are an attorney, a police officer, or a security manager, it is most likely that you have had to complete a comprehensive course of study to obtain licensing or certification. These credentials are considered "prequalifiers" in your field and should be stressed.

For instance, if you are a law student, stress your class standing or other academic honors. If you are an attorney, you can follow your name with "Esq." or "JD" at the top of your resume for emphasis. Or, if you are a paralegal, you can begin your resume with your Education section or Certification sections.

Similarly, if you hold other specialized credentials relevant to your career goal, such as Notary Public or a government clearance, you should highlight this information.

Some Pursue A Non-Legal Career

It is interesting to note that some professionals earn law degrees, but then utilize them in very different fields entirely, e.g., business management, health care, not-for-profit. They view their legal education as a basic foundation, or even combine their law degrees with an M.B.A. or a Ph.D. If you are in this position, you should write your resume to reflect the requirements of your industry, rather than your degree.

Keep Current

As a legal professional, you impact significantly on other people's lives. Your clients, co-workers, and professional boards of registration expect a high level of knowledge, skill, and professionalism. It is, therefore, critical that you keep current in your particular area in order to meet that expectation. Remember to reflect your continued involvement in professional education, organizations, or activities on your resume.

ATTORNEY (General Counsel)

WILLIAM KENFIELD, JD

203 Thorton Street
Shawnee Mission, KS 66202
913/ 555-4257

Education:

JURIS DOCTOR
Baker College School of Law
Baldwin City, KS (1979)

BACHELOR OF SCIENCE IN POLITICAL SCIENCE
University of Kansas
Lawrence, KS (1976)

MEMBER
Kansas Bar (1979 to present)
Second Circuit Court of Appeals (1980 to present)

Professional Experience:

GENERAL COUNSEL
Freeman Properties
Kansas City, KS (1989 to present)

Direct day-to-day legal activities for this residential, commercial, and industrial development and management company with holdings in excess of $800M.

LEGAL PRACTITIONER
The Law Offices of William Kenfield, PC
Bethel, KS (1979 to 1989)

Specialized in commercial and real estate law. Represented real estate companies and banks including Leavenworth Bank, Sage Banks, and Wyandotte County Bank.

Professional and Personal References available upon request

✔ William emphasizes his desire for confidentiality at the top of his resume.
✔ He immediately establishes his credentials by listing his degree after his name.
✔ William's resume is similar to a C.V. in its simplicity and conciseness.

ATTORNEY (International Law)

RALPH JACKMAN

17 Black Rock Road
Mobile, AL 36601

Residence: 205/ 555-8033
Business: 205/ 555-4550

EDUCATION:

Spring Hill College School of Law • Mobile, AL
Juris Doctor, May 1991

Research: The Geneva Convention
Activities: International Law Society
Internship: Corporation Counsel for the City of Mobile

Faulkner University • Montgomery, AL
Bachelor of Arts – French, May 1985

Semester abroad: Nice, France

EXPERIENCE:

1991 to present

Associate – Pierrat Law Offices, Mobile, AL
Advise and represent corporate clients in matters of international law and relations relating to commerce and trade.

1990 to 1991

Judicial Law Clerk – Honorable George Winston
First District Court, Prichard, AL
Researched and wrote opinions and orders, prepared jury instructions, and performed immediate evidentiary research.

1989 to 1990

Legal Aid – Amnesty International, Mobile, AL
Performed legal research for all committees.

Law Clerk – Harper & Barnes, Chickasaw, AL
Performed research and wrote memoranda for small, prestigious international law firm.

Judicial Law Clerk – Federal District Court, Mobile, AL
Researched and wrote legal memoranda on landlord-tenant, immigration, search and seizure issues. Served as French interpreter in court proceedings for Haitian residents.

LANGUAGES:

Fluent in French. Knowledge of Italian and German.

References available upon request

✔ Ralph's interest in and preparation for a career in international law is supported throughout his resume, e.g., research, activities, semester abroad, various professional experiences, and languages.

ATTORNEY (Law and Communications)

MALCOLM BOBKER
736 Division Avenue
Richfield, MN 55423
612/ 555-0477

OBJECTIVE

Career position which will utilize a dual expertise in law and communications

---

EDUCATION

AUGSBURG COLLEGE SCHOOL OF LAW   MINNEAPOLIS, MN
Juris Doctor magna cum laude   **1980**

BETHEL COLLEGE   ST. PAUL, MN
Bachelor of Arts   **1976**

PROFESSIONAL EXPERIENCE

Communications Experience (6 years) encompassed design/editing/writing / production of business and professional articles, reports, newspapers, brochures, and media spots; speech writing; coordination of media briefings; fund raising; budget preparation; staff supervision.

MINNEAPOLIS POLICE DEPARTMENT   MINNEAPOLIS, MN
ASSISTANT DIRECTOR OF COMMUNICATIONS   **1988 to present**

B&D FINANCIAL SERVICES CORP.   ST. PAUL, MN
EDITOR OF INTERNAL NEWSLETTER   **1985 to 1988**

Legal Experience (5+ years) includes planning strategies; drafting documents; and representing clients in the areas of corporate law, estate planning, probate law, real estate transactions, and wills and trusts.

PRIVATE PRACTICE   BLOOMINGTON, MN
ATTORNEY   **1983 to 1985**

LAW OFFICES OF WALLACE & VICKERS   EDINA, MN
ASSOCIATE   **1980 to 1983**

✔ Malcolm's Objective signals his desire for a non-traditional law career.
✔ His expertise in both law and communications supports his Objective.
✔ Malcom's Experience section effectively summarizes his 10+ years of experience.

ATTORNEY (Litigation)

NANCY HILDEGARD, J.D.
117-D Aston Way
Chandler Heights, AZ 85227
501/ 555-9541

OBJECTIVE: Associate specializing in civil and criminal litigation

PROFESSIONAL EXPERIENCE:

VERNAGLIA, LEY & YOUNG   SCOTTSDALE, AZ
Associate Attorney (1990 - present)

Concentrated experience in litigation of general liability actions encompassing district court trials, superior court jury trials, and small claims cases. Duties include arguing motions, obtaining depositions, and preparation of pleadings, motions, and briefs. Gaining criminal, probate, and appellate experience.

VOLUNTARY PROSECUTORS' PROGRAM   MESA, AZ
Volunteer Prosecutor (1989 - 1990)

Gained trial experience while in third year law school. Tried 8 jury-waived cases and assumed responsibility for preparation and investigation of the cases for trial.

PHOENIX LAW LIBRARY ASSOCIATION   PHOENIX, AZ
Assistant Law Librarian (1987 - 1990)

EDUCATION:

WESTERN INTERNATIONAL UNIVERSITY   PHOENIX, AZ
Juris Doctor (1990)

UNIVERSITY OF ARIZONA   TUCSON, AZ
BSBA (1987)

ACTIVITIES:

Volunteer, Legal Aid Society

Town Meeting Member, Chandler Heights, AZ

REFERENCES:

Personal and professional references available upon request

✔ Nancy's Objective is short and pinpoints her expertise.
✔ Her Experience includes paid and volunteer positions during law school.
✔ Nancy also lists current Activities which are related to her career.

ATTORNEY (Of Counsel)

MARTIN TABOR
391 GLEASON STREET
BROOK PARK, OH 44142   216/ 555-3735

OBJECTIVE: Corporate General Counsel

PROFESSIONAL EXPERIENCE:

SHUMAN, WASHBURN & DUGGAN   CLEVELAND, OH
Of Counsel (1988 - present)

Provide counsel to corporate clients on corporate legal matters. Heavy emphasis on banking regulations, employee issues, and preparation, administration, and maintenance of corporate records. Represent bank clients in loan transactions and mortgage lenders license applications. Negotiate and consummate the acquisition of companies.

MIDAS MUFFLER   CLEVELAND, OH
General Counsel (1984 - 1988)

Functioned as Company's Chief Legal Officer representing all legal matters. Handled corporate litigation, business acquisitions, merger agreements, and franchising operations. Reviewed and approved all legal documents and contracts with final authority. Provided management consulting regarding legal ramifications of corporate planned action. Centralized and directed activities of ten attorneys, three corporate Assistant Secretaries, an office manager, nine secretaries, and two legal interns.

BEALE TRANSPORTATION COMPANY   LAKEWOOD, OH
Staff Attorney (1979 - 1984)

AFFILIATIONS:

Admitted to practice of Law in Ohio, Federal District Court - Ohio, Federal First Circuit Court of Appeals, and the United States Supreme Court

Member of Ohio Bar Association

EDUCATION:

CASE WESTERN RESERVE LAW SCHOOL   CLEVELAND, OH
LLB (1979)

CAPITAL UNIVERSITY   COLUMBUS, OH
BSBA (1975)

REFERENCES:

Personal and professional references available upon request

- ✔ Martin's resume reflects a solid career growth in corporate law.
- ✔ He details his comprehensive experience in both management and law.
- ✔ Martin's liberal use of all capital letters makes a strong visual statement.

ATTORNEY (Personal Injury)

MONA DONAT, Esq.
1148 Park Row Drive
Arlington, TX 76010
817/ 555-2438

EDUCATION:

Texas Christian School of Law • Fort Worth, TX
JURIS DOCTOR magna cum laude   1991
Class Standing: 18/143
Bar Status: Admitted to Texas Bar (Dec 1991)
Honors: Washburn Scholar (1990)
          Dean's List (1990, 1991)
          U.S. Journal of Civil & Criminal Confinement (1988)

University of Texas • Arlington, TX
B.A. POLITICAL SCIENCE cum laude   1988

EMPLOYMENT:

Norumbega Legal Associates • Dallas, TX
ASSOCIATE   1991 to present
Represent clients in various stages of personal injury claims for a 12-attorney general practice law firm.

Hogarth Law Firm • Fort Worth, TX
LEGAL ASSISTANT   1988 to 1991
Performed research and provided general assistance to attorneys in a civil litigation firm concentrating in contract law. Prepared, wrote, and answered pleadings, discovery, motions and supporting memoranda.

MEMBERSHIPS:

American Civil Liberties Union

Anti-Defamation League

LANGUAGES:

Fluent in French and Spanish

TRAVEL:

Well-travelled throughout Europe, Africa, and the Middle East

ACTIVITIES:

Politics, fitness, music, literature

REFERENCES:

Available upon request

✔ Mona begins with her Education because of her scholastic achievements.
✔ She only briefly describes her current position because her duties are assumed.
✔ Memberships, languages, and travel enhance her professional credentials.

ATTORNEY (Tax Law)

NEIL WASSERMAN
48 Bridgeton Place
Wilkinsburg, PA 15221
412/ 555-3054

OBJECTIVE: Associate in a law firm specializing in tax law

PROFESSIONAL EXPERIENCE:

INDEPENDENT TAX CONSULTANT (1988 - present)

Provide tax consultation and preparation services for partnerships, trusts, and individual clients. Experienced in the research and analysis of tax liabilities and the preparation of federal and state tax returns and related schedules, estimates, and detailed depreciation attachments. Keep current in the field through independent study.

LAW OFFICES OF BENNING & MOORE   PITTSBURGH, PA
Attorney (1985 - 1988)

Specialized in servicing tax clients for this general practice law firm. Handled collection cases and conservatorship cases including court appearances. Gained exposure to law and issues related to wrongful death, consumer protection, landlord / tenant relations, will and estates, and corporate contracts.

INTERNAL REVENUE SERVICE   BRADDOCK, PA
Volunteer Income Tax Preparer (1983 - 1985)

AFFILIATIONS:

Admitted to practice of Law in Pennsylvania, Federal District Court, Federal Court of Appeals, and U.S. Supreme Court

Member of Pennsylvania Bar Association

EDUCATION:

DUQUESNE UNIVERSITY LAW SCHOOL   PITTSBURGH, PA
JD (1985)

CARLOW COLLEGE   PITTSBURGH, PA
BSBA (1983)

REFERENCES:

Personal and professional references available upon request

✔ Neil presents his area of specialization up front in his Objective.
✔ He describes both his tax duties and other related legal experience.
✔ Neil de-emphasizes dates because the other information is more important.

DAVID ROTHSTEIN
19 Rainbow Pond Drive
Irvine, CA 92664
714/ 555-0288

PROFESSIONAL EXPERIENCE

WILLOWICK LEGAL ASSOCIATES, Costa Mesa, CA (1987 to present)
Business/Manager. Manage total operation of an active law firm comprised of seven attorneys, three adjusters, three law clerks, and five secretaries. Oversee daily functioning of office staff and accounting records to insure the efficient and profitable operation of the business. Hire attorneys and administrative staff, assign and monitor caseloads, and provide liaison between attorneys and clients. Supervise disbursement records and implement collection procedures.

TECH GRAPHICS, Santa Ana, CA (1982 to 1987)
Owner/Manager. Established and managed a 10,000 square foot high-volume graphic arts firm in a large high tech industrial park. Supervised all aspects of this sole proprietorship including purchasing, inventory, production, advertising, accounting, customer service, and maintenance.

LAGUNA HILLS STATIONERS, Laguna Hills, CA (1980 to 1982)
Manager

EDUCATION:

UNIVERSITY OF CALIFORNIA, LOS ANGELES (1980)
Bachelor of Science in Business Management

UNIVERSITY OF CALIFORNIA, IRVINE (1987 to present)
Part-time Legal Studies

INTERESTS:

Stamp collecting, hot air ballooning, international travel

REFERENCES:

Available upon request

✔ David's resume balances his management experience with his interest in law in both his Experience and Education sections.
✔ He includes an Interest section because his activities are unusual.

CLAIMS ADJUSTER

HELEN HIGHTOWER
2401 Cherry Hill Park Road
Fair Lawn, NJ 07410
201/ 555-2009

EXPERIENCE:

PRUDENTIAL INSURANCE COMPANY   PATERSON, NJ
Claims Adjuster   **1990 to present**

Investigate and settle claims related to bodily injury, property damage, liquor liability, and commercial vehicles. Interact with claimants, attorneys, physicians, appraisers, and mechanics.

TRAVELLERS INSURANCE COMPANY   WAYNE, NJ
Claims Adjuster   **1988 to 1990**

Investigated and settled claims related to bodily injury, general liability, and public liability. Handled special investigations involving fraud and questionable circumstances. Interacted with claimants, attorneys, mediators, and physicians.

EDUCATION:

HOWARD UNIVERSITY   WASHINGTON, DC
B.A. in International Relations *cum laude*   **1988**

Planning to pursue a J.D. degree part-time.

PERSONAL:

Single; willing to travel and relocate.

Travelled throughout Africa and the Orient.

Breed and show purebred cats.

REFERENCES:

Available upon request.

✔ Helen highlights prominent companies and university in capital letters.
✔ She emphasizes her plans to continue legal studies by using italics.
✔ Her Personal section reveals unique activities which will spark interest.

CONVEYANCING COORDINATOR

CANDACE HATCH
570 Cerrillos Road
Espanola, NM 87532
505/ 555-4712

EXPERIENCE:

LAW OFFICES OF GOLUB & BUSA • SANTA FE, NM
Conveyancing Coordinator (1991 to present)

> Oversee all phases of residential real estate closings for this general practice law firm. Provide continuous liaison to banks, attorneys, buyers, sellers, and brokers to quickly resolve unique problems and ensure a timely closing process. Trained and supervised secretary in computerized document preparation.

TRABERT, HAWKINS & RASKIND, P.C. • LOS ALAMOS, NM
Domestic Relations Paralegal (1987 to 1991)

> Supported a general practice law firm in the administration of 100+ ongoing domestic relations cases. Prepared pre-trial documentation including complaints, summonses, motions, interrogatories, memoranda, separation agreements, and financial statements. Provided ongoing liaison between law firm, clients, and opposing attorneys. Researched, selected, and implemented computer system for all business functions.

COLLEGE OF SANTA FE • SANTA FE, NM
Instructor / Domestic Relations Litigation (1988)

EDUCATION:

LOS ALAMOS COMMUNITY COLLEGE • LOS ALAMOS, NM
Mediation Certificate (1989)
Paralegal Certificate (1987)

CONTINUING EDUCATION: Real Estate Law, Management Effectiveness

ACTIVITIES:

NEW MEXICO PARALEGAL ASSOCIATION, INC.
Director of Continuing Education

TOWN OF ESPANOLA, NM
Board of Selectmen

✔ Candace describes her knowledge of legal practice as well as her ability to problem-solve, meet deadlines, train staff, and utilize a computer.
✔ Her Education and Activities indicate her commitment to her profession.

HUMAN RESOURCES CONSULTANT

MARSHA BAINBRIDGE
217 Oak Springs Drive
Allandale, TX 78756
512/ 555-0365

EXPERIENCE:

TEXAS INSTRUMENTS COMPANY • AUSTIN, TX
(Worldwide electronics company • $3B annual sales • 27,000 employees)

Human Resources Consultant (1989 to present)
Employee Relations Manager (1986 to 1989)
Employee Relations Specialist (1983 to 1986)

HIGHLIGHTS:

- Provided pro-active counseling to staff and line management, significantly reducing number of lawsuits and minimizing liability/costs of third party actions.

- Developed an employee handbook of updated policies and procedures to improve communications and establish adequate foundation for defending future lawsuits.

- Successfully defended discrimination charges and suits before administrative agencies, state and federal courts.

- Developed and monitored $380K department budget, achieving year-end results of 15% below plan.

- Negotiated conclusions to government compliance reviews with 100% success rate.

- Implemented a systematic approach for awarding funds to non-profit arts and civic groups, enhancing the company's image in the community.

EDUCATION:

UNIVERSITY OF TEXAS SCHOOL OF LAW • AUSTIN, TX
Juris Doctor (1986)

UNIVERSITY OF HOUSTON • HOUSTON, TX
Bachelor of Arts in Psychology (1983)

✔ Marsha describes her prominent company to cue the reader.
✔ She condenses all of her experience onto one page by listing job titles and highlighting only her most important career achievements.

JOSEPH ESCALANTE
1805 La Jolla Vista Drive
Ventura, CA 93001
818/ 555-5597

INDUSTRIAL SECURITY SPECIALIST

Professional Experience:

INDEPENDENT CONSULTANT

Industrial Security Specialist   1989 to present
Assist civilian contractors in establishing and maintaining secure industrial facilities in compliance with DoD requirements. Utilize technical knowledge and problem-solving ability to ensure a smooth operation and a positive working relationship between each contractor and the DoD. *Major clients include Boeing Military Airplane Corporation, Hughes Aircraft, Bell Helicopter Company, and Northrop Corporation.*

- Perform preliminary surveys and recommend necessary strategies.
- Review pertinent corporate data regarding by-laws, organization, and officers.
- Assist in the construction of closed areas to house computer hardware.
- Conduct personnel background investigations.
- Monitor contract specifications.
- Present security workshops to management and staff.
- Closely coordinate with clients' corporate Security Officer and CEO.
- Primary resource in security education and classification management.

DEPARTMENT OF DEFENSE (DoD)
INDUSTRIAL SECURITY SERVICE

Senior Special Agent   1984 to 1989
Planned and supervised daily workflow for ten Field Agents performing background and security investigations within thirteen counties in southern California. Provided liaison with federal and state law enforcement agencies. Planned and monitored budget for equipment, supplies, and personnel. Maintained a consistently high performance level among staff. *Promoted from Field Agent (1980 to 1984).*

Education:

CALIFORNIA STATE UNIVERSITY, SAN BERNARDINO
B.S. in Criminal Justice   1979

✔ In lieu of an Objective, Joseph uses a heading to state his career field.
✔ Bullets are critical in organizing his lengthy job description for easy reading.
✔ To avoid repetition, Joseph does not describe his position as a Field Agent.

LAW STUDENT (Domestic Law)

ANNE TOLAND
1806 Bluemound Drive
Appleton, WI 54911
414/ 555-0947

OBJECTIVE: Associate with a general practice firm specializing in domestic law

EDUCATION:

LAWRENCE UNIVERSITY SCHOOL OF LAW   APPLETON, WI
JURIS DOCTOR   **1991**

- Graduated #1 in class of 125

- President, Law Student Division of the American Bar Association

- Volunteer, Law Students Against Domestic Violence

UNIVERSITY OF MINNESOTA   MORRIS, MN
BACHELOR OF ARTS IN SOCIOLOGY   **1988**

- Phi Beta Kappa

- Chairperson, Student Government Rules & Regulations Committee

- Volunteer, Samaritan Hotline and New Chance Women's Shelter

EXPERIENCE:

LAW OFFICES OF H. BREWER   OSHKOSH, WI
LAW CLERK   **1990 to 1991**

DEPARTMENT OF HEALTH, EDUCATION & WELFARE   WASHINGTON, DC
LAW INTERN   **Summer 1989**

References available upon request

✔ Anne's Objective targets her desired area of legal specialization.
✔ Her Education section stresses her scholastic achievements and her participation in activities directly related to her career goal.

GEORGE ATKINS

Permanent Address:
6 Priscilla Lane
Omaha, NE 68104
402/ 555-2003

Present Address:
119 Snowline Road
Hanover, NH 03755
603/ 555-4185

OBJECTIVE: Associate specializing in litigation with a general practice firm

EDUCATION: **Dartmouth College Law School**
JURIS DOCTOR CANDIDATE, 1992

- *Journal of Legislation* – Editorial Staff Member (1991 - 1992)
- *Moot Court* – National Team Competition (1990 - 1991)

Daniel Webster College
BACHELOR OF ARTS – Political Science, 1989

- *Dean's List (4 years), Gerard Fellowship Recipient*
- *The Collegian News* – Editor-in-Chief (1986 - 1989)

EXPERIENCE: **Office of the District Attorney**
Manchester, NH (Summer 1991)

Prepared and prosecuted a varied caseload of criminal offenses and civil infractions encompassing motor vehicle violations, property damage, drug offenses, and larcenies. Participated in arraignments, bail hearings, plea bargains, sentencing, and discovery motions. Conducted investigations; researched and submitted briefs; conferenced with victims and police, civilian, and expert witnesses; determined restitution and probation.

Law Offices of Mendlebaum & Nuri
Concord, NH (Winter 1991)

Supported in research and case preparation for this small litigation firm specializing in contract law. Researched case facts, case precedents, statutes, and code sections. Drafted interrogatories and attended depositions. Complied with motions for discovery and requests for production of documents; assisted in creating and enforcing wills and private trusts.

REFERENCES: Available upon request

✔ George provides his school address and home for the reader's convenience.
✔ His Education is his major credential, so he presents this section first.
✔ Part-time positions are directly related to his career Objective.

LEGAL SECRETARY

JANICE DE MARCO

1409 Crossman Avenue
Windsor Heights, IA 50311
515/ 555-9892

Objective:

LEGAL SECRETARY IN LARGE CORPORATE LAW OFFICE

Education:

A.S. DEGREE IN SECRETARIAL SCIENCE
Grand View College
Des Moines, IA (1987)

NOTARY PUBLIC
Current

Professional Experience:

LEGAL SECRETARY
Clive Harding & Associates
Des Moines, IA (1989 to present)

LEGAL SECRETARY
Law Offices of Peter Cooperman, PC
Urbandale, IA (1987 to 1989)

Coordinate and organize large caseloads for legal offices specializing
in corporate law; currently preparing 1000 new age discrimination-related
cases for litigation. Provide liaison with partners, senior associates,
lawyers, paralegals, and other secretaries within the office as well as
outside medical, legal, and corporate personnel. Train paralegals and
new associates in office procedures.

References:

AVAILABLE UPON REQUEST

✔ Janice's Objective is highlighted as a banner at the top of her resume.
✔ To avoid repetition, one job description applies to both positions.
✔ Janice's resume is asymmetrical for easy scanning down the left side.

PETER BULMER
1801 Duke Street, 4-B
Alexandria, VA 22305
703/ 555-2807

SUMMARY:

B.S. in Criminal Justice • Loss Prevention experience in diverse business environments • Solid record of planning and implementing programs to insure the safety and security of facilities, personnel, and inventories • Knowledge of OSHA and related regulations • Expert at investigating, reporting, and testifying on work-related incidents • Able to interact with staff and management.

PROFESSIONAL EXPERIENCE:

ACE HARDWARE DISTRIBUTION CENTER   ANNANDALE, VA
LOSS PREVENTION SUPERVISOR   **1990 to present**

- Oversee the security and safety of a 100 person, 375,000 sq. ft., three-building facility housing $35M in inventory.
- Directly supervise one Loss Prevention Officer and three Security Guards in security and safety checks, and general loss prevention duties.
- Collaborate with Operations Management during inventory processing.
- Conduct company-wide safety meetings to insure proper work habits.

GAINES PROTECTIVE SECURITY SERVICES   ARLINGTON, VA
INVESTIGATOR   **1987 to 1990**

- Performed close surveillance watches on subjects and areas to detect fraudulent claims, theft, illegal entry, and bodily harm.
- Conducted interviews and gathered information at places of public record to provide intelligence for investigations.
- Received Executive Protection assignments.

U.S. DEPARTMENT OF COMMERCE   WASHINGTON, DC
WORK STUDY ASSIGNMENT   **10 months between 1985-1987**

EDUCATION:

GEORGE MASON UNIVERSITY   FAIRFAX, VA
BACHELOR OF SCIENCE IN CRIMINAL JUSTICE   **1987**

✔ Peter's opening Summary describes the most important aspects of his career.
✔ His job descriptions provide detailed information about each position.
✔ Peter lists Work Study experience because of his prominent assignment.

SHEILA MAGUIRE
3472-D N.W. 22nd Avenue
Opa Locka, FL 33054
305/ 555-2256

SUMMARY OF QUALIFICATIONS:

- Associate of Science in Business Administration
- Paralegal Certificate
- Notary Public
- Diverse experience as a paralegal and legal secretary in large law firms
- Excellent secretarial skills including shorthand, typing, and word processing
- Strong research, writing, interpersonal, and organizational skills
- Ability to work independently, manage various tasks simultaneously, and meet deadlines

---

EMPLOYMENT:

GORFINE, DAVIS & McDERMOTT • Miami, FL   1990 to present
  Civil Paralegal / Legal Secretary

LAW OFFICES OF L. MILLER • Miami Beach, FL   1986 to 1990
  Civil Paralegal to Litigation Partner and Associate

JOSEPH FLAVIN, PC • Coconut Grove, FL   1983 to 1986
  Legal Secretary to Contract Law Attorney

ROGATZ-LANE LEGAL ASSOCIATES • Key Biscayne, FL   1980 to 1983
  Legal Secretary to Attorneys for Real Estate Company (Litigation)

EDUCATION:

MIAMI SHORE COMMUNITY COLLEGE   1983
  Associate of Science in Business Administration

BARRY UNIVERSITY   1976
  Paralegal Certificate (A.B.A. Approved Program)

CONTINUING EDUCATION
  Business Law, Accounting, Managing a Legal Office

✔ Sheila's Summary presents important credentials in a scannnable format.
✔ To avoid repetition, she lists her job titles, but does not describe positions.
✔ She highlights job titles and degrees by indenting them and using italics.

PARALEGAL (General Law)

JOHN BALDWIN
902 Ashford Dunwoody Road
Chamblee, GA 30005
404/ 555-3118

OBJECTIVE: Paralegal with a general law office

EDUCATION: SPELMAN COLLEGE • Atlanta, GA
Paralegal Certificate (1991)

GEORGIA STATE UNIVERSITY • Atlanta, GA
Bachelor of Science in Criminal Justice (1989)

ASSOCIATION: Member of Georgia Paralegal Association

EXPERIENCE: WESTIN HOTEL • Atlanta, GA
Senior Security Officer (1989 to present)

- Supervise five Security Officers in the maintenance of a secure environment for guests and employees.

- Direct control center operations: dispatch officers for service calls, document shift activities, monitor a sophisticated security system.

- Patrol hotel, conduct fire watch tours, and investigate and report criminal activity, security breaches, and fire and safety hazards.

- Assume responsibilities of Director in her absence.

- First Responder.

- Employee of the Year, 1990.

HOLY FAMILY HOSPITAL • Atlanta, GA
Security Officer (Internship, 1987)

References available upon request

✔ John's Education and Association sections precede his Experience section because they are closely related to his opening Objective.
✔ His Experience section demonstrates responsibility and competence.

PARALEGAL (Insurance Law)

GLORIA TRAINER

49 Oxford Street
Orem, UT 84057
801/ 555-5233

EMPLOYMENT:	**LAW OFFICES OF JANES & GRANT** **Provo, UT** **Paralegal** **1991 to present**

Perform a wide range of paralegal activities for insurance defense law firm specializing in medical malpractice. Duties encompass client interview, legal research, document review and analysis, monitoring schedules and deadlines, and drafting legal correspondence.

EDUCATION:

WEBER STATE COLLEGE
Ogden, UT
Certificate in Paralegal Studies   **1991**

UNIVERSITY OF TEXAS
San Antonio, TX
Bachelor of Arts in Political Science   **1990**

G.P.A.: 3.85

Activities:

"Semester at Sea" (1989)

Student Government President (1989, 1990)

Student - Faculty Representative (1988)

Certified Crisis Counselor (1988, 1989, 1990)

Volunteer Tutor, Martindale Women's Reformatory (1988)

Varsity Tennis Team (M.V.P., 1990)

INTERESTS: International Relations, Travel, Foreign Languages

---

✔ Gloria's first job out of school is in her field so her Experience section comes first.
✔ Since she has only held one job, she embellishes her Education section.
✔ Gloria lists Interests because they might help qualify her for a position.

PARALEGAL (Real Estate)

DENNIS LANGLEY
119 Outwater Lane
Garfield, NJ 07026
201/ 555-6661

PROFESSIONAL EXPERIENCE

NOYES REAL PROPERTIES CORPORATION, Nutley, NJ (1990 to present)

Analyst. Perform comprehensive real estate and legal analyses of prospective real estate investments nationwide. Review and abstract all documents associated with the investments including leases, partnership agreements, loan agreements, operating histories, title abstracts, insurance policies, and service contracts. Closely collaborate with Investment Committee from submittal through closing. Travel nationwide to insure compliance at closings.

TATE REAL PROPERTIES CORPORATION, Hoboken, NJ (1987 to 1990)

Regional Coordinator / Investment Division. Directed leasing and operations of single and multi-tenanted shopping centers, office buildings, and industrial buildings. Provided supervision and liaison with on-site management personnel and developers. Completed Real Estate Training Program for commercial and residential property appraisals.

HEINNEMAN PROPERTY MANAGEMENT, Newark, NJ (1985 to 1987)

Managing Agent. Managed commercial and residential properties in New Jersey and a 420,000 square foot shopping center in New York. Administered lease stipulations, maintenance, rent collections, and tenant relations. Closely collaborated with attorneys regarding property foreclosures, work-out situations, and litigation.

EDUCATION:

LE MOYNE COLLEGE (1985)
Bachelor of Science

FELICIAN COLLEGE INSTITUTE OF PARALEGAL STUDIES (1987)
Certificate

NEW YORK UNIVERSITY REAL ESTATE INSTITUTE
Real Estate Finance, Management and Operating Techniques for Residential Properties, Managing Building Maintenance, Principles and Practices of Real Estate, Negotiating Commercial Leases for Profit.

✔ Dennis' resume shows solid experience and growth in his specialized area.
✔ In each position, Dennis mentions only his most impressive responsibilities.
✔ His Education section demonstrates his desire to progress in his field.

POLICE CHIEF

HENRY COBB
2903 State Street
Ridgeland, MS 39157

Residence: 601/ 555-3317   *Office:* 601/ 555-1212

PROFESSIONAL EXPERIENCE:

POLICE DEPARTMENT OF MADISON, MS   1987 to present

Chief of Police
Manage 26 full-time sworn personnel and a $1M budget. Madison was cited in Law Enforcement Magazine (1990) as being the safest community in the Jackson area.

POLICE DEPARTMENT OF CANTON, MS   1980 to 1987

Deputy Chief in Command of Operations

Lieutenant –Commander of Internal Affairs

Sergeant – Squad Leader of Burglary / Robbery Investigation Squad

Sergeant – Supervisor of Uniform Patrol Squad

EDUCATION:

JACKSON STATE UNIVERSITY GRADUATE SCHOOL   1983
Master of Public Administration

LOUISIANA STATE UNIVERSITY   1979
Bachelor of Science in Criminal Justice

ACTIVITIES:

COMMENDATIONS • 2 Bravery Citations, Excellent Arrest Award

VICE PRESIDENT • Jackson Law Enforcement Council

COMMITTEE MEMBERSHIPS • Grievances, United Way , Educational Development

INSTRUCTOR • Mississippi Criminal Justice Training Division

✔ Henry only outlines his current position because his duties are assumed.
✔ To avoid repetition, he lists all previous positions, but does not describe them.
✔ Henry's dual degrees and numerous activities attest to his professionalism.

POLICE INVESTIGATOR

RONALD LA ROCHE
4309 Claiborne Avenue
Chalmette, LA 70043
504/ 555-0239

Education: **B.S. in Criminal Justice**
SOUTHERN UNIVERSITY • New Orleans, LA   1987

Training: **Municipal Police Officers Training**
STATE POLICE ACADEMY • Metairie, LA   1989

Certificates of Completion
CRIMINAL JUSTICE TRAINING COUNCIL   1987 to 1988

Search & Seizure • Interview & Interrogation • Applied Patrol
Techniques • Rape Prevention • Motor Vehicle Law • Courtroom
Testimony & Procedures • Lighting • Civil Rights Violation • Police
Civil Liability • First Responder • Controlled Substances & Drug
Paraphernalia • Criminal Law & Procedures • Breathalyzer • Basic
Firearms • Homicide Investigation

Experience: **Police Investigator**
CITY HOUSING AUTHORITY • New Orleans, LA   1989 to present

- Investigate, resolve, and report public safety issues at inner-city developments housing 150,000 residents.

- Respond to criminal situations and enforce applicable laws, statutes and ordinances.

- Conduct surveillances and investigations.

- Develop and maintain sources of information to deter crime.

- Received Public Safety performance commendation.

Auxiliary Police Officer
UNIV. OF N.O. CAMPUS POLICE • New Orleans, LA   1988 to 1989

Security / Special Police Officer
JEFFERSON DOWNS RACETRACK • New Orleans, LA   1987 to 1989

✔ Ronald presents Education and Training first as "prequalifiers" in his field.
✔ He bullets specific duties of his current job for easy scanning.
✔ Ronald's previous positions required less responsibility, so he only lists them.

POLICE OFFICER (Patrolman)

MICHAEL O'MARA
118 West Shore Road
Warwick, RI 02888
401/ 555-9076

Education:

RHODE ISLAND STATE POLICE ACADEMY
Certificate of Completion   **1991**

- Breathalyzer, radar, nightstick, field sobriety testing
- 2nd in class

JOHNSON & WALES UNIVERSITY
A.S. in Criminal Justice   **1990**

Employment:

CRANSTON POLICE DEPARTMENT   Cranston, RI
Patrolman   **1990 to present**

Perform all patrolman functions in this working class suburban community. Duties include traffic enforcement, domestic disputes, warrant service, summons service, and interviews.

WARWICK POLICE DEPARTMENT   Warwick, RI
Patrolman   **p.t., 1989 to 1990**

In addition to regular patrolman duties, performed booking procedures and criminal investigations.

LECHMERE SALES   Providence, RI
Store Detective   **1988 to 1990**

Implemented store security policies in order to apprehend shop lifters and reduce loss of inventory. Represent Lechmere Sales at court hearings. Train new security staff.

References available upon request

✔ Michael's Education section includes college degree and special training.
✔ He presents varied aspects of his law enforcement experience in all positions.
✔ Michael uses large left margins and double spacing to fill the page.

POLICE OFFICER (Special Detail)

GARY PHILLIPS
301 Hinesburg Road
South Burlington, VT 05401
802/ 555-9622

OBJECTIVE: Special Detail Police Officer

EDUCATION: **BS in Criminal Justice Candidate**   **1992**
UNIVERSITY OF VERMONT   BURLINGTON, VT

- <u>Coursework</u>: Psychology, leadership, communication

- <u>Activities</u>: Security escort service, varsity football

Finance 100% of education and personal expenses through employment.

EXPERIENCE: **Police Officer**   **Summers, 1990 and 1991**
CITY OF SOUTH BURLINGTON, VT

- Perform preventative patrol in assigned territory and special detail at community and private functions.

- Maintain positive relations with the public and state and local agencies.

- Conduct preliminary and follow-up investigations.

Resident Advisor   **1988 to present**
UNIVERSITY OF VERMONT   BURLINGTON, VT

- Manage residence hall of 75 men.

- Provide academic and personal counseling.

- Oversee maintenance and administrative functions.

- Select professional and student staff members.

- Liaison between students and Office of Residence Life.

References available upon request

- ✔ Gary is seeking employment while still in school, so Education comes first.
- ✔ His summer employment as a Police Officer directly supports his Objective.
- ✔ As a Resident Advisor, Gary demonstrates maturity and responsibility.

SECURITY MANAGER (Contractor)

MARY GRIGGS
1004 St. Charles Road
Elmhurst, IL 60126

Residence: 312/ 555-6209   *Business:* 312/ 555-9090

QUALIFICATIONS:

- Certified Protection Professional; B.S. in Security Administration.
- 10+ years progressive management experience in security operations.
- Accountability in finance, marketing, operations, and administration.
- Established network of clients in manufacturing, medicine, and education.
- Hands-on experience in physical security, audits, and inspections.

EXPERIENCE:

NELSON SECURITY SERVICES COMPANY   CHICAGO, IL
(National contractor of security personnel • 5th largest in the U.S. • 3,000 employees)

District Manager - Chicago, IL   **1990 to present**
(Direct a staff of Operations, Human Resources, Training, and Audit Managers in delivery of services to 30 major manufacturing accounts within highest producing territory • 400 employees • $12M budget)

District Manager - Oak Park, IL   **1988 to 1990**
(Directed a staff of Operations, Human Resources, Training, and Audit Managers in delivery of services to 12 medical and educational institutions in the Cook County Medical Area • 250 employees • $5M budget)

Area Manager - Gary, IN   **1985 to 1988**
(Directed 5 supervisors in the delivery of services to 5 commercial accounts • 100 employees • $75K budget)

Facility Supervisor - South Bend, IN   **1983 to 1985**
(Operational responsibility for the uniformed security services at St. Joseph's Hospital and Medical Center)

EDUCATION:

INDIANA UNIVERSITY NORTHWEST
SCHOOL OF LAW ENFORCEMENT AND SECURITY   GARY, IN

Bachelor of Science in Security Administration   **1983**

✔ Mary's opening Qualifications summarize her entire career.
✔ She describes her company because of its prominence in the industry.
✔ A brief description of each position quickly explains her scope of authority.

JAMES DREYFUS
56 Louise Avenue
Sioux Falls, SD 57101
605/ 555-8544

PROFESSIONAL EXPERIENCE

COLLINS AVIONICS COMPANY   Sioux Falls, SD
Director of Security and Safety   **1990 to present**
Assistant Director of Security and Safety   **1987 to 1990**

- Manage ten in the operation of a Government Security Department.
- Direct plant physical security operations for sixteen buildings.
- Administer $1.6M budget.
- Interface with contract security service.
- Implement Safety and Right to Know procedures.
- TOP SECRET clearance.

Production Manager   **1984 to 1987**
Production Supervisor   **1982 to 1984**

- Directed assembly and testing of high-accuracy avionics equipment.
- Used Just-in-Time methods to increase workflow and reduce inventory.
- Increased productivity by 85% during a 3-year period.

EDUCATION

NATIONAL COLLEGE   Rapid City, SD
Bachelor of Arts / Business Administration   **1982**

U.S. DEFENSE SECURITY SERVICE
Certificate / Security Manager Courses   **1986**

MEMBERSHIPS

Association of Industrial Security • American Society of Security Managers

---

Personal and Professional References available upon request

✔ James presents an overview of his current job, as daily duties are assumed.
✔ He includes professional memberships which are important in his field.
✔ Centering section headings allows the reader to focus on important areas.

SECURITY MANAGER (Hospital)

SAMANTHA FREMANIS
223 Pierce Road
Bangor, ME 04401
207/ 555-0681

EXPERIENCE

CITY HOSPITAL • Bangor, ME
Director of Security, Safety, and Communications (1987 to present)

Plan and manage day-to-day operations pertaining to the security, safety, and telecommunications for a 300-bed hospital facility including 4 parking lots and a 6-vehicle motor pool. Recruit, train, and supervise 33 special police officers, 11 switchboard operators, and 7 receptionists. Prepare and oversee an annual budget exceeding $750K.

Highlights:

- Continually professionalize Security & Safety Department by upgrading positions, implementing specialized training, and redesigning policies and procedures.

- Provide ongoing staff training in security equipment usage, maintenance, loss control prevention, and industrial safety.

- Perform quality assurance studies related to security and safety.

- Serve as Chairperson of the Fire Prevention and Safety Committee.

Senior Security Guard (1981 to 1987)

Security Guard (1980 to 1981)

EDUCATION

HUSSON COLLEGE • Bangor, ME
Bachelor of Science in Law Enforcement (1983)

References available upon request

✔ Samantha has progressed within the organization, but to avoid repetition she only describes her most senior level position.
✔ She provides an overview of the operation and bullets important tasks.

Management 12

Competence, Competence, Competence

Regardless of your level, industry, or management style, as a manager you are charged with leading, fostering productivity, accomplishing a task. If you want to progress in your management career, your resume must reflect competence.

Present Yourself As A Manager

The graphic presentation of your resume is extremely important in projecting competence. You can select any number of effective formats, but keep in mind a few simple suggestions:

- Emphasize company names, brief company descriptions, and your job titles.
  The prestige of the company will reflect positively on your own career.

- Devote the most space to your highest level management position.
  To avoid repetition, list, but do not describe lower-level positions.

- Set off achievements with bullets.
  Supply specific facts and figures when appropriate.

- Select a simple, uncluttered style of lettering.
  Avoid script or other "artsy" styles.

- Choose white, ivory, or a light pastel bond paper.
  Base your choice on personal preference and industry propriety.

- Use matching letterhead and envelope for your cover letter.
  Include a business telephone number if you can speak privately.

Consider The Big Picture

When describing your management position, think in terms of your achievements and your contributions to the company as a whole. Consider the big picture and do not dwell on every detail of your job description.

In fact, the higher up you are on the management ladder, the *less* you may want to include on your resume. Much about your position can be assumed from your job title and a description of the company itself. Information that is too elementary or too redundant to make an impact should be omitted. For example, as Vice President of Sales & Marketing, you should not take up space describing what a VP does on a daily basis. Instead, describe your territory, new product launches, and sales increases.

Include All Your Important Credentials

If you are like many managers, you may also excel in a specific business area, e.g. sales & marketing, software development, accounting. To combat the competition, it is very important to equally emphasize management and technical accomplishments on your resume. Remember to include all your business education and technical training. For example, a dual B.S. in computer science and business, or an M.S. in engineering in conjunction with numerous business course credits can distinguish you from other candidates.

Key Considerations

Management of a department, program, product, project, or technology can often be broken down into discrete responsibilities, e.g., staff, budget, time, equipment.

Consider the scope of your duties, and elaborate:

- *Staff*

    - How many staff members were under your direction?

    - Did you manage supervisory, administrative, technical, or clerical personnel?

    - At what level were they – exempt, non-exempt, union, part-time, contracted?

    - Did you recruit, hire, train, motivate, schedule, and evaluate?

- *Budget*

    - What was the annual dollar figure of your budget?

    - Did you have P&L responsibility?

    - Did you analyze, plan, forecast, or administer the budget?

    - Were you ever responsible for reducing the budget through cost savings?

- *Time*

    - Did you plan budgets, pricing, strategy, development, or promotions?

    - Did you schedule staff, shipments, development, or promotions?

    - Did you save time in development, assembly, manufacturing, or delivery?

    - Did you meet deadlines?

- *Equipment & Materials*

    - Did you supervise the selection and purchase of equipment or materials?

    - Did you modify equipment?

    - Did you maintain or repair equipment?

Age - The Supreme Irony

It takes many years of experience to successfully grow into the role of leader, decision-maker, manager. Therefore, it is not uncommon that among the ranks of management one can find many competent older job candidates. Unfortunately, despite the rapid graying of the baby boomers, in many industries age remains a "Catch 22" for managers seeking upward mobility or even a lateral move.

While it is evident that experience and maturity are key contributors to your career success, they can also be contributors to your career downfall. With aging comes myths about declining health and lowered productivity. With aging comes age discrimination. So, with aging also comes the need for an energetic resume.

To infuse energy, ask yourself what you accomplished in your position that someone else, even someone younger, holding the same position might not have. Describe yourself as self-motivated, results-oriented, a team player. Use strong action verbs to describe your achievements, e.g., "directed, implemented, initiated, spearheaded."

Some managers are very comfortable conveying their age right up front. They would not work for a company that would discriminate against them because of their age.

However, for those of you who feel that age might be an unfair pre-qualifier, pay special attention to your resume. While omitting *all* dates usually raises a "red flag" with a prospective employer, the following subtle modifications can be effective:

- Include only your most recent ten years of experience.

- Omit a direct reference to your date of birth.

- Avoid listing any dates from which your age can be readily inferred, such as date of college graduation.

- Include a Personal section with contemporary and active interests.

- Do not include a picture.

DEREK CARLSTROM
716 Spring Valley Road
North Las Vegas, NV 89030
702/ 555-8002

EXPERIENCE:	**Vice President of Administration**	**1985 to present**
	Operations Manager	**1980 to 1985**
	ARGOS MICROWAVE	LAS VEGAS, NV

Manage daily administrative operations for a national distributor of microwave components. Report to President.

Significantly contributed to growth of firm from $3M to $10M annual sales through the implementation of automated systems for production and administration.

Successfully assimilated a newly-acquired competitor through the smooth integration of personnel, backlog, and debt.

Set up and operated three corporate subsidiaries.

Identified and rectified software problems in an accounting practice.

Assumed roles of both Controller and MIS Director resulting in annual cost savings of $100K.

Primary areas of responsibility:

- A/R, A/P, payroll, financial statements, annual audits
- Hiring, training, supervision of personnel
- Policy and procedures
- Payroll, employee benefits
- Compliance with federal regulations
- Health and business insurance
- Support of software development

EDUCATION:	**BSBA**	**1985**
	WILLAMETTE UNIVERSITY	SALEM, OR

Planning to pursue M.B.A. at University of Nevada

✔ Derek describes both his areas of responsibility and achievements.
✔ To avoid repetition, he lists both positions but combines their descriptions.
✔ Derek's plans to pursue an MBA show his desire to advance.

GRACE LATHAM
334 Glacier Way
Horace, ND 58047
701/ 555-4309

PROFESSIONAL EXPERIENCE:

RAYMOND INSURANCE COMPANY   FARGO, ND
(Regional private mortgage insurance firm • 110 employees)

Vice President of Administration   **1/90 to present**
(Manage daily operations of Claims Administration, Claims Settlement, Customer Service, Xerographics, and Word Processing Departments • 25 employees • $ 500K annual budget)

Supervisor - Customer Service   **2/88 to 1/90**
(Staffed, managed, and documented activities of Customer Service Department • 15 employees)

Customer Service Representative   **7/87 to 2/88**

PROFESSIONAL HIGHLIGHTS:

- Established goals and objectives, developed policies and procedures, recruited and trained staff, and initiated and enhanced automated systems. *Turned around "problem areas."*

- Analyzed and improved departmental operations resulting in increased productivity. *Implemented in-house billing system for inter-department xerographic services.*

- Defined and closely monitored short- and long-term goals and objectives for all departments. *Prepared monthly staff presentations to senior management reviewing departmental status.*

- Attended corporate planning meetings and *assisted in writing policies and procedures.*

- Collaborated with Management Information Systems personnel to design and implement computerized systems. *Researched and implemented a new database management system for the Claims Administration Department which significantly increased its efficiency.*

EDUCATION:

NORTH DAKOTA STATE UNIVERSITY   FARGO, ND
Bachelor of Science in Business Management   **1987**
(Coursework included Business Management, Business Communication, Human Development, Personnel Management, Marketing, Economics, Financial Analysis, and Accounting Theory)

✔ The varied type sizes and styles accentuate important information.
✔ A short description under each position summarizes company information.
✔ Horizontal lines segment information into scannable sections.

BRANCH MANAGER (Manufacturing)

JOSHUA BRECKER
84 Clematis Lane
Hallandale, FL 33009
305/ 555-3378

Professional Experience:

J.P. BASCOM COMPANY
(Leading distributor of industrial products • $2B annual sales • 250 branches • 750,00+ customer base • 5 regional distribution centers • Strong customer service orientation)

Branch Manager	**Miami, FL (1990 to present)**
Assistant Branch Manager	**Miami, FL (1988 to 1990)**
Management Trainee	**Miami, FL (1987 to 1988)**
Sales Supervisor	**Hollywood, FL (1985 to 1987)**
Inside Sales	**Hollywood, FL (1983 to 1985)**

Achievements:

- Successfully managed company's largest branch, with sales of $20M.
- Increased sales from $15M to $20M in a twelve month period.
- Developed and maintained $500K+ budget for payroll and non-payroll expenses.
- Recruited and directed staff of 80 in distribution, operations, and sales management.
- Developed new credit procedure resulting in 7.5% improvement in receivables in six months.
- Revitalized personnel training procedures and warehouse operations workflow.
- Forecasted and improved inventory levels from $2.1M to $2.8M in six month period.
- Increased customer service timely pick-up rate from 53% to 92% in six month period.
- Consistently exceeded sales and service level goals.
- Received President's Club Award.
- Member of Business Development Committee.

Education:

FLORIDA ATLANTIC UNIVERSITY
BSBA (1983)

✔ Joshua briefly describes his company's credentials because they validate his own career accomplishments.
✔ He highlights his achievements by using bullets to present his experience.

MARY COLLIER
790 Holyoke Street
Broomall, PA 19008
215/ 555-6112

EXPERIENCE:

EXECU-SEARCH CORPORATION   PHILADELPHIA, PA

Branch Manager   **1988 to present**
Opened and operated new branch for this leading placement firm.
Assumed major responsibility for P&L, strategic planning, budgeting,
sales and marketing, and personnel. For three months simultaneously
managed second branch. *Spearheaded sales from $0 to nearly $400K
in a new and highly competitive market.*

MARKLINE BUSINESS SYSTEMS   BALA CYNWYD, PA

Account Representative   **1986 to 1988**
Developed new business and managed established accounts for the
largest regional office equipment dealer in the U.S. Utilized telemarketing, direct mail marketing, and individual and small group presentations to sell a multi-product line. *Top sales producer in 1988.*

TUCKER'S   DREXEL HILL, PA

Store Manager   **1983 to 1986**
Recruited to turn around poorly performing locations for this leading
sporting goods chain. Improved inventory control and staff training
procedures resulting in the increase of sales by 32%. *Consistently
earned bonuses for outstanding performance.*

EDUCATION:

DREXEL UNIVERSITY   PHILADELPHIA, PA

B.S. in Psychology cum laude   **1983**

MADISON SALES TRAINING COMPANY   MARPLE, PA

Management Training Courses   **1985 to 1989**

✔ Mary highlights company names because of their renown.
✔ Her short job descriptions end with solid achievements emphasized in italics.
✔ Management Training courses compensate for her lack of a business degree.

CHARLES NORTON

14 Cumberland Drive
Pawtucket, RI 02860

401/ 555-7003

EXPERIENCE HURST CONTROLS COMPANY   PROVIDENCE, RI

Mar 88
to
present

President and Chief Operating Officer

Direct Sales, Service, R&D, Manufacturing, and Administration. Spear-headed organization from 85 employees to more than 300 with an increase in annual revenues from $8M to more than $50M.

METRONICS INCORPORATED   ATTLEBORO, MA

Jan 86
to
Mar 88

Vice President   **Weigh Systems Group**

Directed worldwide Business/Product Planning, Marketing Development, R&D and Manufacturing for Process Controls generating $250M in annual revenues. Successfully launched the WeighStar Process Controlling System.

GILES MONITOR COMPANY   WARWICK, RI

Apr 80
to
Dec 85

General Manager   **Monitoring Systems Division**

Directed eastern third of U.S. industrial Process Monitor sales, service and support organization consisting of 220 personnel. Eastern Operations generated more than $350M in annual revenues, achieving number one standing nationwide in 1982 for overall revenues, bookings and expense goal attainment.

EDUCATION BROWN UNIVERSITY   PROVIDENCE, RI

Jun 84

M.B.A. in Industrial Management

Jun 70

B.S. in Chemical Engineering

✔ Charles highlight essentials of his current positions, not details.
✔ He omits his earliest jobs because of their relative insignificance.
✔ Dates in the margin are de-emphasized by abbreviating the months.

CONSTRUCTION MANAGER (Residential)

JOHN SHALES

2003 104th Avenue
Bellevue, WA 98004
206/ 555-1594

EXPERIENCE:

Construction Manager   **1989 to present**
FALCO CONSTRUCTION COMPANY   SEATTLE, WA

Direct a $12M residential development project in Renton. Successful in meeting time and budget constraints and overcoming a "soft" market.

- Acquire town *building permits.*
- Calculate and finalize *job costs.*
- Locate *subcontractors*; negotiate contracts, payment terms and conditions; establish work completion dates.
- Select *project specifications*, e.g., finishes and colors, lighting, trim, tile fixtures, cabinetry, and landscaping.
- Personally *manage site* including scheduling, coordinating, and overseeing work of subcontractors.
- Collaborate with *loan officer* and *construction inspector.*
- Oversee *town inspections.*
- Support real estate brokers in *sales activities.*

Partner/Construction Manager   **1986 to 1989**
BABBETT PROPERTIES   TACOMA, WA

Directed development of a $2M, twenty unit condominium in Bothell. Oversaw all aspects of construction management, scheduling, specifications, and sight inspections.

- Acquired town *and state permits.*
- Negotiated *construction loans.*
- Collaborated with *architects, brokers, and attorneys.*
- Established rules, bylaws, and fees for *condo associations.*
- Resolved inquiries and problems for *buyers/owners.*

EDUCATION:

Bachelor of Arts   **1986**
SEATTLE PACIFIC UNIVERSITY   SEATTLE, WA

✔ While both of John's positions are similar, his current project is much larger in scope, so he explains it in greater detail.
✔ The two horizontal lines focus the reader's eyes on the Experience section.

JAMES LONERGAN

2337 Valencia Drive
Del Paso Heights, CA 95838
916/ 555-0318

PROFESSIONAL EXPERIENCE:

PIZZA PARLOR CORPORATION   SACRAMENTO, CA
RETAIL CONSTRUCTION & PROPERTY MANAGER   **1985 to present**

Direct construction functions and supervise coordinators in the management of properties throughout the entire Pacific coast. Locate contractors, negotiate construction contracts, participate in lease negotiations, coordinate store openings, and oversee repair and maintenance.

Highlights:

- Achieved 93% on-target store opening dates.
- Decreased build out expense by 8%.
- Rewrote comprehensive building specifications.

SALE KING MANUFACTURING COMPANY   LOS ANGELES, CA
PRODUCTION MANAGER / Promotional Items   **1980 to 1985**

Directed the planning and operation of two technical production departments including management of five supervisors and a $750,000+ budget. Closely coordinated with all departments on new products, displays, and catalogues. *Successfully implemented new production systems, personnel programs, and product ideas which significantly improved production efficiencies and contributed to 35% annual growth in company sales.*

Highlights:

- Reduced department costs by 18%
- Reduced quality rejects from 6% to below 2%.
- Developed training program which reduced training curve by 20%.

EDUCATION:

UNIVERSITY OF CHARLESTON   CHARLESTON, WV
BACHELOR OF SCIENCE   **1979**

✔ James' positions appear dissimilar, but both demonstrate management skills.
✔ He devotes equal space to both positions, which enhances their importance.
✔ His Highlights are very specific and supported by percentages.

FLORENCE DRUCKER

572 Lincoln Road
Portland, OR 97242
503/ 555-1560

EXPERIENCE

Area Contracts Manager (1989 to present)
STATE OF OREGON
DEPARTMENT OF TRANSPORTATION

Initiate, maintain, and monitor contract documents for an Area office with a $10M budget. Provide technical assistance and training to vendors and in-house staff to insure compliance with state procedures and regulations. *Received Certificate of Performance Recognition Award.*

Highlights:

- Performed cost analyses and payroll projections to accurately plan budgets.
- Co-authored policy to track expenditures for special budget fund.
- Consolidated contract processing resulting in increased efficiency.
- Identified potential savings and revenue enhancements.
- Initiated a post-audit procedure to improve vendor performance.
- Conducted random audits at vendor locations to insure contract compliance.
- Developed and implemented post-audit corrective action plans with vendors.
- Directed office relocations including space planning and landlord negotiations.

EDUCATION

BSBA (1988)
LEWIS AND CLARK COLLEGE
SCHOOL OF MANAGEMENT

Planning to pursue an MBA.

REFERENCES

Available upon request

✔ Florence has only held one job, but her resume is not sparse because she describes her position in depth and makes excellent use of section headings.
✔ The Highlights section is a very effective way to utilize space on a resume.

CORPORATE LOGISTICS DIRECTOR

MICHAEL MANCUSO
6821 SECOND AVENUE
NEW YORK, NY 10014   212/ 555-6476

PROFESSIONAL EXPERIENCE:

CHARLESTON CLOTHING CORPORATION   NEW YORK, NY
$400M subsidiary of largest U.S. retailer of men's outerwear with $1B in annual sales.

Director of Corporate Logistics (1988 to present)
Direct staff of 15 in the importation, movement, and distribution of raw materials and finished product. Manage centralized billing, inventory control, fabric lab, pattern and marker departments, and computer-aided design area.

Director of Operations (1986 to 1988)
Procured raw materials from domestic sources for manufacturing at U.S. facilities. Established central cost engineering function for company.

BARTON MANSFIELD COMPANY   NEW YORK, NY
$175M manufacturer of children's apparel.

Vice President of Administration (1985 to 1986)
Appointed to 5-member Executive Board. Established policies and directed staff of 21 in managing the flow of information and product throughout the company.

Corporate Operations Manager (1984 to 1985)
Developed and monitored Master Operating Plan adopted as model within the industry.

Legal Counsel (1980 to 1984)

EDUCATION:

COLUMBIA UNIVERSITY BUSINESS SCHOOL   NEW YORK, NY
M.B.A. / Taxation (1984)

SKIDMORE COLLEGE LAW SCHOOL   SARATOGA SPRINGS, NY
Juris Doctor (1978)

COLGATE UNIVERSITY   HAMILTON, NY
BSBA (1975)

REFERENCES: Available upon request.

✔ Michael's heading reminds the reader to keep his job search confidential.
✔ His high level of responsibility requires very little elaboration.
✔ Michael's Education is so impressive that he could choose to present it first.

CREDIT MANAGER

LAUREEN MACKENZIE
99 Freedom Way
Rossmoyne, OH 45236
513/ 555-9539

EXPERIENCE:

Credit Manager	**1985 to present**
Accounting Supervisor	**1983 to 1985**
GLEASON COMPANY	CINCINATTI, OH

Plan and manage credit, collections, accounting, accounts receivable, and accounts payable operations for this $10M manufacturer of testing devices. Report to Controller.

Primary areas of responsibility:

- **Credit** - Develop and implement company credit policies and procedures. Determine terms of credit for small to large companies, both foreign and domestic.

- **Accounts Receivable** - Monitor A/R both for U.S. and Mexican offices. Reduced D.S.O. through comprehensive account analysis and aggressive strategizing.

- **Accounts Payable** - Supervise all A/P functions.

- **Accounting** - Generate daily sales reports, horizontal analysis of balance sheets and income statements, monthly A/R analysis, and closed jobs reports. Prepare journal entries and month end closing including A/R, order entry, and general ledger. Sign off on monthly financial package for corporate headquarters.

- **Computer Systems** - Collaborate with programmers to customize Data General and IBM systems. Organize in-house computer systems training for accounting and administrative personnel.

Credit & Collections Representative	**1981 to 1983**
Outside Sales Representative	**1980 to 1981**
ACE AUTOMOTIVE COMPANY	YOUNGSTOWN, OH

EDUCATION:

B.S. in Accountancy	**1983**
UNIVERSITY OF AKRON	AKRON, OH

- ✔ Laureen opens with her job title rather than the less important company name.
- ✔ Her areas of responsibility are easily scanned when highlighted in bold.
- ✔ Prior positions are listed to demonstrate career growth.

CUSTOMER SERVICE MANAGER

TANYA BRICE

22 Bennington Avenue   Garland, TX 75040
214/ 555-7843

PROFESSIONAL EXPERIENCE:

GRACO ELECTRICAL CORPORATION • Dallas, TX
($33M warehouse distribution center • Inventory of 65,000 electrical lighting parts)

Customer Service Manager (1987 to present). Spearheaded the successful turn-around of this department into the company's strongest through the evaluation and improvement of personnel, procedures, and technologies.

- Fostered a new team approach to increase productivity and morale. Redesigned physical environment to promote comfort and more effective departmental coordination.

- Streamlined the job flow into one team-approach group. Reduced staffing requirements by 35%, increased efficiency and job satisfaction, and eliminated turnover problem.

- Developed product reference manual encompassing product applications, pricing levels, and special promotions.

- Created staff training program including screening devices, training manual, and taped simulation practice procedures.

SAMUELS ASSOCIATES • Highland Park, TX
(Manufacturer's representative for telecommunications products)

Sales Coordinator (1985 to 1987). Performed a wide variety of sales and marketing functions designed to identify new target markets.

BREWER MORTGAGE BANKS • Dallas, TX
(Corporate headquarters for 20-branch bank)

Sales & Marketing Administrator (1982 to 1985). Reported directly to corporate V.P. Marketing in the coordination of advertising programs for 7 banks. Performed market research, developed marketing plans, and provided liaison among corporate office, advertising agencies, and sales offices during Vice President's frequent travel.

EDUCATION:

IOWA STATE UNIVERSITY • Ames, IA
Master of Science (1987)
Bachelor of Science (1980)

✔ Tanya's opening statement describing her current position is a gem.
✔ She quickly describes her companies within parentheses.
✔ Each bulleted highlight is specific and emphasizes her management ability.

ELLEN TANZI
46 Jackson Parkway
Midfield, AL 35228
205/ 555-9331

SUMMARY OF QUALIFICATIONS

- Ten years of experience managing and coordinating services within a high volume Data Processing Department.
- Proven ability to train, motivate, and supervise staff.
- Solid record of implementing time-saving workflow procedures.
- Demonstrated ability to interact effectively with key personnel.
- Excellent organization, communication, and problem-solving skills.

PROFESSIONAL EXPERIENCE

MED-SAFE CORPORATION • Birmingham, AL
($22M medical shelving manufacturer)

Data Processing Manager (1986 to present). Train and supervise Data Processing Coordinators; consistently achieve accuracy rate of 98% • Provide direct support for Inside Sales and Accounting Departments; verify orders, process changes, generate bills, and rectify problems • Interact daily with corporate MIS departments • Assisted in the lengthy conversion to an IBM mainframe; recommended procedures to compensate for system inadequacies.

Data Processing Coordinator (1982 to 1986). Assisted in the conversion from a manual to a fully automated inventory system necessitated by a 30% increase in customer base • Trained new departmental employees and inside sales personnel • Provided support to Sales, Fabrication, Purchasing, Accounting, Shipping, and Operations Departments • Generated daily computer reports for management; coordinated annual and semi-annual inventories.

EDUCATION

SPRING HILL COLLEGE • Mobile, AL
Business Management Coursework (1981 to 1985)

✔ Ellen's Summary includes pertinent capabilities of a DP Manager.
✔ Her job titles in bold demonstrate career growth within the same company.
✔ Bullets between sentences in the Experience section provide a natural pause.

DISTRIBUTION CENTER MANAGER

ARTHUR LARKIN
821 Griggs Lane
Ashland, NE 68003
402/ 555-7855

EXPERIENCE:

Clarkson Automotive Parts Company   Lincoln, NE

Distribution Center Manager (1989 to present). Direct 50 personnel in the daily operation of distribution center processing more than 1,500,000 parts annually. Productivity of facility increased 15% in one year.

Regional Manager (1985 to 1989). Directed store managers at 17 retail automotive parts stores generating $7.3M in annual sales. Implemented training and development and human resources programs. Developed sales projections, store audits, and semi-annual written evaluations of 180 employees. Collaborated with managers to develop successful sales promotions.

Achievements:

- Managed #1 cost efficient territory in U.S.
- Increased sales from $4M to $6.3M within 4 years.
- Received (3) "Highest Sales Increase Awards" and (2) "Customer Service Awards."
- Significantly reduced employee turnover through effective employee motivation strategies.
- Supervised all aspects of (4) store openings including construction, sales projections, inventory, and staffing.
- Delivered presentations on employee motivation and cost control at regional management conferences.

Previous positions (1976 to 1985) included **Retail Store Manager**, **Assistant Store Manager**, and **Sales Assistant**.

EDUCATION:

Nebraska Wesleyan University   Lincoln, NE

A.S. in Retail Management (1976)

REFERENCES:

Available upon request

✔ Arthur's job titles in bold emphasize steady career growth.
✔ Achievements describe his successful management projects.
✔ He cites the company name only once but lists all positions.

ENTREPRENEUR

PROFESSIONAL OVERVIEW

GEORGE BLACKWOOD
717 Royal Crest Apartments
Reading, MA 01867
617/ 555-7116

Equally comfortable performing in Fortune 1000 companies or retail ventures, marketing technical or consumer products, servicing OEM's or local customers, I have proven my ability to develop policies and programs, manage people, satisfy customers, and generate profit.

- **PARTNER**
  Blackwood Lithographers (1988 to present)

  Researched local opportunities with the goal of purchasing a premium, recession-proof business. Selected a thriving, independently-owned print shop, negotiated purchase price, prepared business plan for bank financing, and facilitated smooth ownership transition.

  Currently function as a hands-on manager with staff of 15. Throughout ownership, maintained maximum profits despite increased competition. Fully repaid $400,000 loan in 1990.

- **MARKETING MANAGEMENT AND SALES POSITIONS**
  Wang Laboratories (1984 to 1988)

  Throughout a 4-year affiliation with Wang, established reputation for the ability to analyze operational areas, allocate and coordinate resources, and follow-up efficiently resulting in increased sales and top quality service. Gained technical competence, traveled internationally, received rapid promotions, and earned early monetary reviews.

- **NATIONAL SALES ADMINISTRATOR**
  Hytron Manufacturing (1980 to 1984)

  Administered sales programs resulting in timely preparation of quotations, precise auditing of product sales, high-profile promotions, and sales training programs.

  Instrumental in re-organizing distribution system for high-demand computer product which satisfied distributors and end-users. Performed direct sales in New England.

✔ George's unique format combines a cover letter and a resume.
✔ Entrepreneurship combined with diverse management and sales positions at well known firms to distinguish George from other candidates.

EXECUTIVE DIRECTOR

NANCY TAGGERT
731 Monadnock Road
Manchester, NH 03101

Residence: 603/ 555-2332

Business: 603/ 555-0900

EMPLOYMENT:

EXECUTIVE DIRECTOR • NH Department of Social Services   1990 to present
(Personnel, program, and fiscal management for a human services agency)

MANAGEMENT CONSULTANT • Bond Associates   1988 to 1990
(Assessment and restructuring of employment program to meet federal requirements)

EMPLOYMENT COORDINATOR • National Job Finders Program   1985 to 1988
(Management of major federal jobs program servicing 800+ individuals annually)

EXPERIENCE:

Policy & Procedural Development - Designed and implemented new policies and procedures within new, established, and under-productive environments

Budget Preparation & Administration - Developed and administered $9M+ annual budget • Assumed P&L responsibility within non-sales environments requiring strict fiscal management.

Personnel Management - Recruited, trained, and supervised professional and administrative staffs. Managed scheduling and workflow.

Program Development & Administration - Designed format, protocol and training program for a prototype crisis peer counseling program • Established a comprehensive vocational assessment, recruitment and career development programs.

Contract Negotiations & Compliance - Conducted negotiations for state and federal contracts • Ensured compliance with contracts from key federal agencies.

Grant Writing & Administration - Generated 130% increase in grant monies from businesses and foundations within one year • One of three regional facilities to receive federal grant monies following a rigorous applications process.

EDUCATION:

BACHELOR OF ARTS • New Hampshire College   1985

✔ Nancy defines her jobs with parenthesized descriptions.
✔ She stresses her key management functions by using bold letters.
✔ Bullets between sentences segment information into scannable units.

FACILITIES MANAGER

FRANK STINSON
66 Amberwood Street
Burlington, MA 01803
617/ 555-4188

OBJECTIVE: Facilities Manager

EMPLOYMENT:

Facilities Manager • HAMILTON MANUFACTURING   1988 to present
(Corporate headquarters • 300,000 square foot building • 26 U.S. locations)

Facilities Maintenance Manager • TEXTEK INDUSTRIES   1984 to 1988
(500,000 square foot building • Four remote plants)

Plant Engineer • FABTRON CORPORATION   1982 to 1984
(Printed circuit board fabricators)

EXPERIENCE:

Expert in commercial and industrial facility operations, maintenance, and management.

- Managed $2M budget for salaries, utilities, expenses, repairs, and maintenance.
- Supervised up to 15 building managers, administrators, tradespeople, and CAD operators.
- Managed space planning and design for 26 locations nationwide.
- Established budget for facility construction projects; acted as construction manager.
- Planned and managed a $4M renovation of corporate offices.
- Designed and installed automated, electronic energy management and security systems.
- Performed energy audits on commercial facilities, resulting in $1.8M cost savings.
- Researched and purchased services and equipment.
- Established and implemented plant safety, security, and hazard waste handling programs.
- Insured compliance with federal, state, local, OSHA, EPA, and insurance regulations.
- Member - National Facility Managers Association, American Institute of Plant Engineers.

EDUCATION:

BSME • UNIVERSITY OF MASSACHUSETTS   1984

✔ Frank's resume is well-targeted toward his Objective.
✔ Describing the facilities allows the reader to better understand his capability.
✔ His Experience section summarizes specific areas of accomplishment.

FOOD SERVICES MANAGER

JULIA RINGWOLD, R.D.
56 Mockingbird Lane
Paradise Valley, AZ 85251
602/ 555-2752

Professional Experience:

PHOENIX HOSPITAL — PHOENIX, AZ
Manager - Food Services — 1989 to present

Manage the day-to-day line operation of food production for patient, cafeteria, and extended services use exceeding 3,000 meals per day.

- Oversee standardized meal preparation and develop modified menus.
- Hire, train, supervise, and evaluate a staff of 50 production employees.
- Implement stringent quality assurance programs and sanitary procedures.
- Monitor a large capital operating budget and prepare annual budget reports.
- Train and supervise dietetic interns.

DARLINGTON HOSPITAL — TEMPE, AZ
Chief Clinical Dietitian — 1986 to 1989

Managed the primary nutritional care for a critical care/surgical patient population.

- Established departmental policies and procedures.
- Initiated quality assurance program.
- Supervised staff of dietitians, diet technicians, and food services employees.
- Conducted community classes and educational programs.
- Provided educational services for outpatient population.
- Participated in discharge planning rounds.
- Served on Nutritional Advisory Committee and Infection Control Committee.

SOUTHWESTERN MEDICAL COLLEGE HOSPITALS — PHOENIX, AZ
Dietetic Intern — 1986

BROOKHAVEN ELDER CARE COMPLEX — MESA, AZ
Nutritionist — 1985 to 1986

Education:

SOUTHWESTERN COLLEGE — PHOENIX, AZ
Bachelor of Science In Nutrition — 1986

- ✔ Julia's title reflects her growth from Nutritionist to Food Services Manager.
- ✔ Her general introductions to each position are followed by specific management responsibilities encompassing staff, budget, and QA programs.

CAROLYN SWEENEY
803 Pine Ridge Road
Berea, SC 29601
803/ 555-2743

Professional Experience

PRICE RIGHT FASHIONS - Greenville, SC
Director of Franchises / Mid-Atlantic Region (1989 to present)

- Opened 15 stores in first year.
- Achieved 22% increase over sales projections during first 6 months.
- Recruited, hired and trained all management personnel.
- Implemented merchandising and sales training procedures.
- Promoted management from within including 3 District Managers.
- Initiated sales incentive programs and management seminars.

THE FASHION PLACE CORPORATION - Spartanburg, SC
Director of Store Merchandising (1987 to 1989)
(23 stores • $19M annual sales • 62% initial markup)

- Increased sales by 33% for 3 consecutive years.
- Researched, negotiated, and established new petite sportswear lines.
- Implemented initial Merchandise Planning Department.
- Devised Promotional management training program.
- Closely collaborated with Regional and District Managers through weekly meetings, feedback reports, and physical store "work-throughs."
- Designed and coordinated all print and catalogue advertisement.

District Manager (1984 to 1987)
(9 stores • $12M annual sales • 2nd highest sales volume in company)

- Maintained highest percentage of sell-through per product category.
- Directed inter-store transfers and analyzed trends for entire chain.
- Supervised all aspects of store operations throughout the district.
- Initiated Supervisor Training Program.
- Coordinated store renovations, openings and special promotions.

Supervisor, Assistant Manager and Store Manager (1980 to 1984)

Education:

WINTHROP COLLEGE - Rock Hill, SC
BSBA Candidate (35 credits completed)

- ✔ Carolyn's resume reflects solid achievements in 3 management positions.
- ✔ She lists lower-level jobs to show rapid career growth.
- ✔ Carolyn's pursuit of her BSBA indicates her industriousness.

CHRISTOFER DUCAT
367 Alexander Street
McKeesport, PA 15134

Residence: 412/ 555-8024   *Business:* 412/ 555-8200

Professional Experience:

REED MANUFACTURING COMPANY   PITTSBURGH, PA
General Manager   **1988 to present**
Production Manager   **1986 to 1988**

Manage daily operations for this international manufacturer / distributor of glassware with $3.8M in annual sales. Doubled sales within 3 years.

Assume P&L responsibility for entire company. Reduced manufacturing costs by relocating production facilities to Mexico.

- **Direct sales programs via a network of manufacturing agents -** hire, train, and evaluate reps; travel nationally to conduct sales presentations for key accounts; establish pricing policies; design new packaging and marketing programs.

- **Supervise purchasing function -** oversee buyers' location of vendors; negotiation of contracts; scheduling of ship dates; instituted inventory control system; established efficient international routing program for raw materials.

- **Oversee accounting / credit / collections processes -** computerized office functions including A/R, A/P, G/L, and Order Entry; prepare for quarterly audits; utilize Lotus 1-2-3 to create monthly budget and 3-year financial plan.

- **Directed manufacturing and R&D -** introduced new consumer products; initiated "just-in-time" manufacturing procedures; performed production scheduling; researched new / used equipment and their efficiencies.

- **Negotiated bank financing -** researched and selected new commercial lender; changed from fully conforming asset-based financing to monthly reviewed financing; control $1M line of credit.

Education:

CARNEGIE MELLON UNIVERSITY   PITTSBURGH, PA
M.S. in Industrial Engineering   **1985**
B.S. in Industrial Engineering   **1983**

✔ Christofer combines his two management positions in one explanation.
✔ He begins his job description with primary achievements in italics
✔ He identifies key areas of responsibility and explains them.

DEBORAH TRINGALE
38 MacPherson Drive
Harwood Heights, IL 60656
312/ 555-0388

SUMMARY:

Doctorate in Health Care Administration • Administrative and clinical health care experience in both public and private sectors • In-depth knowledge of mental health and substance abuse, lifecare care, daycare, recreation, and HMO's • Expertise in program development, planning and evaluation, policy analysis, regulatory approvals processes, corporate needs assessments and feasibility analyses, writing and editing, and large group presentations • Record of planning and achieving organizational goals through team building and group consensus.

PROFESSIONAL HISTORY:

CHICAGO HMO (CHMO)   CHICAGO, IL
PROJECT MANAGER, NEW PRODUCTS   **1989 to present**
DIRECTOR OF PLANNING   **1986 to 1989**

- **Extended Care Project Manager:** Studied lifecare and prepared initial analyses of long-term care insurance options for CHMO. Developed the program and wrote a successful proposal for the CHMO center at Barat College.

- **Workplace Eldercare Project Manager:** Directed CHMO's participation in a study by two corporations of ways to help employees care for elderly relatives.

- **Recreation Project Manager:** Supervised the development and implementation of a network of corporate Recreation Centers.

- **Childcare Project Manager:** Task force leader in the comprehensive study of childcare options for CHMO employees.

- **Internal Consultation** toward the improvement of substance abuse services.

- **Creator & Editor - The CHMO Digest,** a monthly summary for senior managers of current articles in health policy and trends in the workplace.

HEALTH CARE MANAGER (continued)

BETTER HEALTH COMPANY   ELMWOOD PARK, IL
ASSISTANT DIRECTOR   **1984 to 1986**

INDEPENDENT CONSULTANT   SKOKIE, IL
SUBSTANCE ABUSE PROJECT SPECIALIST   **1983 to 1984**

UNDERHILL COUNSELING CENTER   MORTON GROVE, IL
DIRECTOR OF MENTAL HEALTH SERVICES   **1980 to 1983**

EDUCATION:

UNIVERSITY OF CHICAGO   CHICAGO, IL
DOCTORATE IN HEALTH CARE ADMINISTRATION   **1986**

UNIVERSITY OF CHICAGO   CHICAGO, IL
MASTER OF ARTS IN SOCIAL SERVICE ADMINISTRATION   **1980**

LAKE FOREST COLLEGE   LAKE FOREST, IL
BACHELOR OF ARTS IN POLITICAL SCIENCE   **1978**

AFFILIATIONS:

Association of Health Care Administrators   Director - Self Help, Inc.

References available upon request

- ✔ Deborah's Summary is an overview of 10+ years of management experience.
- ✔ She outlines her most important management projects at the HMO.
- ✔ Prior experience is listed only to reflect career growth.

HOTEL MANAGER

DENNIS WHITMAN
447 Gladstone Street
Portsmouth, VA 23705

Residence: 804/ 555-1028   *Business:* 804/ 555-8990

EXPERIENCE:

RED BANNER HOTELS   Norfolk, VA
(135 employees • 181 rooms • meeting facilities for 300)

Guest Services Manager (1990 to present)
Front Office Manager (1987 to 1990)
Front Desk Manager (1986 to 1987)

Direct the operations of the front desk, reservations, auditing, communications and bell staff, and transportation services. Plan and schedule manpower, equipment, and supply requirements and maintain accountability for the cost, utilization, and performance of staff and equipment. Coordinate activities with all departments.

Received letter of commendation for service from V.P. of U.S. Hotel Operations.

- Control room availability and rates to maximize occupancy level and revenue.
- Plan and oversee $2750M annual budget.
- Developed training program and 160-page policies and procedures manual.
- Reconcile daily hotel revenues for comparison with departmental budgets.
- Perform billing, credit, and collections functions for all accounts.
- Utilize a variety of custom computer systems to track reservations, transmit revenue information, create work inventory sheets, perform billing, process receivables, and provide guests with information about special activities.

PREVIOUS EMPLOYMENT in sales and customer service (1982 to 1986)

EDUCATION:

NORFOLK STATE UNIVERSITY   Norfolk, VA
15 credits in Hotel & Restaurant Management (1984)

HIGH SCHOOL DIPLOMA (1981)

✔ Dennis describes only relevant hotel management experience.
✔ Previous Employment from 1982 to 1986 can be explained in an interview.
✔ Because he lacks a formal degree, he lists his high school diploma.

HUMAN RESOURCES MANAGER

SHARON KRUGER

Human Resources

2-C Locust Place
Los Alamos, NM 87544

Residence: 505/ 555-3222
Business: 505/ 555-6600

EXPERIENCE:

MEDI-SCAN CORPORATION • Santa Fe, NM
(Small R&D firm specializing in medical imaging equipment)

1985 - present

Human Resources Manager. Instituted a human resources function within a growing high tech firm. Develop and direct all human resources activities to meet the needs of an evolving organization. Report directly to company CEO and participate in strategic and management planning sessions. Function in coaching and problem-solving role for staff and management on issues of employee relations and organizational development.

- Formulated and updated HR policies and procedures based on extensive research of similar organizations.
- Established recruitment and hiring function for all employees including the development and promotion of company image.
- Initiated wage and salary structures, benefit packages, EEO procedures, and employee relations programs.
- Trained and managed HR support staff.
- Introduced in-house training courses.

1981 - 1985

Executive Assistant. Performed a variety of administrative tasks to support corporate goals and objectives:

- Personnel recruitment and coordination
- Administration of corporate security program
- Facilities and space planning
- Purchasing of equipment and supplies
- Management of administrative support services
- Supervision of technical publications

EDUCATION:

SPECIALIZED EDUCATION - Employee Relations, HR Strategies, Interviewing Techniques, Benefits Administration, Time Management, Needs Assessments, Supervisory Training.

1980

COLLEGE OF SANTA FE • Santa Fe, NM
Associate of Arts in Human Resources Management.

AFFILIATIONS:

HR Network, Employment Management Association

✔ In her present position, Sharon uses the past tense to describe duties no longer performed.
✔ Sharon's previous position shows her progression within the company.

LOSS MITIGATION V.P.

NELSON WILDER
76 Eastgate Mall Road
Shawnee, KS 66203

Residence: 913/ 555-7721   *Business:* 913/ 555-4567

PROFESSIONAL EXPERIENCE:

HART MORTGAGE INSURANCE COMPANY   KANSAS CITY, KS
V.P. / Real Estate Operations   **1991 to present**
Asst V.P. / District Claims   **1988 to 1991**

Collaborate with brokers, appraisers, investors, and lenders to evaluate real estate, negotiate sales, and effect workouts on distressed projects. Travel nationwide to assess market conditions, investigate claims for fraud and misrepresentation, and supervise field personnel.

Manage in-house claims servicers and administrative staff in loss mitigation operations. Designed and implemented comprehensive program of compliance policies and procedures.

Reduced 1990 losses by more than 62% over previous year, substantially exceeding corporate objectives. Contributed to success in exceeding competitors in pre-approved sales and claim dollars saved.

Director of Real Estate   **1986 to 1988**
Real Estate Manager   **1984 to 1986**

Managed REO acquisition, negotiation, evaluation, and disposition. Acquired, managed, and disposed of 75 properties valued at nearly $1.3M. Arranged solutions on major default concentrations.

Doubled percent of pre-approved sales of all claims settlements.

CITY ASSESSOR'S DEPARTMENT   SHAWNEE MISSION, KS
Supervisor of Appraisers   **1983 to 1984**

NELSON REAL ESTATE   SHAWNEE MISSION, KS
Manager   **1980 to 1983**

EDUCATION:

KANSAS WESLEYAN UNIVERSITY   SALINA, KS
Bachelor of Science   **1979**

✔ Nelson's four positions at Hart Mortgage indicate career growth, but to avoid repetition they are condensed into two main job descriptions.
✔ Prior positions are included because they are relevant to his career .

ALFRED NEELON, III
1770 North Avenue
Wauwautosa, WI 53213
414/ 555-2885

SUMMARY

Manufacturing Manager with a solid record of achievement **establishing** and **managing** total production operations. Introduced all systems and controls necessary to transform an R&D Division into a profitable manufacturer. Strengths in:

• R&D	• Product Engineering	• Product Development
• QA	• Production Scheduling	• Material Control
• Accounting	• Purchasing	• Sales Support
• Recruitment	• Training	• Budgeting

EXPERIENCE

TECHMED, INC. / Medical Instruments Division	MILWAUKEE, WI
Manager of Manufacturing	**1989 to present**
Project Engineer	**1985 to 1989**

Established a new production facility to augment manufacturing operation for the company's medical instrumentation product lines, representing $30M in annual sales or 85% of product shipments.

Key Results:

- A flexible manufacturing capability producing multiple product lines.
- A reputation for product quality recognized industry-wide.
- A computerized integrated manufacturing information system encompassing a material control system, an engineering document/product configuration control system, and a production control system.

EDUCATION

UNIVERSITY OF WISCONSIN	MILWAUKEE, WI
M.B.A. Candidate	
B.S. in Mechanical Engineering	**1985**

✔ Alfred's impressive Summary is strengthened by the use of bold type and bullets to emphasize his specialty areas and aid scannability.
✔ Alfred describes his accomplishments in terms of the company's bottom line.

MARKETING & SALES DIRECTOR

KRISTIN HANSFORD
48 Barrington Road
Waltham, MA 02154

Residence: 617/ 555-2469   Business: 617/ 555-2220

SUMMARY

Marketing & Sales Executive with a proven track record in real estate development • Bottom-line achievements based on sound analytical skills, decision-making, strategic planning, and creative solutions • Solid manager, team builder, and motivator.

EXPERIENCE

Director of Marketing and Sales   **1989 to present**
WEDGEWOOD ESTATES   Lexington, MA

Design and implement sales and marketing programs for a 90-unit luxury retirement community. Successful in retaining market share in an increasingly competitive market. Grew facility's waiting list by 35% within 6 months; on target for doubling list within one year.

Sales and Marketing Director   **1987 to 1989**
LUFKIN DEVELOPMENT COMPANY   Winchester, MA

Managed a 175-unit residential condominium development project from construction phase through sales and marketing activities. Successfully completed Phase I and II on time and within budget, with 55% of units sold.

Regional Manager   **1985 to 1987**
GREENE STATIONERS   Boston, MA

Independently opened and assumed P&L responsibility for 10 retail stores generating an annual sales volume of $2.4M and employing 70 personnel. Implemented all operations including personnel recruitment, accounting, advertising, distribution, staff development and training, and budgeting.

EDUCATION

Bachelor of Arts
BOSTON UNIVERSITY

✔ Kristin isolates titles and companies from cities and dates to improve her resume's readability.
✔ She omits the date of college graduation to avoid age discrimination.

MATERIALS MANAGER

STEVEN GILLIAN
974 Babineau Street
Marrero, LA 70072
504/ 555-3821

DIRECTOR OF MATERIALS MANAGEMENT

Summary of Qualifications

- 10+ years progressive experience in health care materials management (HCMM).

- Background in purchasing, inventory control, sterile central supply, distribution, forms, courier, mail, and transportation services.

- Expertise in management, training and development, negotiation, and budgeting.

- Knowledge of automated materials management systems.

Achievements

- Automated entire HCMM operation.

- Consolidated HCMM functions of four health care facilities into one streamlined organization following corporate merger. Directed HCMM activities of staff of 125.

- Developed comprehensive forms management program including procedures for bidding, analyzing bids, and negotiating contracts for printing requirements.

- Instituted computerized mailing system, resulting in significant increase in efficiency. Directed cost justification studies, purchasing of equipment, staff recruitment, and creation of policy and procedures.

- Investigated, audited, and managed unofficial inventories throughout hospital.

Employment

WORTH HEALTH SERVICES • New Orleans, LA
Director of Materials Management (1985 to present)

PIERRE COCHET MEMORIAL HOSPITAL • Metairie, LA
Purchasing Manager (1980 to 1985)

Education

LOYOLA UNIVERSITY • New Orleans, LA
MS in Health Services Management (1983)
BS in Business Administration (1979)

✔ Steven's Objective is short and simple, and appears as a heading.
✔ He includes very specific information which supports his career goal.
✔ His section headings are large and bold to highlight his credentials.

KATHERINE DURENBERGER

18 Hampton Place • Wheaton, MD 20902 • 301/ 555-9253

Experience:

DIRECTOR OF OPERATIONS
FRANKLIN PARTNERS • Washington, DC   1989 to present

Plan and direct day-to-day operations for this national consulting firm. Establish and implement comprehensive policies and procedures. Hire and train administrative staff. Plan and control operational and program budgets.

Plan and direct major consulting projects encompassing significant client interaction and statistical analysis.

Significantly contributed to continued growth of firm through strategic planning and penetration of new markets.

Major Responsibilities:

- Write business plans to secure financing.

- Consult with clients to develop action plans.

- Forecast project costs and generate price quotations.

- Select and coordinate project staff.

- Compile results for statistical analysis.

- Research, select, and customize computer systems.

Computer:

Hardware: IBM-PC compatibles (MS/DOS)

Software: dBase, Lotus 1-2-3, Microsoft Word

Education:

B.S. IN MARKETING MANAGEMENT
GEORGETOWN UNIVERSITY • Washington, DC   1989

References:

Available upon request

✔ Katherine uses bold capital letters to highlight her very prestigious title, company, degree, and college.
✔ Her computer expertise is a significant credential and merits its own section.

PAUL GARABEDIAN
277 Salem Street
Malden, MA 02148
617/ 555-2908

EXPERIENCE

JOHNSON HOME FURNISHINGS CENTER   MEDFORD, MA

Vice President of Operations	**1989 to present**
General Manager	**1985 to 1989**
Sales Specialist	**1982 to 1985**

Direct financial, administrative, and support functions for all locations and distribution center. Collaborate with President and department managers to forecast budgets and plan long-range strategies. Installed new procedures for inventory control, distribution, and staff motivation.

Redirected marketing thrust to capture retail segment and increase cash flow. Reduced payroll, expenses, and dead inventory resulting in the significant increase of gross margin.

<u>Areas of responsibility</u>:

Purchasing:

- Purchase a multi-product line including hardware, paint, kitchens, and bath.
- Coordinate with vendors on product delivery and pricing, training, credits, buy-back programs, and special orders.
- Negotiate display, payment terms, and sales support to stores on all products.

Advertising:

- Execute all aspects of annual advertising campaigns including flyers, yellow pages ads, and help wanted ads.
- Developed a contemporary logo and numerous promotional collaterals.
- Conduct market research and coordinate advertising projects with ad agencies.

Merchandising:

- Instituted weekly promotional bulletins to establish uniformity in all locations.
- Conduct regular product training sessions with store management.
- Provide liaison with all stores to monitor consumer trends and company image.

EDUCATION

NORTHEASTERN UNIVERSITY   BOSTON, MA
B.S. in Management   **1982**

- ✔ Paul's growth within the company is evidenced by his job titles.
- ✔ He highlights primary achievements in italics.
- ✔ He segments his management responsibilities into three major areas.

OWNER

RICHARD KRUPKA
93 Fulbright Street
Jasper, OR 97401
503/ 555-3344

PROFESSIONAL EXPERIENCE:

GENTLE CARE REFINISHING COMPANY — EUGENE, OR
OWNER — **1985 to present**

Direct technical and administrative operations of this firm specializing in the refinishing of antique furniture. Firm has established itself as a leader in quality of workmanship and service.

- Refinish antiques and reproductions for custom executive work-spaces.
- Train and supervise six finishers.
- Present seminars at Antique Furniture Guild and area vocational schools stressing use of proper equipment and shop safety.
- Considered a leader in establishing shop safety records.
- Continually studying and perfecting the technical aspects of the finishing process in order to improve quality and performance.
- Utilize PC's for graphic design, word processing, data base management, and accounting functions.
- Certified by Antique Furniture Guild as Master Tradesman.

FALL CREEK FINISHERS — FALL CREEK, OR
FINISHER — **1975 to 1985**

EDUCATION:

EUGENE COMMUNITY COLLEGE — EUGENE, OR
33 CREDITS; ACCOUNTING MAJOR — **1983 to 1985**

GOSHEN HIGH SCHOOL — GOSHEN, OR
DIPLOMA; VOCATIONAL AND BUSINESS STUDIES — **1974**

Personal and professional references available upon request

✔ Richard's resume equally stresses his business and technical expertise.
✔ References from a former employer will be outdated, so he offers to provide current professional and/or personal references if asked.

TRICIA STEVENS
134 Pond Street
Greensboro, NC 28208

Residence: 704/ 555-2562   *Business:* 704/ 555-7000

PROFESSIONAL EXPERIENCE

PIEDMONT INDUSTRIES

Product Manager   1989 to present

- Oversee complete production of knits for petite women's lines.
- Design and develop styles; approve colors; source yarns and fabrics.
- Develop budgets; establish item costs; approve samples and fits; coordinate South American production and shipments to U.S. Distribution Center.

Manager of Domestic Sourcing   1987 to 1989

- Directed the sourcing of factories, fabrics, and yarns for lines of cut & sew.
- Established costs; negotiated package deals with contractors.
- Generated patterns and markers; specified finished garments.
- Supervised the production, quality, and shipping for catalogue division.

QUALITY GARMENT COMPANY

Quality Control Manager   1984 to 1987

- Managed the production of garments for children's lines at domestic facilities.
- Coordinated production of sample lines for showrooms and salesmen.
- Monitored returns and communicated with buyers regarding quality problems.
- Directed testing of yarns and finished fabrics at in-house finishing plant.

GRAINGER INDUSTRIES

Technical Services Supervisor   1982 to 1984
Process Engineer   1980 to 1982

EDUCATION

WINTHROP COLLEGE
BS in Textile Technology   1980

WOFFORD COMMUNITY COLLEGE
AA in Textile Design   1978

✔ Tricia assumes that the prospective employer is familiar with her industry, so she omits descriptions of her company.
✔ She conveys career growth and breadth of responsibility.

GENA DESCHAMPS

8-D Holton Street
Bexley, OH 43209
614/ 555-0982

Areas of Expertise

PRODUCTION SUPERVISION • PURCHASING • INVENTORY CONTROL

QUALITY CONTROL • PRICE QUOTATIONS • SHIPPING

Professional Experience

MEDICAL INDUSTRY FABRICATORS   COLUMBUS, OH
Production Supervisor (1987 to present)

- Supervise the assembly and packing of high volume, short order runs.
- Hire, train, and evaluate production personnel.
- Oversee production planning, scheduling, and expediting.
- Control inventory and handling of raw materials.
- Support sales in the generation of price quotations.
- Coordinate with warehouse to improve production flow and delivery.
- Maintain consistent record for improving production runs.
- Implement QC programs to reduce customer complaints.

Production Assistant (1986 to 1987)

Education

OHIO UNIVERSITY   CHILLICOTHE, OH
Bachelor of Science (1986)

✔ Gena is unsure of a specific career goal, so she emphasizes many areas.
✔ She omits explanation of Production Assistant as it would be repetitious.
✔ She omits her degree concentration as it's totally unrelated to her field.

LEONARD ERVING
4167 Glendale Canyon Drive
Scottsdale, AZ 85257
602/ 555-7366

Experience:

SATELLITE NEWS NETWORK • Phoenix, AZ
(Fastest growing regional news cable network)

Program Manager (1986 to present). Plan and direct daily trafficking and inventory operations for all commercial advertising and on-air promotions. Provide hands-on management for long-range forecasting & planning, program acquisition, marketing, and consumer relations. *Award-winning programming 1989-present.*

* Administer $800K budget in network's largest department.

* Supervise Traffic Coordinator and Programming Assistant in the administration and troubleshooting of on-air programming.

* Closely coordinate with sales, marketing, public relations, technical, and product managers to ensure the highest quality programming, service, promotion, and product awareness.

* Assisted in the automation of daily operation logs and the research, selection, and development of a computerized commercial insertion system.

* Participate in the expansion of programming and services resulting in increased customer satisfaction and sales.

Production Assistant (1984 to 1986)

Administrative Assistant to President (1982 to 1984)

Education:

UNIVERSITY OF CALIFORNIA • Los Angeles, CA

BS in Business Administration (1982)

Activities:

* Member of Cable News Programming Association.
* Advocate for Association for Senior Citizens.
* Participate in skiing and fitness activities.

✔ Leonard emphasizes his company's success, which validates his own.
✔ His many years in the company establish breadth and depth of experience.
✔ Professional, community, and personal activities show commitment.

RESTAURANT MANAGER

JOHN TEDESCO
7 Whitcomb Avenue
Oak Knoll, MN 55343
612/ 555-2948

OBJECTIVE: Manager of full-service, quality restaurant

EDUCATION: CONCORDIA COLLEGE • St. Paul, MN
Restaurant Management Studies

Certificates in Purchasing, Managing People, Food Service Management and Control, Effective Communication, Total Bar and Beverage Management, Helping Employees Grow, The Guest Experience.

AMERICAN RESTAURANT ASSOCIATION

Seminars in Increasing Sales, Front of the House Management, Dining Room Management, Legal Workshop, Basic Supervision.

EXPERIENCE: CRABTREE'S • Minneapolis, MN   1987 to present
General Manager

Manage day-to-day operations of popular 220-seat seafood restaurant generating $2M total annual sales. Recruit, train, supervise, and motivate a team of 53 servers, cooks, kitchen staff, and maintenance crew. Order food, beverages, and dry goods. Over-see QC operations. Plan menus and promotions. Perform customer service.

BEEF & BREW CAFE • Minnehaha, MN   1984 to 1987
Assistant Manager

VIKING PUB • Minneapolis, MN   1980 to 1984
Bartender

References available upon request.

✔ John's resume is targeted toward one specific career objective.
✔ Numerous career certificates and seminars are important.
✔ Horizontal lines segment information into scannable sections.

TOBY WEBB
289 Trull Brook Road
Fairview, AL 35208
205/ 555-9283

SUMMARY:

Progressive management experience in high-volume gift shops • Extensive knowledge of system operations, staff training and development, management procedures, organizational development, purchasing, MIS, customer service, and P&L • Solid record of performance-based promotions.

PROFESSIONAL EXPERIENCE:

THE TREASURE TROVE   BIRMINGHAM, AL
MANAGEMENT POSITIONS   **1989 to present**

- Within one year progressed from Assistant Manager to Manager.
- Accountable for P&L.
- Direct a staff of eighteen in a high-volume environment.
- Oversee training, inventory control, and advertising.
- Developed employee incentive and task monitoring programs.
- Established a training program and departmentalization of tasks.
- Assisted in a store remodel and new store construction.

WESTON JEWELERS   BESSEMER, AL
ASSISTANT MANAGER   **1986 to 1989**

- Supported in management of a staff of nineteen in a large jewelry store.
- Directed ordering, scheduling, training, and inventory levels.

OLSON'S DISCOUNT DEPARTMENT STORES   BIRMINGHAM, AL
SUPERVISOR   **1983 to 1986**

- Supervised nine in small gifts department of a local department store.
- Assisted in order, pricing, merchandising, ordering, and sales.

EDUCATION:

SAMFORD UNIVERSITY   BIRMINGHAM, AL
BSBA with honors   **1982**

✔ Toby emphasizes promotions and P&L responsibility in both Summary and Experience sections because of their importance in the retail industry.
✔ She combines management positions at Treasure Trove in one description.

GARY NORBERT

Sales and Marketing Executive

17 Saddle River Road
Lincoln, MA 01773

617/ 555-4238

SUMMARY:

Dynamic manager with sales & marketing achievements in entrepreneurial and established high technology environments • Keen understanding of the critical relationships between operations and sales & marketing • Demonstrated ability to analyze complex situations, design practical solutions, and implement cost-effective plans • Proven ability to recruit and motivate sales staffs and rep networks • Strong belief in company loyalty and professional integrity.

PROFESSIONAL EXPERIENCE:

Vice President of Sales & Marketing   **1987 to present**
GENERAL ELECTRIC COMPANY - ENGINE DIVISION   BEDFORD, MA

- Spearheaded sales from $0 to $2M in three years; gained 63% of market share.
- Created a high-impact, low cost advertising campaign to launch new product.
- Developed a top national network of sales representatives in three months.
- Contracted the production of machined parts by a foreign manufacturer.

Vice President of Marketing   **1982 to 1987**
RAYTHEON CORPORATION - MISSILE GROUP   WILMINGTON, MA

- Increased annual sales from $300K to $15M in five years.
- Significantly diversified customer base to include international market.
- Hired and trained management and sales staff using a team approach.
- Initiated a detailed cost accounting system by product and area.
- Designed product catalogue, direct mailers, brochures, and ads.

EDUCATION:

Bachelor of Science   **1975**
MASSACHUSETTS INSTITUTE OF TECHNOLOGY   BOSTON, MA

✔ Gary's resume sells his sales and marketing expertise across two industries.
✔ Companies and college are assumed to need no further description.
✔ Positions prior to 1982 are omitted to keep the resume to one page.

KEVIN SHAUGHNESSY
560 El Mundo Drive
Chula Vista, CA 92010

Residence: 619/ 555-8743   *Business:* 619/ 555-9090

Professional Experience:

PACIFIC TELECOMM TESTING DEVICES COMPANY   SAN DIEGO, CA
Service Manager   **1989 to present**

Plan and manage daily activities of in-house and on-site service programs for this leading firm specializing in the distribution, calibration, and repair of communications test equipment. Consistently meet or exceed time, budget, and quality standards. Achieved 30% growth in billings and a significant increase in customer retention over FY '90.

- Monitor 270 service contracts and 750 monthly calibration/repair jobs.
- Hire, schedule, supervise, and evaluate 10 technical and administrative personnel.
- Generate quotes on service contracts and repair work.
- Approve and expedite ordering of parts.
- Collaborate with Q.A. Manager to maintain quality and conform to military standards.
- Contract with outside vendors for subcontract work.
- Maintain excellent customer relations on special requirements and service issues.

BEACON ANALYZER COMPANY   EL CAJON, CA
Bench Technician   **1988 to 1989**

Calibrated and repaired a wide variety of HF test equipment including modulation distortion analyzers, oscilloscopes, pulse power sources, power meters and mounts, and attenuators.

EQUIPMENT LAB   US NAVY - CORONADO, CA
Technical Supervisor   **1985 to 1988**

Trained and supervised a six-man section in the alignment, repair, and calibration of precision test equipment to meet the specifications of the National Bureau of Standards.

Education & Training:

COMMUNITY COLLEGE OF THE NAVY   **1982 to 1984**
55 credits in Communications Technology

MOBILE COLLEGE   **1980 to 1982**
31 credits in Computer Science

✔ Kevin's resume emphasizes both technical and management proficiency.
✔ Whenever possible, he includes facts and figures to strengthen explanations.
✔ Kevin's Education is particularly important because of its technical nature.

EDWARD ROTMAN

27 Monroe Street
San Francisco, CA 94123

Residence: 415/ 555-9378
Business: 415/ 555-6100

EXPERIENCE: NEWSEDIT CORPORATION SAN FRANCISCO, CA
VP, Technical Development **1986 to present**

Direct all firmware development and QA programs for this firm specializing in newspaper pagination products. Grew the Technical Development area to 75 people with an annual budget of $6M, approximately 92% of company's billable staff and 81% of its total operating budget.

Participate in strategic corporate decision-making, development of corporate policy, and preparation and presentation of departmental budgets and forecasts. Manage systems programming and operations and assume responsibility for Human Resources function.

Chaired an intercompany task force on state-of-the-art technologies resulting in company savings exceeding $300,000. Currently leading a new-venture planning effort for a major new high-tech business proposed by a client company.

GRAVES MANAGEMENT CONSULTANTS CUPERTINO, CA
Senior Consultant **1982 to 1986**

Consulted on the planning, organization, and management of complex software development projects and strategic technology planning for diverse industries. Key clients were major high-tech, insurance, and publishing firms.

CYBERSOFT COMPANY SAN JOSE, CA
Manager of Software Development **1980 to 1982**
Project Manager **1978 to 1980**

EDUCATION: STANFORD UNIVERSITY STANFORD, CA
MBA **1977**
BA in Computer Science **1975**

✔ Edward's 15 year career fits comfortably onto one page.
✔ His first paragraph addresses programs, budgets, staff, and achievements.
✔ Prior positions evidence his managerial and technical competence.

WILLIAM STAFFIER
40 Norwood Avenue
Clifton, NJ 07015
201/ 555-9543

TRAFFIC MANAGEMENT

Professional Experience:

KAWASAKI ELECTRONICS • PATERSON, NJ
(International video equipment firm with annual sales of $950M)

Corporate Traffic Manager (1987 to present). Direct staff of thirteen in freight and customer support operations. Coordinate the transfer of product among plants, third party distribution centers, and domestic and international customers. Oversee the import and distribution of freight from overseas vendors. Manage $18M budget and contribute to company record of maximum efficiency and high cost savings.

Highlights:

- Negotiated contracts with van lines, freight payment and air freight services at lowest possible cost while maintaining highest level of service.

- Shipped 25 million pounds and processed 187,000 freight bills in 1990.

- Developed and implemented duty drawback program for import business.

- Established low tariff import program with Taiwan-sourced video products.

- Tripled savings on international freight in one year.

Traffic Supervisor (1985 to 1987). Supervised staff of eight in directing inbound freight to manufacturing facilities and outbound freight to domestic and overseas sites.

Import/Export Manager (1982 to 1985). Arranged entire dispatch of international shipments and administered company-wide export license program.

Education:

ST. JOSEPH'S UNIVERSITY • PHILADELPHIA, PA
Bachelor of Arts (1981)

References:

Available upon request

✔ William's heading allows him to pursue many positions in Traffic Management.
✔ He highlights his outstanding achievements in a separate bulleted section.
✔ Prior experience in the company is summarized in one sentence per position.

JOSEPH NEWPORT
109 Harvard Street
Dunmore, PA 18512
717/ 555-3961

SUMMARY

Senior Executive with 20+ years of management experience with a $10 million international food processing firm

EXPERIENCE

U.S. FOODS CORPORATION • SCRANTON, PA

Vice President (1987 to present)

Director of Operations (1977 to 1987)

Director of Administration (1974 to 1977)

Highlights:

- Formulated and implemented corporate-wide policies and procedures.
- Managed subsidiary P&L responsibilities with a large corporate framework.
- Member of Executive Committee (1987 to present), Strategy Board (1980 to 1987), and Compliance Review Committee (1984 to 1987).
- Developed new corporate image including name, logo, and promotional materials to spearhead new marketing direction.
- Directed operations through major mergers, acquisitions, and restructurings.
- Initiated major investments and established key strategic alliances.
- Negotiated multi-million dollar contract to develop a line of low-fat products.

EDUCATION

TEMPLE UNIVERSITY • PHILADELPHIA, PA

MBA Candidate

BSBA (1974)

✔ Joseph's Summary is a concise description of his complete professional history.
✔ Key career highlights are consolidated to avoid repetition and save space.
✔ Studies toward his MBA are important to include at his senior level.

Sales and Marketing 13

Varied Paths To A Sales Career

A college degree cannot prepare you for a sales career. In fact, there is no degree in sales offered at any college or university. How do people get into sales, then? Some sales professionals consciously decide right out of high school or college to pursue sales as a career, and some grow into it after succeeding in entry-level customer service or telemarketing positions. Most, however, change to sales from another field entirely, e.g., sports, graphic design, education, or engineering. They combine their specialized expertise with their interest in sales, and start a whole new career. Many continue growing to management level.

Describe Your Effect On The Bottom Line

You might love your sales and marketing position, but are you successful? As a sales and marketing professional, whether entry-level or management, selling a product or service, enthusiasm and energy are not enough to succeed. In fact, you are only considered successful relative to your positive effect on a company's bottom line. It is essential, therefore, that you understand the role that sales and marketing plays in an organization, and sell yourself accordingly.

On your resume, always describe yourself in terms of how you contributed to your company's bottom line, and how you will be able to achieve similar, or even better results for a new company. For instance, instead of writing "I'm a great negotiator," it's much more powerful to describe the successful results of your negotiations, such as "Negotiated exclusive $50M contract with Fortune 50 computer manufacturer." Your resume is your marketing tool. Sell yourself!

Prospective Employers Want Specifics

Writing your resume to obtain a sales and marketing position should be relatively simple because in your field you can easily and accurately describe the *range of your responsibilities*, e.g., territory, products, accounts, marketing programs, and the *scope of your achievements*, e.g., sales revenues. There are usually few gray areas. The following lists will help you define your position and select pertinent information for your resume that will interest a prospective employer. They will also help you prepare for any interviews.

If you're in sales, your resume should answer some of these key questions:

- What product or service did you sell?

- What was your sales approach?

- What was the length of your typical sales cycle?

- Were you on commission?

- Did you meet or exceed quota?

- Did you win sales performance awards?

- What was the dollar amount in sales revenues you generated?

- In what time frame were your sales made, e.g., $5M in 1st year?

- What percent did you expand business?

- Did you sell during poor economic times?

- Where was your territory?

- Did you travel locally, nationally?

- Did you secure new accounts?

- Did you service established accounts?

- Did you cold call, telemarket?

- What industries did you sell to? Government? The Military?

- What were the company names of your key accounts?

- Did you sell to key accounts only?

- What were the titles of the decision-makers to whom you sold?

- Did you negotiate pricing?

- Did you negotiate contracts?

- Did you know facts about competitive companies and products?

- Did you attend trade shows?

- Did you write proposals?

- Did you make group presentations?

- Did you implement new sales strategies?

- Did you take sales training courses?

- Did you use computerized systems for order entry, lead tracking?

- Do you have other computer skills, e.g., word processing, spread sheets?

- Did you collaborate with other departments or sales reps?

- Did you manage staffs, or programs, or products?

- Did you train new sales staff?

- Did you have P&L responsibility?

- Did you participate in forecasting?

- How big was your budget?

If you're in marketing, your resume should answer some of these key questions:

- Did you plan, budget, forecast?

- Did you perform market or trend analysis?

- Did you perform test marketing?

- Did you participate in product launching or positioning?

- Did you create ads, brochures, press releases, technical notes?

- Did you work with advertising agencies?

- Did you place ads?

- Are you skilled in writing, photography, desktop publishing?

- Did you design premium promotions?

- Did you design in-house or sales incentive programs?

- Did you collaborate with sales, management, R&D, manufacturing?

- Did you attend marketing courses?

- Did you create exhibits or booths for trade shows?

Creative Resume Ideas

Since creativity is inherent in most sales and marketing positions, it is appropriate for you to show a degree of flair in designing your resume. A standard resume format can be transformed simply through the selection of quality, color and size of paper; letter style; colored ink; or graphics in the form of a border, logo, drawing, or even your photo.

Consider these other unique alternatives:

- A short resume on the reverse side of a business card

- A biographical sketch summarizing your background

- A fact sheet highlighting your sales achievements

- Press kit incorporating your writing samples or sales figures

A word of caution: Only a very fine line exists between creativity and poor taste.

For Your Convenience

The Sales and Marketing section is arranged by job title as well as by industry.

JULIA GREER

34 East Lakes Road
Woodland, MN 55803

218/ 555-2996

SKILLS:

- Administration
- Vendor Relations
- Staff Training
- Computers
- Bookkeeping
- Meeting Planning

EXPERIENCE:

Customer Service Representative
STATESIDE INSURANCE CO. • Duluth, MN   1990 to present

- Support Insurance Brokers in servicing new accounts.
- Expedite applications and generated proposals.
- Provide clients with pertinent information.
- Perform efficient troubleshooting of account problems.
- Prepare all correspondence relating to client services.

Administrative Assistant to the President
CARR INSURANCE CO. • Duluth, MN   1989

- Recruited at on-site job fairs.
- Planned site and interior design of new office location.
- Compiled figures and generated sales reports.
- Drafted and prepared President's correspondence.
- Participated in both executive and staff meetings.

Office Systems Manager
GRAFF MANUFACTURING • Fond Du Lac, MN   1987 to 1989

- Created initial position for the new Central Division.
- Coordinated all details during establishment of new office.
- Directed office support activities re: staffing and equipment.
- Interviewed and trained administrative support applicants.
- Interviewed vendors; evaluated equipment and services.
- Provided liaison to Corporate office.

EDUCATION:

Bachelor of Arts in Business
HAMLINE UNIVERSITY   1987

✔ Julia summarizes her customer service and administrative skills up front.
✔ Her most recent position demonstrates her range of customer service duties.
✔ Prior experience supports her general business knowledge and capabilities.

DIRECTOR OF SALES & MARKETING

GERROLD MANCHESTER
566 Admirals Way
West Glen, IL 61614
309/ 555-2894

EXPERIENCE:	**Director of Sales and Marketing**	**1989 to present**

COMPU-CO
$6.5M computer products and services firm

Direct the positioning, packaging, pricing and selling of all computer products and services. Develop and implement sales and marketing plans for a variety of disciplines and industries, including finance, engineering, education, direct mail, contract management of manufacturing facilities, and government agencies.

Independent Marketing Consultant	**1987 to 1989**

Consulted to numerous software engineering companies on the research, design, and packaging of products and services for OEM and consumer markets.

Marketing Manager	**1982 to 1987**

GELBART SCIENCES INC.
$95M computer consulting and services firm

Directed the national marketing of customized computer systems. Developed and implemented comprehensive marketing plans; established and supported national dealer network; designed product advertising and promotional literature; prepared technical proposals; prepared and delivered sales presentations; planned trade shows. Clients included corporate end users and OEM accounts.

Marketing Representative	**1980 to 1982**

UNICOMM SOFTWARE COMPANY

EDUCATION:	**BS in Business Administration**	**1980**

Concentration in Marketing

REFERENCES: **Available upon request**

✔ Gerrold's job titles are in bold to emphasize his management positions.
✔ He briefly describes his companies to give the reader a "mind set."
✔ Gerrold's resume reflects solid career growth in his field.

DISTRICT SALES MANAGER

RAYMOND LO PRESTI
234-G Rio Caliente
Huntington Beach, CA 92646
714/ 555-4776

OBJECTIVE	SALES, MARKETING OR PRODUCT MANAGEMENT

EXPERIENCE HD COMPUTER ACCESSORIES   SANTA ANA, CA

(Industry leader in computer peripherals)

Sales Manager (1988 to present). Direct staff of six in the OEM and distribution sales of printers, CRT terminals, and associated accessories to accounts in southern California.

Key Account Manager (1985 to 1988). Directed local sales and program administration for the largest single OEM customer for Letter Quality Printers generating total revenues exceeding $83M.

ELECTRO VIEW CORPORATION   LOS ANGELES, CA

(CRT Tube Division • $50M manufacturer of CRT screens)

Regional Sales Manager (1981 to 1985). Established Regional Sales office for sales of RGB Monitors to OEM's of computer action arcade games.

ROTRON CORPORATION   LOS ANGELES, CA

($18M manufacturer of photolithograpy equipment)

Field Sales Engineer (1979 to 1981). Generated $2M in sales to semiconductor fabricators in NJ, PA, and NY.

EDUCATION CALIFORNIA INSTITUTE OF TECHNOLOGY   PASADENA, CA

BSEE (1978)

✔ Raymond's Objective encompasses three related areas.
✔ He highlights companies in capitals because of their industry prominence.
✔ Similarly, he highlights job titles in bold to show management positions.

DOROTHY HARDING

6 Trojan Way
Ashland, NE 68003
402/ 555-1549

OBJECTIVE:	Outside Sales Representative

EDUCATION:	**UNIVERSITY OF NEBRASKA**	**Lincoln, NE**
	Bachelor of Science in Management	**1989**
	Associate of Science in Chemistry	**1987**

Planned and administered fund raising, budgeting, public relations, and social activities at Pi Eta Kappa Sorority.

PERSONAL: Highly motivated, energetic, and results-oriented. Proven ability to work hard, take initiative, and produce high quality work on time. Excellent communication and interpersonal skills. Both a leader and a team player.

EMPLOYMENT:	**WHALOM WATER FILTER COMPANY**	**Lincoln, NE**
	Sales/Service Representative	**1989 to present**

Provide technical and support service to 350 established customers. Develop new business through the use of cold calls, referrals, and leads generated by advertising. Maintain a successful closure rate and a low cancellation rate. Keep current in field through extensive reading. Consistently receive excellent performance reviews.

ADCO COPIERS COMPANY	**Lincoln, NE**
Account Representative	**1987 to 1989**

Prospected, sold, and serviced accounts locally for the Color Copiers Division. Acquired technical expertise in the operation of a line of business equipment.

References available upon request

- ✔ Dorothy's Objective reflects a specific career direction.
- ✔ Her Personal section consists of important attributes for a sales career.
- ✔ Her present employment is an excellent stepping stone to outside sales.

INSIDE SALES SPECIALIST

ALBERT PRENTICE

Inside Sales Representative

1616 Linden Park Drive
Waverly, MI 48917

517/ 555-9577

Professional Experience:

Inside Sales Specialist   **1989 to 1990**
TELECTRON CORPORATION   LANSING, MI
($25M manufacturer of automatic test equipment)

- Performed inside sales, customer service, telemarketing, and product applications.

- Assessed client needs and recommended appropriate products or modifications.

- Assessed product viability and planned product improvements and modifications.

- Tracked industry trends to alert marketing group to new product direction.

- Coordinated with a national network of manufacturer's representatives.

- Frequently assumed responsibility for Sales Department.

- Consistently received excellent performance evaluations.

Seeking a new position due to company relocation.

Sales Representative   **1987 to 1989**
ODESTA PLOTTER COMPANY   LANSING, MI

Education:

AS in Business Administration   **1987**
MACALESTER COLLEGE   ST. PAUL, MN

Continuing Education includes Sales & Marketing, PC/MS-DOS, Lotus 1-2-3, MS Word, Dbase, and IBM AS 400 mid-range computers.

References available upon request

✔ In lieu of an Objective, Albert uses a title under his name.
✔ The two last bullets in his job description emphasize his performance excellence.
✔ He openly tells the reader why he's out of work and seeking a new job.

GARY WEISS
39 Squire Road
Lincoln, MA 01773
617/ 555-2903

EXPERIENCE:

BIOMED INSTRUMENTS • WAKEFIELD, MA
Director of International Sales (1987 to 1991)

Directed sales, service, and customer support of medical products in six western European countries. Successfully negotiated a $550,000 contract with Germany for ultrasound monitoring equipment and introduced blood analyzers to the Ministry of Health, France.

- Supervised sales representatives and service engineers.
- Represented company to 15 distributors; travelled often to their headquarters.
- Interacted with domestic and international manufacturers.
- Obtained quotations and supplies, and ensured timely service and support.

BIOFILTRATION PRODUCTS • ELKHART, IL
Manufacturing Representative (1983 to 1987)

Maintained total sales responsibilities for medical and scientific membrane microfiltration products. Obtained first time contract with the state of California over competitors who previously had exclusive rights.

- Provided dealer assistance, training and complete support functions.
- Interfaced with representatives from all major scientific products distributors.

VWR SCIENTIFIC • WALTHAM, MA
Instrumentation Specialist - hospital accounts (1981 to 1983)
Field Service Representative - medical equipment line (1980 to 1981)

EDUCATION & TRAINING:

UNIVERSITY OF MASSACHUSETTS • AMHERST, MA
Bachelor Degree in Arts & Sciences (1980)

TECHNICAL SERVICE SCHOOLS
Dionics, Cordell

SALES TRAINING
IBM - Professional Selling Skills
Tom Hopkins Sales Training Course

- ✔ Gary describes specific duties, products, territories, and sales revenues.
- ✔ His earliest positions are listed to show career growth.
- ✔ Sales training and technical training are important listings under Education.

EVANDER GREENE

14 Dunster Street
Brunswick, IN

(219) 555-1842

PROFESSIONAL EXPERIENCE:

Manager of Marketing Services
AHEAD ELECTRONICS • Gary, IN (1984 to present)

- Direct a technical staff of 23 in the design and creation of communications materials for a 31-division electronics company with $750M annual sales.

- Initiated a Corporate Advertising Program which incorporated the use of a graphic style guide in order to achieve consistency of presentation among the divisions.

- Supervise the creation and production of magazine ads, brochures, catalogues, slide presentations, and trade show graphics.

- Utilize working knowledge of 4-color printing, photography, and color lab services.

- Negotiate advertising rates with industry journals.

- Administer a marketing data base program to enhance sales efforts.

- Designed and installed large domestic and international trade show exhibits.

- Develop and administer divisional budgets totalling $3M.

- Grew department from a tech publications operation to a marketing services group.

EDUCATION:

BS in Communications
BUTLER UNIVERSITY (1984)

REFERENCES/PORTFOLIO:

Available upon request

✔ Evander uses graphic design elements in his resume heading.
✔ He cites both management and technical accomplishments.
✔ Dates are de-emphasized because only one job experience is listed.

MARKETING CONSULTANT

DEREK JONES

90 Damon Road
Tampa, FL 33602
813/ 555-4452

QUALIFICATIONS:

- Results-oriented manager with 15+ year record of outstanding sales, managerial, promotional, and public relations achievements in the sports industry.

- Excellent negotiation skills with clients, players, and management.

- Ability to implement effective, creative ideas for leagues, teams, and individuals.

PROFESSIONAL EXPERIENCE:

TAMPA BAY BELTERS (SBL)   **Tampa, FL**
President & General Manager   **2/89 to 6/91**

Spearheaded initial development and implementation of a successful new Southern Baseball League franchise under two ownership changes.

- Designed, purchased, and developed physical facility including baseball diamond, scoreboard, scorers table, and seating arrangement.

- Managed a seven person staff in the development of a team name, logo, sponsorship packages, promotions, player relations, and public relations activities.

NATIONAL LEAGUE (Baseball)   **Kansas City, MO**
Director of Marketing & Communications   **3/86 to 2/89**

Accepted newly created position and developed league marketing plan and brochure for 47 year old baseball organization following meetings at all league cities.

- Developed and implemented "Baseball Highlights" programming for the NL.

- Designed and coordinated successful weekly NL program, "Baseball Players Profile," airing on syndicated cable sports channels throughout the US.

Derek Jones page 2

INDEPENDENT SPORTS CONSULTANT 1982 to 1986

Provided marketing, promotional, and sales consultation to prominent sports celebrities, management, colleges, player representatives, companies, radio, and television.

NATIONAL LEAGUE (Baseball) Philadelphia, PA
Vice President of Team Services 1980 to 1982

Functioned as a liaison between the NL and its member teams in implementing marketing, promotions, public relations, and sales programs.

- Created and implemented innovative marketing concepts - movable signage, team personnel sweepstakes, celebrity autograph program, and training clinics.

- Coordinated and executed contractual agreements between sponsors and the NL.

- Designed and directed sales & marketing seminars for franchise personnel.

HARTFORD HAMMERS Hartford, CT
Director of Marketing/Sales/Promotions 1975 to 1980

Established and administered a multi-faceted program of sales and promotions.

- Developed strong company associations to the Hammers through innovative ticket and promotional programs.

- Directed giveaway campaigns, licensing program, college nights, retirement ceremonies, half-time shows, old timers game, clinics, and ticket promotions.

- Spearheaded Hammers achievement of Number 1 standing in NL group sales for three consecutive years.

EDUCATION:

CONNECTICUT COLLEGE New London, CT
29 Graduate Credits 1978 to1980

NORTHEASTERN UNIVERSITY Boston, MA
Bachelor of Science 1975

✔ Derek's impressive career in major league sports deserves two pages.
✔ His use of bullets, italics, white space, and short horizontal lines to break up sections still allows the reader to scan the two pages easily.

MARKETING COORDINATOR

BRENDA MULCAHY

52 Sutton Woods Road
Concord, NH 03301

Residence: 603/ 555-2897
Business: 603/ 555-0808

SUMMARY: High energy marketing professional with experience in:

- Budget administration
- Media planning
- Promotional materials
- Promotional programs
- Community relations

- Staff supervision
- Marketing analysis
- Press releases
- Vendor relations
- Computers

EXPERIENCE: CONCORD TRUST COMPANY   CONCORD, NH
(Full service bank with 13 branches and assets exceeding $600M)

Assistant Marketing Director   **1983 to present**

Plan and implement comprehensive marketing programs resulting in new business and improved company image. Receive excellent appraisals in the areas of flexibility, organization, follow-through, interpersonal relations, and job knowledge. Assume responsibilities of Marketing Director in his absence. Elected to Board of Directors in 1989.

Coordinate activities of the Community Relations Committee and provide liaison between the public and the bank. Monitor competitive marketing efforts. Support in the planning and administration of marketing budget. Negotiate contracts with media reps and coordinate schedules. Write media press releases. Coordinate with in-house graphic artist in the production of ads, posters, brochures, and reports.

EDUCATION: CHARTER OAK COLLEGE   FARMINGTON, CT
AS in Business Administration   **1983**

RELATED: Advertising Club of New Hampshire
New Hampshire Bank Marketing Association

✔ Brenda's Summary stresses her marketing experience, not banking experience, so that she will be considered for positions in many industries.
✔ Her job description conveys her professional standing at the bank.

MARKETING INTERN

MAUREEN HEGARTY

12 Glen Springs Road
Hanover, MD 21201
301/ 555-2764

EDUCATION:

Bachelor of Science in Marketing	**May 1990**
GEORGETOWN UNIVERSITY	WASHINGTON, DC
GPA: 3.8	

HONORS:

- Marketing Internship Program
- National Marketing Honor Society
- Dean's List - 4 years

ACTIVITIES:

- Chaired 45-member Fund Raising Committee
- Student Rep - National Marketing Association
- Graphic Arts Director - Georgetown U. Gazette
- Advertising Chairperson - Special Events Committee
- Facilitator for freshman development course
- Trained peer counselor - Lincoln Dormitory

EXPERIENCE:

Marketing Assistant - Intern	**Sep 1989 to May 1990**
SEBASTION WINE IMPORTERS	BALTIMORE, MD

(Wine importer to both wholesale and retail markets)

- Trained in sales, product knowledge, and marketing skills.
- Promoted company/product to retailers and wholesalers.
- Conducted market research of industry competition.
- Planned for and assisted at regional trade shows.

Night Manager	**Oct 1988 to Apr 1990**
COLLEGE CAMPUS CENTER	WASHINGTON, DC

Customer Service Representative	**Summer 1989**
CAMPUS HOTEL	WASHINGTON, DC

Sales Representative	**Summer 1988**
NU-WAY GARDENING PRODUCTS	BALTIMORE, MD

COMPUTERS:

Software:	Order Entry 2.2, Lotus 1-2-3, Word Perfect
Hardware:	MS-DOS computers, WANG VS Word Processor
Languages:	FORTRAN

✔ As a college senior, Maureen's resume stresses activities related to her major.
✔ Her Marketing Internship exposed her to diverse facets of the field.
✔ Computer expertise is a plus in any career.

CURTIS ACKERSLEY

29 Notting Hill Road • Concord, MA 01742   508/ 555-6533

SUMMARY:

- BSEE with 12+ years professional experience in "high-tech" marketing.
- Record of achievement promoting intellectual properties in competitive markets.
- Expert in business analysis & planning, marketing, and technical support.
- Experienced in delivering presentations to high-tech community.
- High energy, results oriented, self-motivated team player.

ACCOMPLISHMENTS:

- **Expanded markets for worldwide leader in information marketing services.**
  Established productive new relationships with major high tech companies leading to long-term contracts. Projecting increase of 13%+ in high tech market sales in FY '91.

- **Rapidly positioned a software start-up within marketplace.**
  Devised new penetration strategies for intellectual properties including marketing activities, sales tools, pricing strategies, acquisition of beta sites. Secured $300K contract for the company within 8 weeks.

- **Successfully penetrated two high-tech markets for electronic components maker.**
  Planned and directed marketing programs to penetrate the SCADA (Supervisory Control And Data Acquisition) and LAN (Local Area Network) markets. Oversaw pricing and selling strategies, trade shows, and advertising decisions.

- **Participated in conference presentations and chairing activities.**
  Presented at Communication '90 and chaired a presentation session at Speech '89.

EMPLOYMENT:

Director of High Technology Marketing (1985 to present)
IN-FORM CORPORATION • Cambridge, MA

Strategic Marketing Director (1979 to 1985)
ADVANCED TECHNOLOGIES • Bedford, MA

EDUCATION:

BSEE (1977)
WORCESTER POLYTECHNIC INSTITUTE • Worcester, MA

- ✔ Curtis effectively condenses 12 years of experience onto one page.
- ✔ His Summary identifies his key educational and professional qualifications.
- ✔ Accomplishments include impressive facts and figures from both positions.

LUCILLE BERANEK
742 Seaworthy Drive
Richmond Beach, WA 98160
206/ 555-3645

MARKETING MANAGEMENT

Professional Experience:

BERANEK ASSOCIATES • Seattle, WA   1988 to present

Principal. Direct the efforts of marketing specialists in the development of operational solutions for leading real estate franchise companies.

- Conduct market surveys to determine market penetration and recommend changes in advertising strategy and company marketing literature.
- Coordinate the design, development, and implementation of computerized property appraisal analyses and client/customer data bases.
- One client increased market share by 7% in 6 months and was recognized as #1 multiple office franchise in the Pacific Northwest.

TAU BETA CORPORATION • Redmond, WA   1984 to 1988

Marketing Manager (1986 to 1988). Directed senior product managers and design engineers in the manufacture of supercomputer-based data processing systems accounting for 12% of total company sales ($60M).

- Introduced sophisticated parallel-processing computer system within 16 months of initial design. Test site culminated in a $17M commitment.
- Increased sales by $3M within eight months by introducing a new application of an established product.
- Eliminated unprofitable product with $1.1M annual savings.
- Collaborated with engineering on project priorities, cost estimates, and schedules.
- Developed effective professional relationships with key industry decision-makers.

Asst. Marketing/Product Manager (1984 to 1986). Developed and implemented market and product strategies for numerous product lines and market segments.

Education:

CALIFORNIA STATE UNIVERSITY • Sacramento, CA
BSBA in Marketing Management   1984

✔ Lucille's resume can be used to secure new clients or a new position.
✔ Her introductory heading specifies a career direction without limiting options.
✔ She highlights the marketing management component of her own business.

WALTER MILLS
105 Dyer City Drive
Henderson, NV 89015

Residence: 702/ 555-9357   *Business:* 702/ 555-0030

PROFESSIONAL EXPERIENCE:

NEVADA BANKS   LAS VEGAS, NV
NATIONAL SALES MANAGER, SHAREHOLDER SERVICES   1988 to present

Direct national sales force in new business development for stock transfer agent. Manage four Regional Managers selling services to major corporations, smaller companies on the threshhold of their Initial Public Offering, and corporations engaged in merger and acquisition activity.

Established a formal sales organization requiring the formulation and implementation of pricing decisions, marketing plans, territorial analysis, product promotion, sales training, and sales performance measurements.

COMPUTER KNOWLEDGE COMPANY   LAS VEGAS, NV
MANAGER, FINANCIAL SERVICES   1986 to 1988

Directed a $24M sales organization targeted to major domestic financial institutions in Los Angeles. Developed business in key accounts with sales emphasis on applied telecommunications business solutions.

ASST. MANAGER, INTERNATIONAL BANKING   1984 to 1986

Directed a $5M sales organization focused on new business development in international banking. Implemented shift from traditional consultative sales to software-oriented sales.

EDUCATION:

OCCIDENTAL COLLEGE   LOS ANGELES, CA
B.S. IN COMPUTER SCIENCE   1984

MBA COURSEWORK
MARKETING, FINANCE, COMPUTER SCIENCE

✔ Walter's resume is highly targeted to a specific field, and should be sent to only those decision-makers acquainted with his area of expertise.
✔ Walter's current MBA studies reflect all the components in his career.

REGIONAL SALES MANAGER

CARL NARDONE
717 Bainbridge Street
Roselle Park, NJ 07204
201/ 555-1074

PROFESSIONAL EXPERIENCE:

NEW JERSEY OFFICE EQUIPMENT SPECIALISTS • Elizabeth, NJ
$27M distributor of business communications equipment and supplies

Regional Sales Manager / Facsimile Division (1987 - present)
($6M in sales • 3 branches • Sales force of 45)

Branch Manager / Newark and Elizabeth (1985 - 1987)

Branch Manager / Paterson (1982 - 1985)

Sales Supervisor / Paterson (1978 - 1982)

Key Account Representative (1976 - 1978)

PROFESSIONAL HIGHLIGHTS:

- Directed recruitment, training, and remuneration programs for regional sales force.
- Developed product pricing, sales forecasts, and profit forecasts for regional division.
- Initiated employee "lead program" which generated $510K in new business in six months.
- Established three new branch operations.
- Negotiated contract which generated $21K profit within two months of operation.
- Exceeded profit forecasts by 18% in six consecutive years.
- Spearheaded Facsimile Division to top U.S. dealership in four consecutive years.
- Named to VIP Club for sales achievements.
- Achieved ranking as top 10 sales representative out of 2,750 in U.S.

EDUCATION AND TRAINING:

TRENTON STATE COLLEGE • Trenton, NJ
Business Administration Studies (1974 - 1976)

SALES COURSES: Tom Hopkins Sales Training, Key Account Selling, Sales Management

---

✔ Carl's resume conveys solid career growth in one company.
✔ His Professional Highlights section is a strong statement of accomplishment.
✔ Education which does not culminate in a degree is still worth mentioning.

GAIL SHARP

647 Longboat Avenue • Monona, WI 53716   608/ 555-8921

SUMMARY OF QUALIFICATIONS:

More than thirteen years progressive experience encompassing sales administration, customer service, and office management • Demonstrated success communicating with managers in key companies • Proven ability to manage simultaneous projects, work independently, and meet deadlines • Effective training skills • Outstanding problem-solving ability.

PROFESSIONAL EXPERIENCE:

Regional Sales Administrator   1980 to present
STEELMADE OFFICE PRODUCTS COMPANY • Madison, WI
($43M annual sales in regional office • Largest sales volume in U.S.)

- Process, expedite, and troubleshoot orders with Plant and Purchasing managers for 45 key accounts in the office furniture industry.
- Closely collaborate with R&D, Production, Accounting, and Shipping Departments to keep informed and prevent/resolve problems. Monitor inventory levels and quality control status.
- Assist customers with design and color matches of artwork.
- Provide liaison with Sales, Manufacturing, Research, and Customer.
- Develop new reporting systems with MIS personnel.
- Update sales estimates in line with production orders, new products, and actual sales. Assist in forecasting and budgeting processes.
- Develop training manuals for administrative/sales support staffs.
- Generate correspondence and special reports for sales personnel.

Promoted from position of **Sales Correspondent**.   1978 to 1980

EDUCATION:

Accounting and Business Studies   1980 to 1981
EDGEWOOD COLLEGE • Madison, WI

Planning to complete Bachelor of Arts Degree in June, 1991.

REFERENCES:

Available upon request

✔ Gail's opening summary quickly identifies her key administrative strengths.
✔ Her long job history in one company has afforded her a breadth of experience.
✔ Her candidacy for a BA degree indicates industriousness and professionalism.

**Sales
Marketing
Advertising**

SANDRA BOROWIAK

81 Ridge Road • Warwick, RI 02887 • 401/ 555-5668

Experience:

CONDOMINIUM SALES COORDINATOR
PAGE PLACE • Warwick, RI   1990 to present

Assist Director of Marketing with strategy planning sessions for advertising and marketing programs to promote sales of 240 units priced up to $265K.

MARKETING ASSISTANT
DeCOSTA'S • Providence, RI   1987 to 1990

Performed all aspects of marketing and customer support for this distributor of upscale pasta products.

- Prospected individual, corporate, and retail accounts through cold-calling, telemarketing, trade shows, and professional networking.
- Monitored sales programs, planned new marketing strategies, and devised creative product applications.
- Assisted customers with product, pricing, and delivery information.

GRAPHIC ARTIST
HT GRAPHICS • Cumberland, RI   1986 to 1987

SALES REPRESENTATIVE
LIVING DESIGNS • Providence, RI   1983 to 1986

Education:

ASSOCIATE OF ARTS IN INTERIOR DESIGN
BRYANT COLLEGE • Smithfield, RI   1982

✔ Sandra identifies her areas of career interest in the upper left corner.
✔ Her sales, marketing, and graphics experience all support her career interests.
✔ Sandra's format utilizes space without making her text appear scanty.

IRA LITTLEFIELD

167 E. 30th Street, Apt. 4-C
New York City, NY 10016

Residence: 212/ 555-5769   *Business:* 212/ 555-9100

SUMMARY:

High-energy marketing, sales, and training professional with a solid record of achievement in both start-up and established hi-tech environments • Keen understanding of the critical relationship between the marketing function and sales performance • Demonstrated ability to analyze complex situations, design practical solutions, and implement workable plans • Highly qualified to develop aggressive marketing programs based on a thorough knowledge of reseller environment and product applications.

PROFESSIONAL EXPERIENCE:

Sales Instructor   **1988 to present**
ALTEC COMPUTER   NEW YORK CITY, NY

- Develop and conduct comprehensive sales training courses for resellers at 1,650+ sites throughout the United States.

- Devise strategic plans to identify and support specific business training needs of resellers. Courses include sales training, presentation skills, interviewing skills, inventory management, and creating a business plan.

- Recruit and oversee department managers in the coordination of in-house training of newly hired sales personnel.

Sales & Training Consultant   **1985 to 1988**

- *Radio Shack:* Developed new corporate accounts for micro-computer systems sales in an attempt to test new market.

- *BioComp Corporation:* Consulted to scientific and research professionals on hardware, software, and system configuration to meet their informational needs.

- *McBride Publishing:* Provided software training to corporate end-users.

Ira Littlefield

Key Account Executive   1981 to 1985
APT SOFTWARE COMPANY   NEW YORK CITY, NY

Account Executive   1980 to 1981
CUTTING EDGE CORPORATION   WASHINGTON, DC

Marketing Communications Manager   1977 to 1980
GOVERNMENT ACCOUNTING OFFICE   WASHINGTON, DC

Formerly held sales, marketing, and public relations positions in Boston:

* CASTLETON GROUP - *Marketing Communications (3 years)*
* PRITCHER PROMOTIONS - *Public Relations (1 year)*
* LIPTON & SEDGEWICK - *Sales (2 years)*

EDUCATION:

Bachelor of Arts in Business Administration   1971
BOSTON COLLEGE   BOSTON, MA

Computer Science, Marketing, and Sales Training   1977 to 1981
AMERICAN UNIVERSITY   WASHINGTON, DC

Continuing Education Coursework   1985 to present
NATIONAL ASSOCIATION OF MARKETING PROFESSIONALS, U.S. TRAINING AND DEVELOPMENT ASSOCIATION

References available upon request

✔ Ira's Summary is targeted and hard-hitting.
✔ Although his experience spans 20 years, Ira provides details only about his two most recent positions because the others are not relevant to his career path.

SALES MANAGER (High Tech)

ROSA SANCHEZ
5663 Overlook Drive
San Bruno, CA 94066
415/ 555-6949

SALES MANAGEMENT

Professional Experience:

SALES MANAGER • Regal Computer Company • S. San Francisco, CA   1989 to present
($3M regional computer hardware and peripheral distributor)

- Manage day-to-day sales activities of 4 outside sales representatives and 2 sales support personnel. Develop sales projections, marketing plans, and operational budgets. Design sales literature and represent company at computer trade shows.

- Develop and maintain more than 325 end-user accounts throughout northern California resulting in $850K annual sales revenue. Troubleshoot accounts and provide excellent customer service. Key accounts include major universities and Fortune 500 companies.

- Negotiate large contracts with vendors. Perform inventory, credit, and A/P functions.

ACCOUNT EXECUTIVE • Computer Accessories • Mountain View, CA   1986 to 1989
($10M international computer hardware and peripheral distributor)

- Generated $750K in annual sales of computer hardware and peripherals.

- Developed new territory from Stockton to Sacramento.

- Introduced Uninterrupted Power Supplies to new and existing Fortune 500 accounts.

- Utilized media campaigns, telemarketing activities, cold calling, and follow up.

ACCOUNT REPRESENTATIVE • Hi-Line Suppliers • Novato, CA   1982 to 1986
($2M division marketing a complete line of computer supplies)

- Generated $600K in annual sales. Acquired largest single order of $65K.

- Developed extensive marketing channels through dealer outlets and retail stores.

- Negotiated proposals, bids and contracts through DP managers and Purchasing Agents of major corporations, universities, hospitals, and state agencies.

Education:

BSBA IN MANAGEMENT • Menlo College • Atherton, CA   1982

✔ Rosa's resume reflects steady career growth within one industry.
✔ In lieu of an Objective, she uses a heading to describe her career interest.
✔ Rosa emphasizes specific facts and figures whenever appropriate.

SALES MANAGER (Promotions)

CYNTHIA ST. GERMAINE
34 Briley Avenue
Fort Wayne, IN 46802
219/ 555-6345

SUMMARY:

Results-oriented manager with solid experience in all aspects of manufacturing, particularly sales promotion and production • Proven ability to recruit, train, and motivate staff • Strong communication skills with staff, management, and customers • Established record of improving quality and reducing costs of manufactured goods • Demonstrated ability promoting company goals and image.

PROFESSIONAL EXPERIENCE:

INDIANA ATHLETIC INC.   FORT WAYNE, IN
($95M manufacturer of 4 lines of top quality sporting goods)

Manager of Sales Promotion   **1988 to present**

- Developed a national cooperative advertising program for 5,000 clients.
- Established new program for statistical measurement of client advertising usage; evaluated sales records and trends for future planning.
- Designed and implemented successful direct mail campaigns, advertising scripts, media, and in-store promotions.
- Created innovative sales promotions for major accounts.
- Coordinated preparation, installation, and breakdown of trade show exhibits.

MANAGEMENT TRAINEE PROGRAM   **1987 to 1988**

Scheduling Manager/Buyer

- Developed production schedules and purchasing requirements for 3 product lines. Improved communication among Sales, R&D, and Engineering.
- Sourced and imported component parts from international vendors.
- Oversaw factory production in three states.
- Insured that inventory levels were adequate to meet sales needs.

EDUCATION:

MARIAN COLLEGE   INDIANAPOLIS, IN
AS in Liberal Arts   **1987**

✔ Cynthia's Summary ties together her sales and manufacturing savvy.
✔ She further describes specific achievements that contribute to the company.
✔ Cynthia's Mgmt. Trainee Program compensates for her lack of a BS degree.

PHILLIP MAHONEY
2989 Pacfic Coast Highway
Santa Monica, CA 90406

Residence: 213/ 555-3702   *Business:* 213/ 555-2000

PROFESSIONAL EXPERIENCE

KRAMER'S - CORPORATE HEADQUARTERS   LONG BEACH, CA
(34 store west coast retail chain • $930M+ annual sales)

Senior Marketing Manager / Small Appliances - Jun 89 to present

- P&L responsibility for second largest department with $150M sales.
- Selected to Key Management Group for consistent sales achievements.
- Devised strategic plan to reverse downtrending sales/margin.
- Introduced several new business categories and expanded others.

Buyer / Consumer Electronics - May 85 to Jun 89

- Spearheaded 600% gain in sales volume to $33M within a three year period.
- Established a "Lowest Price" policy which positioned company as a leader.
- Planned and executed the creation of a 16,300 square foot consumer electronics department for new Santa Rosa store, now the chain leader.

COOPER ELECTRONICS COMPANY   IRVINE, CA
Purchasing Agent - 1981 to 1985
(Purchased stereo equipment for retail consumer electronics store • $4M yearly sales)

HOLLYWOOD HIFI   LOS ANGELES, CA
Founder/Manager - 1979 to 1981
(Personalized, high-volume HIFI equipment firm • Sales concept unique to Los Angeles market • $1.5M+ annual sales • Negotiated profitable sale of company)

EDUCATION

CALIFORNIA STATE UNIVERSITY   LONG BEACH, CA
MBA Candidate

CHAPMAN COLLEGE   ORANGE, CA
Bachelor of Arts - 1976

- ✔ Phillip's importance to Kramer's is evidenced in his impressive achievements.
- ✔ Earlier positions are summarized to show his breadth of experience.
- ✔ Pursuing a graduate degree is important to career growth in management.

MELISSA DEVENS
616 Jagged Reef Road
Coral Gables, FL 33134
305/ 555-9385

Professional Experience:

NEW BRIDE MAGAZINE • Miami, FL   1989 to 1991
Advertising Sales Representative

- Developed and managed quality retail accounts for this newly-formed publication.
- Ranked #1 in sales out of 6 Sales Representatives.
- Within first six months, generated $75K in monthly sales.
- Within first year, generated $170K in monthly sales.
- Maintained high renewal rate and low cancellation rate.
- Trained and motivated new sales representatives.
- Selected by management to participate in Seminar in Magazine Management.
- Contributed ideas in all other areas of publishing operations.

FAMILY FITNESS MAGAZINE • Miami, FL   1987 to 1989
Advertising Sales Assistant

- Assisted Senior Sales Representative in day-to-day administration of sales office.
- Qualified prospective advertisers for Arts & Entertainment Section in a difficult market.
- Served as initial contact for new advertisers.
- Performed account analysis and prepared comparison reports.

JACKIMAN & LOWE • Fort Lauderdale, FL   1984 to 1987
Support Staff - Advertising Department

MEDIA MARKETING COMPANY • Key Bicayne, FL   1983
Public Relations Intern

QUIGLEY ADVERTISING COMPANY • Miami, FL   Summers 1982 and 1983
Marketing Intern

Education:

NOVA UNIVERSITY • Fort Lauderdale, FL
Bachelor of Arts in Marketing Management   1984

- ✔ Melissa's resume traces her steady career growth in advertising sales.
- ✔ Internships are listed to show breadth of experience in various companies.
- ✔ Bullets highlight achievements to make reading easier.

ADVERTISING SALES (Media)

LESLEY SAGER LEVINE

54 Graham Avenue • Irving, TX 75060 • 214/ 555-3006

SUMMARY:

- Top producer in multi-media sales and marketing.
- Able to qualify prospects and generate new business.
- Experienced in vendor support and co-op programs.
- Skilled in media planning, copywriting, and design.
- Team player with excellent leadership ability.
- Strong customer service orientation.

EXPERIENCE:

Senior Advertising Account Executive   **1989 to 1991**
KBSE- *A CBS Affiliate*   DALLAS, TX

Generated $200K new business from local and national accounts in 6 months. Won top sales achievement award.

Advertising Account Executive   **1988 to 1989**
BOISE CABLEVISION - *CNN, USA, ESPN*   IRVING, TX

Increased sales five-fold to local and regional accounts in 6 month period. Named top sales producer.

Advertising Account Manager   **1986 to 1988**
INFOBOOK   DALLAS, TX

Developed from entry-level sales position to firm's top producer and area manager. Recruited, trained, motivated, and supervised 7 outside sales reps. Tracked statistics on contract renewals for planning and evaluation purposes.

Advertising Account Executive   **1982 to 1986**
DALLAS BUSINESS NEWS   DALLAS, TX

Sales leader for weekly magazine with 800,000 circulation.

EDUCATION:

AA in Advertising   **1982**
UNIVERSITY OF TEXAS   ARLINGTON, TX

✔ Lesley's Summary addresses key qualifications of an advertising executive.
✔ Instead of repeating general descriptions for each similar position she held, she includes short, specific achievements from each job.

CIRCULATION SALES

RODNEY GROVER
224 MacGregor Lane
Cary, NC 27511
919/ 555-2911

PROFESSIONAL EXPERIENCE

Circulation Director • THE TRIANGLE • Chapel Hill, NC   1989 to present
(Bi-monthly magazine with circulation of 67,000 bi-monthly)

- Manage new subscriber acquisition telemarketing and direct mail promotions. Coordinate the design, production, and printing of 450,000 pieces of direct mail annually. Direct list research, collaboration with computer house and mail house, response analysis, data processing and fulfillment, and billing functions. *Prepared for audit by Audit Bureau of Circulation.*

- Establish and maintain budgets with sensitivity toward revenues derived from subscriptions, renewals, and newsstand/vending machine sales, and expenses incurred from direct mail programs (mailing lists, postage, printing, outside services), and other promotions. *Spearheaded active campaign to convert subscriptions from free to paid.*

Distribution / Sales Manager • HUNT PUBLISHING • Durham, NC   1986 to 1989
(Sports magazine publisher with single copy sales exceeding $2M annually)

- Processed and expedited orders from 30 distributors and 1,100 retail stores nationwide. Key accounts included WaldenBooks, Wordsworth, and Lauriat's.

- Monitored 3,000 accounts to insure prompt payment. Processed accounts receivable, credits, and returns. Resolved customer problems.

- Increased single copy sales 200% in 3 years through utilization of cold calls, direct mailings, and follow-up. *Performed all aspects of list management.*

- Supported in personnel hiring, training, supervision, and evaluation.

Circulation Manager • BLUSHING BRIDE • Charleston, SC   1984 to 1986
(Women's magazine publisher with sales of $1.5M annually)

EDUCATION

Bachelor of Arts • NORTH CAROLINA STATE UNIVERSITY • Raleigh, NC   1984

✔ Rodney's job descriptions encompass his scope of sales programs, major interfaces, key accounts, sales figures, and management duties.
✔ He highlights important information in italics.

BRUCE BIBEAU
79 Fremanis Avenue
Cincinnati, OH 45209
513/ 555-8896

SALES & MARKETING

Professional Experience:

Andrus Corporation • Portland, OR   1990 - present
(Worldwide leader in sales of highly sophisticated microcomputer-based page make-up systems)

DISTRICT SALES MANAGER

- Expanded Ohio territory into Indiana and Kentucky.

- Sell primarily to corporate marketing, video production, communications, graphics, and audio visual departments as well as to large production houses and graphic design firms.

Fisher Financial Systems • Cleveland, OH   1988 - 1990
(National leader in sales of computer-based stock trading systems)

ACCOUNT REPRESENTATIVE

- Sold $700K during FY '89 with average system sale of $50K.

- Exceeded $500K quota within first 6 months, earning incentive award trip.

- Sold primarily to financial and consulting companies.

Dawn Computer Corporation • Santa Clara, CA   1984 - 1988
(Manufacturer of dedicated word processing systems)

ACCOUNT REPRESENTATIVE

- Exceeded first year $350K quota by 167%, earning incentive award trip. Successfully met second year $600K quota, highest in the branch. Average system sale was $23K.

- Expanded territory and managed two major accounts. Primary contacts were MIS directors, presidents and vice presidents of manufacturing, consulting, and service companies.

- In 1985 opened largest new area account for 32 word processing systems.

- In 1987 received award for highest sales volume of 14 sales representatives.

Education:

MBA CANDIDATE • University of Cincinnati • Cincinnati, OH

BACHELOR OF SCIENCE • Warner Pacific College • Portland, OR   1984

✔ Bruce clarifies his career experience by describing each company.
✔ He does not explain all job duties, but instead outlines key achievements in easy-to-read bulleted statements.

EQUIPMENT SALES (Industrial)

SCOTT NEWMAN
589 Hampshire Avenue
Riverdale, OH 45405
513/ 555-2674

EXPERIENCE: QUINT INDUSTRIAL PRODUCTS   DAYTON, OH
(Distributor of warehousing equipment and systems)

Outside Sales Representative   **1987 to present**
Independently established new three-state territory. Achieved first year sales of $400K in a highly competitive industry. Employed cold calling, developed key promotional programs, implemented outstanding customer service practices, and maintained thorough product knowledge in order to expand customer base. Frequently assessed customers' warehousing equipment needs, recommended products and methods for improved operations, and performed equipment troubleshooting.

Inside Sales Representative   **1986 to 1987**
Recruited from prior company for this telemarketing/sales position due to excellent knowledge of the industry and sales techniques. Assessed customers' needs, recommended products, and quoted pricing. Assisted Purchasing Agents of major corporations as well as owners of small manufacturing companies.

LASERTRON CORPORATION   CINCINNATI, OH
(Leading manufacturer of laser printing equipment)

Telemarketing Sales Representative   **1984 to 1986**
Sold Laser printing equipment and accessories on a commissioned basis to the electronic publishing industry nationwide. Assessed and qualified customers' needs, closed sales, and provided customer service. Met or exceeded quarterly quotas.

EDUCATION: CHATHAM COLLEGE   PITTSBURGH, PA
BSBA with honors   **1984**

REFERENCES: Available upon request

✔ Scott emphasizes career growth in sales, from telemarketing to inside sales to outside sales by highlighting his job titles in bold.
✔ Scott's recruitment to inside sales is an endorsement of his capabilities.

EQUIPMENT SALES (Medical)

MARTHA NICKERSON

78 Shady Hollow Road   512/ 555-8622
Alamo Heights, TX 78209

OBJECTIVE: Medical Equipment Sales Representative

SUMMARY:
- Hospital Account Specialist for a fetal monitoring product.
- 11 years experience training physicians, technicians, and students in use of highly technical medical equipment.
- Knowledge of medical equipment for OB/GYN, Neonatal, Cardiac, Vascular, and Neurological applications.

EXPERIENCE: MEDI-Q CORPORATION   SAN ANTONIO, TX
                   (Medical equipment company with $9M annual sales)

Hospital Account Specialist   **1988 to present**
- Sell fetal monitoring equipment to hospitals in the northeast.
- Implement direct marketing campaigns to promote new business.
- Deliver and install equipment; train users on-site.
- Conduct training/teaching seminars for physicians.
- Doubled sales in lowest producing territory in less than one year.
- Received Sales Award in 1990 for generating $2M in sales.

ALAMO HMO   SAN ANTONIO, TX
Ultrasonographer   **1986 to 1988**
Operating Room Radiologist   **1983 to 1986**
Radiologic Technologist   **1981 to 1983**

EDUCATION: UNIVERSITY OF TEXAS   AUSTIN, TX
                   BS in Health Technology   **1983**
                   AS in Radiologic Technology   **1980**

REFERENCES: AVAILABLE UPON REQUEST

✔ Martha's resume stresses her technical training and sales accomplishments.
✔ She limits her Objective to medical sales, but can sell other product lines.
✔ The use of capitals, bold, and bullets makes it easy to read.

Sales
Marketing
Customer Service

ELIZABETH FRANKSTON

317 James Road • Karns, TN 37921 • 615/ 555-7399

Experience:

BUSINESS SYSTEMS INC.	**Knoxville, TN**
Facsimile Sales Representative	**1990 to present**

- Solicit 200+ accounts per week.
- Improve appointment scheduling by telemarketing
- Deliver presentations at product launch meetings.

JG OFFICE SYSTEMS	**Knoxville, TN**
Inside Sales Assistant	**1988 to 1990**

- Provided inside sales and administrative support.
- Received telephone customer service training.

BELKS DEPARTMENT STORES	**Knoxville, TN**
Commissioned Sales Associate	**1986 to 1988**

- Opened 400 new accounts in first six months.
- Assumed numerous storewide sales positions.

Education:

CARSON-NEWMAN COLLEGE	**Jefferson City, TN**
B.A. in Business Administration	**1986**

- Resident Assistant
- Student Liaison to Alumni Association
- Student Housing President
- Rho Omega National Sorority

References: Available upon request

✔ Elizabeth is still relatively new to sales, so she briefly sketches the scope of her duties and training rather than accomplishments.
✔ With her next position, she can eliminate college activities from her resume.

WILLIAM O'MARA
819 Francis Kennedy Drive
Azalia, MI 48110
313/ 555-7103

PROFESSIONAL EXPERIENCE:

SALES REPRESENTATIVE • **OHS Supply Co.** • Ann Arbor, MI   1988 to present
(Distributor of industrial safety equipment)

- Develop and service established accounts within four-state territory. Received *Sales Achievement Award* for top sales during 4th quarter of 1989.

- Assess prospect's needs, develop appropriate equipment and training proposals, and deliver major presentations to corporate *Safety Policy Committees.*

- Primary contacts are *Production Managers, Safety Engineers,* and *Directors of Human Resources.*

- Knowledgeable about *OSHA requirements* and insurance liabilities related to safety and medical issues within the industry.

- Promote health and *wellness training programs.* Present large group seminars on the treatment and prevention of back injury.

MARKETING REPRESENTATIVE • **Polaris 2000** • Strathmoor, MI   1985 to 1988
(650 member full-service athletic facility)

- Planned and implemented marketing programs to increase membership and program enrollment. Oriented prospective members to facilities and program options. *Increased membership sales 23% annually.*

- Sold athletic equipment, nutritional supplements, and sporting accessories to patrons. *Familiar with varied product lines.*

SALESPERSON • **Motor City Sports** • Detroit, MI   1983 to 1985

EDUCATION:

BACHELOR OF SCIENCE
Wayne State University • Detroit, MI   1983
(Concentration in Sports Medicine and Sport Fitness Administration)

✔ William has developed his background in fitness training into a sales career.
✔ By using italics throughout his job description he highlights key territories, awards, programs, contacts, product lines, and regulations.

MICHELLE CHENG

399 Regent Wharf • San Francisco, CA 94123   415/ 555-4908

EXPERIENCE:

CLEARVIEW HOTEL   SAN FRANCISCO, CA
Sales Manager/Meetings & Functions   **1988 to present**
Solicit business from state, regional, and national association market. Maximize profit potential by evaluating business to meet hotel needs. Prepare annual overnight group rooms budget for 322-room property. Develop quarterly departmental action plans. Consistently generate sales 25% or more above monthly quota and revenues of a minimum of 15% above expected budget.

FESTIVE OCCASIONS   MILL VALLEY, CA
Functions Manager   **1987 to 1988**
Assisted owner in function planning, set-up, and supervision. Decreased food costs by 17% by developing inventory control for retail operation. Created point-of-purchase material and displays in retail establishment resulting in increased sales.

FROGEN YOZURT   SAN FRANCISCO, CA
Account Executive   **1985 to 1987**
Maintained 200+ retail accounts south of San Francisco ranging from small independent markets to a large convenience store chain. Analyzed and interpreted purchasing trends to implement sales at a higher price/unit ratio resulting in increased profits. Assisted in formulating promotions and establishing competitive pricing to a variety of target markets. Increased sales more than 25% per quarter.

TRACKER FOODS   OAKLAND, CA
Sales Representative   **1984 to 1985**
Generated sales in 63 new commercial accounts within local area by presenting full product line directly to end-users. Increased sales to end-users through developing point-of-purchase materials and displays. Educated distributor account sales representatives in techniques to promote entire food service product line.

EDUCATION:

ARMSTRONG COLLEGE   BERKELEY, CA
BA in Economic Management   **1984**

AFFILIATIONS:

HOTEL SALES & MARKETING ASSOCIATION   ASSOCIATION FOR CONVENTION MANAGERS

✔ Michelle describes the scope of each position and resulting accomplishments.
✔ Frequent job change is typical behavior for sales professionals.
✔ Michelle's involvement in industry associations is a great networking opportunity.

I L E N E   C E N N A M O

OBJECTIVE   Sales & Marketing Representative • Graphic Arts

EXPERIENCE   **April 1992 to present**
Independent Marketing Consultant
Trendsetters • Marketing for the future
Services: corporate identity programs, market research, marketing
plans, direct mail campaigns, public relations

January 1991 to present
Instructor • Business skills for graphic designers
Paier College of Art

January 1991 to April 1992
Sales Representative
Cliffhouse Studios • Corporate identity/photography
Achievements: Established 36 new major accounts, doubling an-
nual sales. Developed and implemented high power direct mail and
telemarketing campaigns.

January 1990 to January 1991
Sales Representative
Rappaport Advertising • Advertising/promotion
Achievements: Consistently exceeded monthly sales quotas, earn-
ing Rookie of the Year award. Trained 3 other sales representatives
in sales prospecting techniques.

Previous Positions
Sales Rep • Picture Yourself • Do-it-yourself picture framing
Photographer • Heathrow Studios • Corporate photography

EDUCATION   **June 1989**
B.S.B.A. • Graphic Arts/Business
Paier College of Art
Activities: 3.8 G.P.A., Founder/President of Marketing Forum,
Editor/Photographer of Yearbook

435-F Manomet Road
Whitneyville, CT 06517
203 • 555 • 2096

✔ Ilene's graphically-oriented format demonstrates creativity.
✔ Bold highlights and short, clipped phrases communicate information quickly.
✔ All information on her resume supports both sales and graphics strengths.

INSURANCE SALES

BRENDAN FORBES

82 Mesquite Road
Pulaski Heights, AR 52205

Residence: 501/ 555-9428
Business: 501/ 555-3434

EXPERIENCE

UNITED MUTUAL HEALTH INSURANCE   LITTLE ROCK, AR

Regional Sales Director   **1987 to present**

Manage 87 accounts representing $21M+ annual premium income including 1990 sales of $7.3M.

Implemented strategies to increase penetration of target markets and profitably maintain Executive Life Insurance accounts.

Specialized in alternative funding arrangements, e.g., administrative services only and minimum premium plans.

HEALTH CARRIER, U.S.A.   LITTLE ROCK, AR

Major Account Group Consultant   **1986 to 1987**

Developed major accounts from prospect to point-of-sale.

Served on the new product development task force responsible for budget and sales forecasts and benefit determination.

AETNA INSURANCE COMPANY   NORTH LITTLE ROCK, AR

Group Insurance Sales Representative   **1983 to 1986**

Sold employee benefit programs to senior corporate management through consulting firms, insurance brokers, and agents throughout region. Account size ranged from 50 to 5,000 employees.

EDUCATION

HARDING SCHOOL OF MANAGEMENT   LITTLE ROCK, AR

Bachelor of Science   **1983**
Concentration in Marketing

REFERENCES

AVAILABLE UPON REQUEST

✔ Brendan has worked for major companies, so he emphasizes their names.
✔ Career growth is demonstrated through job titles from Sales Rep to Director.
✔ He describes products, account size, revenues, and key client contacts.

Angela Carlson

227 Burlington Road
Falcon Heights, Minnesota 55113
612/ 555-3823

EXPERIENCE

Business Interiors, Inc.
St. Paul, Minnesota
District Manager
1991 to the present

Promote and sell office furnishings and systems to end users and architects / designers for a multi-line service dealer. Manage all steps of the sales cycle including cold calls, sales presentations, specifications, price quotation / negotiation, order fulfillment, shipping, installation, and troubleshooting. Secured 45 new accounts among Fortune 500 companies resulting in substantial repeat business. Established universities, publishing companies, and health care facilities as major markets. Key accounts include the 5th fastest-growing company in the U.S. Generate $1.4 million in annual sales; consistently meet or exceed sales quotas. Serve as corporate representative to ASID, IBD, and MN Council.

Steelcase, Inc.
Minneapolis, Minnesota
Architect and Design Representative
1988 to 1991

Prepared and delivered presentations to the architectural and design community and to facility managers of large corporations including 3M and Rosemount Company. Developed new accounts and expanded existing accounts through telemarketing, direct mail campaigns, networking and cold calling. Assisted the branch manager in providing product training presentations to end users.

Sales Representative
1987 to 1988

Managed all aspects of the sales function from prospecting through installation and customer service for a manufacturer of systems and casegoods. Key accounts included Kaiser Health Plan. Consistently exceeded sales goals in Minneapolis / St. Paul territory and established long-term relationships with customers, resulting in significant repeat business. Top rookie performer.

EDUCATION

Concordia College
St. Paul, Minnesota
A.S. in Interior Design
1987

✔ Angela's unconventional format promotes her creative side.
✔ White space and bold lettering highlight well-known company names.
✔ Job descriptions include key accounts, annual sales, and territories.

Roberta Manchester
941 Kings Way
Lebanon, NH 03766
603/ 555-2879

PHARMACEUTICAL SALES

Professional Experience:

MEDIGEN CORPORATION • Providence, RI
Hospital Products Specialist (Jun 90 to present)
Hospital/HMO Representative (Apr 88 to Jun 90)
Sales Representative (Aug 83 to Apr 88)

Currently develop and manage accounts in New Hampshire for this Fortune 1000 pharmaceutical manufacturer. Primary contacts are physicians specializing in medicine, surgery, and cardiology as well as hospital pharmacists.

Highlights:

- Top Sales Producer, 1986 - 1987.
- Outstanding Sales Representative's Award, 1985.
- Increased sales from $1M to $2M in 4 years.
- 2nd highest sales volume of vasodilator product in hospital/HMO territory, 1990.
- Introduced new vasodilator product; developed market from $0 to $550K in 3 years.
- Highest sales volume of vasodilator product in non-hospital territory, 1980 - 1981.
- Develop and present seminars on sales territory management.
- Participate in training of newly hired sales representatives.

WARREN LABORATORIES • Kenilworth, NJ
Major Account Representative (1981 to 1983)

RHEIM PHARMACEUTICALS • Hackensack, NJ
Sales Representative (1979 to 1981)

Education:

NOTRE DAME COLLEGE • Manchester, NH
Master of Science in Management (1990)
Bachelor of Science in Business Administration (1978)

✔ Roberta's 10+ years in pharmaceutical sales is effectively condensed.
✔ Her climb within a prominent company is supported by sales achievements.
✔ Roberta's Master's degree sets her apart from other sales candidates.

JUDITH COLES

4 MacKenzie Drive
Tempe, AZ 85281

602/ 555-8754

EXPERIENCE:

FOLSOM REAL ESTATE COMPANY
Sales Associate

PHOENIX, AZ
1986 to 1991

Generated $3M+ in annual commercial property sales through the effective management of all aspects of real estate transactions including legal and financial negotiations.

Performed market research and pricing; developed substantial customer/client base; negotiated between client and customer; provided liaison among banks, attorneys, and clients; compiled and updated statistical data; trained new brokers.

- Member of Million Dollar Sales Club.

- Vice President of National Association of Realtors.

KPTO RADIO
Sales & Marketing Representative

SCOTTSDALE, AZ
1980 to 1986

Researched, identified, and successfuly sold to potential advertisers for targeted upscale market. Planned and implemented special promotional events, utilized extensive cold calling, and presented marketing presentations to develop new and existing business.

COMMUNITY AFFAIRS ASSOCIATION
Public Relations Coordinator

TEMPE, AZ
1978 to 1980

Oversaw media publicity and special events to promote community and philanthropic programs for local retailers. Researched and wrote product and retail industry stories, articles for annual reports, and items for local and regional newspapers.

EDUCATION:

SOUTHWESTERN COLLEGE
Bachelor of Science in Advertising

PHOENIX, AZ
1978

REFERENCES:

AVAILABLE UPON REQUEST

- ✔ Judith has built her sales career on an advertising and PR background.
- ✔ Using bullets, she punctuates her current job description with major sales accomplishments to leave a positive impact on the reader.

KEITH WELCH

23 Rollins Road
Maitland, FL 32751

Residence: 407/ 555-3118
Business: 407/ 555-4550

EXPERTISE:

- Sales & Marketing
- Public Relations
- Project Management
- Market Research
- Marketing Plans
- Media Campaigns

- Budget Preparation
- Contract Negotiations
- Financial Negotiations
- Staff Supervision
- Presentation Skills
- Problem Resolution

EXPERIENCE:

SEMINOLE DEVELOPMENT • Orlando, FL (1988 to present)

Sales Director - Cottonwood Condominiums, Conway, FL
Manage the planning and day-to-day operations of a 15-person on-site sales office for this $75M condominium development project. Direct in-house marketing program and pre-construction sales activities resulting in the sale of 250 of 400 units within three months. Report directly to Principals.

ARK DEVELOPMENT COMPANY • Orlando, FL (1985 to 1988)

Project Manager - Palm Place, Pine Hills, FL
Managed on-site sales center primarily engaged in resale activities following condominium conversion of 600-unit complex.

Project Manager - Lakeside Estates, Ocoee, FL
Performed pre-construction sales, marketing, and management functions related to 275-unit new condominium development.

Assistant Project Manager - Palm Aire, Altamonte Springs, FL
Supported marketing and sales effort during pre-sale, public sale, and resale phases of a 550-unit condominium conversion.

EDUCATION:

ROLLINS COLLEGE
Bachelor of Science in Psychology (1984)

ROLLINS BUSINESS SCHOOL EXTENSION PROGRAM
Real Estate Broker's License (1986)

✔ Keith's Expertise section targets skills he can use outside of real estate sales.
✔ He defines the scope of each condominium project to convey the size of the project he managed.

CHERYL NEWTON
769 River Road
Bethesda, MD 20014
301/ 555-5691

Objective:

Sales Associate / Sales Manager within the retail industry

Professional Experience:

PETERSEN LEATHERS • Washington, DC
(Fine leather goods retailer • 18 regional branches • $3.2M annual sales within branch)

Assistant Manager	1987 to present
Sales Associate	1985 to 1987

Hired as first sales associate in new Hillside branch. Built personal sales from $0 to $600K annually, 19% of store revenues. Consistently attain #1 sales ranking in store as well as top four standing in entire company.

Management responsibilities:

- Hire, schedule, and supervise 17 employees.
- Train sales and management staff for all branches.
- Supervise operation of the customer service and repair desks.
- Collaborate with buyers on customer buying pattern.
- Implement display and merchandising strategies.
- Resolve customer problems.

ATKINS JEWELERS • Chevy Chase, MD
Sales Associate   1983 to 1985

Training:

IN-HOUSE TRAINING
Certificates of Completion • sales, security, and product knowledge

NATIONAL MANAGEMENT ASSOCIATION
Certificate of Completion • retail sales management

✔ Cheryl's Objective gives her flexibility to accept a non-management position.
✔ In her job description, she highlights her management responsibilities to increase her chances of securing a management position.

MARGARET PAULUS
90 Locust Street
Irvington, IN 46219

Residence: 317/ 555-3299   *Business: 317/ 555-4440*

SALES & MARKETING EXECUTIVE

• Research	• Sales	• Training
• Direct Mail	• Trade Shows	• Telemarketing
• Communications	• Forecasting	• Planning

EXPERIENCE

REGAL INCENTIVES	**Indianapolis, IN**
Account Executive	**1985 to present**
-and-	
GREAT IMPRESSIONS	**Indianapolis, IN**
Account Executive	**1980 to 1985**

- Market and sell a wide variety of promotional products & programs used throughout industry. Products include executive & employee gifts, awards, trade show specialties, premiums, incentives, and commemoratives.

- Collaborate with key personnel to identify, analyze, and plan specific program objectives. Research and recommend customized products, packaging, and distribution techniques. Customers range from small businesses to Fortune 1000 companies.

- Develop new accounts through cold calling within an open territory. Successfully grew a local account into a major customer.

- Top sales performer at Great Impressions, a $100M national firm.

- Sales Person of the Year at Regal Incentives, a $15M regional firm.

EDUCATION

BUTLER UNIVERSITY	**Indianapolis, IN**
Marketing Coursework	**1979 to 1982**

✔ Margaret's resume is an eye-catcher because of bullets and lines.
✔ In the opening section, she identifies her current key responsibilities.
✔ She combines the descriptions of her two similar positions to avoid repetition.

SUSAN HOSKINS

Sales & Marketing Manager

12 Morgan Way   Ralston, NE 68127   314/ 555-6892

Experience:

Marketing Manager   **1991 to present**
MEDISOFT / HOSPITAL SYSTEMS DIVISION ▪ Omaha, NE
(Leading supplier of PC-based medical support software)

- Plan and manage national marketing strategy for PC-based system designed to integrate software and hardware in the health care administration setting.

- Direct all aspects of sales, installations, and customer support.

Sales Representative   **1987 to 1991**
C.A.R.E. CORPORATION ▪ Council Bluffs, IA
($15M+ national distributor of computer software for medical records administration)

- Five-time Regional Sales Rep of the Month.

- Produced $1.5M in sales during first year.

- Consistently earn quarterly performance bonuses.

- 1987 and 1989 President's Club Member for exceeding sales quota.

- 1989 Top Sales Performer nationwide.

- 1987 and 1988 Award for highest order sold.

Systems Consultant   **1986 to 1987**
COMPU-MED SYSTEMS ▪ Omaha, NE
(Microcomputer sales and systems configuration for the medical market)

Telemarketing Sales Representative   **1985 to 1986**
COMPUTER NECESSITIES ▪ Omaha, NE
(Manufacturer of microcomputer peripherals)

Education:

B.A. in Management / Marketing   **1984**
IOWA STATE UNIVERSITY ▪ Ames, IA

✔ Susan's top heading serves as an alternative to an Objective.
✔ She cannot yet cite achievements in her present job because of her short duration in the position, so she elaborates on prior sales achievements.

EDWARD GRAVALESE
419 High Ridge Road
San Diego, CA 92114
619/ 555-2238

TECHNICAL SALES & MARKETING

SUMMARY OF QUALIFICATIONS:

Sales & marketing experience within high tech environments • Proven ability to utilize consultative sales to successfully sell tangibles and intangibles within competitive markets • Demonstrated proficiency targeting, developing, and expanding markets through cold calling, trade shows, and advertising campaigns • Knowledge of mainframes, minis, and microcomputers as well as popular business software.

PROFESSIONAL EXPERIENCE:

Sales Representative • Tomlinson Consulting   *1987 to present*
(Contract programming and project consulting services for mainframe computer systems)

- Establish sales networks with senior management in Fortune 500 companies.
- Assess client needs through on-site technical discussions.
- Penetrate vertical markets including Banking, Publishing, and Weather Services.
- Locate, screen, interview, and liaison with key contract personnel.

Marketing Manager • Humboldt Heat Sensors, Inc.   *1985 to 1987*
(Manufacturer of temperature measurement equipment)

- Managed marketing communications budget of $300K and a staff of 7.
- Penetrated new markets resulting in sales growth from $2M to $4M in 2 years.

Marketing Specialist • POS Systems   *1983 to 1985*
(Developer of order entry software)

Marketing Administrator • Monitron Corporation   *1982 to 1983*
(Manufacturer of weather systems for government agencies)

Contracts Administrator • Dielectric Substrates Corporation   *1980 to 1982*
(Manufacturer of ceramic materials)

EDUCATION:

Bachelor of Arts in Management • National University   *1979*

- ✔ Edward's top heading emphasizes his specialized sales and marketing area.
- ✔ His Summary highlights pertinent areas of expertise in technical sales.
- ✔ Positions in diverse companies increase his marketability.

David Fisher
66 Spy Pond Road
Weymouth, MA 02188
508/ 555-0033

TELECOMMUNICATIONS INDUSTRY

Capabilities:

- Develop sales/marketing strategies and training programs.
- Establish comprehensive leads network within the telecommunications industry.
- Promote Other Common Carrier (OCC) service to major potential users.
- Utilize extensive knowledge of network competitive services and call accounting systems.
- Manage large staffs of sales and telemarketing professionals.
- Research, analyze, and resolve corporate telecommunication problems.
- Develop, monitor, and upgrade network facilities with sensitivity toward cost effectiveness.

Achievements:

SALES

- Spearheaded growth of sales of long distance service from $0 to $12M within 3 years.
- Personally increased customer base for major OCC by 40%.
- Sold $415K of telephone equipment in the first year of the industry's infancy.
- Closed 12 new hotel accounts generating $75K monthly revenues for long distance carrier.

SALES TRAINING

- Designed and implemented sales training programs for long distance carriers.
- Hired and trained sales and customer service agents and area managers.
- Taught telemarketing techniques to long distance carrier representatives.
- Provided on-the-job supervision of telephone equipment sales representatives.

SALES MANAGEMENT

- Wrote 5 major business plans for long distance carriers and call accounting OEM's.
- Managed sales and marketing programs for long distance carriers and call accounting OEM.
- Supervised 52 outside sales representatives, sales managers, and telemarketing staff.

Employment:

INDEPENDENT CONSULTANT • TC Consulting, Weymouth, MA (1989 to present)
AREA MANAGER • InfoComm Corporation, Boston, MA (1985 to 1989)
MARKETING REPRESENTATIVE • US Quik-Call, Woburn, MA (1983 to 1985)

Education:

BACHELOR OF ARTS • Boston College, Boston, MA (1983)
Honor Society; "Who's Who Among Students in American Universities"

✔ David's heading indicates the industry he's targeting, but not the specific job.
✔ The body of his resume divides his solid experience into three functional areas so he can pursue a new position in any one of those areas.

SHEILA GAYNOR
422 West 28th Street
New York, NY 10011
212/ 555-3059

EXPERIENCE

XANADU TRAVEL   NEW YORK, NY
Sales Representative   **1989 to present**

Perform a wide variety of sales, marketing, and public relations functions for this large travel wholesaler. Credited by management with strengthening company image within the travel community.

Scope of responsibilities:

- **Sales Support** - Support outside sales representatives in effectively resolving problems for client agencies. Effectively interact with all company departments, e.g., reservations, operations, and accounting.

- **Seminars** - Plan, coordinate, and conduct seminars for client agencies. Handle details including pricing, fliers, and reservations.

- **Marketing Support** - Disseminate brochures and discuss newly established tours with existing accounts. Established new system for regular brochure distribution among 2000 agencies. Compile results of post-tour surveys for review by management.

- **Familiarization Tours** - Conduct familiarization tours for client agencies throughout Bermuda, The Caribbean, Mexico, Hawaii, and The Bahamas.

- **Trade Shows** - Represent company at regional industry trade shows.

- **Training** - Train newly hired Sales Representatives.

BEACOM MEDICAL SUPPLIES   BROOKLYN, NY
Outside Sales Representative   **1986 to 1989**
Inside Sales Representative   **1985 to 1986**

EDUCATION

SAINT FRANCIS COLLEGE   BROOKLYN HEIGHTS, NY
AS in Business Management   **1988**

✔ Sheila begins with a general statement of responsibility and achievement.
✔ She clusters her experience into six distinct areas to ease scanning.
✔ Prior experience is listed to show customer support background.

ALEXANDER PLATT
3387 Seventh Avenue - Apt. 2D
New York, NY 10021
212-555-9572

SUMMARY

Dynamic Travel Sales Manager with in-depth industry experience • Strong background in market research and strategic planning • Solid foundation in contract negotiation, conference planning, staff supervision, and product training • Outstanding sales record based on ability to develop new markets and nurture long-term relationships.

EXPERIENCE

BRITISH AIRWAYS
Account Manager - Passenger Sales • New York, NY   **1989 to present**

Increased travel agency sales to British Airways and developed new travel alliances with corporate accounts. Cited as top 5 sales producer nationwide in 1992.

- Increased travel agency sales 25% through the successful negotiation of group movements, tour operator agreements, and convention contracts.
- Spearheaded an increase in annual sales to one tour operator from $100K to $1.5M and to another from $200K to $3.7M.
- Generated contracted revenues of $2.8M from corporations and professional associations through the negotiation of special fare agreements.
- Created and presented product seminars for trade professionals and consumers.
- Represented British Airways at all business and trade functions.

Account Executive - "Reserve Plus " • Washington, D.C.   **1986 to 1989**

Marketed and sold reservation software and training packages to travel agencies. Increased client base by 50% in three years.

CIRCLE TRAVEL AGENCY
Manager • Washington, D.C.   **1983 to 1986**
Assistant Manager • Baltimore, MD   **1980 to 1983**

Planned and managed daily operations of two high volume travel agencies.

EDUCATION

GEORGE WASHINGTON UNIVERSITY   **Bachelor of Arts**   1980

✔ Alexander's Summary consolidates the many aspects of his career.
✔ Job descriptions emphasize sales production with figures and percentages.
✔ To save space, Alexander lists all college information on a single line.

Students 14

Students Face a Special Challenge

Lack of work experience is the special challenge students face in trying to develop a personalized, eye-catching, informative resume. This drawback can be minimized by emphasizing the many strengths you do have, such as:

- academic excellence
- volunteer work
- community involvement
- computer expertise
- leadership roles
- internships
- travel
- other extracurricular accomplishments
- part-time jobs
- practicums
- languages

Remember - energy, enthusiasm, and maturity are also pluses!

Choose an Individualized Format

Do not assume that because you and your roommate are both marketing majors that you should use the same resume format. You require an individualized format because your education, accomplishments, extracurricular activites, and goals are unique.

The resumes in this section are indexed by major for your convenience, but you can easily adapt any of the formats to your specific needs. Several resumes are geared toward graduate students, and one resume format is also included for a student who has completed some college coursework and some specialized training, but has no degree.

Stress Your Qualifications

The section which demonstrates your strongest qualification should be presented first, whether it be Education, Certification, Experience, or Volunteer Activities. Within your Education section, if the name of your college is more prestigious than your degree, list the college first. Similarly, within your Experience section, decide whether the company name or your job title is more impressive, and then list the more important information first.

Emphasize Your Contributions

Even if most of your experience has been acquired through part-time employment, do not just list your responsibilities. Communicate what you contributed to special projects, or what technical skills you acquired, or the level of company personnel with whom you interacted.

Include a Personal Section

It is advisable for students to include a personal section which describes leadership roles, special skills, characteristics, or interests. This information compensates for an understandable lack of professional experience, and at the same time, communicates that you are a well-rounded, active, interesting candidate. It also serves as an ice-breaker for the interviewer.

De-emphasize Any Weaknesses

Concentrate on describing all your positive credentials instead of calling attention to your weaknesses. De-emphase or omit the valleys in your college career, such as a poor G.P.A., disciplinary probation, or job termination.

Ask For Help

You've already taken a first positive step by utilizing this book as a reference guide. Follow up by discussing questions with someone who understands business well and knows you personally, e.g., a parent, professor, placement office counselor, business colleague, or former boss.

A Reminder

Before you begin writing, review all the tips in Chapter 1. It's time well spent.

ACCOUNTING

Ned Hedison
25 Bond Lane
Kenwood, MN 55811
218/ 555-3972

EMPLOYMENT:

Junior Accountant   **1989 to 1990**
GRAMBLE & HINES   DULUTH, MN

Compiled and reviewed financial statements for small to medium business clients. Performed bank reconciliations, computed federal corporate and individual taxes, and implemented computerized accounting systems for clients. Trained in-house staff on computerized system. Maintained confidential client information. Interacted with clients on a daily basis.

Administrative Assistant   **1985 to 1989**
ACCOUNTS, INC.   HILLSIDE, MN

Provided administrative support to this recruitment firm specializing in software professionals. Calculated and disbursed payroll checks, updated records, trained staff, and interacted with applicants in person and via telephone.

COMPUTER SKLLS:

Hardware: HP, Prime, Apple, Vectra
Software: Accounting Plus, Pre-Audit, Micro Tax, Financial Reporting, Lotus 1-2-3

EDUCATION:

BS in Accountancy with honors   **12/90**
NORTHWESTERN COLLEGE   ST. PAUL, MN

SILVER KEY AWARD FOR EXCELLENCE IN ACADEMICS AND EXTRA-CURRICULAR PARTICIPATION

Activities: Accounting Society, Campus Activities Board, Student Advisory & Evaluation Committees, Student Government

REFERENCES: Available upon request

✔ As a Junior Accountant, Ned has valuable employment experience beyond the typical graduate, so he starts his resume with the Employment section.
✔ Computer skills and academic honors are always crucial to highlight.

Edith Hewson
462 Coral Drive
Bidwell, NY 14222
716/ 555-8997

EDUCATION:	**WILLIAM SMITH COLLEGE** **GENEVA, NY**

WILLIAM SMITH COLLEGE   **GENEVA, NY**

EDUCATION:

WILLIAM SMITH COLLEGE   **GENEVA, NY**
BA in Business Administration   **1991**

- Working knowledge of Word Perfect, Lotus 1-2-3, Pascal.

- Financed 100% of education through part-time employment.

- Planning to pursue graduate studies.

Courses:

Financial Policies of Corporations, Marketing, Business Policy, Productions and Labor Relations, Management and Organizational Behavior, Business Law, Business Seminar

Activities:

Senior Hall President; Intramural Basketball (M.V.P.), Softball, Hockey, Volleyball; Intramural Basketball Referee and Umpire; Volunteer for Campus Projects; Disc Jockey, WWPV-FM; Color Commentating for Women's Lacrosse games - Cable Network

EMPLOYMENT: **NIAGARA TELEPHONE CO.**   **NIAGARA, NY**
Service Order Assistant   **Summers 1987 to 1991**

Supported in the completion of numerous projects to insure quality of database management systems. Researched, verified, and corrected service orders. Trained and assisted new hires. Displayed excellent attention to detail, the ability to work independently, and a high degree of motivation.

INTERESTS: Athletics, reading, politics, finance

✔ Though short on business experience, Edith's school activities invite interest.
✔ She shows maturity by assuming 100% financial responsibility for her education.
✔ Planning for graduate studies is always a strong credential.

JOAN SILLARI

122 Bryant Road
Baton Rouge, LA 70821
504/ 555-4529

SUMMARY:

Career-oriented with employment in responsible positions requiring maturity, energy, flexibility, decision-making, team work, communication, and creativity • Experienced living and travelling abroad • Fluent in English and French • Diverse interests encompassing athletics, music, fashion, and crafts.

EXPERIENCE:

KLIB-TV   **DALLAS, TX**
Production Assistant   **1990 to present**

Produced television segments and public service announcements for air time. Researched topics, interviewed subjects, wrote scripts, shot footage, and edited clips. Coordinated with executive producers, hosts, and cameramen.

FRENCH CONSULATE   **DALLAS, TX**
Advocate   **1989 to 1990**

Acted as an advocate to the French population for the French consulate. Assisted immigrants with translation, education, and housing problems.

ACTON PRODUCTION COMPANY   **HOUSTON, TX**
Producer / Fashion Shows   **1987 to 1989**

Planned, organized, and marketed seasonal benefit fashion shows. Selected clothes; hired models; choreographed, scripted, and directed productions.

EDUCATION:

SOUTHWESTERN UNIVERSITY   **GEORGETOWN, TX**
Bachelor of Arts in Classical Civilization   **1991**

KLIB-TV Fellowship Scholarship; Coordinator, Internship Program; President, Design Group; Public Relations Manager NAACP chapter; Law Advisory Board; French/Latin Tutor; Mentor, College-Bound Program; Paraprofessional Leader.

✔ Joan sells her cosmopolitan background up front with a summary section.
✔ Her unique employment in t.v. and fashion are eye-catchers.
✔ School activities support her claims of maturity, creativity, energy, etc.

COMMUNICATION

CHARLENE KLAYMAN
3 Page Village
West Lebanon, NH 03784
603/ 555-8778

EDUCATION

degree:

BS in Speech Communication
BOSTON UNIVERSITY   1990

minor:

Sociology

coursework:

Advertising, Copywriting, Newswriting, Persuasion

projects:

Personal interview with television newscaster re: issues of media confidentiality. Development of multi-media ad campaign for cosmetic product.

Weekend News Broadcaster - WTDC 104.9

EXPERIENCE

advertising:

Co-op Placement
BROWN-DAVIDSON • Woburn, MA   1989
Pasted up help wanted ads and movie directory ads. Consulted with clients to prevent/rectify problems. Performed special projects requiring client contact.

general business:

Shift Supervisor
LUCINDA'S RESTAURANT • Woburn, MA   1987 to 1989
Opened and closed store. Scheduled and supervised employees. Resolved all customer problems.

ACTIVITIES

Earned numerous awards as a **Gymnast** in regional competitions for 8 years. Developed maturity, ability to handle pressure, flexibility, high energy, and pride in accomplishment.

Also enjoy skiing, swimming, and sailing.

References available upon request

✔ Charlene's numerous projects closely relate to her major.
✔ Her excellence as a Gymnast demonstrates maturity and dedication.
✔ Headings in the left margin help zero in on her most important credentials.

COMPUTER SCIENCE

ERNEST FLAHERTY
4223 East Causeway Road
Cleveland Heights, OH 44118
216/ 555-9377

OBJECTIVE: Programmer/Analyst with an interest in new products.

SUMMARY:
- Able to build, install, and debug quality software systems, each containing a high concentration in graphics, for the editorial and classified newspaper markets.

- Strong oral and written communication skills. Delivered presentation at an International Seminar and reviewed new customer and in-house documentation for an editorial product.

- Flexible, quick learner. Work easily and confidently.

EDUCATION: ANTIOCH COLLEGE • Yellow Springs, OH
B.S. in Computer Science   *1989*

COMPUTERS:

programming languages COBOL, C, FORTRAN, PASCAL, BASIC
ReGIS (Remote Graphics Instruction Set)

operating systems DOS on a PDP-II; ATEX-DOS on a PDP-11
UNIX on the SUN and XYVISION workstations

related studies
- Computer Graphics
- Operating Systems
- Compiler Design
- Logic Design

EMPLOYMENT: VEXAN, INC. • Akron, OH   *part-time, 1988 to present*
Customer Support Specialist. Provide telephone support to the customer database and Field Application Engineers. Interact with Test and Development engineers concerning new research.

KASK INSTRUMENTS • Toledo, OH   *part-time, 1986 to 1988*
Systems Engineer. Built, installed, and debugged unreleased graphics software systems for customer beta sites. Provided in-house technical support and expertise.

Software Engineer. Coordinated and tuned software modules to create a customer-specific production environment.

✔ Ernest's Objective is short, clear and concise.
✔ His Summary demonstrates essential technical and communication skills.
✔ Each part of Ernest's resume strongly supports his overall Objective.

CRIMINAL JUSTICE

FRED DAWSON
1369 Mountain Drive
Bay View, CA 91424

Residence: 415/ 555-2336   *Business: 415/ 555-6822*

EDUCATION: **MS in Criminal Justice summa cum laude (1991)**
ARMSTRONG COLLEGE • Berkeley, CA

BS in Criminal Justice (1986)
CALIFORNIA STATE COLLEGE, CHICO • Chico, CA

Certificate of Completion (1988)
DEPARTMENT OF CORRECTIONS Basic Training Course

EXPERIENCE: CONCORD CORRECTIONAL FACILITY • Concord, CA
(Reception and diagnostic center for Corrections Department)

Supervising Counselor (1988 to present)
Supervise 8 Correctional Counselors in the administration of large caseloads of new commitments, parole violators, and inmates from the stable population.   Assume responsibilities of Director of Classification in his absence.

* Chair Classification Board Hearings.
* Determine each inmate's classification status.
* Serve as Institutional Furlough Coordinator.

Correctional Counselor (1986 to 1988)
Managed caseload of 64 comprised of population described above. Received excellent evaluations for inmate and staff interaction, reports, attendance, work habits, and crisis management.

* Conducted initial intake interviews, prepared classification reports, and made referrals to mental health, educational and vocational units within the facility.

* Compiled information from county facilities, court systems, police departments, and other criminal justice agencies.

* Facilitated processing under Chapter 123A.

* Developed an individual program participation plan for each inmate utilizing available source information and assessments.

* Member of Classification and Disciplinary Committees.

✔ Fred's resume displays very solid education, training, and experience.
✔ His work history demonstrates professional growth to a supervisory role.
✔ The inclusion of a business phone number strengthens his professional image.

CULINARY ARTS

BENITA HERNANDEZ

Culinary Arts

2030 Ocean Drive
Hallandale, FL 33009

305/ 555-8137

EDUCATION:

Associate Degree in Culinary Arts - 1990
NOVA UNIVERSITY • Fort Lauderdale, FL

Courses: Sanitation Mgmt, Food & Beverage Mgmt, Nutrition Concepts, Menu Planning, Purchasing, Facilities Planning

Certification: American Hotel & Motel Association

6-month Practicum:

Banquet Cook & Waiter
GLOVER INN • Fort Lauderdale, FL
(10-room, 2,100-guest function facility)

A La Carte Cook & Waiter
LA CUCINA HERMOSA • Miami, FL
(138-seat a la carte dining)

Cook & Waiter
BLUE WHALE SEAFOOD RESTAURANT • Miami, FL
(295-seat casual dining)

Diploma - 1987
AUGUSTA HIGH SCHOOL • Augusta, FL

EMPLOYMENT:

Line Cook - 1989 to 1990
VALE RESTAURANT & PUB • Miami, FL
(soup prep, ordering, receiving, kitchen mgmt)

Grill Cook - 1988 to 1989
FRIENDLY'S RESTAURANT • Miami, FL

Line Cook - 1987
PEARL STREET RESTAURANT • Fort Lauderdale, FL

✔ Benita emphasizes both her coursework and the practicum within her field.
✔ The descriptions of her practicum placements show a range of experience.
✔ Benita's commitment to the field is shown by her return to school for a degree.

DENTAL HYGIENE

DORIS GREENBERG
1307 Puffer Street
Akron, OH 44309
216/ 555-0332

EDUCATION

degree: **AS in Dental Hygiene**
                     OHIO UNIVERSITY • Athens, OH   12/90

clinical experience: General prophylaxis; intra-extra oral exams; blood pressure;
                     charting; treatment planning; patient education; ultrasonic
                     scaling; root planing; amalgam polishing; application of
                     sealants; taking, pouring, and trimming impressions;
                     construction of athletic mouthguards; nutritional counseling;
                     patients with special needs.

projects: Taught high school dental health education program.
                     Presented dental health exhibit at Children's Museum.
                     Promoted Dental Health Month at shopping mall.

activities: Student American Dental Hygienist Association.
                     Member of student government: active in fund raising.

continuing education: Practical Infection Control, Periodontal Disease, Patient
                     Education.

PRACTICAL EXPERIENCE

Dental Hygienist
JOAN MEYERS, DMD
Akron, OH   5/90 to 11/90

Dental Hygienist
LAWRENCE GARRON, DMD
Fairlawn, OH   11/89 to 5/90

Dental Hygienist
ROBERT BARRY, DDS
Silver Lake, OH   6/89 to 11/89

✔ Doris' comprehensive degree program encompasses her equally important clinical and practical experience.
✔ Doris lists, but does not describe positions, so avoids repeating information.

ECONOMICS

CARLA HENKEL
77 Ellis Avenue
Brooklyn, NY 11201
718/ 555-9991

EDUCATION

degree: | **BA Economics**
HOFSTRA UNIVERSITY • Hempstead, NY   1991

coursework: | Econometrics, Economic Development in Latin America, Spanish, German, French.

activities: | Fundraising activities for Special Olympics.

Hold school diving record.

SPECIAL SKILLS

languages: | Read and speak Spanish, German, and French.

computer: | Word Star, MacWrite, Multimate word processing software.

EXPERIENCE

business: | **Administrative Assistant**
EUBANKS MEDICAL CENTER • Brooklyn, NY   Summer, 1990
Provided administrative support for a staff of 15 at the affiliated Sanipure Corporation. Drafted correspondence. Routed telephone calls. Processed A/P checks.

Administrative Assistant
DEBCO ENGINEERING • Bronx, NY   Summer, 1989
Provided administrative support for a staff of 32 R&D engineers. Translated blueprints from Spanish to English. Processed forms and price quotation requests. Word processed correspondence. Coordinated travel plans. Handled client inquiries.

interests: | Swimming, camping, sewing.

✔ Carla is a typical graduate with a variety of skills and experiences that, when combined, qualify her for several satisfying career paths.
✔ Of special interest are courses, languages, computer skills, and fund raising.

RITA JORGENSEN

46 Powerline Road
Princeton, NJ 08540
609/ 555-0111

OBJECTIVE:

Elementary Teacher, Grades 5-8

EDUCATION:

SETON HALL UNIVERSITY   SOUTH ORANGE, NJ
Master's Candidate in Education   **Anticipated Date: Spring 1992**

TRENTON STATE COLLEGE   TRENTON, NJ
Bachelor of Science in Elementary Education   **1990**
Minor in Psychology. Concentration in Science.

CERTIFICATIONS:

State Certification in Elementary Education (1-8)

TEACHING EXPERIENCE:

ANDERSON SCHOOL   VINELAND, NJ
5th and 6th Grade Teacher   **Spring 1991**
Implemented curriculum in math, language arts, science, history, and computer science
for foreign female students with low academic skills.

HARDING SCHOOL   CAMDEN, NJ
Practicum - Reading Clinic Collaborative - 7th and 8th graders   **Summer 1990**
Designed and taught non-text comprehension and vocabulary activities.

NEWARK MIDDLE SCHOOL   NEWARK, NJ
Practicum - Grade 6   **Spring 1989**
Taught history and geography, English, math, science, spelling, and reading to multi-
racial students including two non-English speaking children. Incorporated poetry and
juvenile literature into curriculum.

CAMDEN LIBRARY   CAMDEN, NJ
Children's Librarian   **1987 to present**

✔ Rita's resume is a straightforward statement of teaching credentials.
✔ Of primary importance to all hiring school systems is State Certification.
✔ Rita's teaching experience in grades 5-8 successfully supports her Objective.

ENGINEERING

KENNETH DAVIO
788 Seaview Road
Bridgeport, CT 06602
203/ 555-9333

OBJECTIVE: Design Engineer

EDUCATION: **UNIVERSITY OF CONNECTICUT**   Storrs, CT
                   BSEE   1991

                   Engineering G.P.A.: 4.0
                   Overall G.P.A.: 3.8
                   National Dean's List (1988-1991)
                   President of student IEEE chapter

EMPLOYMENT: **NATIONAL MISSILE LABS**   Bedford, MA
                   Engineer-in-Training / Circuit Design   5/90 to 9/90

                   Analyzed auxiliary power supply for missile system to develop
                   trouble-shoot schematics for production technicians. Broke down
                   complex circuits into elementary components to facilitate analysis.
                   Gained engineering experience with start up circuitry, supervisory
                   logic stages, pulse width modulators, drive circuitry, transformers,
                   and linear regulators. Acquired familiarity with steps in the
                   manufacturing process. Frequently interacted with design engineers.
                   Consistently received high performance evaluations.

                   HI PERFORMANCE LABS   Newton, MA
                   Assistant Circuit Designer (Training)   5/89 to 9/89

                   Performed laboratory testing on new circuit designs, updated
                   schematics, designed digital decoder, and used simulation package.
                   Also performed application testing of new components for use in
                   missile systems.

                   DAVIO LANDSCAPING SERVICE   Danbury, CT
                   Founder / Manager   6/86 to 11/88

                   Established landscape business during summer and fall seasons.
                   Recruited and supervised a 4-person crew. Maintained a high rate
                   of customer satisfaction and repeat clientele of 50 customers.

✔ Kenneth's sleek, easy-to-skim resume is packed with credentials.
✔ His two G.P.A.'s, IEEE membership, and training make a strong statement.
✔ Added initiative is demonstrated by his own entrepreneurial venture.

ENGLISH

FRANKLIN DULING
Rolling Heights Boulevard
Knoxville, TN 37920
615/ 555-4592

EDUCATION: BELMONT COLLEGE • Nashville, TN
Bachelor of Arts in English 1990

BRENTWOOD SUMMER SCHOOL • Nashville, TN
Introduction to Journalism 1989

COLLEGE WRITING INSTITUTE • London, England
Writing on the Arts of London Summer, 1988

EXPERIENCE: OLYMPIC TRAINING CENTER • Knoxville, TN Summer, 1990
Intern. Assisted the Communications Director for the U.S. Hockey Federation in all communications projects. As a team member, designed a comprehensive media guide for the U.S. Olympic Festival.

COLLEGE CATALYST • Nashville, TN 1988 to 1990
Sports Editor/Reporter. Directed the planning and layout of entire sports section. Covered sports events; wrote and published stories weekly. Delegated assignments to reporters and photographers.

WEDGEWOOD SWIM CLUB • Brentwood, TN Summer, 1989
Swimming Instructor / Coach / Lifeguard.

THE KNOXVILLE SUN • Knoxville, TN January, 1988
Copy Aide Intern.

ACTIVITIES: EDUCATIONAL LEADERSHIP PROGRAM 1988
Coordinator. Developed and presented experience-based leadership seminars for high school students in the Tennessee area schools.

OUTWARD BOUND LEADERSHIP TRAINING 1988
Coordinator. Recruited twenty prospective leaders for the Outdoor Recreation Committee. Co-led five day seminar consisting of hiking, camping and group dynamics in the Canadian Rockies.

BELMONT COLLEGE ATHLETIC BOARD 1987 to 1988
Committee Member. Selected as one of two students on faculty committee to plan and implement college-wide athletic policies.

✔ Franklin's resume traces a history of writing and action-oriented activities, which could combine into an exciting career.
✔ He also projects competence and maturity by his breadth of responsibilities.

ROBERT FARROW
12 West Boyleston Place
Phoenix, AZ 85018
602/ 555-4276

EDUCATION:	**PRESCOTT COLLEGE**	**Prescott, AZ**
	Bachelor of Science Degree	**1991**
	Concentration: Finance	

COMPUTER: Experienced in full range of electronic spreadsheets, word processing, statistics, project planning and graphic software on the Apple Macintosh and IBM-PC.

EMPLOYMENT: **Athletes Advisory Program Member**   **1989 to present**

United States Olympic Skiing Association Appointment.
Serve on sub-committee for western U.S. Discuss the future options of skiers wishing to enter college. Deliver presentations at Western Championships to U.S.O.S.A. on the activities of the committee. Attend semi-annual meetings to contribute ideas for updating services of program and discussing policy changes.

Alden Catering Service • Tempe, AZ   **1987 to Spring 1989**

Assistant Manager.
Assisted with business operations including inventory control, accounting, staff supervision, and opening and closing of restaurant. Assumed management responsibilities for catering service including job scheduling, on-site supervision, and customer follow-up.

ACTIVITIES: **Olympic Skiing**

Gold medalist. National and International competitor.
Selected by the United States Olympic Skiing Association to represent the United States in the Junior World Championships-1990. Trained in Canada and United States an average of five (5) hours a day year round through sophomore year in college.

INTERESTS: Stock Market, Baseball, Auto Racing, Squash, Music.

REFERENCES: Available upon request

✔ Robert successfully utilizes his special competitive sports activities and employment as a major focus on his resume.
✔ His degree, computer skills, and background convey a seriousness of purpose.

FOREIGN STUDIES

MITRA RAFAZI
73 Bramble Avenue
Longmeadow, MA 01106
413/ 555-4601

EDUCATION: BRANDEIS UNIVERSITY • Waltham, MA
Masters Degree - Foreign Studies 1990
Thesis: "The Middle East: into the 21st century."

UNIVERSITY OF MASSACHUSETTS • Amherst, MA
Bachelor of Arts - International Business 1987

TEL AVIV UNIVERSITY • Israel
Bachelor of Arts - Biblical Literature 1985

HIGHLIGHTS: HANCOCK TRUST COMPANY • Medford, MA
Account Representative

DEPARTMENT OF JUSTICE • Boston, MA
Interpreter - Immigration Courts

HYATT & ROSSI • Boston, MA
Paralegal

MINISTRY OF COMMUNICATION • Israel
Translator

PERSONAL: Raised in a traditional Middle Eastern community. Completely financed education in top universities in the Middle East and the U.S.

Fluent in English, Arabic, and Hebrew. Well-travelled throughout the U.S., Europe, and the Middle East. Comfortable adapting to and successfully competing within new cultures.

Familiarity with law, banking, and public relations.

Interest in international relations, computers, sports, and travel.

Single; willing to travel and relocate.

References available upon request.

✔ Mitra stresses her unique upbringing, experiences, and education in order to spark a prospective employer's special interest.
✔ Dates are omitted from her Highlight Section as all positions were short-term.

GERONTOLOGY

AMY ROBERTSON
245 Beach Street
Margate City, NJ 08402
609/ 555-5456

Summary of Qualifications:

- Bachelor of Science in Gerontology.
- Gerontology training and work experience in a variety of therapeutic settings.
- Background encompassing direct service, case work, and team treatment.
- Excellent communication, analytical, and problem-solving skills.
- Proven ability to work independently and meet deadlines.

Education:

BRYN MAWR COLLEGE • Bryn Mawr, PA
Bachelor of Science in Gerontology (1989)

Coursework: Principles of Rehabilitation, Interviewing and Counseling, Developmental Psychology, Maturity and Old Age, Psychology of Aging, and Group Process.

Internship: Day Center Facility serving aged clients with primary psychiatric illness

- Planned and implemented recreational therapy and self-esteem groups for clients.
- Provided case planning and participated in weekly treatment team meetings.

Experience:

JAMISON HOSPITAL, INC. • Philadelphia, PA

Utilization Review Assistant (1988 to 1989)

- Created guidelines and procedures to meet requirements of third party vendors.
- Gained familiarization with operation of Admissions Department.
- Coordinated and maintained documentation/team conference status.

Gerontology Unit Aide (1987 to 1988)

✔ Amy's resume demonstrates that she has the education, training, and personal attributes necessary to enter the field of Gerontology.
✔ She mentions employment in her field while at school.

GOVERNMENT

THOMAS BILLINGS

952 Crescent Circle
Annapolis, MD 21401
301/ 555-9274

EDUCATION:

Trinity College • Washington, DC
Bachelor of Arts (May, 1990)

- Majored in Government. Minored in History.
- Academic Honors (1986-1990)

INTERNSHIPS:

Office of the U.S. Senate Majority Leader
Processed and responded to constituent mail, conducted related casework and represented the office at various hearings and committee meetings. (Spring 1990)

U.S. Public Interest Research Group
Conducted research in the Clerk's Office on corporate lobbying for a major bill. (Fall 1989)

Office of U.S. Attorney General
Gained knowledge and understanding of the procedures and practices of the federal courts through observation and discussions with the Magistrate, attorneys, and other judges. (Spring 1988)

Virginia Attorney General Office
Mediated for the Complaint Section offices. Negotiated with both businesses and dissatisfied consumers in attempting to reach out-of-court settlements. (Fall 1988)

ACTIVITIES:

- Member, Judicial Review Board
- Chairperson, Orientation Committee
- Vice-President, Student/Faculty Council
- M.V.P., Varsity Tennis
- Member, Delta Kappa Gamma
- Resident Assistant
- Travel throughout Europe and the U.S.

REFERENCES:

References from all internship supervisors available.

✔ Thomas' internships and other school activities directly relate to his government major and more than compensate for his lack of paid employment.
✔ References from government officials will be extremely influential.

GUIDANCE

HELEN MAPLES
55 High Street
Westwood, CO 80219
303/ 555-0049

OBJECTIVE:	Guidance Counselor (grades 5-12)	
EDUCATION:	**MA in Counseling Psychology**	**May 91**
	REGIS COLLEGE GRADUATE SCHOOL	DENVER, CO
	BA Sociology *magna cum laude*	**1989**
	REGIS COLLEGE	DENVER, CO
CERTIFICATION:	Guidance Counselor (5-12) pending	
EXPERIENCE:	**Counselor Intern**	**Sep 90 to Jun 91**
	MONTCLAIR HIGH SCHOOL	MONTCLAIR, CO

Counseled students of diverse ages, ethnicity, socioeconomic status and educational ability, individually and in groups, on academic, personal, college and career issues.

- Developed expertise in academic and career planning.
- Co-led 3-week freshman orientation workshop.
- Member of Drop-in Room Advisory Committee.
- Interpreted Harrington O'Shea Interest Inventories and College Board scores.
- Attended team evaluation meeting and professional development workshops.
- Assisted Coordinator of suicide prevention program.
- Consulted with parents about financial aid issues.

	Parent Aide (Practicum)	**Jan 89 to Jun 89**
	COUNCIL OF SOCIAL CONCERN	DENVER, CO
	Advisory Committee	**1989 to present**
	LOWRY PUBLIC SCHOOLS	LOWRY, CO
AFFILIATIONS:	AACD, ASCA	
REFERENCES:	Available upon request	

✔ Helen's resume lists her major credentials first - degree and certification.
✔ The description of her Internship program demonstrates exposure to all areas of school counseling, e.g. working with students, teachers, and parents.

DOUGLAS HACK
214 Mission Calle Pedro
Santa Rosa, CA 95402
707/ 555-0229

EDUCATION:

BS/BA in International Business (1991)
STANFORD UNIVERSITY • Stanford, CA

- Concentrations in Japanese and Marketing.
- Member of Japanese Young Professionals Society.
- Knowledge of Japanese culture, language, and business.
- Well-travelled throughout Japan, Europe, and India.
- Plan to pursue an MBA in International Marketing.

EXPERIENCE:

Senior Account Executive - Marketing (1989 to 1991)
INTERNATIONAL ASSOCIATION FOR BUSINESS STUDENTS

Train and supervise a staff of 16 in the marketing of IABS's business internship programs to executive decision-makers of major companies. Finalize contracts. Direct public relations efforts. Key accounts include Fortune100 high tech and financial services firms.

The San Francisco chapter and its Marketing Department are now recognized as leaders in this worldwide organization.

Market Research Assistant (1988)
BENNINGTON REAL ESTATE • Presidio, CA

Developed and administered survey to solict customer satisfaction information for use in future planning by a real estate development firm. Analyzed and presented results to principals.

Marketing Representative (1987)
RYCO MEDICAL PRODUCTS • San Francisco, CA

Coordinated and attended trade shows in Miami, Dallas, and Seattle. Supported in the design, set up and break down of booths; creation of product literature; and customer liaison.

REFERENCES:

Available upon request

✔ Douglas' major is supported by his concentrations in Japanese and Marketing.
✔ His mastery of Japanese language and business combined with his solid marketing experience enhance his chances to win an international position.

JOURNALISM

NANCY JEWISON
499 Steele Drive
Belleville, NJ 07109
201/ 555-2388

EDUCATION:

Bachelor of Arts in Journalism (1990)
Fordham University • New York, NY

- Minor in Human Relations
- Concentration in Magazine Editing
- Member of Society for Communications Majors

EXPERIENCE:

Communications

REPORTER/COLUMNIST • Newark News • Newark, NJ (1990 - present). Report on local news for weekly town paper. Conduct interviews, cover town meetings, and research new developments. Write opinion and experience pieces.

STAFF WRITER • Century Publications • Newark, NJ (1986 - 1989). Performed writing, production, and sales for a daily newspaper, semi-annual literary journal, and yearbook.

Administrative

BRIGHAM PUBLISHING COMPANY • Irvington, NJ (1988). Assisted in the computerization of publications in the technical information center. Utilized data entry skills.

ADMORE COMPUTER COMPANY • Nutley, NJ (1986). Provided switchboard support and performed data entry for the Marketing department.

ABBOTT LABORATORIES • Newark, NJ (Summer, 1985). Acted as information liaison for corporate representatives abroad. Assisted in the compilation and distribution of promotional materials, requiring a Security Clearance.

PERSONAL:

Single: willing to travel and/or relocate • Well-travelled throughout Europe and Canada • Fluent in Spanish and French • Active member of University Alumni Committee.

✔ Nancy's degree in Journalism is supported by two job experiences in her field.
✔ She highlights nationally-known company names in the Administrative section.
✔ Nancy's languages and her willingness to travel are pluses in her field.

ARNOLD HART

4581 Market Street
Castor, PA 19149

Residence: 215/ 555-7822
Business: 215/ 555-4409

EDUCATION:

Drexel University School of Law • Philadelphia, PA
JURIS DOCTOR CANDIDATE   1991
Evening Division
Class Standing: 4/117

Honors: Scholar (1990)
Dean's List (1988, 1990, 1991)
Staff, Journal of Civil & Criminal Confinement (1989)
Reinholt Scholarship, Local Bar Association (1988)

Duquesne University • Pittsburgh, PA
BACHELOR OF ARTS IN POLITICAL SCIENCE magna cum laude   1986

**LEGAL
EMPLOYMENT:**

Haig & Spencer Counselors at Law • Philadelphia, PA
LEGAL ASSISTANT   Aug 1988 to present
Perform research and provide general assistance to attorneys in a litigation firm concentrating in civil liberties law. Prepare, write, and answer pleadings, discovery, motions and supporting memoranda.

**NON-LEGAL
EMPLOYMENT:**

U. S. Bank & Trust • Philadelphia, PA
CUSTOMER SERVICE REPRESENTATIVE   Jun 1987 to Aug 1988

Hyatt Hotel • Logan, PA
SECURITY OFFICER   Aug 1984 to Jan 1987

ACTIVITIES:

Astor Associates
TREASURER of a committee to elect a local political candidate

Association for Retarded Citizens
HUMAN RIGHTS COMMITTEE

Mensa Society
MEMBER OF AMERICAN CHAPTER

Office of State Representative • Philadelphia, PA
CONGRESSIONAL INTERNSHIP PROGRAM - Spring 1985

REFERENCES:

Personal and professional references available upon request

✔ Arnold has distinguished himself from the competition through his class standing and impressive list of honors and activities.
✔ Segregating his Legal Employment lends it the importance it deserves.

LIBERAL ARTS

LOUISE BELSKI
22 Springer Road
Brookline, MA 02146
617/ 555-0209

EDUCATION

degree:	**Bachelor of Arts Candidate - Liberal Arts**	1991
	Northeastern University • Boston, MA	
honors:	**Dean's List** • **G.P.A.: 3.7**	
activities:	**"Semester Abroad" Study Program**	Spring 1990
	Travelled worldwide while earning academic credit for a full semester of study.	
	Delta Delta Phi	1988 to present
	Project Outreach	Fall 1989
diplomas:	**The High School** • Brookline, MA	1987
	Hebrew High School • Brookline, MA	1987
honors:	**National Honor Society**	
	Outstanding Achievement in German Award	
activities:	**German Club / German Exchange Student Program**	
	Lived and studiedwith a host family in Germany. Hosted a German student.	

RELATED SKILLS

languages:	**German, Hebrew, French**
computers:	**Macintosh, Apple IIC, IBM-PC**
visual arts:	**35 mm photography, dark room techniques**

EMPLOYMENT

Hostess	
Casa Di Fior • Reading, MA	Summer 1989
Catering Assistant	
Kitchen Catering • Medford, MA	Summer 1988

✔ Louise traces her educational history back through high school because of her numerous honors and interesting activities during that time period.
✔ Her technical and communication skills reflect her Liberal Arts background.

MANAGEMENT / SPANISH

MARIA MARTINEZ
12477 Paso Roble
Paradise Hills, NM 87114
505/ 555-3365

EDUCATION:

BA in Management/Spanish (1990)
NEW MEXICO STATE UNIVERSITY • Las Cruces, NM

- *Dean's List:* 4 years
- *Honors:* National Collegiate Foreign Language Award
- *Activities:* Spanish Club, Accounting Tutor
- *Computer Skills:* IBM, Macintosh, Dbase III, Lotus 1-2-3
- *Interests:* Skiing, golf, tennis, fitness
- *Travel:* Europe, Ireland, Puerto Rico, Mexico, Canada

EXPERIENCE:

Project Coordinator - Intern (1989 to 1990)
COOPERATIVE NATIONS WORLDWIDE ASSOCIATION

- Coordinated international career forums for 400 students.
- Compiled monthly CNWA newsletter.
- Responded to inquiries from the public and membership.
- Assisted Educational Programs Coordinator with seminars.
- Trained and supervised junior interns.

Accounts Receivable Administrator (Summer 1989)
RICHARDSON STATIONERS • Alameda, NM

- Controlled receivables and reports for retail shop.
- Deposited daily receivables of $15,000.
- Assumed responsibility for office in owner's absence.

Administrative Assistant (Summer 1988)
GAST MANUFACTURING CORPORATION • Albuquerque, NM

- Performed numerous database projects for Marketing Dept.
- Assisted in processing client mailing list orders.
- Performed QC and QA of database update.

✔ Maria's polished resume equally supports both areas of her dual major.
✔ Her Education section highlights language and academic accomplishments.
✔ Her Experience section succinctly describes her business exposure.

MARKETING

C H I P L. R O G E R S
67005 Barrington Lane • **Cicero, Illinois 60650** • **312/ 555-2948**

OBJECTIVE	Market Researcher with a consulting firm
EDUCATION	**B.S. in Marketing cum laude (1993)** **ILLINOIS STATE UNIVERSITY (ISU)**
Projects	**Market Research:** Researched utilization patterns of local amusement park by tourists and area residents. Interviewed employees, investigated guest book entries, and surveyed local residents. Presented findings.
	Advertising: Devised a print and radio advertising campaign for an area bank. Collected and analyzed financial and marketing data, determined target markets, and developed appropriate advertising budget.
	Business Policy: Conducted extensive research for positioning a major grocery chain in the marketplace. Interviewed corporate President, reviewed financial and management data, and analyzed strengths and weaknesses of proposed buy-out. Generated comprehensive report of analyses and conclusions.
Internship	**The Comet:** Created and designed advertisements in a weekly college newspaper for local retail businesses. Closely collaborated with sales and graphics staff.
Activities	**American Marketing Association:** ISU Chapter V.P.
EMPLOYMENT	**Market Researcher (1991 to 1993)** **Capitol Bank**
	Telemarketer (1992 to 1993) **Sparkle-Rite Window Washers**
	Showroom Sales Rep (1989 to 1991) **Service Merchandise**

✔ The use of creative graphics is consistent with Chip's marketing major.
✔ As a recent graduate, he correctly emphasizes his Education section.
✔ His employment demonstrates hands-on experience in his major.

MEDICINE

Curriculum Vitae
of

CLINTON YERBA, M.P.H.
124 Boot Spur Lane
River Oaks, TX 77019
713/ 555-2371

EDUCATION:

                    RICE UNIVERSITY SCHOOL OF MEDICINE
                    Combined M.D. and M.A. in Anatomic Pathology   1991

externship: **ARLINGTON INSTITUTE OF PATHOLOGY**

activities: Coordinator of Anatomy Practice Practical Examination; Student Committee on Medical Student Affairs

                    RICE UNIVERSITY SCHOOL OF PUBLIC HEALTH
                    Master of Public Health   1987

concentrations: Health Law, Environmental Health Sciences

activities: Curriculum Committee

                    AUSTIN COLLEGE
                    Bachelor of Arts Degree   1984

major: Biology

activities: President of Biology Club; Tutor in Anatomy and Biology
Beta Beta Beta Biological Honor Society

EXPERIENCE:

                    CARTER MEMORIAL HOSPITAL • Houston, TX
                    Pathology Department Assistant

                    KINWOOD GENERAL HOSPITAL • Kinwood, TX
                    Research Assistant - Magnetic Resonance Imaging
                    Research Assistant - Nuclear Medicine / CT Scan
                    Russian Interpreter

MEDICINE (continued)

Clinton Yerba, M.P.H. page 2

HARPER CANCER INSTITUTE • Houston, TX
Department of Communications
Community Liaison - Cancer Prevention Education

LAW OFFICES OF KARP & KARP • Houston, TX
Medical Library Researcher

PROFESSIONAL ACTIVITIES:

MEDICAL SOCIETY

Interspecialty Committee
Public Health Committee
Student Section Publications Representative
Medical Student Section Governing Council
Medical Student Section Chairperson
Coordinated Student State Assembly Meetings: "Diagnosing AIDS Patients: The Medical Student Issues" and "Anatomy of An Addiction: Physical Signs."

AMA MEDICAL STUDENT SECTION

Alternate Delegate - Rice University School of Medicine
Delegate - Rice University School of Medicine

PROFESSIONAL AFFILIATIONS:

Texas Medical Society • American Medical Association • American Cancer Society • American Public Health Association • Hellenic Medical Society • American Society of Law and Medicine.

AWARDS:

LANGE MEDICAL PUBLICATIONS AWARD
Community Service/Extracurricular Activities

SCHWARTZ AWARD
Second Prize - "Refusing Nutrition and Life-prolonging Medications."

✔ Clinton's Curriculum Vitae lists only essential facts about his qualifications.
✔ A Curriculum Vitae is standard in the fields of law, medicine, and academia.
✔ A Curriculum Vitae is credential-heavy and can run even more than 2 pages.

Public Relations
Market Research
Communications
Music

JANICE ROSEN

32 Elm Street • Dayton, OH 45401 • 513/ 555-8288

Summary:
- Self-starter with music and PR expertise.
- Able to relate to creative and technical staffs.
- Sensitive to time and budget goals.
- Proficient with computer hardware and software.
- Solid communication and problem-solving skills.

Education:
B.S. in MUSIC / PUBLIC RELATIONS
Ohio State University • Columbus, OH   1991
Dean's List; 4 year full tuition scholarship

Experience:
PUBLIC RELATIONS COORDINATOR
Dayton Symphony • Dayton, OH   5/89 - present

Perform market research and public relations activities for this respected orchestra to increase its regional visibility. Achieve goals on time and within budget.

- Increased ad revenues through research and effective target marketing of local merchants as prospects.
- Generated an active public relations campaign in the news media consisting of performance program notes.
- Planned and implemented direct mail campaigns to encourage financial support by benefactors.
- Created a monthly in-house newsletter composed of internal orchestra news and external events effecting the symphony, e.g., local Arts funding and cutbacks.
- Edited performer biographies and handled the layout for special concert programs.

PRIVATE PIANO TEACHER
Ohio State University • Columbus, OH   1987 to 1990

✔ Janice's fields of interest listed in the upper left corner attract attention.
✔ Her Summary section, immediately following, includes her many strengths.
✔ These techniques allow Janice to pursue varied positions with her dual major.

NURSING

LINDA LEWIN
76 Dogwood Court
Raleigh, NC 27602
919/ 555-4999

OBJECTIVE

Community Health Nurse

EDUCATION

BS in Nursing (Community Health Specialty)
DAVIDSON COLLEGE OF NURSING • Davidson, NC   May 1990

CLINICAL EXPERIENCE

Community Health Rotation
VISITING NURSING ASSOCIATION • Durham, NC   Spring 1990

Performed home care and weekly assessment of chronic patients in the community. Major focus on assessment skills and patient teaching.

Medical-Surgical Rotation
GREENSBORO HOSPITAL • Greensboro, NC   Spring 1989

Provided total nursing care of the patient including administration of medications, treatments, monitoring IV's, and patient teaching. Assessed, planned, implemented and evaluated nursing care. Specialty units included ICU, OR, RR, and ER.

Pediatric Rotation
DUKE UNIVERSITY MEDICAL CENTER • Durham, NC   Fall 1988

Provided total nursing care of acute pediatric patients and those in the Pediatric ICU.

Prenatal Rotation
GREENSBORO HOSPITAL • Greensboro, NC   Spring 1988

Mental Health Rotation
GREENSBORO HOSPITAL • Greensboro, NC   Fall 1987

✔ Linda's Objective is well-focused and supported by her other credentials.
✔ Her varied clinical placements demonstrate depth of experience.
✔ Centering section headings allows the reader to focus on important areas.

PAULA AMICO
87 Lakewood Drive
Collinwood, OH 44110
216/ 555-2789

EDUCATION

degree: CLEVELAND STATE UNIVERSITY • CLEVELAND, OH
Bachelor of Science in Nutrition (May, 1991)

honors: Hospital Food Service Directors Association scholarship

activities: Nutrition Faculty-Senior Student Liaison Committee

RELATED EXPERIENCE

LAWRENCE REHABILITATION HOSPITAL • EUCLID, OH
Dietetic Intern (7/90 to 12/90). Completed American Dietetic Association's qualifying experience in food service, clinical and community nutrition.

GREEVES HOSPITAL • SHAKER HEIGHTS, OH
Diet Technician *per diem* (Spring, 1990). Planned menus, supervised workers, prepared tube feedings, and assisted patients with menus.

HEAD START PROGRAM • CLeveland, OH
Teaching Assistant (Spring, 1989). Planned and taught weekly nutrition classes to preschoolers.

BEACHLAND HOSPITAL • BEACHLAND, OH
Production Aide (Summer, 1989). Gained broad exposure to kitchen operations through rotating assignments - setting up and delivering patient trays, preparing foods, and cleaning kitchen.

LIVINGSTON HOSPITAL • SOLON, OH
Field Work (Spring, 1988). Assisted a clinical dietician chosen to research the literature and design tables for publication of an article entitled, "Nutritional needs of cardiac patients." Wrote an additional paper based on research findings for presentation to a faculty panel.

✔ Paula's resume combines employment and internship experiences under the heading "Related Experience," as they are all of equal importance.
✔ Her experience is broad, covering food service, teaching, and research.

OCCUPATIONAL THERAPY

SUSAN CRAIGIE

33 Salt Mine Road
Kearns, UT 84118
801/ 555-6233

EDUCATION:	**B.S. in Occupational Therapy** *cum laude*	**1991**
	BRIGHAM YOUNG UNIVERSITY • Provo, UT	
	<u>Activities</u>: Student Activities Committee, Big Sister Volunteer	

LICENSES:	**OTR/L**	**1991**

INTERNSHIPS:	OGDEN MEMORIAL HOSPITAL • Ogden, UT	**7/90 to 9/90**
	(32-bed adult open in-patient psychiatric unit)	
	TORREY CITY HOSPITAL • Torrey, UT	**4/90 to 5/90**
	(21-bed locked in-patient adult psychiatric unit)	
	MURRAY REHAB HOSPITAL • Murray, UT	**1/90 to 3/90**
	(Mixed population including geriatric, stroke, hemaplegic, and paraplegic patients displaying a variety of physical dysfunctions)	

Under minimal supervision, performed a full range of treatment planning, programming, implementation, documentation, and reporting activities at the above internship placements. Conducted assessments to evaluate patient mental and functional status. Provided individual, small group, and large group therapy sessions. Participated in treatment planning meetings with multi-disciplinary medical personnel. Received excellent performance evaluations.

EMPLOYMENT:	**Home Health Assistant**	
	ALTERNATIVE CARE COMPANY • Salt Lake City, UT	**7/90**
	Administrative Assistant	
	SCHOOL OF GOVERNMENT	
	BRIGHAM YOUNG UNIVERSITY • Provo, UT	**6/85 to 12/89**

✔ Susan segments her credentials into short sections to aid scanning.
✔ She clusters her internships together with one description, avoiding repetition.
✔ In Susan's field, a license is required, so it merits a separate section.

ANDREA FIDURCO

23B Skidmore Avenue
Sheffield, MO 64125
816/ 555-2967

EDUCATION:

Rockhurst College   **Kansas City, MO**
BACHELOR OF SCIENCE IN PHYSICAL EDUCATION   Spring 1991
(Specialization in NATA-approved curriculum in athletic training &
sports medicine. Major interest in conditioning, nutrition,
biomechanics, and rehabilitation.)

g.p.a.:

3.9

honors:

Helvetia Sophomore Honorary Award
Dean's List

coursework:

Orthopedic Assessment, Therapeutic Modalities, Anatomy,
Cadaver Lab, Physiology, Kinesiology, Rehabilitation, Emergency
Care, Issues in Athletic Training, Independent Study

varsity sports:

Tennis - 1988-1991

certification:

NATA Certification Test - January 1991

Antioch High School   **Antioch, MO**
DIPLOMA   Spring 1987

g.p.a.:

3.85

honors:

National Honor Society
Antioch High School-sponsored Scholastic Award
Davidson Company-sponsored Scholarship Award

varsity sports:

Tennis - Captain
Cross Country - Captain

awards:

MVP, Tennis - 1987
Most Valuable Cross Country Runner - 1986
Coaches Award - 1987
Sportsmanship Award-1987

PHYSICAL EDUCATION (continued)

EXPERIENCE:

Park College   Parkville, MO
STUDENT TRAINER   1988 to 1989
RESIDENT TRAINER   1989 to 1990

Leeds Hospital - Sports Medicine Clinic   Leeds, MO
PHYSICAL THERAPY/SPORTS AID INTERN   Spring 1987
(350-hour volunteer internship)

Camp Campabello   Kirkwood, MO
TENNIS DIRECTOR   Summers 1985 to present
TENNIS INSTRUCTOR   Summers 1983 to 1985

Park College   Parkville, MO
Wedgemere Racquet Club   Parkville, MO
TENNIS INSTRUCTOR   1987 to 1988

USTA Schools Program Volunteer   Leeds, MO
(Tennis Instructor for local public school students)   1990

Hazelton Arms Estates   Raytown, MO
HEAD LIFE GUARD   Summer 1988

CERTIFICATION: Life Guard - Red Cross certified
CPR - Red Cross certified
First Aid - Red Cross certified
SCUBA - PADI certified

AFFILIATIONS: Active member of NATA, USTA, MAHPERD, RED CROSS

ACTIVITIES: Marathon Runner
Triathlete
Tennis
Hiking

REFERENCES: Personal and Professional References available upon request

---

✔ All of Andrea's credentials are impressive and relevant, meriting 2 full pages.
✔ Andrea patterns her resume after a Curriculum Vitae, presenting factual information only, which facilitates scanning.

PRADIP RAMASHAN
899 Massachusetts Avenue
Cambridge, MA 02139
617/ 555-7112

EDUCATION:	**RENSSELAER POLYTECHNIC INSTITUTE**	**Troy, NY**
	Bachelor of Science in Physics	**1991**

Strong background in chemistry
Dean's List - 4 semesters

COMPUTERS:

Hardware

IBM 3081, IBM-PC, Apple II-C, DEC Rainbow

Software

Q SYSTEM, Enable

Operating Systems

MS/DOS, UNIX

Languages

BASIC, FORTRAN 77, FORTRAN WATFIV

EMPLOYMENT:	**REFAB TESTING COMPANY**	**BUFFALO, NY**
	Assistant Inspector	**Summer 1989**

Work involved ND testing. Prepared, processed, and inspected aerospace parts using Florescent Penetrant, Magnetic Particle and X-ray methods.

CHISWICK INDUSTRIES	**CRANFORD, NY**
Materials Handler	**Summer 1988**

SAFEWAY SECURITY COMPANY	**BUFFALO, NY**
Security Officer	**Summer 1987**

WANG COMPUTER CORPORATION	**LOWELL, MA**
Materials Handler	**Summer 1986**

REFERENCES: Available upon request

✔ Pradip's academic success at a prestigious college is his major credential.
✔ His range of computer expertise is fundamental to his field.
✔ Only the summer employment relevant to his major warrants description.

POLITICAL SCIENCE

ROBERTA RILEY

---

37 Heath Street • Alexandria, VA 22313   703/ 555-0624

EDUCATION:

ROANOKE COLLEGE • Salem, VA   1990
Bachelor of Arts in Political Science
Concentration: International Business
Activities: Delta Sigma Pi, Teaching Assistant

ECOLE INTERNATIONALE • Paris, France   10/89 - 6/90

SPECIAL SKILLS:

Language: Proficient in French language - speaking, reading, writing

Computer: Multimate, Microsoft Word, Wang, WordPerfect, MacWrite, DECMate

WORK EXPERIENCE:

ECOLE INTERNATIONALE • Paris, France   10/89 - 6/90
Student Liaison. Organized and coordinated numerous events for 145 college students enrolled in a foreign study program. Facilitated orientation, participated in field study trips, and planned special events.

NEW WORLD CENTER • Roanoke, VA   9/88 - 9/89
Student Coordinator. Coordinated lecture and host placement activities for the International Visitor Program. Interacted closely with international dignitaries.

ROANOKE COLLEGE / STUDENT ACTIVITIES OFFICE • Salem, VA   9/88 - 9/89
Student Accounts Business Manager. Oversaw accounting procedures for 65 student organizations. Assured compliance with state alcoholic beverage regulations.

LEADERSHIP EXPERIENCE:

ROANOKE COLLEGE / WORLD RELATIONS ASSOCIATION • Salem, VA   9/87 - 9/88
President. Established the Association on campus to promote international awareness within the student body. Enlisted professors to conduct discussion groups.

ROANOKE COLLEGE / ACTIVITIES COUNCIL • Salem, VA   11/86 - 9/87
President. Administered professional contracts for campus-wide lecture series, cultural and social events. Managed $45,000 budget and 43 peers.

✔ Roberta's resume is a breeze to write because she has so much experience.
✔ Small margins and long lines of information are space-saving techniques.
✔ Roberta presents a very strong resume that will get noticed.

WILLIAM LUKENS
7668 Providence Road
Cranston, RI 02910
401 / 555-9863

EDUCATION

degree:

BA Psychology
BROWN UNIVERSITY   1990

coursework:

Research Methods, Statistics, Experimental Psychology, Abnormal Psychology, Developmental Psychology, Learning and Motivation, Psychopathology, Personality.

activities:

Psychology Association, Commencement Committee

EXPERIENCE

directed study:

Researcher / Clinical Psychology Professor
Study comparing male and female sexual patterns.
(Coded research and submitted paper on related topic)

Researcher / Physiological Psychology Professor
Study investigating skin responses to ultra-cold stimuli.
(Compiled, analyzed, and presented data)

research:

Research Assistant / Social Psychology Professor
Longitudinal study of dual-career families.
(Coordinated students in coding transcriptions)

Research Assistant / Biology Professor
Ecological study of South American killer bees.
(Performed coding and statistical analyses of data)

teaching:

Teaching Assistant
INTRODUCTORY PSYCHOLOGY • Providence College
(Presented lectures; proctered and graded exams)

Teacher
RELIGIOUS SCHOOL • St. James Church
(Taught classes for elementary level children)

✔ William's diverse experience in his major - directed study, research, and teaching - is highlighted with markers in the left margin.
✔ Short descriptions generate interest and additional questions from a recruiter.

PSYCHOLOGY (Social)

DELLA JACKSON

Permanent Address:
27 Southgate Road
Castleton, IN 46250
317/ 555-6707

Temporary Address:
44 University Drive, #82A
Terre Haute, IN 47809
317/ 555-4523

EDUCATION: INDIANA STATE UNIVERSITY   TERRE HAUTE, IN

Bachelor of Arts Candidate in Psychology   **1990**

- *Dean's List:* Spring, 1990
- *4-year tennis scholarship:* Team Captain (Fall, 1990), MVP (Fall, 1990)
- *Coursework:* Social Psychology, Abnormal Psychology, Industrial Psychology, Small Group Processes, The Family as a System.
- *Activities:* Student Advisory Council, Volunteer for the Young Adult Retarded Citizens, "Big Sister" to freshman student, Intramural Volleyball.

EMPLOYMENT: RECREATION DEPARTMENT   TWELVE POINTS, IN

Tennis Instructor   **Summer, 1989**

- Trained and supervised two assistant instructors.
- Planned, organized, and taught group tennis lessons to 30 beginners.
- Developed program to emphasize technique, scoring, and court etiquette.
- Designed curriculum to include drills, games, and competitions.
- Stimulated learning through positive reinforcement and creative teaching.

LINWOOD REHABILITATION HOSPITAL   MEADOWS, IN

Team Coordinator - Ambulatory Care   **Summer, 1987**

- Interacted with medical personnel, administrative staff, and patients.
- Obtained patient charts and documentation for multidisciplinary team.
- Researched charts to verify patient status prior to discharge.

PLAYTIME   TERRE HAUTE, IN

Sales Assistant - Crafts Department   **Summer, 1986**

- Assisted both adult and child customers with selections and purchases.
- Recommended ideas to management regarding merchandising.
- Advised management as to inventory levels of specific products.

✔ Della is interviewing while still a senior, so she includes a campus address.
✔ Her academic and employment accomplishments are highlighted by using a pleasing variety of caps, italics, bullets, boldface, lines, and white space.

JULIE ANDERSON, *LCSW*

911 Shady Pines Road
Apple Ridge, MS 39204
601/ 555-0284

EDUCATION:

Master of Social Work	**1991**
BELHAVEN SCHOOL OF SOCIAL WORK	JACKSON, MS
(Advanced Standing)	

Bachelor of Social Work	**1989**
JACKSON STATE UNIVERSITY	JACKSON, MS
(Summa Cum Laude)	

ORGANIZATIONS: National Association of Social Workers

EXPERIENCE:

Social Worker	**9/89 to 8/90**
WESTLAND HUMAN SERVICES DEPT.	WESTLAND, MS

Participated on a multi-disciplinary team providing problem-solving treatment plans for a varied client caseload. Provided counseling for teens and adults focusing primarily on marital, family, and sexual abuse issues.

Social Worker	**5/87 to 8/89**
OUTREACH INCORPORATED	JACKSON, MS

Participated on a multi-disciplinary team to aid families in the development of successful relationships and the establishment of a community support network. Provided support and advocacy including court appearances, daily living assistance, and parenting interventions.

Social Worker	**5/86 to 5/87**
HUMAN RELIEF INCORPORATED	NORTHSIDE, MS

Provided counseling and crisis intervention for abused women and their children. Conducted in-take processing and assisted in teaching educational seminars. Advocated in court for women seeking to obtain restraining orders.

✔ Julie establishes her credentials immediately by using LCSW after her name.
✔ Her credibility continues to grow as the reader scans her academic excellence, professional affiliation, and 5 years of full-time professional employment.

SOCIOLOGY

BONNIE TATE
144 Burlington Road
Bethany, NE 68505
402/ 555-5679

EDUCATION

degree:
Bachelor of Arts in Sociology   **1991**
UNION COLLEGE   Lincoln, NE

coursework:
Social Welfare, Social Services, Social Work, Child Psychology, Research Methods, Ethics.

activities:
Voluntary Action Center, Amnesty International, ASPCA

EXPERIENCE

employment:
Park Supervisor   **1989 to 1991**
BLAIR RECREATION COMMISSION   Blair, NE

- Organized daily activities for 28 young children.
- Recorded attendance, lunch distribution, and events.
- Coordinated bi-weekly citywide events for children.

internship:
Protective Service Intern   **Spring 1991**
DIVISION OF YOUTH SERVICES   Lincoln, NE

- Managed caseload of 8 clients.
- Conducted in-home and supervised visits.
- Maintained files and wrote court reports.
- Actively participated in juvenile court proceedings.
- Extensive interagency contact.

volunteer:
Fund Raising Committee   **Summer 1991**
ATTENTION, INC.   Beatrice, NE

Activities Aid   **Fall 1990**
WILLOWS NURSING HOME   Fremont, NE

Befriender   **Fall 1989**
PINE STREET INN   Lincoln, NE

✔ Bonnie's resume expresses her commitment to the field of Sociology.
✔ Her school coursework and activities, employment, internship, and volunteer activities reflect her social conscience and interest in people.

JAMES H. DUNBAR

34 Elmwood Drive
Riverton Heights, WA 98188
206/ 555-6909

OBJECTIVE: Software Quality Assurance Engineer

EXPERIENCE:

PARSON COMPUTER LABORATORIES • REDMOND, WA
Senior Software Engineer - Software Quality Assurance (1990 to present)
Software Engineer - Software Quality Assurance (1988 to 1990)
Senior Programmer/Analyst - MIS (1984 to 1988)

HIGHLIGHTS:

- Evaluate software via specifications.
- Create test plan or test check list for component level and system level testing.
- Create or enhance regression test suite.
- Create or populate test bed data.
- Review and certify software and documentation.
- Document test results via on-line problem reporting system and test reports.
- Train Customer Service Reps on regression testing.
- Coordinate and create test environment for VS COBOL federal validation.
- Integrate test suites with PBX's.
- Perform black box testing.

EDUCATION:

SEATTLE PACIFIC UNIVERSITY • SEATTLE, WA
Master of Science in Software Engineering Candidate

WASHINGTON STATE UNIVERSITY • PULLMAN, WA
Bachelor of Arts in Computer Science (1984)

✔ As a graduate student, James has already established himself professionally.
✔ His Objective and Experience demonstrate a chosen career path.
✔ The Highlights section summarizes 10 years of experience without repetition.

ALLAN G. DOUCETTE
3227 Holly Drive
Manchester, NH 03101
603/ 555-1373

EDUCATION

MS in Sport & Recreation Management   **Jun 91**
NEW ENGLAND COLLEGE   HENNIKER, NH
Graduate Teaching Assistant: Soccer, Lacrosse

BA in Human Relations *cum laude*   **1988**
RIVIER COLLEGE   NASHUA, NH
Activities: Captain/President Men's Swim Club, Senior Class Representative, Senior Class Publicity Committee, House Council, Class Council, Intramural Sports

---

WORK EXPERIENCE

Intern - Halloween Parade Coordinator   **Fall 1990**
BEDFORD RECREATION DEPARTMENT   BEDFORD, NH

> Planned and directed "first ever" town-wide Halloween Parade with 700 participants. Coordinated publicity, gift solicitation, committee meetings, awards presentation.

Tournament Director   **Fall 1990**
BEDFORD ANNUAL TOWN TENNIS TOURNAMENT   BEDFORD, NH

> Planned and coordinated annual town athletic event comprised of 110 entrants. Oversaw publicity, gift solicitation, committee selections, and awards party.

Swim Team Head Coach   **1988 - 1990**
MANCHESTER YMCA   MANCHESTER, NH

> Coached 100 boys and girls ages 5 to 18. Trained swimmers, planned roster of events and swimmers, coordinated special events, and scheduled AAU swim meets. Division II League Champions.

Intern   **Spring, 1987**
CENTER FOR MISSING & EXPLOITED CHILDREN   MANCHESTER, NH

Snack Bar Supervisor   **Summers, 1986 & 1987**
BEDFORD SWIM & TENNIS CLUB   BEDFORD, NH

✔ Allan's BA and MS degrees are "people-oriented," ideal for his chosen field.
✔ His interest in people and recreation is supported by each of his numerous college activities and work experiences.

TEXTILE DESIGN

SUZANNE HARRINGTON
876 Beechwood Court
Friendly, NC 27404
919/ 555-2464

EDUCATION

Bachelor of Science in Textile Design
Bennett College • Greensboro, NC   1991

RELEVANT COURSES

- Textiles for Interiors
- Design Materials
- Perception: Color & Light
- Visual Thinking
- Experimental Textiles
- Environmental Design

AWARDS

- Handcrafted Paper and Textile Design displayed in Bennett College Art Gallery.
- Hand-knitted Sweater displayed in University Art Gallery.
- Hand-printed Silkscreen Design displayed in Jones Gallery, City, State.

INTERNSHIPS

Interior Design Consultant
Beauty Interiors • Greensboro, NC   Jan - May 1991

- Provided decorating assistance to customers both at in-store and on-site locations.
- Designed store floor displays.
- Mixed paints to complement textile colorations.
- Priced merchandise and samples including mark-up calculations.
- Organized fabric, tile, and wood floor departments of more than two thousand samples.
- Designed wall unit to store carpet and floor samples.

Jewelry Maker
Hopwood Jewelers • High Point, NC   Jan - May 1989

- Designed and handcrafted necklaces and earrings.
- Assisted customers with selections and purchases.

✔ Suzanne's resume presents information in attractive, easy-to-scan units.
✔ Centered section headings draw attention to the Awards section.
✔ A strong graphic presentation is very important in the design field.

NO DEGREE

DINA GIORGIO
9433 Poe Road
Milwaukee, WI 53202
414/ 555-1878

EDUCATION:	**LAKELAND COLLEGE**	Sheboygan, WI
	Business Management (80 credits)	**1989 - 1991**

KING TRAVEL EDUCATION CENTER   Swan, WI
Certificate of Completion   **1989**

Curriculum included domestic and international air ticketing, domestic tour, Caribbean client, SABRE system, ticketing and documentation, and computer reservations.

EMPLOYMENT: **CONCORDIA DATA SYSTEMS**   **Milwaukee, WI**
Sales Administrator   **1989 - present**

Support sales and administrative staff in the smooth operation of the department. Greet customers; prepare, verify, and mail contracts to corporate headquarters; generate sales forecasts and commission schedules; perform billing, banking, and filing functions; utilize Multi-mate on the IBM-PC.

BERKS CLOTHING   **Milwaukee, WI**
THE GAP   **Mayfair, WI**
Sales Associate   **part-time, 1990**

HOLIDAY HEALTH CLUBS   **Harbor, WI**
Assistant Manager   **part-time, 1989**

PRIMO'S   **Milwaukee, WI**
Assistant Manager   **1988**

INTERESTS: Fitness, Travel (Europe, Caribbean, Canada)

Fluent in Italian

REFERENCES: Available upon request

✔ Dina's business and travel education coupled with her sales and management experience will allow career growth despite the lack of a degree.
✔ She is well-qualified to succeed in many management training programs.

COVER LETTER (Dual Major)

88 Torrey Pines Blvd.
San Diego, CA 92101

Date

Mr. Seth Jacobson
Assistant Vice President
Bentley Corporation
221 Old Town Drive
San Diego, CA 92101

Dear Mr. Jacobson:

Can Bentley Corporation use an enthusiastic new college grad who speaks both business and Japanese?

I just earned a management degree at National University with a concentration in Finance and Japanese. This dual focus has enabled me to acquire business knowledge and a comprehensive understanding of Japanese language, culture, and business.

Throughout college, I also worked in various marketing positions. For two years I was Senior Account Executive/Marketing Department for the local Chapter of a worldwide organization which places foreign students in business internships. I gained hands-on experience in program development, staff development, and negotia-tion with top executives.

A position at Bentley particularly interests me because of its policy of training managers in several operational areas. I would welcome the opportunity to further discuss my qualifications and how I might make a contribution at Bentley. I will contact you next week after you've had the opportunity to review my credentials in the enclosed resume.

Sincerely yours,

Frank Baldwin

Encl.: resume

✔ Frank turns his cover letter into a strong marketing tool by presenting himself as a confident, accomplished entry-level business professional.
✔ A good choice of dual majors shows a shrewd business mind.

COVER LETTER (Honors Graduate)

35 Gilbert Street
Bluff Park, AL 35226

Date

Christine Burke
Director of Personnel
Prescott Bottling Company
39 Prescott Place
Birmingham, AL 35203

Dear Ms. Burke:

As an honors graduate in accounting, I am ready to put into practice all I've learned. Your advertisement for a Junior Accountant particularly interests me because of the diverse opportunity it offers to work with both corporate and individual clients.

As the enclosed resume indicates, I recently received a B.S. in Accounting from the University of Alabama where I maintained a G.P.A. of 3.9.

Through related employment I gained experience using Lotus 1-2-3; maintaining A/R, A/P, and payroll records; preparing Financial Statements; reconciling Bank Statements; and supervising staff.

I would welcome the opportunity to further discuss my qualifications and am available for a personal meeting at your convenience. I will contact you next week to discuss this possibility.

Sincerely yours,

Deborah Jason

Encl.: resume

- ✔ Deborah opens by stressing her strong academic standing.
- ✔ She describes specific skills she's acquired in accounting.
- ✔ Deborah also discusses why she's interested in that particular position.

COVER LETTER (Referral)

11 Irvine Street
Eugene, OR 97401

Date

Ms. Sarah J. Lopez
Vice President
The Brighton Company
Farwood Place
Eugene, OR 97401

Dear Ms. Lopez,

Edward Chang, Employment Manager at your subsidiary, The
Brighton Safe Deposit & Trust Company, strongly suggested I
apply for a position as a Mutual Fund Performance & Business
Analyst.

Mr. Chang knows of my academic achievements as a finance major
at Reed College and of my background as a world-ranked gymnast.

Through my college studies I acquired strong analytical, quantitative, research and writing skills coupled with a working
knowledge of PC's, financial software packages, and business
operations. I am able to work independently, am highly motivated,
and can communicate effectively.

My sports activities demonstrate my discipline, energy, and desire
to work hard and succeed.

I would welcome an opportunity to discuss my qualifications and
learn more about the Brighton Company. I will call you next week
to determine the possibility of scheduling an appointment at your
earliest convenience. If you have any questions prior to that time
about the enclosed resume, please feel free to call.

Sincerely,

Harriet Somerson

Encl.: resume

- ✔ Harriet wisely uses the name of the specific manager who referred her.
- ✔ She stresses her academic and sports achievements.
- ✔ She expresses an interest in learning more about company operations.

Career Changers 15

Career Change Is Here To Stay

Once thought of as almost shameful, a sign of instability or failure, career change is now viewed by most experts as a natural part of career development, and many people welcome the trend as a vehicle to self-fulfillment. Whatever the motivation - layoffs, burn-out, boredom, relocation, or a myriad of lifestyle considerations, it is a fact that more and more people are changing careers.

Utilize As Many Methods As Possible To Effect The Change

Successful career changers, like successful job seekers, use many methods to open up career avenues. Among them are:

- Advanced education

- Re-training

- Library research

- Career testing and counseling

- Informational interviewing

- Networking

- Professional associations

- Internships

- Volunteering

- Part-time work

- Turning hobby into career

- Family business

- Entrepreneurship

Any of these methods, alone or in combination, will allow you to learn more about your chosen new field and hone the credentials necessary to not only make the change, but succeed in the new field.

Focus Is Key To Developing A Powerful Resume

Whether planned or involuntary, changing careers can be a daunting undertaking. The obvious impediment to transitioning easily to a new career is lack of direct experience and/or other necessary credentials. Unfortunately, this same drawback can also hamper you in constructing a powerful resume.

Before you begin writing your resume and cover letter, you need to identify what your new career will be, why you have chosen it, and why you will be good at it. This knowledge will help you pick out relevant experiences and expertise from your past which can be emphasized on your resume. In other words, this exercise will provide you with focus.

It is extremely important that you "let go" of past experience that is irrelevant to your future career choice. For instance, you might need to omit a hard-earned M.B.A. or downplay your success in your role as manager. This task is extremely difficult because in our culture "who we are"is often based on "what we do." We see ourselves as being "a secretary" or "a marketing executive" or "an entrepreneur." Without that identification we feel insecure, somewhat lost as to how we stand among our peers. Beginning from the bottom in a new endeavor is not easy on the ego at first.

A few key points might be helpful to remember when focusing your resume in a new direction:

- An Objective at the top can provide both you and the reader with an immediate focus. There is no doubt where you're headed.

- A Summary of Qualifications section will allow you to introduce many professional credentials and personal qualities geared toward a new career.

- If your education is a strong qualifier for a new career direction, begin your resume with your Education section, despite the length of your employment history.

- List your work history out of chronology if it is necessary to emphasize a particular position which is not current.

The Cover Letter Tells Why You Will Be Successful

Despite your best efforts, when viewed alone, your resume might still appear sparse. The more radical your change, the less likely there will be convincing data to document your resume. However, when your resume is linked with your cover letter, together they can paint a picture of you as a competent, focused, enthusiastic professional who is motivated to make a change and who is confident that the change will be successful.

It is essential that you write your cover letter in such a way that it is both professional and personal. Include references to who you know in the company or industry, what you know about the company or industry, why you have decided to enter this new profession and, most important, *why you will be successful*. You need to convince a prospective employer that you have given much thought to your decision to change careers and your new venture is very doable. Convey a highly positive, confident, and energetic tone so that there can be no doubt in the reader's mind that your career change is not just pie in the sky.

In this chapter we have provided you with samples of resumes for a variety of typical career change situations, e.g., transitioning from teaching to business, leaving the military, combining two careers, turning a hobby into a career. We have also included sample cover letters as companion pieces to the resumes.

Your Efforts Will Be Rewarded

Throughout our many years in the resume-writing business, we have assisted numerous clients in changing their careers. Some changes, such as speech and language pathologist to technical writer, were achieved easily. Others, such as accountant to hospitality director of a trendy ice cream manufacturer, were more difficult. While even others, monk to model and financial executive to owner of pet-sitting service, were inspirational!

The common denominator in all success stories is enthusiasm about the change and willingness to work hard to achieve it. You can do it too.

CARLOS F. GUERRERO
73 Naples Drive - Apt. 11
Rockymount, North Carolina 27801
919-555-6104

OBJECTIVE: Language Arts Teacher - Secondary Level

SUMMARY: North Carolina certified secondary teacher with strengths in:

- Literature/Poetry/Theater
- Curriculum Design
- Skills Assessment & Development
- Communication Skills
- Creativity/Innovation
- Effective Discipline

TEACHING EXPERIENCE:

CARY JUNIOR HIGH SCHOOL	CARY, NC
Language Arts Teacher / Grades 7, 8, 9	**1985 to present**
TECHNICAL HIGH SCHOOL	RALEIGH, NC
Remedial Reading Teacher	**1983 to 1985**
PRIVATE TUTOR	RALEIGH/DURHAM, NC
Students in Grades 8-12	**1983 to present**
YOUTH JOB CORPS	GREENSBORO, NC
Youth Counselor (Ages 14 & 15)	**Summers, 1985 to 1987**

OTHER EMPLOYMENT:

HILLSIDE CONFERENCE CENTER	ROCKYMOUNT, NC
Assistant Dining Room Manager	**p.t., 1992 to present**
FIRST NATIONAL BANK	DURHAM, NC
Customer Service Representative	**1980 to 1983**

EDUCATION:

DUKE UNIVERSITY	DURHAM, NC
Bachelor of Arts in English	**1980**

✔ Before his career change, Carlos tailored his resume toward teaching.
✔ He obtained a part-time position as the first step in his career change.
✔ Carlos' revised resume will de-emphasize all of his teaching experience.

CARLOS F. GUERRERO
73 Naples Drive ■ Apartment #11 ■ Rockymount, NC 27801 ■ 919-555-6104

Summary of Qualifications:

Dynamic manager with diverse experience in business and education ■ Effective relating to multi-cultural staff and clients at all levels ■ Skilled in managing multiple tasks, problem-solving, and implementing solutions ■ Successful in following through and meeting time and budget deadlines ■ Solid background in staff training, supervision, and development ■ Strong customer service focus with training in TQM.

Professional Highlights:

BUSINESS

Assistant Dining Room Manager
HILLSIDE CONFERENCE CENTER - Rockymount, NC (p.t., 1992 to present)

Plan and manage V.I.P. functions and special events for a world-class residential executive conference facility catering to national and international CEO's and dignitaries. Hire, train, schedule and supervise staff of 27 Servers and Supervisors. Frequently update personnel training manual. Assume total reponsibility for facility during Manager's extended absence.

Customer Service Representative
FIRST NATIONAL BANK - Durham, NC (1980 to 1983)

Assisted commercial and retail customers in a wide range of sales/service areas. Trained tellers, cross-sold products/services, and attended seminars on new business development.

TEACHING / COUNSELING

Language Arts Teacher, Reading Specialist, Private Tutor
JUNIOR & SENIOR HIGH SCHOOLS - Raleigh/Durham/Cary, NC (1983 to present)

Youth Counselor - Ages 14 and 15
JOB CORPS - Greensboro, NC (Summers, 1985 to 1987))

Education:

Bachelor of Arts in English
DUKE UNIVERSITY - Durham, NC

Professional Development
Personnel Management & Motivation, TQM, Customer Focus, Business Law, Accounting I

✔ To effect a career change into business, Carlos writes a strong Summary of Qualifications that highlights business experience.
✔ He de-emphasizes teaching jobs by omitting position descriptions.

BRIGIT D. SWENSON
1322 Long Prairie Drive
Windom, Minnesota 56101

Date

Carolyn Anderson
Deputy Director
Minnesota Dept. of Education
243 Kennedy Drive
Minneapolis, MN 55401

Dear Ms. Anderson:

With a dual career background in teaching and business administration, and numerous years as coordinator of several local community programs, I feel highly qualified for the position of Assistant Program Director of Minnesota's acclaimed EDUCATION 2000 program.

Since its inception ten years ago, EDUCATION 2000 has been publicized everywhere - *American Educator, New York Times, PBS.* I never get tired of hearing about the remarkable accomplishments of its young participants.

I feel I know the program in a more hands-on way as well. For several months last year I collaborated with your former colleague, Mel Ackerman, in the early stages of developing Windom's YouthCorps for America program. I believe we were highly successful in our efforts to incorporate many ideas from EDUCATION 2000.

After reviewing my resume, I hope you agree that my understanding of adolescents, my ability to shape concepts into programs, and my effectiveness in bringing together community forces will enable me to successfully undertake the Assistant Director position.

Sincerely yours,

Brigit D. Swenson

✔ Brigit immediately describes her dual career.
✔ She establishes a strong personal connection.
✔ Brigit ends with a statement of her strongest credentials.

BRIGIT D. SWENSON

1322 Long Prairie Drive
Windom, Minnesota 56101
(507) 555-1262

SUMMARY

15+ years in teaching and business administration • Creative thinker with strong organization, communication, and problem-solving skills • Mature and responsible • Flexible and forward-thinking • Able to work independently or with a team to "get the job done" • Leader in numerous community service programs, e.g., Meals on Wheels, YouthCorps for America.

EXPERIENCE

Long-term Substitute Teacher (Daily, 1990 to present)
PUBLIC SCHOOLS • Windom, MN

Completed long-term teaching assignments at the middle and high school levels. Familiar teaching in diverse learning environments including open classroom, self-contained classroom, resource room, library, and computer lab. Comfortable teaching individual, small group, or whole class lessons. Adept at individualizing curriculum to meet the learning styles and psychosocial levels of all students including multi-cultural and special needs.

Office Manager (1979 to 1990)
PEDIATRIC MEDICAL ASSOCIATES • Springfield, MN

Managed daily operations of small private pediatric medical practice specializing in patients from ages 2 to 18. Computerized and administered patient records and billing, prepared monthly financial statements, and purchased supplies and equipment. Functioned as liaison between office and community hospital and agencies.

EDUCATION

B.S. in Business Administration (1994)
IOWA WESLEYAN COLLEGE • Mt. Pleasant, IA

A.S. in Secretarial Studies (1979)
LORAS COLLEGE • Dubuque, MN

Personal and professional references available

✔ Brigit's resume presents a balanced career history of teaching and business administration which allows her new options in program management.
✔ She offers personal references because of her close ties to the community.

DEPARTING THE MILITARY (Cover Letter)

RONALD L. ANSARA
32 Fillmore Street
Brookville, Ohio 44403

Date

Robert Avery
Manager of Quality Assurance
Applications, Inc.
765 Cerles Street
Columbus, OH 43216

Dear Mr. Avery:

As the enclosed resume indicates, I hold a B.S. in Electrical Engineering Technology from Wentworth Institute and have several
years of experience as a Q.A. Technician with M/A-COM, a leading
manufacturer of telecommunications equipment. I also worked for
two years as a Surface Sonar Technician with the United States
Naval Reserve.

Between 1991 and 1994 I was an Officer in the United States Marine Corps, where I was second in command for the training, supervision, and evaluation of 250 Marines.

Since my honorable discharge last month, I have been investigating
engineering positions. Your advertisement in the IEEE newsletter
interested me because the position is similar to the one I held at
M/A-COM, and also offers management potential.

I am very knowledgeable about the cutting-edge technologies that
Applications, Inc. utilizes and know I could undertake the position
with minimal learning time.

I would welcome the opportunity to further discuss my qualifications at a personal meeting and will contact your office next week
to determine the status of your interview schedule.

Sincerely yours,

Ronald L. Ansara

- ✔ Ronald summarizes his major "civilian" strengths in his opening paragraph.
- ✔ He describes his military experience only in terms of his leadership role.
- ✔ Ronald displays his current knowledge of the company and its technologies.

RONALD L. ANSARA
32 Fillmore Street
Brookville, Ohio 44403
(513) 555-0945

EDUCATION

B.S. in Electrical Engineering Technology   **1989**
WENTWORTH INSTITUTE   Boston, MA

Officers Training   **1991-1992**
THE UNITED STATES MARINE CORPS   Quantico, VA

COMPUTER SKILLS

Hardware: VAX, PC   **Languages: Fortran, Pascal, Assembly**

MILITARY EXPERIENCE

Anti-Armor Platoon Commander   **1992-1995**
UNITED STATES MARINE CORPS   Camp Lejeune

Surface Sonar Technician   **1989-1991**
UNITED STATES NAVAL RESERVE   San Diego, CA

EMPLOYMENT

Q.A. Technician   **1986-1989**
M/A-COM   Burlington, MA

Tested in-circuit test programs to detect manufacturing faults and aided in the design of ATE test fixtures and test harnesses.

Technician   **1985-1986**
FLEET COMMUNICATIONS   Bedford, MA

Prepared and installed cellular phones and trunked two-way radio systems.

✔ Ronald's degree is his chief credential for a career as an engineer, so he lists Education first despite substantial years in the military.
✔ He stresses technical and leadership background without using military jargon.

EMPHASIZING INTERNSHIP (Cover Letter)

Ann P. Diamond
4 Nassau Drive
Bloomfield, Nebraska 68718

Date

Susan G. Egan
Director of Marketing
GENERAL FOODS
FAX: 914-555-3880

Dear Ms. Egan:

Rich Lewis of your Market Research group suggested I contact you.

Upon graduation from Harvard College in 1987 with a degree in management (marketing), I secured a summer marketing research internship at General Foods. Rich was my direct supervisor.

Now, seven years later, I am a practicing attorney with a strong desire to return to the field of marketing.

In contemplating this career change, I have determined that my major area of interest is consumer marketing and my major strength is market research.

General Foods has now reached beyond food products by acquiring other consumer product lines. As we enter the year 2000, the possibilities are endless for products that seniors, singles, working parents, latchkey kids, and other major demographic groups will need. I can be valuable in compiling and analyzing data to determine market trends and profit potential.

I have included my resume for your convenience and will call you next week to answer any questions and discuss potential openings at General Foods.

Sincerely yours,

Ann P. Diamond

✔ Ann "woos" General Foods when she mentions the name of her former supervisor and describes her positive experiences during her internship there.
✔ She demonstrates her knowledge of the company and how she can contribute.

EMPHASIZING INTERNSHIP (Resume)

ANN P. DIAMOND   4 Nassau Drive • Bloomfield, Nebraska 68718 • 402/ 555-0729

Qualifications:

Dual degrees in law and managememt • Solid foundation in marketing, statistics, and psychology • Strong interest in consumer markets • Excellent oral & written communication skills • Effective problem solver • Solid research & analysis skills • Highly polished image.

Experience:

Associate Attorney   **Lyons & Lyons, P.C.**   **1990 to present**

- Interview and counsel individuals regarding employment law issues.
- Analyze client situations to determine client rights and legal strategies.
- Negotiate with clients' employers to promote out-of-court settlements.
- Plan and conduct litigation on behalf of clients.

Research Assistant   **John J. Finn, Attorney-at-Law**   **Summer 1989**

- Researched and analyzed civil rights cases and topics.
- Wrote articles for newsletter describing legal issues with a focus on gender discrimination.

Assistant Buyer   **Lord & Taylor**   **1988**

- Planned sales and profit goals for growing Maternity market.
- Analyzed sales performance against long-term and seasonal projections.
- Evaluated competitive retail organizations.

Marketing Research Intern   **General Foods**   **Summer 1987**

- Analyzed long-term consumer trend data and calculated market share of two product lines.
- Compiled data on interviews, expected costs, and actual costs.
- Drafted sections of analysts' report to senior management.

Education:

J.D. *cum laude*   **Harvard University Law School**   1990

B.S. - Management (Marketing)   **Harvard College**   1987

✔ Ann's Qualifications qualify her to enter many areas of business.
✔ Her present job description incorporates transferable skills .
✔ Ann includes an earlier summer internship because it is marketing-related.

HOBBY TO CAREER (Cover Letter)

MARYANNE A. CHOU
245 Crestview Avenue
Harrisburg, Pennsylvania 17105

Date

Patrick O'Neill, V.P. of Sales
A Roomful of Dolls
1322 Macon Parkway
Macon, GA 31201
FAX: 912-555-7990

Dear Mr. O'Neill:

As a lifelong doll collector, I was delighted to read of your store's imminent arrival in Lancaster. I visited your stores in both Atlanta and Miami, and hoped the North Atlantic region would be next.

For your convenience, I am faxing you a current resume which outlines my years in management. While focused on the produce industry until now, I am excited about undertaking a new challenge, and would love it to be A Roomful of Dolls.

What my resume does not explain is my love of dolls. I have an extensive collection, including one-of-a-kind miniatures. I keep current in the field through attendance at shows and subscriptions to Antique Dolls, Dolls Through The Ages, and Doll Collecting.

My fascination with doll collecting continues to grow, and at this juncture in my life I would love to combine my hobby with my career. In addition to extensive product knowledge, I offer strong experience in sales, customer relations, merchandising, and staff management.

I would welcome the opportunity to further discuss my qualifications and can make myself available for a personal meeting at your convenience. I will contact your office next week to answer any questions about my resume.

Sincerely yours,

Maryanne A. Chou

✔ Maryanne's opening is a personal "hook" which connects her to the reader.
✔ Paragraph two briefly, and positively, explains her wish to change careers.
✔ She continues to "sell" her love of the industry with her expertise.

MARYANNE A. CHOU

245 Crestview Avenue
Harrisburg, Pennsylvania 17105
717/ 555-4880

SUMMARY:

Hands-on manager with a significant record of achievement in retail, wholesale, and distribution operations. Consistently exceed goals, impacting significantly on a company's bottom line:

Areas of expertise:

- CUSTOMER RELATIONS
- QUALITY CONTROL
- STAFF TRAINING & MANAGEMENT
- PRICE NEGOTIATIONS
- MARKET CONDITIONS
- TELESALES

- VENDOR RELATIONS
- PRODUCT KNOWLEDGE
- MERCHANDISING
- COMPETITIVE MARKETS
- INTERNATIONAL MARKETS
- PURCHASING

EMPLOYMENT:

General Manager	**1988 to present**
UNDERWOOD PRODUCE CO., INC.	Harrisburg, PA
Senior Sales Representative	**1984 to 1988**
SHERMAN PRODUCE BROKERS, INC.	Lancaster, PA
Sales Representative	**1981 to 1984**
BALLARD & ASSOCIATES	Lancaster, PA

EDUCATION:

Bachelor of Science in Business	**1981**
FRANKLIN & MARSHALL COLLEGE	Lancaster, PA

✔ Maryanne's Summary widens her appeal to prospective employers because she lists expertise which would also be valuable in other industries.
✔ She further de-emphasizes her current industry by omitting position descriptions.

JANET B. DICKINSON

631 Ellerton Avenue
Fremont, California 94536

PHONE/FAX: 510-555-3841

Date

TO: Hiring Manager
      SAMPSON INDUSTRIES
      FAX: 408-555-8900

Dear Hiring Manager:

Following is a current resume in support of my application for the position of Registration/Exhibits Manager.

I have had eight years of experience as a Registration Manager at the conference company International Productions, where I managed registration, mailing list and exhibitor services for international trade shows and expositions.

While my career has taken a recent detour into real estate appraisal, I am eager to return to conference management.

I would welcome the opportunity to further discuss my qualifications and the position at a personal meeting.

Sincerely yours,

Janet B. Dickinson

✔ Janet addresses FAX to "Hiring Manager" as no contact's name was provided.
✔ Her second paragraph concisely describes relevant experience only.
✔ Her third paragraph acknowledges her career change in a positive manner.

JANET B. DICKINSON

631 Ellerton Avenue
Fremont, California 94536
510-555-3841

PROFESSIONAL SUMMARY

Eight years of experience in all aspects of conference planning registration • Solid planning, organization, problem-solving, and follow-through skills • Proven ability to train and supervise staff • Able to work independently or as part of a team.

WORK EXPERIENCE

Registration Manager   **1982 to 1990**
INTERNATIONAL PRODUCTIONS   SAN FRANCISCO, CA

- Managed registration for six international technical conferences annually.
- Developed database of Fortune 500 attendees, projected attendance levels, and administered invoicing, receivables, and collections.
- Ordered and compiled registration/conference materials and coordinated with promotional staff in the development of brochures and signage.
- Supervised large on-site staffs in registration operations.

Licensed Real Estate Appraiser   **1990 to present**
PACIFIC APPRAISAL COMPANY   SAN JOSE, CA

- Determine fair market value of residential properties valued at $50K to $1M.
- Conduct interior and exterior inspections of residential properties.
- Research and locate assessment values of comparable properties locally.
- Generate calculations and report on values of inspected properties.

EDUCATION

Bachelor of Science   SAN DIEGO STATE COLLEGE

✔ Janet's Summary describes experience related to her career goal only.
✔ She reverses chronology of Experience to emphasize the relevant position.
✔ Janet omits date of college graduation to avoid age discrimination.

Index

C

D

E

T

U, V, W